DWIGHT D. EISENHOWER
National Security Conference
2005

September 27–28, 2005
Ronald Reagan Building and International Trade Center
1300 Pennsylvania Avenue N.W., Washington, D.C. 20004

General Editor
CPT (P) John E. Prior, United States Army

Contributors
Bernard E. Brown, Ph.D.
National Committee on American Foreign Policy

Robert S. Litwak, Ph.D.
Woodrow Wilson International Center for Scholars

Janne E. Nolan, Ph.D.
Matthew B. Ridgway Center for International Security Studies
Graduate School of Public and International Affairs, University of Pittsburgh

Roy Williams
Center for Humanitarian Cooperation

Strategic Studies Institute, United States Army War College

Rapporteurs
Students of John Calabrese's U.S. Foreign Policy Unit for the
2005 Washington Semester Program at American University:
Colin Conerton, Everett DePangher, Paul Schneider,
Susanna Svensson, and Gregor Young

Co-sponsors
Center for Humanitarian Cooperation
Matthew B. Ridgway Center for International Security Studies
National Committee on American Foreign Policy
Woodrow Wilson International Center for Scholars

Contents

INTRODUCTION

As the global war on terrorism enters its fifth year, the efforts of that struggle are beginning to bear fruit. Although democratic elections in Iraq and Afghanistan represent hope for the future, our nation faces grave threats from around the world. Finding answers demands a unique and informed approach.

The 2005 Eisenhower National Security Conference, the culminating event of the 2005 Dwight D. Eisenhower National Security Series®, was held September 27–28 in the Ronald Reagan Building and International Trade Center, Washington, D.C. The conference presentations and discussions worked to accomplish several objectives:

- Provide a broad and unique forum to discuss and debate contemporary and future national security issues;
- Examine and advance ways to focus the instruments of national power more effectively; and
- Contribute to the ongoing national security dialogue while broadening the experience of midlevel and senior Army leaders through exposure to diverse issues, institutions, and perspectives.

Five addresses challenged the participants with diverse viewpoints, which provided for a balanced and informative discussion. The five distinguished speakers were His Royal Highness Prince El Hassan bin Talal of Jordan; Hernando de Soto, president, Institute for Liberty and Democracy; Eliot Cohen, Ph.D., Robert E. Osgood professor of strategic studies, director of the Philip Merrill Center for Strategic Studies, Paul H. Nitze School of Advanced International Studies, Johns Hopkins University; Ambassador Carlos Pascual, coordinator, Office of Reconstruction and Stabilization, Department of State; and U.S. Representative Ike Skelton (D-MO), ranking member, House Armed Services Committee.

Four panel discussions, equally challenging and enlightening, were co-sponsored by the National Committee on American Foreign Policy (NCAFP), the Center for Humanitarian Cooperation, the Matthew B. Ridgway Center for International Security Studies at the University of Pittsburgh, and the Woodrow Wilson International Center for Scholars.

The first panel addressed the question of power and national sovereignty. This panel, co-sponsored by the National Committee on American Foreign Policy, was moderated by Professor Bernard E. Brown, Ph.D., the director of the committee's Transatlantic Relations Project. The panel included the NCAFP's president, George

D. Schwab, Ph.D.; Ambassador Alyson J. K. Bailes, director of the Stockholm International Peace Research Institute; Ambassador Herman J. Cohen, former assistant secretary of state for African affairs and president, Cohen and Woods International; and Ambassador Richard N. Gardner, Ph.D., professor, Columbia Law School.

The second panel, co-sponsored by the Center for Humanitarian Cooperation, provided insight from nongovernmental and humanitarian organizations into the difficult task of operating in today's complex security environment. Roy Williams, president of the Center for Humanitarian Cooperation, moderated the panel. Panelists were Nancy E. Lindborg, president, Mercy Corps; Robert MacPherson, director, CARE Security Unit; Kevin M. Kennedy, director, Coordination and Response Division, Office for the Coordination of Humanitarian Affairs, United Nations; and Geoff Loane, head of the regional delegation for the United States and Canada, International Committee of the Red Cross.

The third panel covered the timely topic of understanding and preventing strategic intelligence surprises. Co-sponsored by the Matthew B. Ridgway Center for International Security Studies at the University of Pittsburgh, the panel was moderated by Professor Janne Nolan, Ph.D., of the Graduate School of Public and International Affairs at the University of Pittsburgh. The panel included David A. Kay, Ph.D., adjunct senior fellow, Potomac Institute for Policy Studies; Carl W. Ford, Jr., executive vice president, Cassidy & Associates; Admiral William J. Crowe, Jr., former chairman of the Joint Chiefs of Staff and chairman of the Board of Advisors, Global Options; and Dennis M. Gormley, senior fellow, Center for Nonproliferation Studies, Monterey Institute of International Studies.

The final panel, co-sponsored by the Woodrow Wilson International Center for Scholars, was moderated by Robert S. Litwak, Ph.D., the center's director of the Division of International Security Studies. The panel explored the nexus of proliferation and terrorism and featured Shahram Chubin, Ph.D., head of Academic Affairs, director of Research, Geneva Centre for Security Policy; Bruce Hoffman, D.Phil., corporate chair in Counterterrorism and Counterinsurgency, the RAND Corporation; and Mitchell B. Reiss, D.Phil., vice provost, College of William and Mary.

SUMMARY

SHAPING NATIONAL SECURITY—
NATIONAL POWER IN AN INTERNATIONAL WORLD

Day One — Global Perspectives

His Royal Highness Prince El Hassan bin Talal of Jordan opened the conference by challenging the participants "to bridge the gap of too many monologues and too few dialogues." To that end, he began by stating that the people of Jordan and the Middle East share with Americans respect for the sanctity of human life, adding that all want peace at home and abroad. Prince Hassan noted that not only war, but also natural disasters and other nonviolent calamities, can shatter peace. Regardless of the cause, all tragedies underline the universal reliance on humanity and community to recover.

The first panel looked at the issue of power and national sovereignty, offering a diverse set of views on the validity of nation-states as the basic unit of international structures. Professor Bernard Brown framed the discussion by asking questions concerning the effects of globalization, the rise of regional organizations such as the European Union, how genocide has impacted the inviolability of national sovereignty, and the dangerous political position faced by the world today as old institutions lose effectiveness and legitimacy without new ones to take their place. Ambassador Richard Gardner argued that sovereign nation-states will continue to be the primary actors in international relations for the foreseeable future, while Ambassador Alyson Bailes noted that the European Union presents a clear model for countries pursuing regional integration at any level. Presenting a third point of view, Ambassador Herman Cohen observed that not all nations are truly a part of this discussion. African governments have not fully consolidated their sovereignty, do not have the organization or consensus necessary to pursue regional unification, and are largely losing out with respect to economic globalization. Closing the discussion, Dr. George Schwab reiterated the concept of pooled sovereignty, which enables individual states to pursue discrete political interests while simultaneously benefiting from shared economic collaboration.

Hernando de Soto, president of the Institute for Liberty and Democracy, focused on property rights, the rule of law, and their link to international security.

He identified three critical attributes for prosperity in successful market economies: legally supported titles to property, business organizations that transcend individuals, and identification systems that link individuals to addresses and income streams. Industrialized countries should focus primarily on the establishment of these basic components rather than democratization and political change, for without these fundamental rights, economies and peoples will remain on the fringes of globalization and political reform.

Roy Williams assembled an international panel to discuss nongovernmental and humanitarian organizations in today's security environment. Each panelist approached the topic from a different perspective, leading to varied conclusions. Nancy Lindborg questioned the concept that today's world presents a "new" security environment. She contended that nongovernmental organizations have operated in a number of insecure environments around the world and that the real issue today, as it has been in the past, is population engagement. In contrast, Robert MacPherson noted that until 2000, the deaths of most humanitarian workers were in accident-related fatalities. Over the past five years, this has changed; deaths are no longer random but directed, with clear evidence of a deliberate process behind the killing. Presenting the United Nations position, Kevin Kennedy made clear that the 2003 bombing of the UN mission in Baghdad strengthened the organization's resolve, leading to better information collection, more staff in the field, and closer collaboration with nongovernmental organizations in operational theaters. All the panelists agreed that regardless of differing perspectives of the past, humanitarian workers today face considerable risk that can be addressed only through cooperation between aid organizations, the United Nations, and belligerents on both sides of conflicts.

The keynote address was delivered by Dr. Eliot Cohen of the Paul H. Nitze School of Advanced International Studies at Johns Hopkins University. Dr. Cohen highlighted the contradictory nature of the world and, consequently, American foreign policy, encouraging reflection on the tensions, contradictions, and their implications, rather than assigning political leaders and policies to specific, definitive schools of thought. Demonstrating that U.S. presidents since John Quincy Adams have been both realists and idealists, Dr. Cohen rejected the idea that foreign policy is based on great principles. Although consistency may or may not be a virtue, it is unsustainable in the long term, as all political leaders find themselves in situations where they must compromise their principles. In conducting foreign policy, American statesmen always have, and still do, navigate through a middle ground where ideas and interests walk hand in hand.

Day Two — Strengthening Essential Capabilities

The second day opened with an address by Ambassador Carlos Pascual, coordinator of the State Department's Office of Reconstruction and Stabilization. Ambassador Pascual outlined four concurrent phases of conflict transformation: stabilization, beginning with the political process of transferring ownership; addressing the root cause of conflict; creating a supply side of governance through the establishment of basic laws and institutions of a market economy; and providing for the demand side of politics by nurturing civil society so as to hold governments accountable. Underscoring the shift in policy with regard to failed and failing states, Ambassador Pascual observed that two decades ago we would have sympathized with societies in conflict, but we would not have intervened or tried to reconstruct them. We now see that even the poorest countries can threaten our national security.

The third panel discussed the topic of intelligence, exploring how the United States can prevent strategic surprises. The panel shared consensus that intelligence failures often stem from policy failures. Admiral William Crowe, Jr., stated that those charged with interpreting intelligence should not shape policy decisions. Conversely, policymakers should not influence analysts or organizations to provide analyses that reinforce only specific policies. Although encouraged by the creation of the post of director of national intelligence, Carl Ford, Jr., proposed a rebalancing of intelligence efforts away from "reporting the news" toward true analysis—identifying the trends and scenarios necessary for the formation of appropriate policy solutions. Moving beyond the pure question of intelligence, Dennis Gormley cautioned that the prospect of strategic surprise has been constant. The real danger of poor intelligence failing to prevent a major attack on the U.S. homeland would be the catastrophic effects on all aspects of our society, including the curtailment of civil liberties.

Focused on the nexus of proliferation and terrorism, the final panel sought to dispel the concept that terrorist access to weapons of mass destruction is inextricably linked to rogue nations. Both Dr. Shahram Chubin and Dr. Bruce Hoffman pointed to examples of terrorist organizations using weapons of mass destruction without any state sponsorship, most notably the 1995 attacks on the Tokyo subway system and the 2001 anthrax mail attacks in the United States. Dr. Chubin went on to say that the direct transfer of weapons of mass destruction to terrorist groups by countries like Iran is highly unlikely because of the danger it would pose to the country providing the weapons. Although established regimes are not likely to transfer weapons technology, Dr. Mitchell Reiss sees "inadvertent" transfer as the most worrisome scenario. Dr. Reiss outlined the possibility of transfer through state collapse, where either chaos or the emergence of a new regime could present a small window of opportunity that terrorist organizations could use.

Congressman Ike Skelton gave a powerful speech to close the conference, addressing the need to meet current security challenges without losing sight of future threats. Iraq and Afghanistan are important. If we fail, those countries are likely to become breeding grounds for transnational terrorist activity. But we must look ahead to other possibilities as well. From Islamic extremism to the proliferation of weapons of mass destruction, asymmetric threats present formidable challenges. At the same time, we must prepare for traditional state conflict, even as we strive to avoid it. China is developing strategic relationships in Africa, Central Asia, and South America, simultaneously improving its military capability. As a result, the

U.S.-Chinese relationship must be constantly managed to ensure success for all. Beyond military action, strategic foresight means preparing for and responding to tragedies like Hurricane Katrina and the Indonesian tsunami. Dedicated, trained professionals willing to serve the nation are the key to current and future capability. Leaders at all levels and in all professions must make a clear and compelling case to encourage our nation's youth to serve. The cost of preparing for the future pales in comparison to the consequences of failing to do so.

CONFERENCE CHARTER

SHAPING NATIONAL SECURITY— NATIONAL POWER IN AN INTERNATIONAL WORLD

The theme for this year's Eisenhower National Security Series and Conference is *Shaping National Security—National Power in an International World*.

Through the advance of global communications, national economies have grown progressively more intertwined; successful diplomacy has become increasingly interdependent as local traditions and cultures permeate distant nations. Correspondingly, the definition of power is changing. Individuals and organizations can now obtain the destructive powers once reserved solely for nation-states. In this context, free nations must determine how to secure their populations and apply national power. What is the correct balance of economics, diplomacy, and military strength? Are some programs, policies, and strategies more important than others? How should nations apply power relative to their neighbors, allies, and competitors?

The Eisenhower National Security Conference is the culminating event of the annual Dwight D. Eisenhower National Security Series, a yearlong progression of seminars, workshops, and conferences that address critical security issues under a unifying annual theme. Participants and audiences include a wide range of current and former national security policymakers, senior military officers, congressional leaders, international security specialists, members of nongovernmental organizations (NGOs) and humanitarian organizations, corporate and industry leaders, and the media.

OPENING ADDRESS

PERSPECTIVES ON HUMAN SECURITY

His Royal Highness Prince El Hassan bin Talal, Hashemite Kingdom of
   Jordan
Introduction by: Susan Eisenhower, Senior Fellow and Chairman
   Emeritus, The Eisenhower Institute

Summary

Susan Eisenhower, Senior Fellow and Chairman Emeritus, The
   Eisenhower Institute

The topic, Perspectives on Human Security, is particularly appropriate to the legacy of President Dwight D. Eisenhower.

During the Cold War, the United States had to contend with the worldwide threat of communism. Today, globalization and terrorism pose numerous tests for the United States. Interdependence has made us more prosperous, yet more vulnerable. The increased movement of goods and people has simultaneously drawn us closer together and degraded our ability to control and police our borders.

The scourge of terrorism is not the only challenge we face. We also confront the challenges of competition for scarce resources, economic protectionism, rising indebtedness, and deterioration of the natural environment.

We cannot afford to be complacent. American predominance is not guaranteed. It is tempting but foolhardy to seek to meet these challenges alone. More than ever, we need partners. This presents new and intriguing challenges, for "we depend not only on new friends, but also on old enemies." There are also pressing domestic problems. We will have to find a way to strike the right balance between these domestic concerns and our international commitments. We cannot live only for today. We must think and plan for tomorrow.

Prince El Hassan bin Talal
_____

- Prince Hassan identified as the overarching purpose of his participation in the conference the desire to help find a way "to bridge the gap from too many monologues and too few dialogues." Toward that end, he began his address by stating that the vast majority of people of Jordan and of the Middle East share with Americans the values of respect for the sanctity of human life. He added that, as individuals, the people of the Middle East believe in peace abroad and peace in the world. Yet, he noted, peace has lately been shattered by such natural disasters as the tsunami. For Americans, peace at home was shattered by the tragedy of Hurricane Katrina. These calamities have underlined universal reliance on humanity and community.

- The body of customary law could lend itself to a "positive peace." In fact, the call for a law of peace has been on the agenda of the UN General Assembly for decades. Attaining positive peace requires addressing two core questions: How should we shape security policy to safeguard human life in our interconnected world? And how should the United States apply its power to allies, competitors, and adversaries? Nonmilitary approaches must be employed and further developed as a complement to military force.

- All of us who collectively form the "moral majority" must work together. Pluralism is an important point of departure for the psychological and emotional reconciliation of war-torn societies. The United States can and must serve as "a beacon of hope."

- Meeting the challenge will not be easy. Millions of Palestinians languish in refugee camps decades after their dispossession. Countless Iraqis are displaced. Hope must be restored to them and countless others. The Middle East has abundant natural resources. To be sure, these resources must be employed to create livelihoods that will give people the trust and the confidence that their future can be better than their past. But what is needed, above all, is "anthropolicy" not "petropolicy."

- Confronting terrorism is not a straightforward task. If the international community focuses strictly on hard security, we will forget the obvious—that it is human beings who create peace and stability. Given political alienation, compounded by authoritarian systems, consistent support for democratic governance will decrease the appeal of terrorism.

- For the most part, primary responsibility for this project lies within Middle Eastern countries, but the United States can, nonetheless, play an important supporting role. However, one must be realistic. The struggle within the Arab world to establish democratic systems is very difficult in light of the institutional deficiencies, including the fact that the leading regional organization, the Arab League, has atrophied. For this reason, we must build from the ground up.

- Western nations can best serve their own interests and the interests of others by adopting a human security approach to political violence. Waging an effective battle for hearts and minds requires understanding the cultural, social, and psychological underpinnings of political violence—the sense of powerlessness, exclusion, and humiliation that drive violence and extremism. Here, an alliance between the media and academia might be useful. In sum, the "policies of peace and security need to be rebalanced."

    • We must encourage moral authority that places religion outside the political box, while maintaining the best that religion has to offer in terms of human values. And we must contain fundamentalism in all its various manifestations.

    • To win the war on terrorism, we must address the alienation of all citizens. It is not enough simply to imprison and kill terrorists, to take the fight "over there." For terrorism is a demand-driven phenomenon, not merely the irrational acts of a few fanatics.

    • We need new counterinsurgency techniques that aim to achieve a positive peace. We need robust peacebuilding efforts that "humanize the relations" between warring parties, lest they relapse into conflict. In this respect, nonviolent communication training and teaching tolerance can be very useful. Citizens groups and nongovernmental organizations (NGOs) that are engaged in such projects need and deserve our support. We need to "mobilize virtuous reality before virtual reality spins our world out of control."

    • Human security is the issue of our time. Building a "social infrastructure" of reconciliation and tolerance is urgently necessary.

Question-and-Answer Period

    • Regarding the future of the West Bank and East Jerusalem: The overarching issue is that of demography. Unless a conference is held and some progress made on the issue of Palestinian dispersion in the entire region, forced and voluntary migration will continue. Over the years, Israeli control of territory and resources has expanded. Rationally, how can the Israeli and Palestinian communities coexist in the light of greater Jerusalem, separation of the West Bank and Gaza, etc.? It is time for creative ideas, explored away from the media spotlight, such as the revival of the Benelux solution based on a notion of "intradependence."

    • Concerning how to integrate religion and religious leaders into the postconflict reconstruction process: Churches and mosques have extension services, and thus the networks to make such contributions. We must support these grassroots initiatives. However, we should think even more broadly in terms of how to support NGOs, including religious NGOs, in peacebuilding undertakings. A multilateral and nondenominational system of "blue overalls" would be a valuable complement to "blue helmets" in peacebuilding endeavors.

Analysis

    Prince El Hassan's entreaty to incorporate dialogue as part of any security issue is noteworthy and prudent. The human tendency to eschew dialogue when conflicts erupt is ultimately counterproductive at all levels of the political spectrum. Because of the passions excited by the conflict, affected states are not disposed to open a dialogue for conflict resolution. In such cases, leading powers and organizations must help the states in conflict to help themselves. As a vehicle, institutions certainly perform an invaluable role for issue linkage, accountability, and reconciliation.

No state or international organization has yet to address properly the militant groups and organizations that view conflict resolution as anathema and actively undercut peace overtures through violence. The cycle of violence, with its tit-for-tat dynamic, bolsters the ultraconservative camps on all sides, providing abundant grounds for continued diplomatic intransigence. One would think statesmen of the world community would take a stand rather than shrugging their collective shoulders.

Advocates of institutions, regimes, and organizations correctly point to the power of norms, laws, and principles in guiding behavior. Nevertheless, the pronounced absence of condemnation regarding terrorist acts and militant apologists establishes a normative behavior as well. Sadly, the United Nations General Assembly has abrogated its moral obligation in this regard. The office of the UN secretary-general possesses the authority to use the bully pulpit for the purpose of giving voice to the moral majority. Too often secretaries-general fail to check the tyranny of the rabble. The point is, changing behavior begins at the top, and if the United Nations fails in this basic duty, diplomatic breakthroughs at lower levels are much harder to achieve and maintain.

Prince El Hassan touched on the United States' potential role in promoting peace processes. Its position as a global power carries with it an expectation of moral authority that transcends its traditional "City on the Hill" archetype. The United States has demonstrated the will and capability to depose tyrannies since September 11, 2001. The denouement of the Iraq insurgency provides an opportunity for the United States to take a leading activist role in peace processes. Relentless pressure on Middle East states to continue with political, economic, social, and cultural reforms, acting through the Arab League, religious institutions, academia, and so on, is the appropriate course for U.S. foreign policy.

As Prince El Hassan implied, the United States can demonstrate as well its nonmilitary power in counterinsurgency to great effect and payoffs. Empowering states to reform themselves may be the most effective means for positive peace, without the need for a U.S. presence in every troubled spot. However, the United States, working through other states and organizations, must accept that some conflicts cannot be resolved by warring factions on their own. In such cases, peace enforcement assumes a moral authority of its own, permitting the process of dialogue to begin in earnest.

Transcript

ANNOUNCER: Ladies and gentlemen, please welcome your master of ceremonies for the Eisenhower National Security Conference, the Army's director for Strategy, Plans, and Policy, Major General Keith W. Dayton.

MAJOR GENERAL KEITH W. DAYTON: Thank you. Ladies and gentlemen, on behalf of the Chief of Staff of the Army, General Peter Schoomaker, welcome to the 2005 Dwight D. Eisenhower National Security Conference. Along with the Army, four distinguished organizations co-sponsored this event. They are the National Committee on American Foreign Policy, the Center for Humanitarian Co-operation, The Matthew B. Ridgway Center for International Security Studies at the University of Pittsburgh, and the Woodrow Wilson International Center for Scholars. Without their participation, this conference would not be possible.

This conference, the culmination of a year-long series of events, brings together some of the nation's top experts in national security policy. The theme for this year's conference, "Shaping National Security—National Power in an International World," is described in your conference materials. We're excited about the panelists, the speakers, and you, the participants, who have assembled to address this complex theme. We have brought together representatives from a variety of organizations—foreign and domestic, public and private—to provide balance and diversity of opinion. Among the 567 registered participants, 45 percent are military, with the remaining participants coming from a variety of backgrounds, including academic, congressional, corporate, governmental and nongovernmental, and the media.

The success of our conference today and tomorrow depends on your participation. We encourage you to ask questions, and we have microphones positioned through the venue to facilitate your involvement. I ask that you identify yourself and your organization when asking questions. Before we begin, please take a moment and make sure that you've turned off any cell phones or pagers or other devices that you may have.

Now at this time, it is my honor to introduce the Chief of Staff of the Army, General Peter Schoomaker. General Schoomaker has served in a variety of command staff assignments, in both conventional and Special Forces operations. He is a veteran of numerous deployments, including DESERT ONE in Iran, URGENT FURY in Grenada, JUST CAUSE in Panama, and DESERT SHIELD and DESERT STORM. He is a leader who has been actively engaged throughout his career in the struggle against terrorists and terrorist organizations. Ladies and gentlemen, the thirty-fifth Chief of Staff of the United States Army, General Peter Schoomaker.

GENERAL PETER SCHOOMAKER: Thanks very much. Thanks, Keith. Good morning everyone, and welcome. This year's theme, "Shaping National Security—National Power in an International World," is timely. It addresses issues of a globalized world and the application of national power, while acknowledging the threat posed by non-nation-state adversaries. It is now possible for individuals, groups, and organizations to leverage destructive powers exclusive in the past to nation-states. We all understand the many benefits of a globalized world. However, there are also many challenges worthy of examination. Given the unprecedented degree to which we are connected, it is imperative that free nations actively determine how to collectively interact to secure our interests. Our own national security strategy underscores the importance of the theme of this conference, seeking a balance of power that favors human freedom.

President Eisenhower was both a great military leader and statesman, and we honor his legacy with our efforts here today. As we participate in the discussions over the next two days, I ask that you freely participate in the dialogue, explore the challenges we face, and help shape how we deal with these issues that are before us. I would like to thank each of our partners in this conference for their steadfast work on behalf of national and international security. I especially would like to thank the Eisenhower family for their continued involvement and support.

It is now my great pleasure and honor to introduce Ms. Susan Eisenhower. She is accomplished and well-renowned in several disciplines. In addition to being a scholar and best-selling author, she is serving her fourth term on the National Academy of Science's Committee on International Security and Arms Control. It is particularly interesting that in 2000, a year before September 11, she coedited a book, *Islam and Central Asia*, with the subtitle *An Enduring Legacy or an Evolving Threat?* As an expert in nuclear energy and the space program, she has participated in several projects with the Department of Energy. She also serves as director of the Carnegie Endowment for International Peace and the Nuclear Threat Initiative. These are just a few of her many activities and accomplishments. We are extremely privileged to once again have her with us today. Ladies and gentlemen, please join me in a warm welcome for Ms. Susan Eisenhower.

SUSAN EISENHOWER: General Schoomaker, His Royal Highness Prince El Hassan bin Talal, members of the United States Armed Forces, prestigious members of our international academic and political communities, I welcome you to this important event, the fourth Eisenhower National Security Conference. As a member of the Eisenhower family, I would like to say that all my family members and I are deeply proud that the Army has named this conference series after one of their own, a former military leader and president of the United States.

This year's topic is particularly appropriate in the context of Dwight Eisenhower's legacy. Similar to the period after World War II, the global community today is in transition, and the threats are only partially military in nature. As communism and its military ambitions became a new multilayered challenge in the late 1940s and 1950s, globalization and one of its side effects, terrorism, pose an equally puzzling set of dilemmas today. The contemporary world is interdependent in many unprecedented ways. It is both more stable and more vulnerable than it was in the past. It has changed the way we do business, economically, politically, militarily, and commercially. The answers of how to deal with these changes are not altogether apparent, and our experience in the Cold War gives us little training in how to frame even the most urgent issues.

Advances in communications bring people closer together than we ever thought possible and yet, at the same time, amplify the ability of extremists to rip us apart. Scientific advancement has provided us with the means to solve many of humanity's most difficult problems and yet, in the process, has created a whole new set of perils. Increased human interaction and movement has enhanced our ability to positively affect our national security from half way across the world, but has simultaneously degraded our abilities to protect ourselves within our own borders. And ironically, in the hopes of garnering and securing our economic future, we now depend as much on our old enemies and new competitors as we do on our own friends.

As we now know from recent events, the scourge of terrorism is not the only threat that jeopardizes U.S. national security. Competition for increasingly scarce energy resources could, over time, significantly endanger our very way of life. Environmental degradation and global warming concern us as never before, while recent experience shows us that natural disasters can easily expose

Susan Eisenhower

our vulnerabilities and undermine our stability. At the same time, our economic security is being endangered by mounting debt, protectionist practices, and foreign trade pacts antithetical to U.S. interests. In defining our priorities, the United States cannot guarantee that the emerging environment will necessarily fall in our favor. Americans can no longer presume the strength of our nation will forever remain the linchpin of the global system. Complacency and contentment will result in falling behind, while the rest of the world prepares to sprint ahead.

The race has already begun. India is advancing by leaps and bounds in terms of technology and innovation. China is actively seeking new markets that rival our status. Even though the United States is Latin America's top trading partner, continued American dominance is no longer guaranteed as many of our jobs move offshore. We have to be smarter, faster and stronger than ever before. Though the temptation today might be to meet these challenges by ourselves, now more than ever we need our allies.

Dwight Eisenhower often said that our national security relies not just on our capacity of force, but also on the moral and economic conditions within this country. That is why the administration and Congress have rightly stepped up to the plate in lending a helping hand in the hurricane-ravaged South of our country. These costs, however, will bring with them new challenges, especially when added to our commitments overseas. Dwight Eisenhower understood the importance of assigning national priorities, even in the face of unfolding crises. Democracy, he thought, required not only participation, but also collective restraint. Linking economic solvency and security issues, Eisenhower closed his farewell address to the nation by saying, "As we peer into society's future, we—you and I and our government—we must avoid the impulse to live only for today, plundering for our own ease and convenience the precious resources of tomorrow. We cannot mortgage the material assets of our grandchildren without asking the loss also of their political and spiritual heritage. We want democracy to survive for all generations to come, not to become the insolvent phantom of tomorrow. Our capacity to mete out obligations to our countrymen go hand-in-hand with the relationships we have fostered around the world. Nowhere are they more important than in the strife-ridden regions of the world."

So, in that vein, it is my honor to introduce our opening presenter. Drawing from this theme of engaging our allies in the fight for international and national security, our next guest has been integral to countless projects aimed at communications and understanding and fostering trust between the Muslim world and the United States. His Royal Highness Prince El Hassan bin Talal is the younger brother of His Majesty, the late King Hussein of Jordan. Prince El Hassan has served as King Hussein's closest political advisor, confidant, and deputy. And he acted as the regent in the king's absence. He has been decorated by more than twenty countries and holds the Order of Al Hussein bin Ali, Jordan's highest honor. It is my distinct pleasure to introduce now Prince El Hassan, a personal friend of mine and a friend of the Eisenhower National Security Series. Thank you very much.

HIS ROYAL HIGHNESS PRINCE EL HASSAN BIN TALAL: Good morning, ladies and gentlemen. Thank you, Susan, for that generous introduction. I'd like to say that the first encounter between prominent members of our two respective families was when the late King Hussein was received by President Eisenhower in 1959. From the outset, I would like to emphasize that Jordan is the only non-Commonwealth country actually that fought alongside the Allies in two World Wars, and I want to make it clear that we share the values of respect for the sanctity of human life, going back to the Code of Hammurabi in Mesopotamia, to the Charter of Medina, to the Magna Carta, and indeed to the Declaration of Independence. As individuals, we believe in peace abroad and peace in the world. Peace at home, of course, has been shattered by man-made disasters as well as man against nature. Hurricane Katrina and the Asian tsunami have underlined our universal reliance on family and community, our universal consciousness, and our basic need for security and well-being.

In the face of daunting threats, it was in 1981 that the former president of the Red Cross, Alexandre Hay, asked if we could convene a meeting of conversations focused on humanitarian and Red Cross law, which we were introducing at that time to war colleges and military academies. We chose to introduce them to the then-liberation-movements in the world. We felt that the antagonists should be made aware of what the rules of the game were, in terms of man against man. I was encouraged by Alexandre Hay to travel to the United Nations, to bear in mind the absence of a law of peace. It was Professor Lauterpacht the elder of Cambridge University who made it clear to us in his ideas on the law of peace that the body of customary law could lend itself to the creation of a positive peace. We were encouraged by NGOs the world over. (I myself am a nongovernmental organism.) The NGOs presented themselves to me as the body for the powerless. We presented our report in 1988. Our commission included the participation of Robert McNamara; Simone Weil, herself a survivor of the holocaust; and over 28 nationalities. The call for a law of peace has been on the books, as it were, of the United Nations General Assembly from 1988 to 2004, in UN speak, and the call for a new international humanitarian order. And in that context, the early beginnings of our nations, as a prelude to the question you have asked yourself on your video preview, I would like to repeat, "How should we shape security policy to safeguard our nation in today's ever-more-interconnected world?" And I quote again, "How should America apply power in relation to our neighbors, allies, and competitors?"

Prince El Hassan bin Talal

I hope you realize that I have come here as a partner, not as an immediate neighbor, certainly as an ally and the competitor, only trying to offer solutions that are authentically reliable in bridging the gap between monologue and dialogue. I feel that we have too many monologues over the need for dialogue.

All of us who collectively form the so-called moral majority have both the ability and the will to work together to bring global commons and regional commons closer. It was Abraham Lincoln who suggested, and I quote, "I destroy my enemies when I make them my friends." We have different cultures and identities. I, for one, do not believe in the dirty P word—pluralism. Far from it, I believe that pluralism, based on enhancing what is universal in respecting the other, is an important point of departure, not least of all in postwar reconciliation and reconstruction, psychological and educational reconstruction. The challenge, it seems to me, is to develop a beacon of hope, to make America's message universal through finding partners.

We generalize when we speak of Marrakech to Bangladesh, from Casablanca to Calcutta, as the Middle East is sometimes defined. What a definition! We are talking about the most populous, the most dangerous, and the poorest region in the world. Effectively, we should be addressing the subregions—West Asia, Middle East, North Africa, Central Asia, and South Asia. In UN speak, I am an Asian. My Egyptian Arab friend is an African, and my Israeli friend is whatever he wants to be that particular morning. I want to be realistic about the challenge. It will not be easy when only 20 percent of the pledged reconstruction money has been disbursed. Many Iraqis are still too scared to leave their own homes. Those who have left have deluged my small country, Jordan, in large numbers. When millions of Palestinians still languish in refugee camps in Lebanon, Syria, and the West Bank, many decades after their original dispossession, the challenge seems yet more daunting. How can we ensure that all these people are genuine stakeholders in a common future?

In this arc of crisis, there is a wealth of natural resources: 70 percent of the world's known oil reserves and 40 percent of its natural gas. There is a complex interplay between the need for both stability and change. In West Asia alone, it is estimated that 35 million new job opportunities—and I quote the Economic and Social Commission for Western Asia—have to be created over the next decade, or else we will be hot-housing the extremism, the fanaticism that we all claim to fear. Seen in this light, confronting the threat of terrorism is clearly not a straightforward task that can be achieved through purely military means. This is all the more true when we consider the alarming prospect of nuclear terrorism, and Susan told you a few moments ago that we share membership on the Board of Nuclear Threat Initiative. Proliferation experts, in that context, estimate the likelihood of a successful nuclear attack within the next ten years at a 30-percent chance.

My country falls in the middle of the smoking zone, and I'm not talking of nicotine. I speak as someone who has been directly affected by terrorism, who has lost friends. But I feel that in terms of this region, we have to look to the future to develop a step away from "ad hocracy," piecemeal initiatives, to a longer-term strategy. We need, in short, policies to determine our future, and not only politics. Given that climates of political alienation created by authoritarian political systems have contributed to the rise of organizations like al Qaeda, there is no doubt that consistent support for democratic governance in West Asia will create long-term stability. It will reduce the appeal of radical extremisms that are opposed to all our interests. This was acknowledged by Secretary of State Condoleezza Rice on her recent visit to the region and by independent studies such as the Council of Foreign Relations (CFR) Report on Arab Democracy. We all agree that the prevailing political, economic, and social conditions in the Arab world are a security concern and that we must jointly mobilize resources to improve them.

In that context, I was heartened to see Arab assistance to the victims of Katrina. But I was saddened to feel that for twenty years, I have been calling for an Arab and Islamic Relief Fund—incidentally, Arabs comprise only 22 percent of the Muslim world—and yet, where is the altruism, where is the reaching out to help other human beings? Given the fact that 70 percent of the world's refugees are Muslims, often created by violence between Muslims. It is at this point that Jewish, Christian, and Muslim colleagues on the Board of the World Conference for Religions and Peace said to me, Well, you know that such funding has been made more difficult by 9/11, but we need someone like you to assist in setting up a vetting agency for a relief effort. And if you can bear in mind a modular approach, I am in the process of working a white paper with people from all over the world to present to the financiers in our part of the world, including risk analysis; crisis avoidance; a full-fledged multinational, gender-balanced—and let me stress gender-balanced—peace corps. Women today are 62 percent of the population in Iraq. Women should be involved in addressing issues of women in distress. If by the end of the year we present this study and no one picks up on it, at least my conscience will be clear. But I will feel that much sadder that the realities are focused on hard security at the expense of the basic flash of the obvious—that it is human beings who cause insecurity or who build stability, and it is in them that we should invest. I speak of anthropolicy not petropolicy.

Sudden traumatic change, of course, may not be in everybody's interest. Evolution is preferable to revolution. The CFR suggests, and I quote, "Democracy entails certain inherent risks. The denial of freedom carries much more significant long-term dangers. The emergence of more open qualities, greater economic opportunities, and social reform is primarily an Arab project, in which Washington can and should play an important supporting role." I would like to remind you of the difficulty of playing the supporting role in the absence of an institutional umbrella in West Asia, Middle East, North Africa, and the Gulf subregion. The Arab League is facing, it would be unkind to say its death throes, but great difficulties. The Arab League, like the United Nations, is the representative of the combined will of its governments. And governments today tend to be more unilateral than multilateral. So I would like to suggest that we make some sense, in this Eisenhower lecture, of alphabet soup—PFP [Partnership for Peace], PFM [Partnership for the Mediterranean], OSCE [The Organization for Security and Co-operation in Europe], partnership to this, that, and the other, for peace for the Mediterranean—in addressing the possibility of creating a stability pact in our region based on a cohesion fund that looks directly to the issue of building from the bottom up, creating participation and stakeholding.

Independent and sustainable democracies depend on more than just the holding of elections. The challenge is to create a new culture of democratic participation in a diverse region, recognizing the specific characteristics of each country. I believe that our focus has to turn very clearly toward human security approaches to political violence, by recognizing that terrorism is a tactic rather than a definable enemy. We can avoid the pitfall of dehumanizing the other. If we are serious about containing terrorism and reducing its impact on civilian populations, policies for peace and security will need to be fundamentally rebalanced from their existing bias toward military intervention alone. Right now, for example, in the United Kingdom, the budget for conflict resolution is less than 0.5 percent of funding for military intervention.

I was on the stage the other day in the Royal Court Theater in London at a conference entitled "Speaking to Terrorists," and not far away from me was the representative of the British Ministry of Peace. Now that, you may like to know, is not a pop concert. It may be a cubby hole in the Ministry of Defense, I don't know. The Swedes, once upon a time, had a Ministry of the Future, and then they terminated it. I don't know whether they found the future. But in the context of seeking peace, I want to point to the communication strategy for public diplomacy as presented by the Pentagon last year. I do feel that when we're talking about Iraq, Palestine, or al Qaeda, many of the traditional approaches to counterterrorism and conflict resolution are struggling to deal with turbulent, new realities. I'm aware of the excellent paper presented on the lessons of Fallujah, with which your educators in the military are so keenly involved. I had the privilege of speaking at the Marshall Center not so long ago, and I know that the rethinking process is well under way. But I came here to say that military measures alone can only be temporary, unless they are accompanied by a real battle for hearts and minds. As a complement to the military dimension, we also have to understand the social, cultural, and economic context of conflict, the emotional and psychological aspects. Powerlessness, exclusion, trauma, and humiliation are very often key factors in the resort to violence. And this should encourage us to develop new security doctrines based on principles of nonviolence, mutual third parties, mutual respect, and dialogue.

Now let me say that these remarks are directed more to governments in our region than they are directed to the governments of our allies in the Western Hemisphere. I would like to say that we have a duty to understand the nature of the threats we face, including phenomena like suicide terrorism, however repugnant it seems to us. In June of next year, we shall be holding WOCMES—the World Congress of Middle East Studies—which will bring the four study centers or the four study networks of the Western Hemisphere for the first time to Jordan. I hope that we can create alliances between the media and academia, so the media develops a citizen-to-citizen approach. We have 167 satellite frequencies in the Arab world, producing infotainment and infoterror, but no infohumanity or infowisdom that I can detect. Deepening our understanding of violence will, I feel, help us achieve a safer world. We have heard the expression "embedded journalists"; what about "embedded scholars"? I think that the introduction of the Missionary Herald, which was produced for two centuries, of the onsite anthropologist, the pockets of missionaries gave me a greater insight into the rites and customs of people in the nineteenth and late eighteenth century than any sitrep [situation report] I have read by any intelligence service.

To understand, however, is not to sympathize, but to take the first step on the road to prevention. It has become very clear that terrorism is not merely a matter of poverty, political constellations, or religious extremism. It is easy, but inaccurate, to think that suicide bombers are a very recent phenomenon of poor, uneducated, religious fanatics who are depressed and emotionally unstable. But that profile has simply not stood up to scrutiny. The usual motives, in fact, include senses of powerlessness, violation, and injustice, often created by autocratic governments. Preventing further violence, further backlashes in a region where different levels of territoriality and identity—let's remember that acronym TIM, territoriality, identity, and migration—interact, requires that we collectively promote a culture of open participation. We cannot underestimate the influence of fundamentalist beliefs for populations that have been repeatedly traumatized. These beliefs offer a firm philosophy in an uncertain world, the feeling of familiarity and safety and a sense of community and belonging, as strange as that may sound. By helping to dehumanize the enemy and reduce the ability to understand the complexities of human behavior, these conditions can stimulate acute political violence. However, developing relationships with moderate religious leaders is one way of reducing the appeal of radicals or extremists who distort religion for their own political ends.

Let me be clear: Henry Kissinger asked, "What is the address of Europe?" I ask, "What is the address of Islam?" And I believe that in both Mecca and in Najaf, we have to encourage the creation of a moral authority—and in Jerusalem, for that matter—that places religion outside the political box, effectively separates church and state, while maintaining the best that that religion has to offer in terms of human values that we share. For after all, if we all believed in the Ten Commandments, we wouldn't be in this mess in the first place! The politicizing and the privatizing of religious groups and of war by what we now call terrorist organizations is, however, offering an alternative political conversation for some. But please let me emphasize that we must not be fooled. We must not fall into the trap of creating cult heroes of people who have contributed so extensively to the hatred industry. We must legitimize religion in the minds of all. And let me say in that context, we must contain fundamentalism in all its aspects: liberal fundamentalism, secular fundamentalism, and, for that matter, the so-called religious fundamentalism, which in a sense are contradictions in terms.

Foremost in my priorities, I believe, is to address the alienation of ordinary citizens. There's a powerful correlation between humiliation and the desire to restore honor and pride through violence. The first Chechen suicide bomber, a twenty-two-year-old woman, had sixteen of her closest relatives killed by the Russian military during the year before her attack, among them her husband, two brothers, one sister, and several cousins and nephews. With all due respect, ladies and gentlemen, imprisoning or killing a finite number of terrorists is not the only solution. I, for one, am a great fan of the film, Casablanca. "Round up the usual suspects," he said. I do not think that here it is a case of fighting them over there, so that you do not have to fight them over here. Suicide terrorism is not a supply-limited phenomenon. It is not just a few fanatics wreaking havoc wherever they go. It is a demand-driven phenomenon, fueled by the presence of foreign forces in what people see as their homeland. That is why, although previously unheard of in Iraq, it is now at unprecedented levels for any conflict. According to United States statistics, 412 suicide bombings from January to August killed an estimated 8,000 Iraqis. Iraq may not be the root cause of terrorism, but it is now adding fuel to the fire.

If the military presence remains necessary, different approaches can also be considered. And I think these approaches should take into consideration counterinsurgency techniques, like clearing neighborhoods in search of potential suicide bombers and smuggled weapons, which are much more effective when local leaders are consulted. This depends on establishing prior contact, employing Arabic speakers, and respecting local traditions and culture. I remember offhand and apropos nothing very much, but I have to tell you the anecdote—all the best books, by the way, are written in anecdotes—I remember [former President] Bill Clinton and [former Vice President] Al Gore applauding me when I greeted Simon Peres [former Prime Minister of Israel] in Hebrew at the White House. I said to them, "Gentlemen, maybe you should applaud Simon when he can answer me in Arabic." Colonel Douglas Macgregor of the U.S. Armed Forces said, and I quote, "Most of the generals and politicians did not think through the consequences of compelling American Soldiers, with no knowledge of Arabic or Arab culture, to implement intrusive measures inside an Islamic society." Winning the peace in Iraq will require a new approach to counterinsurgency, and I'm not a born-again wiseass. This is exactly what I said at Kensington Town Hall to the then-Iraqi-opposition, many of them in power today.

Sidney Bailey, my dear departed friend, a Quaker, wrote three volumes on How Wars End. I think we have to consider winning a positive peace—nothing provokes like injustice. Systematic efforts to restore a sense of respect, as well as removing daily humiliations—and here I address the issue of Palestine today and the numerous studies by Israelis in Palestine, which I summarize, such as road blocks, intimidating body searches, night raids on houses, etc.—would make a big difference. Efforts could also include creating jobs, encouraging rebuilding, providing access to medical health, reestablishing schools, empowering women, removing hindrances to trade. What is the point of withdrawing from Gaza, if the Gazans do not have a single drop of water to drink? Isn't it time that we recognized the importance of a supranational management of the seventy-mile radius of the conflict with seventeen million people by removing the brand names Palestinian, Israeli, Jordanian, Lebanese, et al.? And focusing on the existential question, "How can these producers and consumers of water coexist?" It is for that region that we are proposing a supranational Water and Energy Commission, the product of studies by LAC, German universities, and Arab and Israeli participation in a conference to be held in Prague, hosted by Vaclav Havel, in the next two months. If Europe started with coal and steel, why can we not start with a policy of energy and water for the human environment?

I was delighted yesterday to talk to NTI about our first conference, agreed upon by all parties in the region, on the management of pandemic flu—in the same way as I was delighted years ago to hold the first conference on chemical weapons, long before it was safe or fashionable to talk about multilateral cooperation. Everyone agrees between closed doors, but in the broad light of day, we need the support of the United States to bring together a template to which we can all step up, of rights and responsibilities in current and basic security, economic and social, as well as cultural and humanitarian issues. In May 2004, a roundtable on human security in the Middle East was held to attempt exactly that. Interdisciplinary—politics, business, the military, academic research, psychology—all contributed their experiences of civil society and peace building in Eastern Europe prior to the Velvet Revolution, as well as in Northern Ireland, and constructed the plan for a civil society network in the Middle East. I am delighted to be able to announce the creation several months ago, if you forgive the acronym, of MECA—Middle East Citizens

Assembly—where we have the participation of everyone, including, believe it or not, Iranians, Israelis, Saudis, and others.

It is vital to differentiate between those who may be open to dialogue and those with whom negotiation is impossible. The International Crisis Group in 2005 issued a report warning against the sledgehammer approach, which refuses to differentiate between modernist and fundamentalist varieties of Islam. I, incidentally, ladies and gentlemen, am a Muslim, not an Islamicist. And I would like to say that there are many questions that we have to address in our conversations. I'm the only Muslim member of the board of the Center for Hebrew Studies at the Yarnton Manor in Oxford. And these questions are common to all our communities. How can we preempt the outbreak of conflict? How do wars end? Why do 50 percent of countries emerging from war fall back on it? How can we address the basic needs of protecting people, reducing violence, and establishing the rule of law, to ensure sufficient space for political solutions?

If you consider the cycle of violence, it goes, as stated in a paper produced by Demos—I work with Peace Direct, with the Oxford Research Group, and Demos in London—something along the following lines: atrocity, shock, fear, grief, anger, bitterness, revenge, retaliation, back to atrocity, and so on. A different kind of intervention is needed before anger hardens into the desire for revenge. For example, in areas of violent conflict, why not set up centers for listening and dialogue, listening and documentation, or truth and reconciliation commissions? When large numbers of people have endured horror, they need the space to humanize their relationships and move beyond demonizing the other.

I had the privilege of hosting on more than five occasions religious leadership from Iraq and visiting Indonesia during the week of East Timor's independence. What we do is talk to the religious leaders. We say, "You are the servants of the community, we are the servants of the servants, how can we develop a conversation?" And I remind you that the noble art of conversation is not a martial art. The physical, political, and psychological securities of those trapped in violence are all equally important. Improved methods of peacekeeping, violence monitoring, disarmament, and gun collection also help to establish a safe environment. It is an incredible fact that in modern wars, over ten civilians are killed for every combatant. Then there is the need for [inaudible] holding. Only legitimate participation in a political process and the prospect of a secure future will stop violence in the long run. Sometimes we'll have to adapt our concepts of democracy and secularity to each particular environment. This, however, is not a cop-out. It is basically an understanding of the fact that patronage does not trickle down. Politicians will mouth in countries all over the world whatever you want to hear, but it will not reach the common man.

As I said at the Defense College yesterday, I was privileged to accompany my friend Rabbi Rene [Shmuel] Sirat, the former rabbi Grand Rabbin of France, to a refugee camp on an unannounced visit. We walked into a class of Palestinian students. He spoke French and I translated into Arabic. They'd never seen a rabbi; he could have been an alien, a Martian. And he said to them, "I was born in

Algeria, and I was refugeed." A fourteen-year-old child said, "Ya Haram, you poor fellow." And I said to him, "Would you get that answer in a banlieue, in a suburb of Marseilles, or in the Bronx?" These kids are beginning to blossom. It's a question of how we guide them and who is closest to them. I took Mo Mowlam, one of the authors of the Good Friday Agreement [Belfast Agreement], God rest his soul, an Irishman-Israeli into a coffee shop. A Palestinian said, "You're English; we hate the English because they victimize us. You're Irish; you'll do because you've been a victim like us. You're an Israeli; you know what we would do to an Israeli if you weren't in the company of the prince." Forty-five minutes later, they were talking. And I think that if opposites can talk, it is largely due to the experience that has been accumulated over many conflicts and many tragedies all over the world.

So, if I may, in conclusion, say that nonviolent communication training, the brainchild of Marshall Rosenberg, is being used to great effect in Israeli primary schools. More than 50,000 schools here in the United States use a program called "Teaching Tolerance." Over in Jordan, initiatives like Project Citizen and Foundations of Democracy, which promote the development of peace and security through active citizenship, start at the primary school level. I would quote Martin Luther [King Jr.], who said upon receiving an award at Morehouse College, "If you succumb to the temptation of using violence in the struggle, unborn generations will be the recipients of a long and desolate night of bitterness, and your chief legacy to the future will be an endless reign of meaningless chaos." So I look to organizations, such as Partners in Humanity, Middle East Citizens Assembly, the creative thinking of what to do in the aftermath of 9/11 put together by many of us at the JFK Library, and say that I hope these initiatives are recognized. I hope that Karen Hughes's four E's—Education, Empowerment, Engagement, and Exchange—are supported, but also let us remember that these are two-way processes.

I feel, ladies and gentlemen, that it is important to mention one fact: that at a time when four members of the UN Security Council are responsible for 78 percent of global exports of conventional weapons—roughly two-thirds of which go to developing countries, countries and regions of conflict—it is also in our interest to reassess arms policies. And I applaud the efforts of Paul Wolfowitz to emphasize education and health as the two prongs of the new approach of IVRD. In weapons, we're talking figures like thirty-seven billion in 2004 alone. I remember a senator saying to me, "Folks like you are bad for business." Well, I've never done business, so I don't know how good I would be even if I tried.

But in conclusion, let me say that we have to mobilize a virtuous reality before virtual reality spins our world out of control. As a moderate or as an aggressive moderate, if you will, from within the West Asian region, we moderates sometimes feel, sadly, as though we are the radicals. Maybe if I had a long beard and the Kalashnikov, I would be easier to deal with, rather than the one who talks back. I hope I'm talking sense. I can't really see you through these lights, so how sensible I'm being, I don't know. I've no doubt that human security is the issue of our time and the science of the future. Postwar reconstruction of buildings is one thing, but postwar reconstruction of social infrastructure is the real task. I was speaking to the mayor of Hannover the other day, and the mayor of Hiroshima was commemorating sixty years since the devastation of their cities. I don't know if you're aware, in the whole of Europe there is only one university that studies the reasons for out-migration: Osnabrück in Germany. In the whole of the Western Hemisphere, there are only two universities that focus on refugee issues: York in Canada, and my alma mater, Oxford. I think the time has come to recognize why people do the things they do.

In 1995, Simon Peres and I went to Brussels to ask for $35 billion to encourage the will to stay, to be spent on twenty-four countries to build infrastructure from Morocco to Turkey. For a decade—$35 billion. The answer was a yawn and first-come, first-served—a shopping list approach. After 9/11, I note ironically, that it was the same figure, $35 billion, but in one day, to develop a fortress mentality. A stitch in time, crisis avoidance, focusing on human dignity are essential as a change to our strategy for the future, and maybe, just maybe, calling for an international law of peace to address the wounds left in the hearts and minds of ordinary people. I think it is in the interests of United States national security, in the interests of all peace-loving people, that serious planning and funding be invested in this approach: nonmilitary ways of managing conflict as a complement to the gallantry and the dedication of the military in many areas of the world. I know, I've been there, I recognize the difficulties. I recognize those in the military who would say, "Well, come down to the street corner and take some fire and then come back and give this speech." I have seen the effects of napalm; I have lost comrades and I empathize. But I conclude with a quote, with two quotes actually—one from my friend Boaz Ganor, who is the Israeli director of the Center for Terrorist Studies at Herzliya, and we both recognize skeletons in our respective cupboards: "No prohibition without definition." Let us examine clearly who are the hard and who are the harder men, in terms of this opposition that we face. Let us examine the reasons, and I would suggest that the words of Edward Gibbon be borne in mind: "When the Athenians finally wanted not only to give to society, but for society to give to them, when the freedom they wished for most was freedom from responsibility, then Athens ceased to be free."

Ladies and gentlemen, thank you very much for listening.

EISENHOWER: Prince Hassan, thank you so much for what was a really a most insightful and thought-provoking presentation. I know I speak on behalf of my family and everyone here in attendance. Our deep appreciation for your words! Would you be willing to answer a few questions?

PRINCE HASSAN: By all means!

EISENHOWER: I think we need a microphone over here.

AUDIENCE - GEORGE MAURER: Prince Hassan, I am amazed at your eloquence and your moral view, but if I could be so presumptuous as to ask a question about your immediate neighbor. What do you foresee in the next five years in the West Bank and in East Jerusalem? And I'm George Maurer, Key West, Florida, retired colonel, Army Reserve.

PRINCE HASSAN: Thank you very much, Colonel. First of all, I'd like to say that we have five neighbors, so we have to have five immunities, if you will. They include the Israelis, the Palestinians, the Syrians, the Iraqis, and the Saudis. Simon Peres once made the justifiable Israeli lament before the peace treaty. He said, "We are surrounded by enemies." I said to him, "You think you've got a problem; we're surrounded by friends!"

Let me take the overarching issue—demography. I think that unless, and time is running out, a conference is held on the issue of demography in the region—not the 1993 conference on assistance to the Palestinian people, which, when I arrived, turned out to be assistance to the Palestinian Authority, which is rather a different matter, but one addressing the dispersion of Palestinians in the region—it is going to be very difficult in the next ten years to see anything other than continued forced or voluntary migrations. And at the end of the day, I suppose they come to the same thing, moving from one place to another.

When I started writing about settlements in the earlier 1970s, there were less than a thousand settlers. When the David Rockefeller Commission—on which I had the privilege of serving with Jacob Javits from this country, Edward Kennedy, Robert McNamara, and others—funded a study entitled Middle East 2000, we spoke about ten million consumers of water between the Mediterranean and the Jordan River. The only person, or one of the very few, who took this study seriously, from my knowledge and conversation, was Ariel Sharon. And I'm not saying that he worked with that objective in mind, but the product of years of occupation has been the gradual growth of the territorial and resource control of the settlers and the settlements, to the point where it is going to be very, very difficult indeed. And I'm speaking rationally. You know, some people in our part of the world think everything will be solved by alchemy. But rationally, how can these communities coexist, given the realities of greater Jerusalem, the separation of Nablos and Hebron, the separation of Gaza and the West Bank? As I said, the withdrawal from Gaza was a courageous and brilliant tactical move. It did not, however, seem to me to be in the context of a strategy.

So you asked me what the future would look like. I do not have a crystal ball, but I would like to suggest that if we can develop a community of creative ideas, preferably, by all means, away from the television cameras, then maybe, just maybe we can talk about the revival of Benelux. Remember Abba Eban in the 1970s. It has to be a Benelux solution, based on intra-independence not interdependence, because interdependence can mean crumbs from your table. It can mean anything you like.

Secondly, I think the overarching issue is refugees, which I touched on. But I would go further. With [Israel's Prime Minister] Yitzhak Rabin, since 1971, when I met him privately in Washington, I always used to say, "You will say 'no' to the right of return, and I will say 'yes' to the right of return. Your 'no' and my 'yes' do not invalidate each other." Because if they do, then what is the validity of Aliyah [immigration to Israel]? What is the validity of talking about free trade area for the free movement of goods, capital, and labor? What is the validity of the claim of Arab Jews to return to Arab countries? And, as you know, the import of Asian labor has taken the place of Palestinian labor.

So I think that the issue of Jerusalem and other overarching issues have to be addressed in terms of sharing holy sites. And I would recommend to you the work of Exeter University in this regard—I think it's Professor [Michael] Dumper of Exeter University—how to share holy sites in Jerusalem [The Politics of Sacred Space: The Old City of Jerusalem in the Middle East Conflict]. Please open our website with Harvard [University] School of Urban [Planning and] Design, on the issue of Jerusalem. The Harvard School and the Royal Scientific Society of Jordan have done some excellent work on what I call "Jerusalem Consciousness." The question of water, as I said, is a regional issue, which I think has to be discussed in the context of the Danube Commission, the Rhine Commission, the Mekong, the Delta—let us look at the whole Rift Valley and not just limit ourselves to historic and legal claims, which will get us nowhere. So, if that is possible, then I think there is hope for the future. If, however, the negative scenario kicks in, then violence will increase in the occupied territories. The temptation, given the neighborhood, to have a go at Syria, or effect regime change without really knowing where it's going to lead to or what the derivatives are, or to have a go at Iran and God knows. . . .

Prime Minister Sharon was saying a few months ago, "It is not yet time." To escape into the future means fragmentations in the plural, and when we get to that point, I think that the region is going to be Balkanized in the worst possible manner. That's why I come here at this time, at this important time, given many factors—domestic and international—and suggest that maybe there is still a window of opportunity to look at the region as a whole. Pakistan, I think, took a brave and a justifiable move in opening conversations with the Israelis, for one reason that I can recall, and that is that the Weapons of Mass Destruction Commission in Cairo, an Israeli in the plenary, said, "Even a comprehensive Arab-Israeli peace is not sufficient to justify a weapons of mass destruction free zone. What about Iran and what about Pakistan?" And my comment was, "Is it for you to move back the goal posts, or can we go back to a day when we look to the United States for guarantees?" Aegis cruisers were a topical reference to monitoring of incoming devices in the '90s. Where is the concept of even what Carl Bildt called a "mission-empty" Stability Pact in the Gulf, in the Balkans, being applied to our region, in the Gulf, and elsewhere? For it is not only the safety of the Gulf that is important, but also of the hinterland. So I hope I haven't raised more questions than given answers, but what you see is what you get. Thank you, Colonel. Thank you.

AUDIENCE - RAY BINGHAM: Your Highness, you spoke of two areas that I'm currently researching: postconflict reconstruction and religion. It appears that civilian and military strategic planners are working hard to integrate religion and religious leaders into the decision-making process. What are your thoughts on how NGOs, policymakers, and military planners can best integrate religion and religious leaders into the postconflict reconstruction process? And I'm Ray Bingham, a military fellow.

PRINCE HASSAN: I had the privilege of talking to Pope Shenouda, the Copt pope, and to the Grand Mufti, the Sheikh of the Ahzab, on the importance of the HACI program—Hope for African Children. This was two or three years ago now, and we said, "You have extension services among those communities, the churches and the mosques." I mean, when I brought together the Iraqi Muslim and Christian leadership, the two Christian bishops said that they had not spoken to each other in ten years, although they lived a few kilometers apart. And to my sadness, when we met at the WFDD, the World's Faith and Development Dialogue, hosted by the World Bank and Lambeth, Jim Wolfensohn, and Archbishop Carey—I referred to our host as "Cash and Carry"—we entreated them to support such grassroots initiatives. The World Bank's reservations were basically, we have to send an appraisal mission; we have to do the job ourselves. And I said, well, why don't you monitor the activity of these churches and these mosques, which are actually a part of what is ongoing? I find it sad that the people who want to do it right face bureaucratic difficulties.

Another example of doing it wrong this time is when you see Wahabis trying to teach—I worked with a leper colony in 1985 in Western Sudan—trying to teach Arabic to people who don't want to learn Arabic or the Koran, for that matter, who basically want their basic existential needs attended to. And then you go to Zanzibar, and you see the poor box in the church with the crosses full of money, and the poor box with the crescent is empty. And after the tsunami, the same kind of trying to buy souls by similar organizations was clear. This is why I am calling for an international effort to develop a relief fund.

The Washington Post suggested before the MDGs [Millennium Development Goals], we need the famine fund. Well, I would like to suggest that your question finds its way to the decision makers: How can we use the network of NGOs, including religious NGOs? We work in Cambodia and Laos with the Asian Muslims Association and the Catholic Bishops Council. One and half million kids sold into the sex-slave trade. Governments don't even want to know. And you go to a family of eighteen and say, "Why have you sold your eighteenth child?" They say, "To save the other seventeen."

In short, again, going back to Simon Peres—and you recognize how long we have been friends—he once said to me, "Why can we not create blue overalls instead of blue helmets?" Keep the blue helmets, by all means, but let us have some form of postwar reconstruction and development effort. And the more, as I said, multinational and nondenominational it is, the more we give credence to our shared commitment to enabling the poor. One of the great tragedies of 9/11 is that we worked in Pakistan with the katchi abadi authorities and India with the Alternative Development Group, in Bangladesh with BRAC [Bangladesh Rural

Advancement Committee], trying to educate rural women. My late sister-in-law was a lawyer in Bangladesh. She worked for twenty years offering free legal advice to women to eradicate legal illiteracy. We talk about citizenship—it just doesn't happen overnight. People have to learn. I speak of communities that were spinning and weaving right up to 9/11 and exporting textiles. 9/11 led to a decision to stop the import of textiles from South Asia, and I asked a congressmen I knew, "Why are you throwing these people into the arms of the drug barons and the war lords?" And the answers were more commercial than they were humanitarian. So I think it's hugely important to look at those three baskets of Helsinki once again: security, economy, and culture. And to develop a strategy to which we can all relate. Otherwise, I have to tell you that most organizations, even the best funded, are searching desperately for much-needed funds. You don't find a Jimmy Carter everyday who focuses on guinea worm and gets the job done.

MAJOR GENERAL KEITH W. DAYTON: Your Highness, let me thank you for an opening address that I think put a tremendous perspective on where we're going with this conference. I think Dwight Eisenhower would agree with the profound observations you made that it's really all about people, and at the same time, there is no purely military solution to any of the challenges we face. In fact, the military may be only one element, perhaps a fairly small element, of national power. And with that introduction that you gave us, I think we are ready to get to work here. So Your Highness, again, thank you very much for, to me, a very profoundly rewarding address. Thank you.

PANEL I

POWER AND NATIONAL SOVEREIGNTY

Co-sponsor: National Committee on American Foreign Policy

Moderator: Bernard E. Brown, Ph.D., Transatlantic Relations Project
      Director, National Committee on American Foreign Policy
Ambassador Richard N. Gardner, Ph.D., Professor, Columbia Law
      School
Ambassador Alyson J. K. Bailes Director, Stockholm International Peace
      Research Institute
Ambassador Herman J. Cohen, Former U.S. Assistant Secretary of State
George D. Schwab, Ph.D., President, National Committee on American
      Foreign Policy

Panel Charter

Is national sovereignty being eroded, and if so, to what extent? Are
nation-states still the basic unit of the international system, or are they being displaced by other players and forces from below (ethnic groups, civil society) and
from above (regional and international organizations)? If the latter, what are the
implications for the use of military and other power?

Discussion Points

Each panelist was asked to focus on one of the following challenges to national
sovereignty:

1. Globalization of the economy. Are nation-states still in a position to make
authoritative decisions concerning fiscal flows, trade, labor relations, and all other
traditional concerns when many problems now arise beyond national borders? Is a
global society (including activists, nongovernmental organizations, and world con-
gresses called by the UN General Assembly) making it difficult or even impossible for
nation-states and intergovernmental agencies to function?

2. The rise of regional organizations, notably the European Union (EU). Does
the EU represent a new kind of "postmodern" power, presaging the "breaking of

Left to right: *Alyson J. K. Bailes, Bernard E. Brown, Herman J. Cohen,*
George D. Schwab, and Richard N. Gardner.

nations" (as in the title of a recent book by Robert Cooper) and a transformation
of the Westphalian system based on the principle of national sovereignty?

3. Genocide. There is widespread desire to prevent genocide and violations of
human rights, particularly in "failed" states. Is the principle of national sovereignty
undermined by intervention of external forces, either by regional organizations or
the United Nations?

4. Political situation. Are we perhaps in that most dangerous of all political
situations, referred to by Emile Durkheim as "anomie"? This occurs when old
institutions and values have lost their effectiveness and legitimacy, but new ones
have not yet been created.

Summary

Ambassador Richard N. Gardner, Ph.D.

   Is the Westphalian system being changed under the forces of globalization? Is
the U.S. ability hindered by the UN and constrained by international law?

• Sovereign nation-states will continue to be the primary actors in international
relations for the foreseeable future. However, in examining the roles that states
can and do play, it is necessary to distinguish between their formal, legal status
(juridical right to establish laws and enforce them on a territory rests with that
state alone) and their actual ability to secure borders, preside over a functioning
economy, and cope with environmental degradation. Performing the latter tasks
requires pooling sovereignty.

• NATO changed markedly at the end of the 20th century in order to adapt to
the needs and opportunities of the post-Cold War world. Through the Euro-Atlantic

Partnership Council, the NATO-Ukraine Council, the NATO-Russia Council and the expansion of the alliance to 26 members in 2004, NATO has worked to extend the sphere of mutually assured defense. NATO reformed its command structures to ensure that all countries wishing to work together on security matters could do so, and it accepted the fact that going "out-of-area" would be necessary to keep the alliance relevant and safe. NATO completed successful missions in Bosnia and Kosovo, knowing that failure would have gravely compromised its international standing and ability to deter potential adversaries.

• The primary security threats today are suicide terrorism and terrorists in pursuit of weapons of mass destruction (WMD).

• The U.S. national economy is substantially affected by the global economy, whether in terms of our sizable energy imports or our external deficit, which exceeds a trillion dollars. Given this dependency, the only way to ensure effective sovereignty is to accept limitations on our formal sovereignty through agreements in which we accept mutual restraints and reciprocal concessions.

• International law certainly constrains the United States. International law involves those "wise restraints" that keep the peace and that make interdependence a viable proposition. This body of law was imposed, but developed through treaties (in some limited cases, through custom) to which the United States gave its consent. One exception to this body of consensual law can be found in Chapter VII of the UN Charter, which empowers the UN Security Council to make law for its members. As one of the veto-wielding permanent members of the Security Council, the United States can block laws proposed by others and can help enact laws that bind others.

• U.S. Ambassador to the United Nations John Bolton takes a different view of international law. He believes that it is a mistake to grant any validity to international law because over the long term, those most dedicated to it are those who want to constrict the United States. Yet this perspective is directly at odds with that of America's historical allies, not to mention the traditional U.S. approach. The hope is that the U.S. government will rejoin the mainstream.

• Should international law override sovereignty where genocide or massive human rights violations are being committed? The international community has a responsibility to protect when the sovereign power is unable or unwilling to do so. The big question is whether UN members, especially the five permanent members of the UN Security Council, will be willing to act in the future in situations like Darfur.

• Anticipatory self-defense cannot and should not be adopted to replace preventive war, which is justified in situations where a threat of attack is imminent.

• The International Criminal Court poses a dilemma for the United States. U.S. policymakers must look at each agreement on its merits to determine whether, on balance, it serves American interests. In this case, because the United States is the world's residual peacekeeper, U.S. military personnel are uniquely vulnerable to frivolous prosecutions. Unfortunately, the United States did not succeed in having the necessary safeguards written into the Rome Treaty.

Ambassador Alyson J. K. Bailes

What relevance does the EU have for issues of sovereignty and pooling of sovereignty?

- In spite of the present crisis of confidence, the European Union is a strong and vibrant family of twenty-five (soon to be twenty-seven) nations. The EU is the primary model for countries pursuing regional integration. Furthermore, the EU still represents America's main partner in addressing new security threats such as terrorism and weapons of mass destruction (WMD) proliferation. Sensible Europeans see that "terrorism strikes at foundations of ordered global society."

- Is the European Union a global power in its own right? Let us recall the unique motives that spurred its creation: the traumas of World War II, shared grief and guilt, fear of falling once again into the abyss, as well as hope. The European enterprise was essentially aimed at avoiding war. The field in which Europeans decided not to collaborate—defense—was essentially outsourced to the North Atlantic Treaty Organization (NATO). This logic prevailed until EU members took their first concrete steps in 1999 to develop an independent European military capability. Yet this is in its infancy; the EU is far from becoming an "antipower."

- There are three drivers of the EU reassessment of its potential and duties in addressing security threats. The first is functional, a shift in the nature of threats to those that arise from within the social sector. The EU has some competence in these fields, such as customs and border and export controls, binding laws that encompass all members across the whole territory. Most ordinary and sensible Europeans are willing to accept this. The second driver is geographical; it stems from the fact that with enlargement eastward, the EU shares a border with Russia, Ukraine, and the Balkans, and thus faces new security challenges. The third driver is political: the United States has gradually scaled down its forces from Europe and at the same time expects its European partners to be more active outside Europe.

- Europe is experiencing growing pains. Europeans are reluctant to give up sovereignty. They are accustomed to patterns and practices inherited from NATO, whereby they never had to give up assets to central command. Nor did they have to adopt common positions for dealing with problems like China and the rest. European politicians have to deal with the ambivalence of their publics.

- What Europe will create through the continuing evolution of the EU will not be an empire. At its core, the EU is based on voluntary membership, dialogue, compromise, rule of law. These attributes are attractive to other countries. But in developing their own regional structures, these countries will have to mold them to their own distinctive security needs.

Ambassador Herman J. Cohen

When does intervention not violate the Westphalian system?

- South Africa is the only African country that has fully consolidated its sovereignty. Most African governments are thus very sensitive to infringements on their sovereignty. Yet, much of the assistance offered by the West is conditioned on African beneficiaries ceding sovereignty. African leaders are very wary, for example, of privatization, which they suspect will build competing power centers.

- It took African leaders thirty years to agree that large-scale violence in any country is the business of all African countries. So fixated on national sovereignty have they been that African Union members didn't intervene in the Darfur conflict until 2003, and even then reluctantly, at which time a mechanism for mediating conflict was created and became operational.

- How can Africans engage in selective globalization so that they can take advantage of these forces? They are largely incapable of doing so because of this preoccupation with sovereignty. They need larger markets—regional common markets—to benefit from economies of scale. Yet they are dragging their feet.

- What implications does this situation have for U.S. interests in Africa? U.S. officials used to look at Africa mostly in humanitarian terms. Now, we look at Africa more strategically. Yet we must tread carefully, considering the sensitive issue of national sovereignty. Two decisions made by President Eisenhower in 1958 will serve us well in this regard: his decisions to treat each African country as sovereign and to rely on the United Nations to deal with peace and conflict. The homage Eisenhower paid to the idea of national sovereignty will enable us to achieve our national objectives in Africa.

- The Geneva Convention demands action on genocide, but the international community's reaction to acts of genocide has been very selective, ranging from a robust military intervention in Kosovo to tepid responses in Africa. We do not really believe in the responsibility to protect.

George D. Schwab, Ph.D.

Is political sovereignty indivisible?

- National sovereignty is inextricably linked to a well-functioning political system. The latter improves the prospects for ensuring order, peace, and stability.

- We must readjust our thinking about state sovereignty. It is possible both to pool sovereignty and to retain it. The European Union, a complex body of twenty-five member states, is a prime example. By joining the European Union, member states continue to articulate their political interests and act accordingly. The EU is not a politically sovereign body, nor does it aspire to become one at this time.

- The state cannot cede its fundamental obligation to protect its territory and people. It can enter treaties and the like, but cannot willingly divest itself of the right to distinguish friend and foe and to act accordingly.

Question-and-Answer Period

• Regarding the safeguards necessary for the United States to accede to the International Criminal Court (ICC), Gardner responded that U.S. Soldiers and public officials must be protected from frivolous accusations. It will be difficult to build adequate safeguards into the present ICC arrangements when there is not yet a sufficiently strong international consensus as to what constitutes aggression and war crimes.

• Regarding the possible impact upon the United Nations of Ambassador John Bolton's tenure as the chief U.S. representative to that body, Gardner said that nobody questions Mr. Bolton's intellect or expertise. However, his temperament and worldview are of great concern. Unless U.S. officials demonstrate a decent respect for the interests and priorities of others in the conduct of diplomacy in the United Nations, no progress can be achieved. Confrontational tactics are bound to backfire.

• Might the forces of globalization lead to conflict? Gardner noted that on balance, globalization serves the interests of others as well as the United States. The best way to avoid wars over scarce resources is to reinforce institutions such as the World Trade Organization (WTO), create and strengthen other mechanisms aimed at transparency, and encourage open markets. With respect to global poverty, the United States and other advanced industrialized states must open our markets to agricultural and other products from developing countries. In addition, mechanisms must be introduced to respond to product surges and hot money flows to guard against the economic destabilization that might ensue and the human consequences of displacement that would follow from it.

• What are those forces at work in Africa that are undermining the very sovereignty that Africans seek? According to Cohen, good governance and the rule of law are precious but scarce commodities in Africa. Upon independence, African states inherited these concepts, but perhaps not the institutions to apply them. As a result, this moderately good base was lost due to greed and corruption. During the Cold War, by making sweetheart deals with African dictators, multinational corporations (MNCs) contributed to this problem. Today, however, MNCs tend not to want to enter a country that is corrupt, since they are fearful of instability and of the consequent loss of investment. With the possible exception of the energy sector, they realize that deals with dictators are not enough to protect their investments.

• Against the backdrop of the sixty-year evolution of the European Union, what are the prospects for subregional integration efforts in the Western Hemisphere, such as the Andean Pact, MERCOSUR, and the like? Bailes observed that the problem with these integration projects is that there are about a half dozen of them, and they overlap. Therefore, it is difficult to locate precisely where the dynamism is. Nevertheless, the good news is that there is more free trade and free investment in Latin America and the Caribbean than ever. There are no more interstate conflicts. Although two costly internal conflicts continue to rage, by and large, neighboring countries are not exacerbating them.

• Regarding U.S. food aid policy, Cohen said that so much aid was funneled into Niger that it threatened the collapse of local agriculture. But it is important to note that when, as in the case of Niger, countries lack sovereignty, they are unable to control the international response. Regional factors must also be taken into account. In the Niger case, neighboring Nigeria's new policies banning the importation of poultry increased domestic demand for grain and distorted the regional market. The United States, too, tends to distort markets by dumping grain into impoverished countries, using food aid as a subsidy program for the American farmer.

• To what extent is the lack of infrastructure a major cause of Africa's development woes? There is a need for infrastructure, Cohen noted, and the United States had poured significant resources into large infrastructure projects in the 1960s and early 1970s. By 1975, the United States became disillusioned. Africans had been so preoccupied with consolidation of power and sovereignty that they had failed to assume responsibility for properly maintaining roads and other infrastructure. Resources are once again being channeled toward port rehabilitation, electric power, and rail transport projects, now that a small number of African countries have begun to respond to the stimuli of the World Bank and the International Monetary Fund (IMF). They are "going back to basics."

• Is the core of the problem of postmodern society the difficulty of sending Soldiers to die for the protection of a national economy? According to Bailes, there is an emotional, cultural dimension of "nationhood." It is difficult to send Soldiers to die to save a common market or the global economy. The motto of the EU is "unity and diversity," and it reflects the desire to retain the "good juice" of national identity. Although it is difficult to ask people to die for something other than their nation, many assume this risk and make the sacrifice. The challenge is not just to motivate the armed forces, but to enable the ordinary citizen to grasp common risks and challenges, and the necessity of common action.

• The European Union sets strict conditions for entry of new nation members, including internal economic and foreign policy issues. Bailes noted that prospective members must be able to implement 80,000 pages of common rules. She would advocate dropping some of the more insignificant rules and putting more emphasis on how countries relate to their neighbors, how they deal with historical claims and problems. Even ancient enemies like Poland and Lithuania have demonstrated the ability to make peace with each other before being offered EU membership.

Analysis

The panelists generally agreed that state sovereignty will remain the basis for international organization, no other formula having emerged from the forces of change. They also agreed, however, that state sovereignty is not what it once was, and pooling sovereignty, along the general lines of that in practice by the European Union, may typify or even serve as a guide to the future. The bedrock issue for the continuation of the concept of state sovereignty is providing security to the population—there is no major impetus to cast that requirement aside. Although none directly addressed the question, "Is a global society making it difficult or even impossible for nation-states and intergovernmental agencies to function?" it was clear that the answer was very situation dependent. None of the speakers addressed the issue of preventive war and anticipatory self-defense.

Ambassador Richard Gardner set the stage with his remarks regarding the continuing centrality of state sovereignty and the absence of a viable alternative. The various threats to state sovereignty mesh nicely, as the threads of both the limiting and empowering force of international law are woven together. The impetus to act against genocide and its equivalent atrocities, for example, illustrates a clear mandate to set sovereignty aside, as does Chapter VII of the United Nations Charter. Ambassador Gardner then held up Ambassador John Bolton as an illustration of a countervailing force demanding a special position for the United States as a country under attack by both terrorists and manipulators of international law.

Ambassador Bailes posited the case for the European Union as a model for what might be termed blended sovereignty, and rightly noted the growing pains of this grouping. Her characterization of the EU as a work in progress was ably supported by enumeration of the continuing changes underway in its attitudes, membership, and security challenges. She gave tacit assent to Ambassador Gardner's proposition that state sovereignty remains central to a functioning world system, but emphasized the attractiveness to other regional groupings of the EU's basis for success—voluntary membership, open dialogue, compromise, and especially the rule of law.

Ambassador Cohen examined sovereignty from an African perspective. He noted that only South Africa could claim to have consolidated its sovereignty. Other African states continue to be extremely jealous of their sovereignty, to the detriment of progress. They now seem to be entering a phase in which the violence of the past three decades may be yielding to cooperative actions that no longer appear to threaten state sovereignty. If the United States continues to follow President Eisenhower's 1958 decision to treat them as sovereign states responsible to the United Nations for dealing with issues of peace and conflict, he said, the concept will endure, although with unique interpretations.

Dr. Schwab tied the preceding observations together, noting the essential nature of the concept of state sovereignty and the adaptation through the idea of pooling currently exhibited by the EU. He closed by giving central emphasis to the idea that a state is first responsible for the security of its peoples.

So, does the European Union represent a case of pooled sovereignty, and perhaps the coming of a new era in which regional organizations replace nation-states? Ambassador Bailes asserted that Europeans have given up national sovereignty in many areas, though not in defense and some other fields. Dr. Schwab denied that Europeans have ceded to the EU the right to determine their political interests.

The disagreement to some extent is semantic, turning on the definition of sovereignty and whether voluntary agreement to accept common rules on the economy and trade falls in the realm of cooperation or authoritative decision making. Dr. Schwab agreed that the EU is an economic superpower that can act as one entity, and Ambassador Bailes conceded that nation-states retain their prerogatives in the critical areas of foreign policy and defense. The failure of the EU to adopt the proposed Constitutional Treaty indicates that the legitimacy of the central institutions of the EU is in question. The progress made toward increasing European unity while retaining diversity nonetheless is one of the most important developments in international relations since World War II.

Are we now entering a period of anomie, wherein existing institutions are undermined and new ones are not (or not yet) effective? Discussion by the panelists led up to but did not confront this issue. The consensus among panelists seemed to be that nation-states remain the leading actors on the world stage, and so far have dealt with new threats and challenges by cooperating among themselves and pursuing their interests within regional organizations and the United Nations. But many warning lights are flashing. Nation-states are finding it increasingly difficult to manage the multitudinous problems created by globalization. The Westphalian system is being adapted to new circumstances and will certainly be changed in important ways, if not transformed, in the process.

In the question-and-answer period, the uniqueness of the U.S. challenges and responsibilities were highlighted several times in regard to the exercise of international law and what some see as an attempt to ride roughshod over the United Nations. Oddly, there was no follow-up to Ambassador Cohen's closing observation that the demand for action on matters as serious as genocide was very selective. These two matters could have borne a great deal more focused attention. Much attention was devoted to Africa, the reasons for its massive failures, and the emerging hopes for its progress. Ambassador Bailes made one of those quietly stunning points that, in regard to the evident benefits of globalization, 80,000 pages of regulations do not make for rapid progress.

Transcript

ANNOUNCER: Please welcome the moderator for our first panel, the Transatlantic Relations project director of the National Committee of American Foreign Policy, Professor Bernard E. Brown.

PROFESSOR BERNARD E. BROWN: I'm just the moderator, so it's a difficult role because, as an academic, I'm programmed to speak for fifty minutes. But fear not, I will just take a few moments. It is my task to simply present the issue and then the panel.

Now the issue we are discussing is national sovereignty and power. National sovereignty means that states have exclusive jurisdiction over their territories and that states exercise a monopoly on the legitimate use of violence. Another way of putting it is that no other state has the right to interfere in the internal domestic policies of that state in its own territory. This is the bedrock principle of international relations. It has been the bedrock principle for at last three and a half centuries. In fact, historians generally agree that it is a principle that was recognized at the Peace of Westphalia, and that is the reason why we refer to the international state system in short hand as the Westphalian system. I mention that because our speakers are going to make references to the Westphalian system.

The Westphalian system did not come out of a vacuum. There was a reason why it emerged. It emerged after a long period, a centuries-long

Bernard E. Brown

period of extraordinary violence that raged all over Europe. There was a confusion of jurisdictions, a rivalry of powers among potentates and petty princes and pretenders to thrones, and included armies in the service of various interpretations of religious faith. There was a murderous religious civil war going on in Europe. And finally, it was simply a consensus that one way out of the chaos was to establish the principle, to recognize the principle of national sovereignty.

Now the question that the panel is going to face is whether and to what extent this principle of national sovereignty is now eroding. Are the states still the basic units of the international state system? The state is being challenged, and this is especially true since the end of the Second World War and the end of the Cold War. The state is being challenged from every side. It is being challenged from below and outside and above. Below and outside, there are powerful multinationals whose capitalization and power sometimes exceed that of even moderate-sized, certainly small states. There are ethnic groups; members of these ethnic groups sometimes feel greater loyalty to their ethnic group than to the state, and these ethnic groups sometimes spill out over borders. There are criminal networks—drug-selling networks and so on—that operate internationally. And the state is being challenged from above, from regional organizations and from the United Nations itself, the international organization that, under certain conditions can't intervene in the internal policies of states and certainly to protect human rights. And there are regional organizations: states are pooling their sovereignty or pooling their authority in order to accomplish certain objectives because, while states are the supreme authorities in principle, they do establish rules of the game among themselves. They do respect a certain code of behavior.

Now, our panelists are going to approach this question from their angles of expertise, and let me just produce a quick check list. We are going to have three major angles of approach, and each angle corresponds to the point I just made about the challenges to the state from below, outside, and above. The first question is that of globalization. There are titanic movements of capital across national borders, movements of people, migration—some of it illegal—movements of labor, instant communications now through computers and the Internet. Do states still have the capacity to establish law and order and to regulate their societies and their economies in this age of globalization? A key question, which we are going to address first. Second, what about the weak or the failed states and the problems that they create? Suppose these weak and failed states cannot protect human rights and maintain law and order within their territories. Suppose they constitute a danger to other peoples. Is there an obligation, a power on the part of the international community to intervene? Does that weaken the Westphalian system? Are we witnessing a transformation of the Westphalian system under the impact of globalization and the problems created by the weak and the failed states? And then third, a special angle—regionalism, the most important example of which is the European Union. Are states pooling their sovereignty in the European Union? Are we seeing the emergence of a new kind of state, perhaps a state that is not based on force and violence—the classic definition of the state is the legitimate use of force and violence—but one based on institutionalized dialogue, constant negotiation, and consensus? What some people have called a postmodern state? For some people, indeed, this is the future of not only regional organizations, but perhaps the international state system. And in this view, the European Union represents the future, and the United States, as a classic state, represents the past. Tocqueville is stood on his head.

Now these are some of the issues that we are going to explore. We have four panelists and I will present each one briefly. At least I think that's our system. What's happening to the panelists? Ah, here come the panelists. I will present each panelist individually because you might forget who they are if I present them all at once. Our first panelist is Richard Gardner, who is on the extreme left. He is a former United States ambassador to Italy and also to Spain. He is now a professor of international law and organization at Columbia University. He is a prolific author; in fact, his most recent book is called *Mission Italy*—I have a copy that I'm supposed to hold up—and it is being published by Roland Publishers. You can order it from Amazon.com or on the Internet. I'm going to present a leading question for each panelist, and the question that I am going to ask Ambassador Gardner to address is the following: Is the Westphalian system, which I described very briefly before, being affected, being changed, perhaps even being transformed under the impact of globalization? And as a follow-up to that, a question that I think would concern many people in this audience, for example: Is the ability of the United

States to defend its national interests hindered or affected by its membership in the United Nations and constrained under international law by, for example, the creation of the International Criminal Court? Professor Gardner. Each panelist will have fifteen minutes.

AMBASSADOR RICHARD N. GARDNER: Thank you, Bernard. It is a great honor to be a speaker at this 2005 Eisenhower Security Conference and to be part of a panel with three old friends, all distinguished thinkers about international affairs. I have been given a question that requires about three hours, but I will do my best in fifteen minutes to respond and hit the highlights.

We live in a world of sovereign nation-states, and this will continue to be true, in my view, for the foreseeable future. We are not going to have a world government. But we have to distinguish between formal, legal sovereignty and effective, real sovereignty. By formal, legal sovereignty, I mean that it will continue to be true that the juridical right to establish laws and enforce laws on a nation's territory will rest with that nation alone. But by effective sovereignty, I mean the ability of any nation—including the strongest in the world, the United States—to secure the physical safety of its people in an age of terrorism, to secure the economic security of its people in an age of globalization, to secure the environmental security of its people in an age of global warming and transnational environmental threats. That power is increasingly diminishing and requires a pooling of sovereignty through international law and organization with other countries if we are truly to be effectively sovereign.

Look at the main threats to the United States today. Suicidal terrorism in pursuit of nuclear weapons: Is there any way the United States can defend itself against that threat without the cooperation of others? Obviously not. Look at our economic situation. I was at a meeting yesterday in which Alan Greenspan, our distinguished head of the Federal Reserve, spoke. He started out with a remarkable statement. He said, "When I try to forecast America's economy, I start with the world economy." He said, "I start with the question of the price of oil; our dependence on foreign oil is such that our situation is now substantially affected by the availability of oil and the dangers of the pass-through of that increased oil price into inflation and reduction of consumer spending." Our external deficit each year, right now has reached $700 billion. We are in debt to the Chinese, Japanese, Taiwanese, Koreans, and others well in excess of a trillion dollars—and that grows every year. So how sovereign are we really, given our financial dependency, our energy dependency? We want to open markets to our products. We want to protect American investors abroad. Again, that requires cooperation from others. So, to sum up this rather obvious point, the paradox is that the only way to assure the effective sovereignty of the United States is to accept limitations on our formal sovereignty by pooling our sovereignty through international agreements, agreements in which we accept mutual restraints and reciprocal concessions from other countries.

I heard our distinguished moderator refer to the principle of noninterference in the internal affairs of other countries. What is an internal affair in an interde-

Richard N. Gardner

pendent world? Let me tell you, when I was ambassador to Italy, much of my time—and I have just written about this in a book, *Mission Italy*, which you kindly referred to—was spent trying to say to the Italian people that if they voted the Communists into power, as seemed very likely when I arrived in Italy in the spring of 1977, given the orientation of the Italian Communist Party—despite Enrico Berlinguer, still pro-Soviet and hostile to the U.S.—that that would have a profound effect on the Western alliance and on the American view, that we had a right to say to the Italians what kind of allies we preferred to have. I also lobbied the Italians to increase by 3 percent their defense spending. I also lobbied them hard to do more to punish the Soviet Union for its invasion of Afghanistan and to help us respond to the taking of American hostages by cutting off trade and credit to Iran. Was I interfering in domestic affairs? When I went as ambassador to Spain, I spent a good deal of my time lobbying Spain to do more to protect American intellectual property, lobbying Spain to take a stronger line in the European Union on GMO [genetically modified organism] foods, which were of great importance to us, and to eliminate certain regulatory barriers affecting Americans. There used to be an old adage: the one thing an ambassador should not do is intervene in the "internal affairs of the country to which he is accredited." Well that advice is wrong. Of course, you don't intervene by CIA dirty trick operations or murdering people or corrupting people. I'm talking about what Joe Nye [former dean, John F. Kennedy School of Government, Harvard University] refers to as "soft power": using persuasion.

Now, international law, very briefly. The question is, does international law constrain the United States? Of course it does. There was a great Supreme Court justice who referred to the role of law in domestic society as embodying those wise restraints that make men free. International law, in our world of interdependence, involves those wise restraints that keep the peace and make interdependence a viable proposition. And I would argue that international law, in that sense, helps America and helps American security. It is, as I said before, something that embodies mutual restraints and reciprocal concessions, which are in the interest of all concerned. This international law is not imposed from on high; it is developed through treaties and, in some exceptional cases, customary rules that we consent to. We use our sovereignty to form these rules, which we then need to comply with.

Now there is one exception to this consensual international law, and that's found in Chapter VII of the UN Charter, and very few people realize this. The Security Council, under the UN Charter, can make law for its members. That's in Chapter VII—they can actually make law, impose law on its members, except the five permanent members, who have a veto. So you have a wonderful situation from the American point of view. We can block any Security Council action imposing an obligation on us. But 186 of 191 members of the UN can't; they have accepted a set of rules under which the Security Council can tell them what to do, and it *is* telling them what to do right now—in resolutions telling them that they must cut off financing to terrorists, that they must arrest terrorists and extradite them, that they must take steps to hold nuclear proliferation, and so on. Seventeen UN peacekeeping operations are underway in places where the U.S. does not want to send its military. Yes, these are imperfect operations. How could they not be, given the difficulty? But the choice would be, if we had no UN, either the U.S. would have to send Soldiers to die there, or these seventeen trouble spots would spiral out of control.

Now I have a problem with time. How much time do I have left? Two minutes. John Bolton, our new ambassador to the UN, has, as you would all understand, a different view than mine. He said in the late 1990s, and I quote, "It is a big mistake for us to grant any validity to international law, even when it may seem in our short-term interest to do so, because," he added "over the long-term, the goal of those who think that international law really means anything are those who want to constrict the United States." John Bolton is a brilliant man, but he is so wrong on this and he is out of the mainstream. Dwight Eisenhower would never have said anything like this; Harry Truman never said anything like this; George Bush's father never, Bill Clinton, others. This is not the American way. We believe in building a rule of law, and I hope—and I am convinced that—our government will rejoin that mainstream.

Just one other thing: there is the question whether, in exceptional circumstances, the United Nations or any regional organization can override national sovereignty—where there is genocide or massive violation of human rights as there was in Kosovo. My own view of that is, it's a difficult question. There is a responsibility to protect people when the national sovereign state is unwilling or unable to do so. And the question is, in the light of recent recommendations by a high-level panel and by Kofi Annan [secretary-general of the United Nations], whether this responsibility to protect will be recognized as an exception to traditional sovereignty, and whether the UN members, particularly the five permanent members—which include, of course, China and Russia—will be willing to act in future situations like Darfur, and in places in Africa. That is a question that is still open.

The United States has an interest in using its military power in accordance with the rules of the game, which essentially say, we can do so when approved by the Security Council or when it's in self-defense, and self-defense includes anticipatory self-defense where there is an imminent threat to the United States. But in my view, and I think most of the countries of the world would support this view that I am expressing, this right of self-defense cannot be stretched from anticipatory self-defense in the face of an imminent threat to preventive war. That doctrine was rejected at Nuremberg [Nuremburg War Crimes Trials], and if it were accepted internationally, would license India to attack Pakistan, China to attack Taiwan, the Arab states to attack Israel. So when we adopt a new theory of the use of American power, and I conclude with this, let us always be careful to be sure that we are prepared to live with the consequences.

I close with a quote from my old friend, Zbigniew Brzezinski. He said in an article that appears this month in a new magazine, *The American Interest*, "America needs to shore up its international legitimacy by a demonstrable commitment to shared political and social goals. We must become the pacesetter in shaping the world that is defined less by the fiction of state sovereignty and more by the reality of expanding and politically regulated interdependence."

BROWN: Could I ask for one more comment. We still have two minutes. What about a comment on the International Criminal Court.

GARDNER: The International Criminal Court presents for someone like me, frankly, a dilemma because I am a multilateralist, as you would gather, but I'm a selective multilateralist. I think you have to look at each international agreement on its merits to decide whether, on balance, it serves our interest. I think it is tragic that in the negotiations for this court, we could not get a few safeguards in there to reassure the United States. Our position is unique and uniquely vulnerable. We have hundreds of thousands of our military all around the world. We are the world's residual peacekeeper, and therefore any system that threatens to hold our military leaders accountable and put them in an international tribunal, or even our Henry Kissingers or Madeline Albrights... But there were some NGOs that said that what we did in Kosovo was a violation of international law and should go to the International Criminal Court. So I would say that the concept that there should be rules applied to war crimes and aggressive war—yes, the concept is good. But I think this particular instrument would have to be amended in significant respects before I could recommend to any president or secretary of state that we ratify. Thank you.

BROWN: Thank you, Ambassador Gardner. Our next speaker is Alyson Bailes, who is a former UK ambassador to Finland, who represented the UK and various security agencies of the European Union before that, and who is now director of the International Institute for Peace Research in Stockholm. I want her to speak on the European Union as a regional organization. And my question for Ambassador Bailes is the following: What is the special relevance of the European experience for the sovereignty issue? Ambassador Bailes.

Alyson J. K. Bailes

AMBASSADOR ALYSON J. K. BAILES: Thank you very much. It's an honor and pleasure to be here, also somewhat scary and difficult to speak about Europe or for Europe when the EU is still in the crisis of confidence following the collapse of efforts for a new constitution. But however that crisis may be overcome, some facts about the EU won't change. It's a family now of twenty-five nations, soon to be twenty-seven, with the addition of Bulgaria and Romania, and some of them are fairly advanced, rich, influential nations. The EU model is actually being imitated by a number of other regional groups that are going for deeper integration in Latin America, in Africa and parts of Africa, and the ASEAN [Association of South East Asian Nations] region. For the United States, the EU already represents its main sparring partner in the area of trade and economic management, and it's fast becoming an active partner in dealing with all the nonmilitary manifestations of new threats like terrorism and proliferation, which have to be tackled essentially by nonmilitary means. So if there is something right about the EU model, a hardheaded U.S. strategy would say, okay, how can we exploit that? And if it has its weaknesses, all those people in other continents who have been, to some degree, inspired by it need to think carefully how they will avoid making the same mistakes that the Europeans have made. I am going to trace this issue just on one particular question, which I think fits with our panel theme here: the EU as a power. Does the EU think of itself as a power in the world? Do others see it that way? What kind of power is it or does it behave like?

To start on that issue, I have to ask you for a moment to jump back sixty years to realize how unique the motives were for creating the European Community movement, which led to the European Union of today. In the past, countries lost sovereignty if they were eaten up by other countries. They became part of an empire or they pulled together in a traditional alliance to combine their strengths for greater strategic impact. But after the traumas of World War II, when everyone shared in suffering and guilt to some degree, the countries that built the European Community did it out of fear as well as hope—fear of falling back into the abyss of their own nationalism—not trying to pool the power or the way of doing things that they'd had up to then, but to leap ahead to a new age in which power relations, at least within Europe, would not entrap them anymore. So it was very much an enterprise about war and about avoiding war again in Europe. But the one area where the European members decided not to cooperate, at least after the collapse of a short-lived experiment in 1953–54, was the area of defense. That was essentially outsourced to NATO, where the Europeans worked with the United States. That strong division of roles between the EU and NATO stood firm right up to about 1999, when the Europeans took the first steps to having a military capability, at least for some limited goals of crisis management. And another point I need to throw in here is that, although NATO was a very strong, integrated alliance, it did not try to have common positions or actions on things happening outside Europe. And so when you think of the EU in these early years, it was, in a sense, an antipower. It was several steps away from playing any kind of traditional strategic role.

But if we fast forward to the present, I can see three main drivers that are forcing Europeans to rethink all of that, to ask themselves about the EU's potential as a power and perhaps its duty to be a power. Now the first reason is functional, that is, the shift of security concern, as we have heard so well explained this morning, to threats of a new kind—terrorism, proliferation, crime, disease, bad weather— that arise in the social and economic field, rather than the traditional defense sector, and can only to a limited degree be checked with military weapons. Now the EU has some competencies in that field. It has policies on things that are important for checking terrorism, like internal affairs and justice, border control, customs, transport security. It has competence of relevance checking proliferation, like industrial regulation and strict export controls. And it has the very interesting power to make binding laws for all its members across the whole territory, and for those transnational enemies who are working at the levels of individuals and corporations, the power to hit them with the traditional tools of executive power. But if you can have an all-embracing law and you can enforce it, you can catch even the smallest, even the most individual of your enemies. And Europe's people—let's not mistake this—they want to use that capacity against threats like terrorism, not just because they know they can themselves become victims of terrorists and all the more because they live in this open, single market without borders of such a huge area of the continent, but because, I think, sensible Europeans see that terrorism is part of a vicious cycle with conflict and bad, inadequate development. They can see that terrorism strikes at the foundations of the ordered global society in which a rich and vulnerable creation like the EU needs to be able to live.

The second driver is geographical. We have expanded our membership and our territory enormously. We have come up against the borders of countries like Russia, Ukraine, and Belarus. It's pretty clear that we are going to have to continue, at least so far as embracing the Balkans region, and that new weight of responsibility would make people take their security responsibilities more seriously. But there are two extra facts in the way that this happened. The nature of the new central European members of the EU, now they understand this point about integration, limiting the bad aspects of their own nationalism; but if they give up sovereignty for a collective group, they want that collective group to go out and act to protect freedom and democracy, not just our own, but other people's. And then there's the nature of our neighbors, Russia, Ukraine, and the rest. They are a strategic challenge. There are problems on the security and the stability front, the spreading of new threats from them. You don't have to posit a military attack to see that there is a security agenda there, and they're a challenge for integration. Some of them now aspire to live the EU way of life, but getting them there is a bigger challenge than we've ever faced. And the EU, frankly, up to now is muffing that challenge, partly because there are very different approaches to Russia, in particular among members of the EU. But the challenge is not going to go away, and one day we will have to meet it.

Then there is the political driver. The biggest influence politically on the EU is still the United States. And if I try and cut through all the emotions and debates about how we affect each other on the different values, let's get through to two important strategic points. First, the U.S. is increasingly withdrawing its direct military engagement from Europe and hoping that Europe, at least on a day-to-day basis, can take on more of its own security burdens. Second, where the EU and U.S. work together, the U.S. expects it to be outside in the world for purposes that go beyond just the narrow defense of our own territory. For both of those reasons, the Europeans have been driven to get their strategic act together, to have some kind of manipulable military potential.

Now why did they choose to work for that in the EU framework as well as in NATO? Because increasingly—and not just because of what they think about the U.S.—Europeans like the idea of sometimes being able to do military operations for their own interests, under their own leadership, in their own way, and that won't necessarily be in ways that hurt the U.S. Let me just take the latest operation that was approved, in the Aceh province of Indonesia. But if you link up these present pressures with the past, I think you can see why Europe has difficulty walking down that road to become a power Its pattern of strengths and weakness was actually inherited from NATO as well as the EU. Because neither in the EU nor NATO have Europeans up to now really had to pool their military forces and give up significant national control in the military sphere or start seriously specializing. Neither in the EU nor NATO have they been required to have common positions on the hard defense issues out there in the rest of the world. Issues like the Middle East conflict, how to deal with the challenge of China, and so on. And both from the U.S. side and from European populations, there is pressure saying okay, cross those last divides, tackle those tough issues. But as we've seen in the votes on the new constitution, the European people, at the same time, are terribly sensitive about giving up what they see now as the last shreds of national sovereignty, which they have retained in the military field, but not in others. How can Europe's politicians deal with that? Well, they have to convince the people that what is at stake here, greater security also against the new and intimate threats—that game is worth the candle; it is worth making these final sacrifices for. And then they have to actually get those results of greater security, effectiveness through both capabilities and coordination, and they have to do this by playing a kind of double act, which no other politicians in the world actually have to perform—that is, they have to be equally clever and good and responsible when acting as part of a collective decision-making community at the EU level, and when they go back to their own people to convince their people that they have done the right thing.

Now personally, I think they will get there. I think the direction of advance is good. I think the speed of advance since 2003 became a bit hectic and rushed, and the leaders tripped over themselves and tripped over public opinion. They are having to pick themselves up and go ahead. But however far they get, I would like to end by stressing, that what they create is not going to be the old kind of power. It is not going to be like an old empire, because its members have joined voluntarily. It is not going to be a military power, because its main strength always lies in the nonmilitary field and because Europe, when it acts in the world, has to be true to those things that keep the Union alive internally, and that is compromise the rule of law and, in principle, the equal treatment of nations.

A final word to those regions that are thinking of copying the EU's example. They live in areas where they don't have the equivalent of a NATO to look after them; they probably never will, the way that history has gone. It has taken the EU sixty years to grapple with its security responsibilities. I think if you live in Latin America or Africa or the ASEAN region, you can't wait sixty years, and I think the integration experiments that are going on there can actually do better than the EU—if they start thinking from a much earlier point about what their strategic responsibilities and their strategic capabilities are. Thank you for your attention.

BROWN: Thank you, Ambassador Bailes. Our next speaker is Herman Cohen, who is a former U.S. ambassador to Senegal and Gambia, and a former assistant secretary of state for African affairs. He is now president of a consulting firm, Cohen and Woods, and an adjunct professor at the Johns Hopkins University. He has been writing a lot recently, including an acclaimed book called *Intervening in Africa*. My question for Ambassador Cohen is this: When the international community intervenes, especially in Africa, but elsewhere as well, in order to protect human rights and to prevent genocide, is this not a violation of the principle of national sovereignty, and what does it mean for the Westphalian system in general? Ambassador Cohen.

AMBASSADOR HERMAN J. COHEN: Good morning, everyone, it's a great pleasure to be here. When I was asked to participate in this panel on national sovereignty, I was rather enthusiastic as an Africanist, because it is my feeling that you really can't understand what's going on in Africa today unless you address the issue of national sovereignty. It's the key to an understanding of Africa. Now why do I say that? In Africa there is only one country that has fully consolidated its national sovereignty. So the essence of most governmental action in Africa today is, how do we get to the point where we have consolidated our national sovereignty, even though we have been independent since 1960?

If you measure national sovereignty country-by-country in Africa on a scale of one to ten, there is one country that has a ten, and that is South Africa, which inherited a well-established system of rule of law, internal security, internal justice, and

Herman J. Cohen

internal administration that is really up to European and American standards. All other countries are still struggling to get to that point. Among the fifty or so countries, all the way down to number one on the scale, which is a failed state, there are a few like Sierra Leone and Liberia, or the Central African Republic. At nine on the scale are countries that are about to get there, like, I would say, Nigeria. But the struggle for national sovereignty really informs the whole issue of how Africa gets along with the rest of the world.

Okay, so you have these countries, and the international community comes to them and says, hey, we have got a lot of goodies for you; but in order to take advantage of these goodies, you are going to have to give up a little bit of your national sovereignty, just like all the other countries are doing, like the U.S. is doing and the Europeans. And the Africans say, wait a second, you are asking us to give up sovereignty; we haven't even got it yet fully. So this is a problem for us.

So how does that manifest itself in practical terms? Well, the World Bank comes in and says, you have severe economic problems; we are going to set up a program of economic reforms for you, and if you go through the whole business over a few years, you will be able to turn around, and some of you will become Asian tigers. So the Africans look at this and they say, well, we can't turn down this money; let's see how we can handle it. So case-by-case, it's a struggle for these African governments not to accept infringements on their national sovereignty while they are taking the World Bank money, and that's why Africa is not advancing as much as other parts of the world. To give you an example: the World Bank says, you all have government-owned enterprises, none of them are making money, there is only one in all of Africa that is making money, and that's Ethiopian Airlines. But all of the rest are losing money. So, the only way to solve the problem, get some revenue, is to privatize. Privatization is extremely slow in Africa. You would think they'd jump on the band wagon and say let's do it. The reason they don't is if you privatize an enterprise, you are setting up another center of power in that country, in the private sector. And the African government says, well, we haven't consolidated our own power yet; why are we setting up new centers of power? So privatization is going very slowly—and this is true across the board in all of the World Bank programs—and that's why they are going so slowly.

Okay, African countries have severe problems, especially those countries that are on the bottom of the scale of national sovereignty. They have internal conflicts, ethnic groups are not happy, they are not getting their fair share of resources—like in eastern Nigeria, where the poorest people living in Nigeria are living right on top of all the oil resources of Nigeria. They say, we are not getting anything, so, we are very unhappy. You have violence in Nigeria, and this is true in many African countries. So how do you handle that? It took the African collective that is known as the African Union—or the Organization of African Unity before that—it took them thirty years before they could agree that internal conflict and violence was everybody's business. Countries were tearing themselves apart and Africans were doing nothing about it. I remember giving a speech at the Africa-America Institute annual conference in 1988, which took place in Cairo, and I chastised them for this. I said, "Look, all this conflict's going on, and who is dealing with the African conflict? It's the United States. We are all over the place, trying to mediate, and you Africans are doing nothing." Well the reason for that is that they are so fixated on national sovereignty, which they don't have yet, that they refuse to intervene in countries of their own continent in order to help solve these problems. So it took them until 1993, when they enacted a resolution in the Organization of African Unity that internal conflict is something that they should be worried about and do something about. So they set up a mechanism for mediating conflict in Africa that became operative. As this became more operative, the United States started backing off and saying, okay you do it, and we'll support you. But until that point, we were the ones dealing with African conflict because of their fear of losing this concept of sovereignty.

Alright now, if you flash forward from there to how does Africa engage in selective globalization so they can take advantage of modernization and move ahead in the world, just as the European Union and other countries are doing, as Ambassador Gardner said, by pooling of sovereignty—are they capable of doing that? My answer today is, they really are not; they really are not capable of doing that because of this fixation on sovereignty. For example, in regionalization, economists will tell Africans, so many of your countries are too small; you need larger markets in order to benefit from economies of scale. So you should have regional groupings, at least common markets. You don't have to pool your politics, but have common markets. There is yet to develop one that is functional. They have organizations—there are at least twenty-seven regional organizations in Africa—but they are not functioning because of this fear of giving up sovereignty and control.

I was talking to the secretary-general of the Francophone union of the seven countries in West Africa [ECOWAS, the Economic Community of West African States]. On paper they have an economic common market. I met him in Bamako [Mali], and I asked, "Is it working? Do you have a common market?" He said, "Well, I'm measuring it in a funny way. When I drive from Bamako to Abidjan [Ivory Coast], I count the number roadblocks, people collecting money from cars and trucks going by. Over the years, they have gone down from fifty-two to about eighteen. But we still haven't gotten there yet, we still don't have that common market." So that's a big problem for them.

Okay, now what does this do for U.S. interests in Africa now that these are increasing? We used to look at Africa basically as a humanitarian project, and we want to help them settle conflicts, we want to help them develop so they can become buyers and sellers and producers. But now we have to look at Africa more strategically. When Professor Brown and I visited NATO headquarters a couple of years ago, they were telling us that the SACEUR [Supreme Allied Commander, Europe] said let's look south, because that's where things are happening in terms of U.S. interests, because 25 percent of crude oil that is imported into the United States comes from the Gulf of Guinea. Well, we have to worry about that. Our problems inside these countries are going to cause us problems in terms of our resource needs. China is now all over Africa because they have tremendous resource needs, and they are trading construction projects for resources. They will go into a country and say, what do you need? And they say, well, we need a road from point A to point B. And China will say, okay, we will build it for you, but we want guaranteed two hundred thousand barrels a day for the next twenty-five years. So, we have to worry about what China is doing, and therefore our relations with Africa matter in terms of our own national interest.

So how do we deal with it? My view is that we deal with it by being careful about the national sovereignty issue, and there we are in very good shape because of two decisions made—rather interestingly because of the name of this conference—by President Dwight Eisenhower in 1958. In 1958 they saw all these countries becoming independent and they said we have to get some policies toward these independent countries in Africa. I've read lots of documents lately on the National Security Council meetings on Africa, and they were presided over by President Eisenhower himself. He made two important decisions. He said, "We will treat all Africans as truly sovereign nations and treat them with dignity. We will place an ambassador in every country. Secondly, we will rely uniquely on the United Nations to deal with instability and peace problems in Africa." Those two decisions by Dwight Eisenhower remain in force today, and because of those decisions, Africans trust the United States. You have U.S. military going all over the place from EUCOM [U.S. European Command]; all over Africa they are welcome all the time, they are not considered threatening. And whenever we deal with conflict issues, as mediators or as advisors, we are not considered threatening. So I feel that if we continue this paying homage to the idea of African national sovereignty, while they are building up their self-confidence, I think we will be able to achieve our national objectives in Africa. The former colonial powers have problems. Where you see French troops in Côte d'Ivoire [Ivory Coast] right now, they seem to be threatening. British troops are in Sierra Leone; they are not so threatening, but still they are uneasy with the former colonial powers being there. But with the United States, it's okay as long as we remember that the Africans are striving for national sovereignty.

Now, Professor Brown asked the question about genocide and intervention. My feeling is that the Geneva Convention, which demands action by the international community in the face of genocide, is really being implemented only selectively. To the extent that the Africans are worried about intervention as a breach of their sovereignty—I think they shouldn't worry about it because the international community is not that active on that issue. Good example: Rwanda. The United States not only failed to intervene, but failed to allow the Security Council to intervene, and President Clinton apologized for that. Look at Darfur today. Our reaction to Darfur has been very tepid, not because we worry about African sovereignty, but because we don't see it in our strategic interest really to have a vigorous, robust response to Darfur. Kosovo—that was different. Kosovo, the ethnic cleansing that was going on there, we couldn't get our resolutions through the Security Council, and we went to NATO and got a resolution authorizing action in Kosovo. So the whole issue of genocide and this embryonic concept of the responsibility to protect populations, even from their own governments, is really not a threat to African sovereignty yet, because we don't really believe in it. Let me be very blunt about it: we believe in it only when it affects our national interest. Kosovo affected our national interest; Darfur and Rwanda did not. So human rights and genocide and that sort of thing has a long way to go before the Africans have to start worrying about unauthorized interventions against their sovereignty. So remember, be respectful of African desire for sovereignty and you'll make headway. Thank you.

BROWN: That was brilliant, terrific. Our last speaker is a noted political theorist and also a close student of foreign affairs and foreign policy. He will bring a European flavor nonetheless to this panel because one of his specialties is German political theory, and he is going to focus on the issue of sovereignty in a fairly large perspective. He will also be something of a discussant, picking up on some of the points made by the previous speaker. Our next speaker is also the president of the National Committee on Foreign Policy, and that's George Schwab. My question for Dr. Schwab is a very simple question, but perhaps it gets to the heart of the issue that we are discussing: Is political sovereignty divisible? Dr. Schwab.

GEORGE D. SCHWAB, PH.D.: Thank you. Thank you, the Eisenhower National Security Series, for having invited us to co-sponsor the session with you. We are delighted to be here with you. The question is, as Bernard Brown said, "Is political sovereignty indivisible?" To answer this question, we must first define what we mean by sovereignty. Traditionally, sovereignty has been inextricably linked with well-functioning political entities, namely states. The sovereign state is one that is in possession of the monopoly of political power with all that this implies, including assuring domestic order, peace and stability, and if existentially threatened, the right to defend militarily its interests.

Since World War II, and especially in the recent past, the state's sovereign authority is being questioned and even challenged as never before by, for example, the globalization trend and by bodies such as the UN, NATO, NGOs, the EU, and other such bodies. Hence, in answering whether sovereignty is indivisible, it appears that we must readjust our thinking.

George D. Schwab

Let us look for a moment at the EU—and Ambassador Bailes has given us a wonderful presentation on the EU. As we all know, it is a complex body of twenty-five member states, but is the EU a sovereign political entity? Have member states either ceded or delegated, fully or in part, their possession of the monopoly of political power? The answer is "no," in short. By joining the EU, member states continue to enjoy the right to articulate a political interest and act accordingly. It follows that the EU is not a politically sovereign body, nor does it aspire to become one at this time. There is no way that a politically functioning sovereign state can cede its fundamental obligation to safeguard its territorial integrity. Yes, a politically sovereign entity can and must enter into all kinds of treaties, understandings with other such political constructs, but it can never willingly divest itself of the right to distinguish friend from foe and act accordingly. Can anyone in this audience imagine the United States' sovereign authority deciding that an existential threat is facing the country and this sovereign authority willingly ceding to the General Assembly or the Security Council of the UN the right to decide what kind of action the U.S. is permitted to take in response? This is inconceivable. And from this perspective I join also Ambassador Gardner, who said that sovereign states continue to exist, will continue to exist, not only for the immediate future. But as far as I am concerned, a state is not really a state unless it is fully sovereign. Of course, in the discussion period we can discuss various gradations, including the nature of failed states and what can be done to prevent failing states from becoming failed states with all that this implies. Thank you very much.

BROWN: We all want to thank George Schwab because the speaker who was supposed to be with us, Gilles Andréani, who's our colleague and friend, unfortunately got involved in an accident on the way to the airport in Paris, and he had to go to a hospital. It turned out that he badly hurt his knee, and he's now immobilized in a bed, with his leg up in the air. And at the last minute, George Schwab agreed to tackle the larger theoretical question of the nature of sovereignty, and I'm grateful to him that he did step into the breach.

Alright we now have a question period. One other point, Ambassador Gardner has a previous commitment, a very important commitment, and it involves a lunch. One hundred fifty other people are waiting for him to speak at this lunch, and he will have to leave at 12.00 noon. So I'm going to ask that members of the audience who have questions for Ambassador Gardner ask their questions now, since he will have to leave us at 12.00 noon. Then we will go on after that until approximately 12.30 p.m., and the other three panelists will be happy to deal with your questions. So I'm going to ask if you take the floor, if you are recognized, to identify yourself first and to pose a question, if possible directed to a specific panelist. And as I just said, we would appreciate it if you have a question for Ambassador Gardner, to pose that question now. Alright, the floor is open now for questions.

ANNOUNCER: Ladies and gentlemen, if you have a question for the panel, please raise your hand and a microphone will be brought to you.

BROWN: Alright, I see someone over here on my right-hand side. Okay, what's your question, sir? Yes, this gentleman; do we have a microphone for him? Yes. Fine, thank you. Could you identify yourself?

AUDIENCE - GEORGE MAURER: George Maurer, retired colonel, Army Reserve, Key West, Florida. Could you discuss for us the interrelationship of status and forces agreements, the International Criminal Court, and the Nuremberg trials, and indicate to us, if you were going to support some exceptions to this jurisdiction of the International Criminal Court, specifically what those exceptions would be.

GARDNER: I was promised only easy questions. No, yours is a very good question, but it would require more time than I have to do justice to it. It is important that our forces overseas be immune from prosecution in local courts. I think it is important that they be immune from frivolous proceedings that might be brought against them for "war crimes or aggressive war," since the definition of both of those things is not very clear. Example, Kosovo: we rightly, in my view, supported NATO's decision to bomb two civilian targets in Belgrade, the television network which Milosevic used to mobilize his population, and the electrical grid. It was only when those two targets, "civilian targets," were knocked out that he stopped his ethnic cleansing, came to the table, and agreed to a settlement. Now was that a war crime to hit those two civilian targets? Amnesty International thought it was—brought a case against us in the then-Yugoslav Tribunal; it was thrown out of court. And then, as you know, the International Criminal Court talks about aggressive war, and we don't have a definition of aggression. Is what we did in Iraq aggression or not? I was against the Iraq war as a matter of policy, but I think it can be defended as a matter of law under UN resolutions 678 and 687, which respectively authorized the UN and its members to use force to expel Saddam Hussein from Kuwait and "restore peace and security in the area." And the truce agreement embodied in 687 said the hostilities would stop conditional upon Saddam accepting UN inspectors. And he proceeded to violate that condition, which, in my view, gave us the option of resuming the use of armed force in order to force the inspectors back. Resolution 1441 of the UN threatened the use of armed force unless he accepted the inspectorate, headed by Hans Blix. My own view was that once Hans Blix was allowed to go back with the inspectors—and that only happened because of the threat of force—he should have been given the additional two months he wanted to find out if there were weapons of mass destruction. He told me that he could have verified in two months that there were none, and we could have kept inspectors in Iraq indefinitely to assure that weapons of mass destruction were not developed. Now that's a little bit of a digression, but what I'm trying to say to you is that this is very complex, that the international community does not have a sufficient consensus on what is a war crime and what is aggression, in my view, to justify our going into the International Criminal Court. I would be very cautious about subjecting our servicemen or indeed our presidents, our secretaries of state, our heads of National Security Council to prosecution in somewhat ambiguous situations.

BROWN: Is there a question perhaps on the left-hand side, on my left-hand side rather, for Ambassador Gardner? Yes, sir. Could you just postpone it for a moment or two. Alright, any question for Ambassador Gardner on any side? Yes, ma'am, right over there. Please identify yourself.

AUDIENCE - BETHANN RITTER: My name is Bethann Ritter. I'm with the GAO. Ambassador Gardner, you mentioned in your talk about the impact of Ambassador Bolton on the United Nations, and I was just wondering what kind of both short-term and long-term impacts you see him having, and , being a multilaterist, what you might see as damage being done, how that might be undone by a future ambassador?

GARDNER: Well, again, I thank you for the question. Now you're going to get me into a controversial area, and it's a little awkward to be criticizing a particular individual, particularly when he is serving currently in a very key post for the United States, but I will answer your question. I know John Bolton rather well. He is a brilliant man. There is no question about that. He was either first or second in his class at Yale Law School. I went to Yale Law School. You don't get to be first or second in your class unless you're very smart. He also knows a lot about the UN because he served as assistant secretary of state for international organizations years ago and, of course, more recently as under secretary for arms control. So there's no question about his brains or his experience. It's his world view and his temperament that worry me. Now let me be very specific—I hadn't intended to say this, but you asked me a question and I'm going to answer it head on. I was following very carefully the run up to this recent head of government UN General Assembly, which was the Millennium Plus Five General Assembly. His purpose was to do two things: to advance progress toward the Millennium Development Goals, which had been agreed to five years earlier—I was at the 2000 assembly that approved those goals as a presidentially appointed delegate—and the purpose of this recent assembly was to assess progress toward those goals and hasten those goals, which were basically the eradication of poverty. The second purpose of this recent General Assembly was to reform the United Nations, okay. Now delegates had been working for months on a consensus document to embody these two things, and a very able acting representative of the United States to the UN, Anne [W.] Patterson, a career foreign service officer, and her career staff had come a long way toward getting a successful document. I saw the document as it existed one month before the UN was to begin, at the time when John Bolton came up to New York. Before John Bolton got to New York, you had a document that had some very specific commitments about the responsibility of countries to advance the Millennium Development Goals and to reform the UN. For example, the document provided for a new Human Rights Commission, which would replace the totally discredited current Human Rights Commission in which you have countries like Libya and Cuba and so on sitting in judgment or basically refusing to allow criticisms of one another. The new Human Rights Commission, this document specified, would be smaller and would require that the members have decent human rights records and be elected by a two-thirds majority of the UN General Assembly. So that was pretty good. It also had a definition of terrorism, which we very much wanted saying any attack on innocent civilians for whatever reason was terrorism and illegal and to be condemned. That was very good, because many Arab countries have said there are exceptions—you know, if they're in occupation like Israel, or so-called occupation of Arab territory, anything goes; you can kill anybody. So the definition of terrorism is in there. We also had in there a very good proposal under which the UN secretary-general would be given more authority than he has now to move people around in the secretariat or move resources around without being micromanaged by a 191-member General Assembly. We also had provisions about better oversight to avoid oil-for-food scandals and ethics committees and full disclosure and transparency and all that. Bolton went up a month before the UN started and he looked at the document. He said he didn't like it. He put in, believe it or not, over 700 amendments. The result was that the so-called developing and nonaligned countries, first thing they saw was that he said we don't want any reference to the Millennium Development Goals and our responsibility to eradicate poverty—even though this administration had accepted that in the consensus document in Monterey in 2002, which provided that there should be common action in the direction, agreed action toward the goal of 0.7 percent of GDP [gross domestic product] in overseas development assistance. That was agreed to by the Bush administration. But all that was rejected. Bolton said we don't want any responsibility to achieve the development goals. But of course, once that happened, the bad guys—the Cubas, the North Koreas, the Zimbabwes, the Venezuelas, and so on—said, oh well, you don't want to promote the things we care about; we'll take off the table all the things you guys want. And thus we lost the strong language about a new Human Rights Commission, about a definition of terrorism, about the management reforms. So what is my point? You don't get your way in the UN or in any multilateral body by confrontational tactics. Unless you show a decent respect for the interests and priorities of others, you will not get others to help you promote your basic interests and priorities. The name of the game is consensus building. I hope that John Bolton will learn from this experience, take the advice of the professionals on his staff, and do a better job in the future. Now that may be something some of you disagree with, but you asked for my view, and I'm no longer in public service, so I'm free to express it. Thank you very much.

BROWN: Why don't you stay here and we'll have one more question. Perhaps one more question for Ambassador Gardner. We don't want him to be late.

GARDNER: Make it an easy one.

BROWN: An easy question this time. In the back, perhaps this gentleman in the last row. Could we get a mic up to this gentleman. Could you identify yourself first.

AUDIENCE - DAVID LOUDEN: Yes, sir, my name is Dave Louden, and I'm retired Navy and now a defense contractor. Ambassador, can you conceive of a situation where a free market economy that takes such advantage of globalization can have the perhaps undesirable effect of negatively impacting national sovereignty? And in a sense, if my history is correct, it would just perhaps prompt some evolution into the conditions that grew out of the Westphalia Treaty, where we no longer fight wars over religion, we created nation-states, but in this economic power base, it's there and can leverage scarcity of commodities. Could you conceive of such an event where that would impact nation-states?

GARDNER: I think the best way to avoid wars over scarce resources is through mutually agreed arrangements through the WTO, the World Trade Organization, other institutions to promote open markets, and a free flow of investment. We had a secretary of state once, Cordell Hull, one of the great founders of the post-war trading system, who said, "If goods can't cross borders, armies will." There was a lot of insight in that statement. As a result, under his leadership and that of Franklin Roosevelt, Will Clayton [assistant and later undersecretary of state under Presidents Franklin Roosevelt and Harry Truman], a lot of great gentlemen, we took the leadership in the creation of the Bretton Woods organizations, the World Bank, IMF, and the General Agreement on Tariffs and Trade. And of course, these are imperfect organizations—and I myself have ideas of how they should be re-formed—but one of the great successes of our foreign policy in the postwar period was not just the Marshall Plan, but the creation of these institutions. There is no chance of moving the Third World countries out of poverty—and we have, as you know, a billion people in the world, two billion people in the world actually, well one billion people in the world living below the poverty line of a dollar a day. No chance of moving them out of poverty unless we open markets to their products and they encourage productive investment by their own people and by foreign agencies. So, I believe that to promote globalization is, on balance, a good thing for both developing and developed countries, although I would have to add—and this is accepted in these international institutions—there have to be some safeguards against product surges and hot money flows that can be destabilizing, there have to be some exceptions, but they should be carefully granted. We face this issue now with this massive influx of Chinese textiles, for example, and we do have an obligation to deal with the human consequences of product surges, and we must do something through domestic arrangements to help workers who are displaced by imports to be retrained and find alternative occupations. So these are difficult issues. But I think, on balance, globalization serves the human interest both in our countries of the developed world and in the developing countries. Thank you all so much for these excellent questions, which have forced me to think very hard.

BROWN: Thank you. Thanks for being so patient with us.

GARDNER: Thank you. Good to see you.

BROWN: Well, a lot of people are waiting for Ambassador Gardner to speak at a lunch elsewhere in Washington, and it was good to see him again. Alright, the floor is now open for questions to any of the other three panelists, and this gentleman, you were going to ask a question to, pose a question to Ambassador Cohen, as I recall.

AUDIENCE - PROFESSOR HENRY FEARNLEY: I'm Professor Hank Fearnley from the College of Marin, a professor of political science, and I'd like to address my question to Ambassador Cohen, if I may. The previous question and answer sort of anticipated what I was going to ask—well, I'll ask it anyhow with respect to Africa. The point that you made about the West having to be sensitive to the needs of African states to consolidate their sovereignty is well taken, but isn't it also true that there are forces at work in globalization, perhaps under the guise of globalization, and perhaps in alliance with corrupt leaders in some cases, that are undermining the very sovereignty that they seek?

COHEN: Yes.

FEARNLEY: And how do you reconcile those two factors?

COHEN: Yes, I would agree with that. One of the reasons that African sovereignty is lagging behind the rest of the world is the absence of good governance, or the absence of rule of law. All of these governments, when they became independent of the colonial powers, they inherited pluralism and they inherited the rule of law, but perhaps they didn't inherit the institutions that are needed in modern societies to maintain, to have sustainable development. But they had a good base, and unfortunately a number of African governments lost these advantages that they inherited because of corruption, because of extreme power, the elimination of democracy—and as they say, power corrupts. So it is quite possible for international entities, multinational corporations, what have you, to make alliances with such persons and therefore retard the growth of national sovereignty.

Having said that, I will also say that in today's society, multinational corporations, businesses of any size, shy away from this now. I would say in the '60s, maybe some of them said, okay, lets make a deal with [Joseph Désiré] Mobutu, or lets make a deal with [President Gbanisengbe] Eyadema in Togo, and everything will be okay. But more and more, most of them will say, we will not go into any country that doesn't have the rule of law that we can rely on—where we can enforce contracts that we've signed—and we will not go into a country because of its corrupt system, which is likely to fall into a state of instability. I remember when I was chargé d'affaires in Kinshasa, in the Congo in 1968. I was chargé d'affaires for a whole year—we had no ambassador—and in come these people from Exxon, minerals, Standard Oil, and they say, we know there's some fabulous copper deposits here. Four percent copper. In Arizona they mine 0.5 percent copper and make money. Can you imagine 4 percent copper ore? That's fantastic! So we worked with them to get a concession from Mobutu—he was the dictator. We said we'd make a deal with Mobutu. Well, five years later, after they spent $250 million developing this deposit, that area around the deposit erupts into civil war. The railway that would carry their ore to the ports is destroyed over on the other side of the border in Angola. So corporations look back at that and they say, oh, we had a sweetheart deal with Mobuto, but, you know, we need other things to protect our interests. So I would say more and more now, they're avoiding this type of commitment, and they want to have modern institutions and systems before they'll invest money. And that's why they invest in Mexico instead of Africa and many countries.

But as Africans develop good governance, you see more investors going in, and more important than foreigners is the local guy. If the local guy invests money, it means he or she is confident. Nigeria has 100,000 dollar millionaires, and that money is not in Nigeria. And if you multiple 100,000 by a million, you'll kind of get the Nigerian revenue from oil for the last two decades basically. So, Africa will not advance until they achieve their sovereignty, with good governance and with pluralism and democracy, because they will not attract investors from their own countries, not to speak of foreign investors. So those are the old days of the '60s where what you described took place, and I've seen lots of these sweetheart deals. Now the only place where corporations have to deal with bad governments are the oil companies, because the oil people will say, we have to go where the oil is; we can't explore for oil in Manhattan. We have to go to Equatorial Guinea, and that government there is the worst you can imagine. We've got to make a deal with that guy. But that's the exception that proves the rule, I would say.

BROWN: Sure go ahead.

FEARNLEY: I really wasn't referring to the '60s. I'm quite aware of that. But some of the contracts that you mentioned in your response are themselves the cause of undermining sovereignty—the imposition in those contracts of agreements that undermine what little rules those countries might have: environmental, financial. Those countries have very little choice but to agree to the demands of some of the corporations—and not all, by any means; I don't want to paint them all with the same brush. So, I'm not talking about the '60s; I'm talking about now.

COHEN: Well, I don't see it happening. I don't see many contracts being signed. Unfortunately, I'd like to see more investments coming into Africa, but they're staying away in droves. The only things that corporations get when they invest these days are tax holidays, and they may get some breaks on real estate. I'm working now for Reynolds Aluminum down in the Congo. We wanted to set up an aluminum plant in the port of Pointe-Noire. Well, they were so anxious to get to this that they gave us 200 acres on the bay, where we can bring ships in, that sort of thing. But that's not corrupt; that's incentives, I think. The problem is that they're not getting these investments because of the instability, lack of rule of law, which is one of the manifestations of the absence of sovereignty.

BROWN: How about a question from the right-hand side? I do this because it's easy for the people with the mics to work one side after another. This lady over here, yes.

AUDIENCE - CATHERINE LOVON: Thank you. My name is Catherine Lovon. I'm from the Embassy of Peru. My question is for Ambassador Bailes. From your point of view, it almost took sixty years to build, to evolve what is the European Union, as it is known right now. What's your point of view on the future for the subregional integration agreements, such as the Andean community or the MER-COSUR, the so-called Common Market of the South, if we take into consideration that there are some internal troubles or internal issues in some of these developing countries. Thank you.

BROWN: Grab a mic.

BAILES: Yes, thank you. I am delighted to take that question. In fact, my institute has published a chapter on developments in South and Central America in our yearbook this year, and it was really addressed to the people who are skeptical, because I think it's always a shame to be skeptical when you see countries trying to do something good. The problem with countries in South and Latin America and the Caribbean is that they've tried to do good too many times over. There are half a dozen regional groups that dedicate themselves in some way to security and economic development, and they overlap. It's quite hard, especially for an outsider, to take one thing like MERCOSUR or the Organization [of American States] or the Andean Pact or the new one that was set up last year and say, this is where the dynamism is.

And yet, with all that skepticism, if you look back on the last twenty years or so in those parts of the world, there has been an opening up to globalization; there has been more free trade and free investment and mobile policy in the economic field. There are no more conflicts between states at the moment. Costly conflicts—there are still two going on, but they have to be considered purely internal conflicts, and by and large, the neighboring countries are not making those conflicts worse. There is a seeming phenomenon going on of a kind of insulating or isolating of the remaining conflicts from the main discourse of cooperation in the area, including cooperation against new threats. And it's hard to say that the existence of the multinational organizations was what caused those good things, but it seems to me it certainly did not hurt, because it created a state of mind one would hope for in the leaderships of most of the countries, which said, let's not go for our own maximum good against the neighbor, let's not kick the neighbor when the neighbor is down and in civil war or something; let's try and work for stability in the continent as a whole. So basically I'm quite hopeful from past experience that good effects of stabilization and corporation can be achieved.

But I'd like to come back here, also, to what I said at the end of my own talk: there's a tendency from the Euro Atlantic area, when we look at another region like the countries belonging to MERCOSUR or the African Union, to say, hey, they're not serious because they haven't even got a right single market yet. But I think they're doing some more imaging there, because in Europe we started with a single market that was the sign of our seriousness. We created a single iron and steel industry—by the way, not really for economic reasons, but so that countries wouldn't have their own iron and steel industry to create a war machine to go to war with each other; that's why we started in that place. That's why the single market was the test of our seriousness. It doesn't necessarily have to be the starting point or the test of seriousness for other regions. When I see a region—and actually, this has happened in Latin America—starting to work out a common policy on a new threat like terrorism or stopping proliferation, for example, then I say, hey, you may be starting in the right place for your continent. You don't have to do it the same way around as in Europe. And if you look at the seriousness with which these regions are adopting policies on the new threats, I find it encouraging. I think we may be seeing a kind of alternative security-first model here. Another reason why it may be happening that way is that the breaking down of national economic borders, which we had to do in Europe through the single market sixty years ago, that breaking down has been done by globalizing forces already. It's been done by the world environment, which is sixty years different from where Europe started.

So that's the very generalized answer. I'm putting it that way because I'm addressing it to all the regions that are engaging in this kind of experiment. I guess my message is, don't be skeptical about what you've already achieved. There is a linkage between general improvements in security and the existence of these multilateral frameworks. Don't think that you have to start in the same place that we started, but do think that when you've adopted a policy, you have to carry it through. Because failing to do that is where the real corrosion will set in.

BROWN: I promised to recognize this lady here.

AUDIENCE - SIMIN CURTIS: I'm Simin Curtis with Greycourt & Company, an investments advisory company in Pittsburgh. I'm also here with the Ridgway Center at the University of Pittsburgh. My question is to Ambassador Cohen. I read recently where there was so much aid that started to come into Niger—it might have been in the *New York Times*—that the prices of the crops of the local farmers were severely depressed, and that this then threatened a new round of famine. I was just wondering if you could comment on that, as that certainly complicates the humanitarian aid that rushes in sometimes.

COHEN: This is extremely important, and it does apply to national sovereignty because when countries are having difficulty, and they don't have the mechanisms and the institutions in order to control the international response, they sometimes suffer for it. And then food security—there are two issues: one is markets, or actually it is markets and Niger had probably two ways. Niger is living next to a 600-pound gorilla named Nigeria. Niger suffered from drought and locusts. I visited Niger during the locust infestation and, believe me, it's horrible. You're driving along a road and your windshield is just covered—there are millions of them. But anyway, they had drought plus locusts, and the crop that was planted came up only 11 percent short of their normal production. Now that's amazing: 11 percent loss despite all the locusts. Next door in Nigeria, which is 120 million people compared to Niger's four or five, they suddenly enacted legislation prohibiting the importation of poultry meat. So that led to an upsurge of domestic production of poultry, which meant that poultry producers went out in the market to buy grain wherever they could find it. So they drained the country to the north of them, Niger, of grain, and the price of grain went up. So the consumers of Niger didn't have enough money to buy food. And that's why there was a lot of famine and starvation, and you saw all of this on CNN and FOX News and that sort of thing. So the international community, one country next door, can distort the markets of another. As you said, the international community responds and brings in a lot of food. The new crop is coming in, and suddenly the farmers find that they can't sell their crop for as much it cost to produce it. Therefore, they just don't go to market or they put it in storage until next year, which further increases famine.

If you look at U.S. food aid policy, it's not calculated really to be a development assistance or a humanitarian assistance; it's really designed to be a subsidy to the U.S. farm community. So when there are surpluses in the U.S. farm community, the U.S. government buys the food and then finds an outlet for it in terms of food aid. And the timing of that may not be the right timing, because it has nothing to do with what's going on in Africa or other countries. Look at the curve: U.S. food aid goes up when there is a lot of production in the United States. U.S. food aid goes down when there is drought in the United States and lower production. So the U.S. impact on Africa tends to be—yes, we're saving lives today, but it distorts markets. And one of the solutions is to not give away anything free, but to make people pay for the food that they get, which tends to work into the local market conditions and therefore is less distorting than other things. But it is a major problem; we look at it mainly for domestic political purposes rather than for foreign policy purposes.

BROWN: Is there a question on my left? To make it easier on the people who are handling the mics. Yes, sir?

AUDIENCE - EUGENE BEYE: Eugene Beye, GAO. If my memory serves, USAID just instituted a policy of actually buying local grains, some portion of local grain, in the local markets rather than using food aid. Do you see that as a positive development?

COHEN: I think that is a very positive development. Sometimes I joke—after I left the State Department, I spent five years in the World Bank and everyone was talking about poverty reduction; that is the objective of what we're doing. I would only half jokingly go around saying, "You know what poverty is? It's the absence of money." Let's stop talking about socioeconomic conditions; people need money. And so I think going out into the market to buy—you're promoting local markets and local farmers, and that's the best way. One of the big setbacks we've had in Africa in the last five years is Zimbabwe. Zimbabwe used to be the breadbasket of east and central Africa. Tremendous grain surpluses. But after all the land seizures and all of the craziness going on there, production has gone way down. USAID used to spend a lot of money in Zimbabwe to provide food aid in Tanzania or in the Congo, but that's not available anymore. So buying food in local markets is not as easy as it used to be, but its still doing it; and I fully approve of that rather than shipping stuff over from the States.

BROWN: All right, I'll go back to my right-hand side now. Yes, back there, that last row, could we get a mic to the gentleman.

AUDIENCE - BILL JONES: Yes, Bill Jones from *Executive Intelligence Review*. Also for Ambassador Cohen: I found your presentation very, very important and a very important issue, but the viability of creating nation-states in Africa is largely dependent on the economic situation. Africa will never develop, will never come out of a situation where it's dependent on food aid or help from abroad, until there is infrastructure on a continental scale. But since the era of Cecil [John] Rhodes, where they talked about Cape to Cairo and Djibouti to Dakar railroads, we have not really spent any effort in trying to deal with this major infrastructure problem. Africa, as you know, is very big; it's very hard to get to some of these countries, and unless these countries can be brought somewhat into a mainstream of international commerce, there is really no hope for the continent as a whole. And it seems to me with the interest in Africa in the United States during the Clinton administration, also reflected to a certain extent in the Bush administration, that instead of thinking of simply giving aid to these countries, we should again revive the idea that what they need is the infrastructural basis for learning, for coming into the world economy and being able to develop on their own. Because it seems to me that without that, we're going to have a problem on our hands for a long time to come. I wish you would comment on that a little bit, because I think that's an important issue.

COHEN: The operative words of your question are "again revive, again revive." I'm a senior citizen and I started my career in Africa in 1961 in Uganda, and this was the era of independence. Lots of countries were becoming independent. The U.S. had a euphoric view of all of this, and we spent a lot of money on infrastructure in those days; and I saw it myself. Thousands of Americans swarming all over the place, building roads, irrigation systems, water systems, electric power; it was big stuff. But by 1975, there was tremendous disillusionment because the Africans were so preoccupied with consolidation of power and national sovereignty that they forgot to do maintenance. And when you don't do maintenance in tropical climates, roads get washed away, electric power declines. I remember the Congo had 1,700 megawatts installed power; they are now producing 300. Why? All the hydro channels are all silted up because they haven't done any dredging. So that's why infrastructure stopped in terms of foreign aid. It's now starting to come back because there's a small number of African countries that are starting to respond to the stimuli of the World Bank and other donors by starting to institute good governance, good systems, good maintenance. The idea of infrastructure is now coming back, and especially through the World Bank. They are now starting to build roads again and starting to do electric power projects, starting to revive port infrastructure. So your point is very well taken. You can't get anywhere unless you have the basic infrastructure, and that's why even the good-governance countries in Africa are not getting investments—because the electric power is not there. If you have electric power only seven hours a day instead of twenty-four, or the water systems are not good, or the road to the port gets washed out, you're not going to get anywhere even with the best government. So infrastructure is coming back. In the jargon of the aid community, they say it's "going back to basics." Going back. And you're absolutely right that it has to be done, or else Africa is going to be left behind. But first comes maintenance capability. Maintenance: I remember the World Bank guy for Africa telling me, we built 580 miles of roads before we realized, hey, they don't have a maintenance department in this country. It all has to come together.

BROWN: Perhaps there could be a question for Ambassador Bailes, who has quite an important role in the building of Europe, and the European Union is a very important part of the world. Would anyone care to ask a question to Ambassador Bailes? Yes, sir.

AUDIENCE - LIEUTENANT COLONEL JEAN-MICHEL MILLET: Lieutenant Colonel Millet, the assistant military attaché at the French Embassy. And I had a question for Ambassador Bailes. I'm a convinced European. But I must say that the concept of nation and sovereignty has been addressed mostly in the legal framework and the economic framework. I think that there is also an emotional and cultural dimension of nations, and as far as Europe is concerned, it is both a problem and maybe a solution. To put it bluntly, it's very difficult to send Soldiers to potential death to save the global economy or even to save the European Common Market. Don't you think that the core of the problem for postmodern regional organizations is the lack of definition, a will to live together and its ultimate expression, the difficulty to send Soldiers to die for a cause?

BAILES: Yes, I take all that extremely seriously, and I would never be a person who spoke against the national idea in the broad sense that you mean. It is true that what a nation means is a great deal more than just its legal definition, and it's very often a force for good if it stands for positive values, belief in one's own culture. The motto of the European Union is "Unity and Diversity," because at least in principle, the people who designed it and the people who run it today want to keep as much as possible of the good juice of the nation, if you like. The positive life energy comes from that, while at the same time restraining the bad side—and we Europeans, above all, know where bad nationalism leads us. Now, to ask somebody to die for something other than their nation is difficult. It's amazing, actually, how many tens of thousands of men and women every year go out on peace operations, sometimes far from any country that they've had any historical connection with, and do face death and risks almost worse than death, injury, tough decisions they have to take, and so on. To some extent, we can appeal to altruism. Altruism and self-sacrifice is part of, I believe, the French national tradition. It's in the great revolutionary idea that we are working for all men and all women. It's somewhere in everybody, I hope, including our armed forces. I certainly think it needs to be backed up by other things. It needs to be backed up by a sober realization that sometimes even in the remotest countries, we are dealing with things that affect our own vital interests. I think it's actually much easier to prove that in a globalized world than in a Westphalian world. You might ask, for instance, why should the security of India matter to us, and why would it be important to stop an annihilating nuclear war between India and the Pakistan? The fact is that many of our communications companies are using call centers in India, that our entire communication system would break down if there was a war there. It gives you a kind of answer that you didn't have sixty years ago, you didn't have in the Westphalian system. It's going to be difficult to make that intellectual point, which anyone in the armed forces could grasp, into an emotional point as well, to realize that there is actually a common interest here.

But my final remark on this would be, if we're talking about living or dying for our values, for the values of our nation or of our multinational community, it's not just a challenge that the military faces today, because the ordinary citizen can die in a terrorist attack. And the ordinary citizen can die in a natural catastrophe, or from AIDS or SARS, if those challenges are not handled properly. So the challenge is not only to motivate the armed forces, but to motivate the citizen to say, you are not just a victim in the face of terrorism or even of natural disaster; there is a way that you could act. There is a responsible way that will make the danger less and that will also be helpful to other human beings who are at risk. So I think the distance between the altruism and discipline of the Soldier on peacekeeping duty is not as far away now as it used to be in history from the altruism and discipline of the ordinary citizen, whom we ask to act in a good way when terrorists strike or natural disaster strikes. It's a journey that all of us, as human beings, are having to take together in the globalized world.

BROWN: I think we have time for perhaps one more question. Well, someone who hasn't asked a question yet, perhaps. Do I see a hand up? Way up in the balcony, how about this gentleman over here? Perhaps we have time for two questions; we'll see.

AUDIENCE - COLONEL PETE MANSOOR: Colonel Pete Mansoor, Council on Foreign Relations. My question is also to Ambassador Bailes. It seems to me that one of the major ways sovereignty is being eroded, at least in Europe, is the conditions that the Europeans sets for entry into the Union, whether you look at Turkey or Serbia or some of the other nations that want in. There are some fairly distinct conditions that are set, not just internally for their economic transformation, but also for solving their nagging foreign policy issues. I'm just wondering if you could comment on that and maybe expand on that. Is there some sort of economic union or model for the rest of the world to solve some of these crucial foreign policy issues, at the same time giving the country something for giving away part of its sovereignty?

BAILES: Yes, thanks. This is a great question. Enlargement policy is a really tough area for Europe, as you've seen. It's one of the things that caused those referendum results that broke down the constitutional experiment. And I think the history of the EU has made this issue especially difficult, because the EU started with this thoroughgoing internal integration and harmonization; it has no less than 80,000 pages of common rules—on stuff like whether you can use your lawnmower after seven o'clock at night. And if the new states are not to come in as colonies almost, as sort of lower, second-class citizens that we just exploit in some way, they have to be capable of implementing those 80,000 pages. Now, it can well happen that there is a state that we need to have in there for security and strategic reasons and to help that state build democracy and stay democratic, but it can't fulfill all those 80,000 pages. What do we do? The EU, up to now, has said, sorry guys, it's the 80,000 pages that matter. It's the culture and the values and the nature of your political civilization that matter. And that's why Turkey, up to now, has always been held up. Although I'm glad to say we are at least opening a formal negotiation process with Turkey in the coming week. That, I personally think, is a pity and is bad for Europe. I personally would drop some of those 80,000 pages and say, you know, let's just accept that you're different in the way that you use lawnmowers. What I would not want to drop is some of the fuzzier criteria about political civilization, because if you don't—well, let's put it this way: We in the EU have opened up to each other so much. We have made ourselves so vulnerable to each other. But if somebody comes in that doesn't respect the rules, it's going to be the cat among the chickens. It can lead to a kind of reversion to competition within our community, reversion to bad national behavior, even in those areas where we had painfully and slowly wiped it out. Right, so certain things about political civilization and the way that you act toward other countries—how you relate to your neighbors, how you deal with your historical claims and problems—that has to be taken into account. I would say let's drop the lawnmowers and let's be even clearer and stricter about what we mean—and that is not coming from me as an anti-enlargement statement. I believe Turkey, in particular, needs to be taken in and will be taken in. What gives me hope that we can solve these issues of political governance is, just look what's happened in central and eastern Europe already. Even before we were really offering EU or NATO membership, ancient enemies like Poland and Lithuania, Hungary and Romania, Romania and Ukraine, they were getting together in the first two or three years of freedom to give up vital parts of sovereignty to make lasting historical peaces with each other. To draw boundaries and leave some of their own minorities outside. Enormous sacrifices were made by those newly democratic countries. And I don't think we should say to a country like Turkey or Ukraine, hey, we rule you out from the start; you are not capable of making those changes and sacrifices. I think that they are, and I think we should keep the door open, and keep the right criteria clear and bright for them, and give them every chance to cross those hurdles.

BROWN: We have strict orders to terminate on time. It is 12:30. On behalf of the panel, we should like to thank you for listening; and on behalf of the audience, I would like to thank the speakers for the presentations.

Luncheon Address

Property Rights, the Rule of Law, Exclusion, and International Security

Hernando de Soto, President, Institute for Liberty and Democracy
Introduction by: Judith A. Guenther, Director, Army Budget Office

Summary

Hernando de Soto

• One of the biggest changes is the worldwide phenomenon of migration. A vast number of people are on the move from rural areas to towns and cities. This is the industrial revolution all over again.

• Of the approximately six billion people who inhabit the earth, five billion live in the former Soviet Union and the rest of the developing world. About 80 percent of these five billion do not have the societal structures in place to be successful. Indeed, most of the world lives outside the rule of law. And this is precisely where terrorists and a multitude of other transnational actors operate.

• In the euphoria of the collapse of communism, we perhaps underestimated how long and how difficult is the road to the establishment of a democratic market economy. Above all, we underestimated the critical importance of "institutions of unity" to the creation of prosperity in successful market economies.

1. Title. The majority of the world's people have assets (e.g., chattel, animals) but have no title to their property. Without titles, there are no incentives and no access to credit. The ability to distribute clean water or energy hinges on being able to identify subscribers. This cannot be done in the absence of titles to property.

2. Business Organization. In the absence of rudimentary business organization, the basic transactions of a market economy become virtually impossible. There can be no asset partitioning (what belongs to whom), no perpetual succession for firms beyond the organic life of the individual, no knowledge of risk, no division of labor, and no known limits of liability.

3. Identity. The lacking of a system of identification that links individuals to addresses or an income stream impedes the development of a market economy. Paper and plastic are vitally important to collaboration, not to mention to the maintenance of law and order.

• In developing societies, extralegal adjudication creates property. Source records do exist. They provide protection of assets and make those assets fungible. Disputes are resolved by being submitted to third parties. The third world, therefore, "is marching toward a market economy." We just have not noticed it. The agenda for the future is to bring those four billion people under the rule of law.

Question-and-Answer Period

• How can people be brought under the rule of law? First, heads of state must be fully committed. Next, they must create special organizations to cut through the thicket of bureaucratic inertia and resistance. Political leaders can be induced to make this commitment. They must be persuaded that there is a constituency for change, the implementation of which will provide democrats with more votes and dictators with more legitimacy.

• Do the political leaders and people of the Andean region support free trade? A large majority appears to favor the creation of a Free Trade Area of the Americas. The biggest problem in achieving this objective is dismantling internal barriers.

• Has the time come for Western countries and international financial institutions to review the concept of privatization? It is time to review not the concept of privatization, but the terminology, and to root it in the local culture so that ordinary people understand that privatization is not a code word for further enriching indigenous and foreign elites.

• Would electronic means expedite the processes of bringing people under the rule of law? Though digitization can ultimately be very helpful, these processes must be "paperized" before they can be "digitized."

Analysis

Mr. de Soto is a gifted speaker with an ability to endear himself to his audience, even as he gently chides them about their governments' shortcomings. He skillfully summarized findings from large, complex research projects and convincingly provided conclusions that were contrary to those probably held by many in the audience. It is not often that a speaker can so effectively address a difficult and complex subject with techniques sufficiently adroit to uplift listeners' spirits by convincing them that there might, in fact, be a solution to what previously seemed overwhelming.

His description of developing countries' current state of title, business organizations, and identity was plausible and supported by his research, although the audience could only glimpse his projects' research methodologies. Unfortunately, Mr. de Soto's recommendations for how to use his information to make societal structures successful for most of the world's population were less impressive than his descriptions of those structures. He asserted that "the agenda for the future is to bring those four billion people under the rule of law," but failed to suggest in any detail how such a lofty goal should be attained.

When questioned about implementing his agenda, Mr. de Soto responded in sweeping terms, such as committing heads of state, cutting through bureaucratic inertia and resistance, dismantling internal barriers, and revising terminology. As is often the case with grand strategies, concepts may well have face validity, but successful implementation of any strategy requires careful operational transformation of those concepts and huge amounts of work and time to implement changes. Mr. de Soto's audiences may be uplifted by his concepts, but may well be daunted when confronted with the difficulty of their application.

Pointing out the magnitude of work left unsaid is not a criticism of Mr. de Soto's research, and he is most certainly aware of how difficult it would be to implement his strategy. His audience needs to understand what they are being asked to support and the large commitment needed by them and their leaders if changes proposed by Mr. de Soto are to be successful.

Transcript

JUDITH GUENTHER: It is my distinct pleasure this afternoon to introduce our speaker, Mr. Hernando de Soto. I could go on for a very long time about his illustrious career, but I won't take all of his time because we know we want to listen to what he has to tell us. So, let me tell you a few things about him. Mr. de Soto is the president of the Institute for Liberty and Democracy (ILD), headquartered in Lima, Peru. As the principal activity, de Soto and the ILD are designing and implementing capital formation programs to empower the poor in Asia, Latin America, the Middle-East, Africa, and the former Soviet nations. The ILD is regarded by the *Economist* as the second most important think tank in the world. Mr. de Soto was the personal representative and principal advisor to the president of Peru, Alberto Fujimori, until he resigned two months before the coup d'état. He has initiated Peru's economic and political reforms. He deals with the world of the informal or extralegal economy. Although he was born in Peru, he was raised in Europe, and he went to school in Geneva, Switzerland, at the Institut Universitaire de Hautes Études Internationales. He had a very successful business career. He went back to Peru at the age of 38, when he could have retired, but decided instead to get involved with helping the poor of the country. He served as an economist with the General Agreement on Tariffs and Trade (GATT), president of the executive committee of the Intergovernmental Council of Copper Exporting Countries, managing director of the Universal Engineering Corporation, a principal of the Swiss Bank Corporation Consultant Group, and a governor of Peru's Central Reserve Bank. Between 1988 and 1995, he and the ILD were responsible for some 400 initiatives, laws, and regulations that modernized Peru's economic system. He is

Judith A. Guenther

the author of several books, and I had the pleasure of having him autograph one of them for me. He has written *The Other Path, Invisible Revolution in the Third World*, and *The Mystery of Capital: Why Capitalism Triumphs in the West and Fails Everywhere Else*, which was placed by *Fortune* on its list of the Seventy-five Smartest Books We Know. He has written several articles, as well. He has received a great number of awards. In 1999 *Time* magazine choose him as one of the five leading Latin-American innovators of the century, and in May of 2004, he received the Milton-Freedman Prize for advancing liberty and a cash award for his contributions to the advancement of private property rights in developing countries. He was also instrumental in defeating terrorists, known as the Shining Path, who were attacking him. He instead defeated, through his economic reforms, these terrorists who were after him and his think tank. So, without further ado, it gives me great pleasure to introduce to you Mr. Hernando de Soto.

HERNANDO de SOTO: Good afternoon. Thank you very much for such an embarrassing introduction. I read before coming here what this conference is all about in the overview to try and make sure that my comments tuned in with your concerns, at least as I perceived them. I was struck by the continual reference in the overview remarks to the fact that the world has changed, that globalization is a new reality, a new framework within which we have to look at things, how that has changed the nature of the world and security problems, of course, and how even local traditions and cultures in faraway lands present different challenges today than they did before. Well, since I happen to be from a faraway land, what I'm going to give you is a faraway-land point of view, and I hope that it is of interest to you: a glimpse of the world as we see it changing, at least as my think tank, my organization, perceives it.

We think that the first big change came about in 1978. The world is more complicated than that, but we have to put milestones when things have been said. "I don't care what color my cat is, as long as it catches mice." That was a formidable change that took place in that part of the world. It continued changing with the fall of the Berlin Wall, and it continued on with the process of decolonization that began in Africa and as different kings and dictators started falling in different parts of the world. The biggest manifestation of this change has been in migrations.

Over the last forty years, in developing countries, the cities and towns have grown on average about fifteen times. It isn't the world that used to be before. Before, all the people that were not part of the Western culture—the kind of people you looked up in *National Geographic* magazine to find out what they were doing, or you tuned into the Discovery Channel, Art Today in the cities—like Oliver Twist they would come, and they're changing us, and they're changing us completely. So I agree with the overview that things have changed.

What is actually happening is, it's the industrial revolution. It's what happened in Europe about the nineteenth century. All of a sudden, people decided that to cooperate better and to create prosperity, whether they knew it or not, they were going to congregate, because the closer they were to each other, the larger would be the scale of businesses. The easier it would be to do what both Adam Smith and Karl Marx talked about—one 150 years ago, another one about 250 years ago—they said it's the new division of labor. People are not just stuck in cottages. They found out that interconnection makes a lot of sense. They move, and as they do that, they change the nature of the world as we know it.

So today we are about six billion people on the face of the earth, of which one billion are in the North Atlantic—that's you people, together with Canadians, of course, and with West Europeans, some East Europeans. We are slowly moving toward Western systems, or some even quickly. Japan, Four Tigers maybe, Australia, and New Zealand; that's one billion. That leaves five billion of us. Those five billion are the former Soviet Union and us developing countries. According to our calculations, about 80 percent—that is to say, about four billion of those five billion—do not yet have the societal structures to make them successful countries, and that's what my conference presentation will be about. In other words, in a country like mine, for example, Peru, we figure that about 20 percent of the population would be like me. We have some notion of English. We know how to travel. We can get passports. We can participate in business. People like me can understand maybe two-thirds of the jokes on *Saturday Night Live*; we're the "Westernized Elite," the kind of guys you talk to. But 80 percent of Peruvians you don't talk to. As a matter of fact, I could even say *we* don't talk to. And it's not only us Peruvians; it's Peruvians and Mexicans.

We just finished what we call a diagnostic for President Fox that was done in a team of 7 Peruvians and 120 Mexicans, and we found out that outside the books, outside the records, there are about 11 million buildings, 134 million hectares, 6 million enterprises, 47 percent of the Mexican population. And if you calculate those who work part-time in the black economy, that makes 80 percent of Mexicans. It's a worldwide phenomenon. We were invited by President Shaakashvili to Georgia—same phenomenon, if not more. In other words, most of the world is outside a system of what you would consider and we would consider "by the book," the rule of law. And in that area is where today's security threats are—at least they were for us as we fought the Shining Path quite successfully in Peru during the 1980s.

Hernando de Soto

The threats to world security don't seem any longer to come from a number of powerful, hostile states. We can't just say it's Beijing, it's the Kremlin in Moscow. It comes from a multitude of poorly known, invisible, nonstate actors who seek refuge and operate in the unorganized, unstructured, non-rule-of-law and failed states, where there are a lot of very discontent and alienated populations that no longer like things as they are today. Those are the people who migrate to the cities. Those are the people who migrate to your country because they're very unhappy where they came from, whether it be Latin Americans or whether it be Africans—just ask the Europeans.

Now, what happened? I mean, this wasn't supposed to occur. As the Berlin Wall fell, as people started becoming reasonable about economics, that the only system that worked was a market economy, weren't we all sort of supposed to get together and be happy and fruitful and identify ourselves and work within the rule of law? Well, the thing is that we have identified what was essentially the collapse of communism, and looking from my think tank, we fell to thinking that it was a victory of democratic capitalism. But we don't think that democratic capitalism has won out yet. Communism collapsed, and we thought that once communism collapsed, a market economy would function. Our thesis is that it's not that easy for a democracy in a market economy to work. It isn't that you just get rid of communists, or you just rid get of the people who were there before. The tendency of people is not to create a market economy unless you actually have basic institutions that support that economy, which was very familiar to your great, great granddaddies in the United States, to your great, great granddaddies in Europe—but you sort of forgot about these institutions that took a long time to come into place. Jesus Christ, himself, 2,000 years ago threw the merchants out of the temple because they had converted it into the market. So Jesus Christ was very familiar with what a market was. But it was a very poor market, a very poor people. That wasn't the interesting market. If that's a market, there are markets in Senegal, there are markets all over the world. There are always people in the casbah, in the streets, wherever you go in a Third World country, trading and buying and selling. That isn't what creates prosperity within the market. What I would tell you is that what creates prosperity within the market, looking from a faraway land toward your country—which in a way sometimes puts me in a better position or at least in a singular position, compared to you—is certain institutions that allow you to organize yourself in a free society. Institutions of what [Edmund] Husserl would call unity, which are responsible for uniting together pluralities into unitary collectives. Flocks of geese get together; shoals of fish gets together—complex social wholes that have accepted rules that allow living human beings to be compounded together into organizations that are more than the sum of their simple parts. And I will argue that the three institutions—and they were not doing enough throughout the world about the missing institutions among these four billion inhabitants—are systems of property rights, systems of business organizations, and systems of identity. I will try and explain how that works.

First of all, the majority of all of these four billion people I am talking to you about—and we worked in Tanzania and we worked in Mexico, as I explained before, and we have worked in the Philippines—have assets, whether they be land, whether they be businesses, whether they be chattel, machinery, animals. But they don't have a written property right, a legal property right to it. And we think when that doesn't happen, a series of things don't work. You don't have the same incentives that everybody else has. Larry Summers once actually summed up John Locke's definition of property rights by explaining that you never wash a rented car; when you have a car that is your own, you wash it. That is property rights. But beyond John Locke and beyond Larry Summers, property rights are also the possibility of using your asset to get credit.

There is no way that you can think of business moving ahead without credit. Now, credit is possible because of property rights, not because of money. For example, in my country we always thought that money came from printing money; that's the reason why we Latin Americans have some of the highest inflation rates in the world. And we now know that just money doesn't create credit. I asked this question some time ago, when I was invited in by the chairman of your Federal Reserve, Alan Greenspan, and I asked if I could be indiscreet about our conservation. I told him, "Mr. Greenspan, how do you know how much money to put into the U.S. economy?" And so he said, "Well, I try and see how many transactions are taking place." I said, "I hear you have very good military intelligence. This probably means that you have got these people in the front of the doors of every shop and every factory, to see how many sofas are going in and out, how many cars are going in and out, and so that gives you an idea of how much money to put in." He said, "No, that isn't the way it works." I said, "All right then, how does it work?" So he said, "Well, the way it works is that there are markets and people trade their stuff back and forth." "The tractors," I said, "the airplanes." "No," he said, of course, "the property rights over the airplanes and the tractors," which, of course, was the reply I was expecting.

So now try and imagine Mexico or try and imagine Peru, where 80 percent of all the assets, or Tanzania, where 98 percent of all the assets, are not on the books. How does Alan Greenspan know how much money to put into the economy? How does the tax man know who to charge for taxes? If Osama bin Laden is among them, how do you know his address? If property rights aren't in place, credit doesn't function, a bunch of other things don't function.

So I asked Mr. Greenspan, "For example, when you now realize how much money is needed in the United States to make the market transactions work and have credit work, how do you pour that money into the markets?" He said, "Well, the way it works is that banks and financial institutions go out and, one way or another, they receive people who solicit credit. And when they receive the solicitation for credit, they secure it one way or another, either with real goods as collateral, mortgages, or they expect to secure it with information about the movement of the goods, or the ownership of the goods, or the tradition of these people, or a salary stream, or whatever it is. Then what we do is, we take that security and we rediscount it." I said, "Well, now imagine a country, like most African countries, where 90 percent of all the assets are not on paper and can't be secured. How do you put the money into the market?" And, of course, Mr. Greenspan didn't have a reply. So the news is this: property rights aren't only the source of ownership; they are also the source of credit. And if most of the world doesn't have property rights, they're not going to have the credit that they require.

Think of capital. When people go out and raise capital—anybody who's got a business and wants to raise capital in your country—what do they do? They've got a company—property—and so then they cut the property of their company up into little pieces, thousands of little pieces, and they go and sell the pieces to different people who buy that piece of property and give an investment against it. Nobody goes and just puts a bag of money on the table. What they do is they buy a piece of property. So try to imagine, in Tanzania, where 98 percent of all enterprises are not registered on the books, or six million enterprises in Mexico that are not registered in the books, how do you go out and raise investment? The reply is, you don't, and so you're poor and you don't have capital. But you would if you started off with a property system.

One interesting thing in the way we came off of this, which might be of special interest to you, was in the 1980s, when we were seeing a terrorist system basically haunt Peruvians and make life very miserable for us. We started to try and find out why it was that people were actually sometimes harboring these terrorists, or hiding them. We always thought it was terror, until we discovered that the terrorists were actually giving services. And the service that they did was basically protecting the assets of the poor. They protected the assets of the poor wherever they produced cocoa, wherever they produced opium. And they protected the assets of the poor where people in the cities, who didn't have property titles, feared that the authorities would evict them. That's why one of the first things we did was organize a massive titling program. We actually displaced the terrorists, and therefore they were unemployed. That's how we were able to take away their constituency. And we learned that they, of course, had learned this from Mao Tse-tung—this was the way that he advanced from Manchuria down, defeating Chiang Kai-shek. He didn't give them private property rights, but he did give them collective rights over things and, therefore, swelled his armies. It was an old Ho Chi Min tactic as well, and therefore we thought it was useful.

It was also very useful, of course, because wherever we've had property rights in place, we also had addresses. Then we actually put in somebody to work with the New York Police Department for a while to find out how you found your criminals. In Peru, it is relatively easy: we put two policemen on every corner, and if somebody goes out running too fast, you arrest them. But what was interesting about you Americans is that you didn't see uniforms all over the streets. I remember once bringing a colleague of mine here to Washington; it was the first time he traveled outside Peru. And he said, you know what's fascinating about these countries, I don't see cops, where are they? So I tried to explain that the tendency of American cops—what I had seen on television shows like *Starsky and Hutch*—was to wear civilian clothes. But despite the significant amount of cops who weren't in uniform, we learned by observing the New York Police Department that they had a system called "skip tracing": a crime is produced; something doesn't work; and by knowing who lives where, you rapidly tie things up. Was this guy living here of such and such an origin? Did he have a cousin? Nobody really commits crimes in areas that they don't know one way or another, so there is a way that you can pick up the information based essentially on information on who is where, who owns what, who is renting to whom, who has been taking airplane or driving lessons, and who hasn't. And that kind of thing allows you to catch them fast. But when you don't have that kind of information, skip tracing is very difficult. You can't even have law and order unless you actually have a system of addresses.

Try to even to think of simple things like electricity, or try and think of things like water. How do you distribute clean water and electricity or any form of energy so that people can produce peacefully? Well, you certainly need some kind of a property rights system, otherwise how would you identify your subscribers? How would you create electricity subscription contracts if you do not know where the houses are, or who owns what house? You may start putting a tube to put clean water into a house or a wire to get electricity, but you've got to find out more than just where the houses are. We in Peru know where all the houses are; we use your satellites all the time. The problem isn't that. The problem is who is in the house and who really owns it and who has got what rights over the house, because they can differ from one place to another. So how would you implement billing systems, meter-reading circuits, collections mechanisms, loss control, delinquent-charge procedures, and fraud control if you didn't have property rights? What I am basically telling you now is that property rights is the first basis of organization of any society. When it is in place, it's not just that he got a title; it's much bigger. It's much bigger than parceling or titling. It basically has to do with an underlying social contract, where everybody has agreed how and according to what rules goods and ideas will be divided in a country, and that provides information. Not information like information technology, which is about communications, but information about how society is basically structured, documented, provided information. When you've got that, then everything starts working.

I have asked, for example, at this time, if my hosts here would be kind enough to get me an apple, and I've got one. A few generals there looking at me have seen me getting an apple, so I've got a lot of good witnesses here; this apple is mine. But no matter how we look at this apple that we all know is mine now, and that I have not yet consumed, there is nothing on it that says that this is Hernando's apple. There is nothing on it that says that I can receive it, I can sell it, I can buy it, I can rent it, I can lease it, I can mortgage it, I can use it as collateral. I can give you a hundred things that you can do with your objects and with everything you've got in the United States that you can't do in my part of the world. In other words, apples are not good enough. If there isn't a law that tells you who it belongs to and what you can do with it, nothing absolutely happens.

I got into the United States and I was being told that this is a country where trust is high. I just read Samuel Huntington; he said the difference between us Northern Anglo-Saxons and you guys is the fact that we trust each other. And I really believe that, in the depth of my heart. So when I got here and I went through Dulles, through immigration, and I said it's so good to see your trusting blue eyes—I told the immigrations officer this—because I know you're going to trust me. And as he asked me to identify myself, I said I'm Hernando de Soto Polarin, I come from (inaudible) 380 years ago, they came from my aunt in Spain. My mother actually comes from Namocaya (phonetic) where they came from, I think, from Swiss-Italy. But here's the interesting part. He said, "Will you just shut up and show me your passport." And I did. And the moment I showed him a title that described me, this man began trusting me. When I went to the hotel—and I have been to this hotel for many, many years—and they said, "Mr. de Soto, so good to see you. How are you doing?" I said, "I'm absolutely fine." "How are you going to pay?" I said, "Properly, as usual." I'm one of these few honest Peruvians who are around town. And he said, "Can I see your credit card." And then I realized that the reason that he always had trusted me was because I was on paper. I was documented. I, of course, couldn't have gotten this credit card if somebody didn't have my address to be able to issue it to and have some idea of what kind of assets I own so I could pay my debts. No property rights, no organization of society. Don't just say it's freed up; it's not going to work.

The second pivot of organization in the world is business organizations. You know, up until 1850 in the United States, before you could actually build a company, you had to get an act from Congress. It was a political act. And in Europe, you needed a charter from the king. Then Dudley Smith changed all of that about 1850 in New York, and it changed in France about 1870 with Cocoalan. The argument against giving people the right to automatically owned forms of association, a very intangible thing, was because they said only government can have that. You see, if you give that right to anything that isn't government, you will be trading states-in-little. And one day, those states-in-little will challenge the world.

As my friend, Jagdish Bhagwati, an American economist of Indian origin, always says, these companies are the B-52s of globalization. The fact that you give people the legal right to organize themselves is just absolutely tremendous, because it gives them a legal right to create a single, controlling, planning coordination. It gives them limited liability, which means that they and you know what their liabilities are limited to. In other words, when you go and talk to an American company, you've got a lot more information of how liable they can be, as opposed to talking to somebody whose status and liability aren't written or cannot be traced on paper. It gives you asset partitioning. You know what belongs to the family, you know what belongs to the suppliers, you know what belongs to the creditors, you know what belongs to the investors, you know what belongs to workers' rights—and all of this is done on paper in abstract. It isn't apples; it's all about paper being put together; it's perpetual succession. It means that the company or the organization will last forever, even when you die. In other words, they go beyond organic life. When you are in the informal sector in the dark economy, in the black economy, in the grey economy of Russia or the black economy of Peru, when you look at whoever you're dealing with, you better look to see how healthy he is, because if he's a goner, there goes your deal. While in the United States, you do a deal with Smith and Company and Smith dies, so what? Smith and Company keeps on going on. So companies give you a whole bunch of things: like long life, like ways of partitioning assets, knowing your risk. It allows you to divide labor; that's the first thing that Adam Smith said.

Talking about the *Wealth of Nations*, Smith said he had just been, I think it was to Glasgow, and saw a couple, a married couple, and they were producing fourteen pins a day between both of them. Sometime later he went to Edinburgh, and he saw eleven people producing much more than that, producing 48,000 pins. How come this increased productivity? And he said it was because they divided labor among themselves. One fellow was in charge of buying the wire, another one of straightening it, another one of cutting it into small equal pieces, another one of drawing a point on one end, another one of rounding the other end so that another one could put the head on that end—and thereby productivity increased enormously. What Adam Smith didn't tell us is that it's very hard to get a family that's got eleven members interested in making pins. You can't just have a family do that. You need to get together all sorts of people with different specialties, and that requires a legal entity called a business association. I repeat: whether you're going to Afghanistan, whether you're going to Tanzania, whether you're going to Mexico, more than eight-tenths of the world doesn't have these business organizations. What you get is, like in my country, you go to a business, it's an informal business, and you get a fellow—very virile with his big black moustache—and you ask, "Who's the boss?" and he says, "I am the boss." And as you look at him, you look with the side of your eyes to his wife, and you understand that she's really the boss. But you don't know who is the CEO, you don't know who is the CFO, you don't know who is organizing what, who's responsible for what, and you don't know how long they're going to live, and you don't know whether they really own what they're telling you they're going to sell. It's very hard to do prosperous business in worlds like that, but that's the way the majority of us citizens actually live. We don't have these statutes now.

Once you've got those two things [property rights and business organizations], there is a third item that is extremely important, which is identity. If you've got an address, if you are connected to some kind of stream of income that comes from some kind of organization, you can be located. The other day my address book had just gotten too thick, and my secretary told me, you can carry everything in a Palm Pilot, let's put it on there. The trouble is I can't put more than 2,500 names. So I said, okay, get me the physical list of people I have met in my life; I will just simply cut it down to 2,000 or 2,500, and the criterion has got to be very easy: who do I remember? I found out I didn't actually remember about 2,000 people, and that's it. We all know about 2,000 people. But you are nearly 300 million Americans. How do you get to know all the other Americans? They may be your brothers and your sisters, but the only way is through identity systems.

All identity comes on plastic or on paper. To come into this country I had to be identified with my passport—and that took some doing, as I told you before. To get into this building, I have my passport. I've got another passport here for the hotel. You Americans are continually issuing identification documents all over the place—and that's how you can collaborate, and that's how you can cooperate, and that's why law and order also work, apart from the rule of law. I mean, Huntington may be right that I need a blood transfusion before I can become developed, but in fact it's essentially a system, a fantastic legal system, that has allowed you to integrate yourself in a social whole.

Now why don't we just do that? I think that it's essentially because there's a prejudice in the world. I think there is prejudice in the world that says you Latins are good at dancing, you African's have got rhythm, you Chinese are subtle, etc. But a really structured system on how to do business is the thing of the northern people. And we really don't talk too much about it because in your country, I understand, it's not politically correct. Thank goodness in my country I can do all the talking I want about it. But here it's not politically correct. So one of the things we have been doing in the world, as governments have called us in—these capital formation projects always start with a president or head of state calling us—and we say, the first thing you've got to find out, Mr. President, is how many people are really governed by the rule of law because, for the reason that I explained before, there is not much you can do [without the rule of law]. We're the only ones in the world so far who do that. So let us count who has got property rights, who has got business rights, and who has got ideas. It's not that difficult.

I'm going to just share with you some images about what we found out in Tanzania. We were told before that these are, of course, societies steeped in tribal organizations; they're not really ready for market economies. We said, well, let's find out. So we fielded a team of about 950 people, and with these 950 people we started finding out the following things. First of all, the legal system was in place. You've got every law that you need. However, if you wanted to buy a plot of land, which was easily done—well, it's not *that* easy to do; it takes about 400 days, but let's forget that. Once you own that plot of land, you decide you want to make a shop, a restaurant, a factory, a garage. Whatever it is, it'll take you roughly eight years, working about eight hours a day each year, I'm trying to find my references on it—I have to look back all the time. Put it another way: you set up a firm and you take out insurance, you register, you change your activities twice, you pay your taxes, you advertise fourteen times, you make provisions for your kids getting the company once you die, little things like that. It will take you, in Dar El Salaam, 32,000 days to do that, So it's no wonder that only 2 percent of Tanzanians are recorded according to law.

Now we went out there to say, well, the rest must be organized by tribes. We didn't find one acre organized by tribes. What we did find, which was extremely interesting, was that the rest of the country, underneath the legal system, had begun organizing. Hopefully that figure is coming out; I don't know if my little thing here is working. There we go. We found that everywhere—just like we found in Latin America, just like we have in Asia—that everywhere in a country that has $270 of gross national product per capita, they have small court systems. Like early on in the United States in the eighteenth and nineteenth centuries, during the California Gold Rush, in Little Miami River, in Arkansas, people get together, and when neighbors have conflicts or have doubts, the neighbors get together and draw up a document that says so and so owns so much, by dispute resolution.

So you may not have a constitution that actually says who has property rights, but all the documents that are necessary in Tanzania to establish a system of property rights are already in place—and we found them just about everywhere we went. I'm waiting for the next picture. And in effect, we have not only seen that there is eased conflict resolutions, but we haven't found one piece of land where there isn't an established mutual agreement on it or where there isn't a document, most of which aren't standardized. Moreover, in every village of the 10,000 villages—the ones that we were able to visit, not, of course, all 10,000, but we did visit about some 1,700 and we got a pretty good sample—we haven't found any one without all the documents about people being born, about people dying, about knowing who owns what, about knowing who has what corporation, who has traded what. All the documents are actually being stored in specific places.

Now supposedly, these are people who don't like private property and these are people who don't like business, but all the institutions of business are already existing. And the titles that they have to their businesses, and their goods and their chattels and how much money they have, are all fungible. In other words, they are not only there to protect themselves from the police, they are also there to be traded—including used as collateral and mortgages, to be able to get credit on the basis of their land. And it goes even so far that we haven't found one piece of land that doesn't have a testament. There you see it, of course, with a fingerprint, because the guy doesn't know how to read. But he has got a friend who does know how to read and, like Americans or Brits 150 years ago, they are the scribes who have to be trusted. They put their fingerprints [on the testaments] so that they establish, quite clearly, that there are individual wills, indicating that most of Tanzania has got just about all the institutions you had at the birth of the United States, including that of associations. That is to say, a collective put together to organize enterprise and to determine its meaning and capture it in statutes, and that lives parallel to the family, to the clans, and to the tribes. It is not contradictory to them. And there is division of labor throughout the whole of the land. And there is a division between management and working classes, even garbage collectors. There is a garbage collection company owned by women, and because they are not strong enough, it's the men who are actually the labor. And they have got all their documents set out in their different villages so that they can be recorded. You will also see that in most companies, there is somebody who actually keeps a record of the assets and distinguishes capital. And last but not least, we haven't found one cow in Tanzania that isn't branded and that doesn't have a private property document right on its hide.

So, what happened to Margaret Meade? Hey, where's Oscar Lewis? Where are all these people who said we Third Worlders were tribal and collective while you are individuals, you get divorce. Where is solidarity? What happened to all of that? Well, I think what's happened since Karl Polanyi, since Levi Strauss, etc., is that we have certain documents of anthropologists and sociologists who have got a very idealistic vision of where we are. Maybe we used to be that way. The news I am trying to bring to you with this part of the flow chart is simply to tell you that whether it's the Philippines, whether it's Peru, whether it is Mexico, whether it's Guatemala, whether it's Honduras, whether it's Ghana, whether it's Tanzania, wherever we have gone, whether it's Egypt—already the world is marching toward a large market economy, and we just haven't actually gotten in touch with it. What we have, on the contrary, are very disorienting attitudes, very noble ones, of giving them charity without actually asking ourselves whether they can actually organize. Because if they do get organized, then, of course, what can happen is that we will have a modern society, and those dark areas where the threats to national security now come from will cease to exist, because people will be organized in a way that we all become accountable to each other and where prosperity is again possible. Capital is possible, credit is possible.

So when you look at the poor in developing countries or in the former Soviet Union, poor isn't really what makes you violent. Generally, most poor people I know are pretty humble and, on the contrary, they keep their heads down low most of the time. The angry people are the excluded people: those who are excluded from the rule of law, those who are assailed every day because nothing is possible. Whenever in the United States or in another developed country people get together, they say, we should be able to do this. I know somebody who can give us credit. I know somebody who is a specialist on this. I know people who want this product. We need some favorable legislation. I know Senator such-and-such; we will be able to go get him. Congressman such-and-such has got to get elected here every two years; we can talk to him. Everything is possible. To be among the four billion of the Third World, nothing is possible. Red tape will drown you out until you finish the day, and it will be right in front of you when you begin the next day. You will not have institutions to turn to. You will not have capital investment. You will have no credit. You will have no identity. You will have nobody protecting you, and somebody will tell you, this is a free market economy, man. Get up, go out and do it. How can he do it? How can she do it if they don't have these institutions? Think of the free trade agreements. What does it take to globalize? To globalize or to export, you have to at least fill in a bill of lading. You have got to write in who you are—identity. You have got to say where you live, you have got to give an address. You have got to put down what company you belong to. Those three things four billion people in the world can't do. So when you talk to them that the world is globalizing, what do you think they think about globalization? It's just a pretty vague word. The only people who can really globalize are you up north, the one billion elites—I am figuring there are one billion; we could only be maybe half a billion, we haven't really counted them. The ones who can fill in a bill of lading.

So these are people who serve, but are not observed, who exist but are not seen. And all their potential, their enormous potential that we have found in the poorest countries of Africa, are hidden. Their entrepreneurship by charity drives by Jeffrey Sachs and these other people who come around and say, "You need to be helped because nature is against you. You need to be helped because you don't have a chance." Nobody actually looks at the fact that there are no institutions there to actually help them. Nobody looks at the fact that this pretty much looks like your country did in the nineteenth century, when you were also a Third World country, but you gave yourself the institutions and you allowed yourself to be pulled together. I was just recently reading—because I was in St. Louis, helping inaugurate an institution within a university—I was remembering one of the speeches that had been given to me. In 1832, when Abraham Lincoln was just a Congressman, he was visiting St. Louis and he was chagrined, he was profoundly struck, as he had been in many American cities, at the horror. As he went into St. Louis with his horse and carriage, he wasn't able to see the sunset because of the amount of corpses hanging on the boughs of trees—like curtains, he said—of people who had been lynched or who people who had been hung because of property conflicts. And he said, when are you going to get yourselves together? Well, you did. You put in thirty-two preemption acts throughout the nineteenth century, the last preemption act being called the Homestead Act, which I think he did himself, and got your country organized. You were a Third World country, and you did it through very good institutions and through making sure that everybody participated in those institutions.

And you thought about it at many opportunities. One of those opportunities, for example, was Japan. We in Peru were always very interested in Japan because we have had a president of Japanese origin, named Alberto Fujimori. Alberto Fujimori was the son of one of the one million Japanese families that crossed the ocean, the Pacific, to come and live in the two South American countries that opened their arms to migration. One of them was Brazil and the other one was Peru, the smaller one. But these one million migrants came, in the '30s and the '40s. Now, that's not really what is interesting. What is interesting is the fact that the Fujimoris came to Peru, the Yoshiamas went to Brazil, but why didn't the Toledos and the Lulas go to Japan? And the reply is, because Japan had a GNP per capita only half of ours. We were twice as rich as they were. To their credit, they had a powerful army—so did Saddam Hussein—you can still be a poor country. And so we got very interested in finding out how come, now that Alberto Fujimori is back in Japan, he is in a country ten times richer than mine. What happened in those last fifty years? So we decided to investigate it. We looked at your books, and we looked at your declassified documents—which are very hard to read because they are very smudged and black, so you can't really get to the background stuff—and we looked at the Japanese books, as well, and it wasn't very clear. So we got a grant and went and studied Japan. What we asked was, who was in charge of the reforms? And we managed to identify, in a joint venture with the International House of Japan, the seven surviving octogenarians who had drawn up the Japanese reforms from 1945 to 1952 and flipped a feudal country and turned it around into a modern, thriving economy that has its difficulties but is still ten times richer than we are.

Now, when we sat down with them, we found out a whole bunch of things. Among other things, they were very much supported by the U.S. occupation forces. As a matter of fact, General McArthur had put, I think in 1942 or 1943, a team working in Honolulu to see what are we going to do with Japan once we actually take over Japan, and the conclusion was, we have to bring in a property system. And we have got to bring in the rule of law. Why? The reason that Japan was expanding was because it was a feudal economy. There have been many revolts in Japan and then, with all these revolts, what the feudal military establishment did was say, well, we need more land. And that was the source of Japanese expansionism. So, if we have a property system, the incentives to do that in the future will die down. Moreover, Mao Tse-tung was coming down from Manchuria, giving away collective property, so the American reply in Japan, in Taiwan, then Formosa, and in Korea was to start putting in the instruments of the rule of law. And they met up with a group of Japanese who were in absolute agreement, who had been trying to do this over time.

I would like to show you two posters out of over a hundred posters that we got from them. Why? Posters are very important because posters are the way that you communicate policies. When you are going to change a country, you have got to tell everybody what you are doing, and before, there was no television. So this is Japan, 1946. These posters try to explain to the Japanese what is going on. At the bottom level you have got the *bakufu*. What they found out is that under the feudal system, the Japanese, in spite of the fact that they paid their feudal lord's rent and they paid taxes, among each other—you know, the de Sotos and the Smiths, etc.—they bought and sold all the way for 400 years, like all people, like Tanzanians today, like Mexicans. So when they told them, now we're going to find a way through compensation to make sure that feudal land also belongs to you and that assets that you have got also belong to us, that shows the people at the bottom—and there they are pointing out—I own this, I own that, he owns this, I'm trading with him, and they can provide the information. Then they elect—that's the second level up—they elect their representatives, who then tell the prefectures—the third level up—what are the rules of the game. So they aren't concocted in Washington. They aren't concocted in New York or in Moscow or in Paris. They found out what the rules of the market are in Japan, very specific to the culture of Japan. And on the fourth level, it's when—because that's what happens in all countries that are not Anglo-Saxon—we have to codify things. They are blocked together in new codes, which create the modern Japanese state. And the next picture, the next poster—we had to photograph it, because they never gave them to us—shows that in one circle, the Meiji Restoration of 1890 is being torn up because it basically consolidated the property rights or, shall we say, the feudal rights of an elite. Then at each level of village it is decided who really owns what since forever and ever, and how the compensations will take place. The third circle is a new law being written up, and then you see the poor Japanese being brought into the system of the rule of law.

So, one of the things that we find very inspiring is, what was the U.S. policy in Japan that was so successful? To me, it's a lot more interesting than the Marshall Plan, because what it basically did, it stuck three needles in the sides of the Chinese and forced Deng Xiaoping to change the system. So, that's one thing. It allowed us, with Abimael Guzman, to pretty much liquidate the Shining Path. I mean, they will be around, they might kill someone, but they are dead as a political movement. It would be very interesting to look into U.S. history, what you did, for example, in California, when California in 1856 was 800 illegal states—which you called, of course, miners' claims, the inspiration of the American people—but there were 800 illegal guys who had swarmed into Latin American territory and taken over outside the law and outside sovereignty, yet they got consolidated into a nation. What did you do? That would be very interesting to find out, because every time we read what we should do from North American authors, they make less sense, and we have looked at your great great granddaddies, who make a lot of sense for us.

Also, get the picture on property. It's not about parcels; it's about constitutions, it's about the rule of law, which is based on grassroots activity. It also means opening up the archives. The World Bank and the Inter-American Development Bank here in Washington have done a lot of work on property. Now, that's the advantage about being an American: when something doesn't work, you bankrupt, you fail, and everybody else knows about it. Last year, you had 1.5 million bankruptcies; now you know where not to go. But what happens with a lot of the money that you send to us via international financial institutions is, we don't know what to do with it. The files aren't open. By the way, I'm not saying that that's the fault of developed countries; it's mainly developing countries on the board that block it. But we have to know where the failures are if we are going to know how to build successes. That's extremely important.

And take the long view on these things. The way we see it is that we are still now fighting a war that started a long time ago with the Enlightenment. The Enlightenment essentially challenged the national romantics and said civilization is written without an s; there is only one civilization and it's the one of humanity. You can have many cultures, but we can all be civilized in the same way. The romantics, like Vico and Herder, came around and said, no, no, what exists are only these national structures, and that is what we inspire ourselves for. That was in battle. The Enlightenment won out against feudalism, the Enlightenment won out against capitalism, against fascism, and in the Cold War, won out against communism. That same battle now has been transferred to globalization, but it's the same battle. And the problem is that it hasn't stood still. Now the kind of people you have to conquer—all those people who were in *National Geographic*, what we mentioned before, in the hinterland, who have now come in to be active citizens—have been told that this is the market economy; there is no centralized planning system. And they have no tools to actually be working in a market economy. There is no way that they can actually be successful. And I think that that's very much part of the agenda for the future. Because if we solve that, I think as we get the rule of law inside—and as I've been trying to explain, hopefully satisfactorily, at least enough to make you think that we make some sense—that's what will actually be the challenge of the twenty-first century: how to bring in the rule of law, and how to make all these people, who are not so poor so much as they are excluded from the rule of law, come into a system using the examples that you set so marvelously during the eighteenth century and the nineteenth century. Thank you very much.

MAJOR GENERAL KEITH W. DAYTON: Okay, I'm going to try to talk without a microphone. We are going to adjust the schedule very, very slightly. At 2:30 we were supposed to break, but I think you'll agree with me that we can talk for maybe ten or fifteen more minutes. Mr. de Soto has graciously agreed to take questions, if we have a few. So if you do have a question, all I ask is that you stand up and address us that way and tell us who you are and all that. So are there any questions out there? I will kind of help moderate this. Yes sir, right here.

AUDIENCE - PETER SHARFMAN: Peter Sharfman of the MITRE Corporation. If the government of Tanzania, to take the example you cited, were to decide to bring the 98 percent under the formal rule of law, how would they go about it, and what difference would it make?

de SOTO: Well, President [Benjamin W.] Mkapa has announced that that's what he will do. That's the reason why I have the right to show these images and talk to you about it. The first thing that you have to do is create an appropriate organization, because you are turning the country over. When the Europeans did this—for example, when the Germans were defeated by Napoleon and became aware of how the British were prospering and the Dutch were prospering, as opposed to themselves—they set up the Stein-Hardenberg Commission, the purpose of which was, as a matter of fact, to change the status of the law so that the benefits of the ownership system, the benefits of the company system, would be equally accessible to all Germans. When the Swiss decided to do it, from about 1898 all the way to 1908, they put up what is called the Eugene Huber Commission—in other words, a whole bunch of people who had to see how the government, the state, was going to be restructured, in the same way that the Japanese had to get organized. Because the existing established structures are, of course, generally in favor of the status quo. The old saying is Louis XIV will never reform himself. So you can't just simply go to the Ministry of Lands of another country or the Ministry of Industrial Production or Commerce of another country; it has to be dealt with at the level of a head of state, because you are talking about a revolution. You are talking about changing the status quo. So what the Tanzanians are planning on doing is creating a special organization that will work at the level of the head of state, where it has been working so far, with whom we have been working. And then we will gradually put up a plan to turn it around, which will involve communications. What is most important, this study in which we joint ventured shows them that they have got a constituency. You see, until you get to know what's actually going on in developing countries, everybody feels that a free market program, a program to be in democracy, is really an idea of the West that was taken up by some people in Third World countries who went to American universities and got very inspired. That doesn't cut it. The only way politicians will move is if they realize that they are serving most people: if they are a democracy, that they will get the most votes, and if they are dictators, that they will get more legitimacy. When that happens, then you can turn around. But you need a special organization, because there is nothing in a developing country, nor in a developed country, that is actually structured to be able to make those changes.

DAYTON: Okay, let me take one over here on this side. Yes ma'm. If you please, get her a microphone.

AUDIENCE - COLONEL ANITO DOMINGO: Yes, sir, I'm Colonel Domingo. Sir, I wanted to ask, in the beginning you mentioned that in order to have a market economy, you must have basic institutions to support a free economy. Do you think the Andean rich nations are ready to come into a free trade agreement?

de SOTO: The Andean region? Yes, I do think that they are ready, and they are very desirous. At least the polls in my country indicate that, I think, two-thirds of the population is in agreement with that. The problems that will come from that is that the distance between those who can fill a bill of lading and those who cannot will grow, because those who will actually connect with you in the United States in these enormous markets that allow for so much specialization will prosper, and it won't trickle fast enough. So that's why we have proposed, in the case of Peru, to think not only of a free trade agreement with the United States, but also a free trade agreement with our poor. Now what you're letting us do is work in your market. What we've got to learn to do now is let our poor get into our own market, which we don't. It's not that anybody's conspired, nobody's actually created a huge wall that doesn't allow the poor to come in; it's the result of bad legislation, bad government practices over time. The Peruvian government, for example, produces 28,000 rules and regulations per year; that means about 106 per day. So it's the interest of him, and it's the interest of her, and they all get put together, and after awhile you've got walls all over the place. Obviously nobody did it on purpose, but there it is. The same way that you create a free trade agreement, you have to dismantle the barriers between the Andean regions in Peru. We've got a lot of internal dismantling to do to make sure that we *all* benefit from the wide market—not just an elite and produce again in our country revolutionary conditions.

DAYTON: Two more. I think I saw a hand up over here. Could you please get him a mic. You've got one, okay.

AUDIENCE - JONATHAN CZARNECKI: Mr. de Soto, Jon Czarnecki, Naval War College at Monterey. E-Bay is an Internet phenomenon in which you can develop a virtual identity as well as have market evaluations available for sellers. Do you have any opinion or view, in terms of Internet websites like eBay and the sellers they provide, do they provide at least part of what you have espoused?

de SOTO: Yes, sir, I do think the fact that information technology has come onto the scene will make things much easier. There is no doubt that information technology will allow us, in many cases, to leapfrog and get ahead. One of the things we've seen, for example, is that when we created our own new property records in Peru, it actually allowed us to, first of all, defeat the Shining Path, and then give a sizable part of the population standards of living that they didn't have before. It was due to the fact that we could digitize rapidly, because we don't have four hundred, five hundred years of property titles to put into the digital system. We could leapfrog. However, one has to remember that before you can digitize, you have to paperize. In other words, I have never seen, so far, a computer with a sort of a vacuum cleaner on the other side, sucking in information. You bring it out from written information, and many of the people in our countries actually have no information. And when they do have information, they may have too much or uncertain information. For example, in our case in Peru, when everybody said "Yeah, what's missing is property titles," we said there are no missing property titles, because we had found that in Lima, on average, there are twenty property titles per parcel of land. Since the conquistadors came in, everybody titled, but the paper was worthless because they never recorded it. Just like the *Doomsday Book*, the whole trick is not to make one inventory, but to make sure that it recycles itself so that it actually reflects the reality of life. In other words, it's a 2005 phone book on Washington, D.C., it's not that of 1918. In other words, it means something, it's relevant to reality. Sometimes it's too many titles, sometimes there are not enough titles—but the important thing is that legal documents are very uncertain under the existing system. So if you don't have a system of law that is well established on paper, or shall we say somewhere, it's very hard to digitize it. But I do agree with you that there are many cases where digitization will allow us to record much more quickly than having paper. Absolutely.

DAYTON: Okay. I have time for probably one more. Sorry, I'll have to go with this gentleman way in the back over here, if we can please. Can you get him a mic.

AUDIENCE - GEORGE MAURER: I don't need a mic, General, thank you. George Maurer from Key West. Mr. de Soto, one of my good friends is Dennis Jett, who until four or five or six years ago was ambassador to Peru and is now the director of the International Center at the University of Florida. He would agree with most of us in Florida that the meeting of the Organization of the American States in Fort Lauderdale a couple of months ago was pretty much a disaster, and the reason being that of the twenty-three countries, I believe, that were attending that meeting, at least ten or eleven of them were bitterly opposed to American efforts to privatize, particularly in Bolivia, where, if I recall correctly, there are tremendous natural gas resources that the natives are most reluctant to give to Enron, to Chevron, and to other people or multinational corporations of that ilk. How do you see the privatization efforts in both South America and Central America?

de SOTO: Thank you, sir. An admirable voice. Thank you. I think you've posed a very, a very important question. First of all, regarding privatization, I think it's time that we reviewed not the concept, but the terminology, and also rooted it in local language and understanding. In to two or three places that we've worked, we've been able to make two interesting polls, but let me tell you about the Peruvian one because then I will not violate the confidence of any of our other clients. We asked a group of the most notable extralegal entrepreneurs—these are people working in that gray market—three questions. The first one: are you a member of the private sector, and the reply of 96 percent was no, which was astounding to us because they were all private—illegal, but obviously private. Second we asked them, then are you a member of the public sector, and they said, "Of course not, public sector is government." And the third question was, who, then, is the private sector, and they replied, "*Los de arriba,*" "those up there," the oligarchy. In other words, as time has gone by in Latin America, and we look at the social pages—the president of the Peruvian Chamber of Commerce shaking hands with one of the big businessmen of the United States or Europe—private sector has meant "the rich." So if that's the understanding of the word "private" among the poor, imagine going to a country and saying "We're going to privatize this industry." What are you telling them? So we recommended a long time ago, over fifty years ago, drop the word "private" because it doesn't mean the same thing in the U.S. that it means in other countries. Check the vocabulary. Do what you did in Japan. Ask them not only who owns what, ask them what they mean by different words. If you had started saying at that time, we want this to be administrated in a way by companies that are not government because of corruption, if you really pitched it right then, it would work. But what happens with many Latin American leaders, of course, is that they don't really understand or have fathomed what is actually meant by revolution toward the market, and therefore they just repeat the *libertadores,* whatever they get from the North, and of course it means something different. Secondly, talking about gas, what happens is the following: you have 80 or 90 percent of Bolivians who don't really know who owns what, who are not really protected by law. They're protected by their own organizations. And all of a sudden, an American or a European company comes along and gets due title to the land, but not only gets due title, he gets the best lawyers in Bolivia or Peru. And they even bring the best notaries and get it all on nice, sealed paper. Not enough, they go to the World Bank to get extra assurance, and they go over and get OPEC. This guy's got no title, and he's just their neighbor—what does he think of property. Now, he doesn't have the notion of property in his head; the only notion he has in his head is sovereignty, and that's when he says, "What are these foreign guys doing in my territory?" Sovereignty he understands. Now, I've got a property title, so I've got no problem. I can distinguish between Americans taking over Peruvian territory and getting an American neighbor, but can everybody else? I don't think so. So the reply to your question is, privatization is good. Markets are good. Democracy is good. But those three words, in my part of the world, may have been eroded to the point that you want to reconceptualize them, and you want to recast them so that they actually work in terms that the majority of people will understand. By the way, regards to Dennis Jett. He was an excellent U.S. ambassador to Peru, fought for all the right things.

DAYTON: Okay, I'm about to announce a break, but just stop and think what we just did here for the last hour. You have a truly international player from Peru who came to talk to primarily a bunch of Americans about national security, but he didn't once talk about the military. He didn't once talk about fighting in the usual sense, but he talked instead about economic relationships. He talked about how you generate wealth around the world. He talked about the four billion people out there whom none of us really think every much about on a day-to-day basis. Now I bring that up because it was not for nothing that we called this the Eisenhower Series. President Eisenhower, former general, was fascinated with the challenge of national security, but he would be among the first to say that a man like Mr. de Soto would be exactly the person who should come and talk to a national security conference, because it isn't about the military. And all of us who are in uniform—and those of you who follow what we do—should understand that as well, especially in this twenty-first-century world that we face. Now, I'm about to declare a break, but our next group is going to be in a similar vein. We're going to talk about humanitarian and nongovernmental organizations in the new security context environment, whatever that is. So along that theme, I hope you'd all join me in one more round of applause, because you don't get the likes of Mr. de Soto everyday. And, sir, we thank you very much for coming here and talking to us today.

PANEL II

NONGOVERNMENTAL AND HUMANITARIAN ORGANIZATIONS IN THE NEW SECURITY ENVIRONMENT

Co-sponsor: The Center for Humanitarian Cooperation

Moderator: Roy Williams, President and Chief Executive Officer, Center
    for Humanitarian Cooperation
Nancy E. Lindborg, President, Mercy Corps
Geoff Loane, Head of Regional Delegation for the United States and
    Canada, International Committee of the Red Cross
Robert MacPherson, Director, Security Unit, CARE
Kevin M. Kennedy, Office for the Coordination of Humanitarian Affairs,
    United Nations

Panel Charter

Most people would agree that recent changes to the world security environment have led to a paradigm shift in humanitarian circles over the basic concept of humanitarian space—a safe and secure environment in which to provide impartial assistance and protection. Most would agree that such space is increasingly difficult to find and maintain. Many humanitarian nongovernmental organizations (NGOs) and international organizations (IOs) contend that the concepts of impartiality, nondiscrimination, and independence from political and military organizations are essential to maintaining NGO/IO neutrality, and therefore security. However, these concepts are not always respected by all of the other actors in every conflict. In many cases, humanitarian NGOs/IOs have become prime targets due to their proximity to conflict and their interaction with military forces.

Discussion Points

This panel studied and discussed the roles, missions, and issues related to nongovernmental and humanitarian organizations in the new security environment. Among the questions the panel considered were the following:

Left to right: *Roy Williams, Nancy E. Lindborg, Geoff Loane, Robert MacPherson, and Kevin M. Kennedy.*

1. What are the elements affecting your agency's decision whether to operate in a conflict environment?

2. What are the overall consequences for humanitarian organizations working in the same area but operating under significantly different security protocols?

3. Is it still realistic to expect protection based on neutrality?

4. What is out there in terms of codes, best practices, lessons learned, and professional capacity building? How can these most effectively be shared and understood among humanitarian and military actors?

5. What changes to military and nonmilitary organizations need to occur to facilitate more effective operations for all parties?

Summary

Nancy E. Lindborg

• How "new" is the current security environment? Are the situations in Afghanistan and Iraq typical or anomalies? NGOs operate in many insecure environments around the world. It is far from clear that the situation they face nowadays is fundamentally different. NGOs devote a great deal of time, training, and resources, seeking to build a "community acceptance strategy" so that staff can navigate these difficult environments. To be sure, Iraq and Afghanistan are lightning rods. They embody important issues of discussion, not least when and how to transition from emergency relief to development.

• Neutrality is not a part of the code of conduct to which many NGOs are signatories. Furthermore, strict neutrality is difficult to maintain in a conflict area. The wrong question for us to consider is the nature of the relationship between the NGOs and the military. The more important question is how development NGOs can serve their local constituents while avoiding excessive dependence on the military. NGOs must also strive to distance themselves from the U.S. government. NGOs link up with local actors to produce positive change. But they cannot do so when they are bound up tightly in a governmental structure. Once NGO personnel are operating behind barbed wire and armed guards, they cannot easily engage civil society.

Geoff Loane

• The International Committee of the Red Cross (ICRC) is legally obliged to work in conflict zones and has accumulated a vast reservoir of experience in insecure environments. However, the ICRC cannot operate without security guarantees. Security is the primary responsibility of the belligerents, whether state or nonstate actors. The ICRC's operational role is to assess the human needs situation generated by conflict. Some belligerents choose to ignore these needs. We must address more effectively the problem of how to "responsibilize."

• Humanitarian work has changed a great deal since the end of the Cold War. The proxy wars of that era were marked by denials by the belligerents that such conflicts were indeed taking place—nonaccess and nonrecognition of humanitarian needs. More recently, especially with the growth of transnational terrorism, conflicts have changed. Terrorists do not aspire to control physical space, their leadership is not accessible, and they do not respect legal and humanitarian frameworks. Consequently, the process of providing for those in need has become very complicated and is sometimes impossible. Meanwhile, humanitarian organizations have been able to negotiate access more successfully than ever before, making countless needy victims of conflict reachable. Yet, with increasing frequency, humanitarian workers have been perceived as having political agendas, which has resulted in the "instrumentalization" (manipulation) of humanitarian work.

• Today we live in a more accountable world where seemingly everything is becoming more transparent. Increased transparency, however, limits the movement of the people working on the ground. For instance, today the ICRC would not be able to replicate some of its work, such as in Somalia, due to higher standards and expectations of accountability.

• It is inevitable that there will be humanitarian crises. The U.S. military has enormous capabilities and is ready to employ them to respond to such crises. Humanitarian organizations must acknowledge this, yet (certainly in the case of the

ICRC) be ever mindful of their obligation to remain neutral in negotiating access to those in great need.

Robert MacPherson

- Security has always been a concern. CARE has 13,000 staff in seventy-two locations. Until about 2000, almost all of the humanitarian workers killed were accident-related fatalities. Over the past five years, this has changed.
- Security is not CARE's core business, but is nonetheless a critical element of everything we do. Deaths are no longer random, but directed. In many cases, there is clear evidence of a method or thought process behind the killing. The objective of targeting humanitarian workers appears to be to disrupt the reconstruction effort and/or gain publicity by attacking the organization.
- It is easy for anyone wanting to disrupt relief or reconstruction efforts to simply point to sources of money or other links to the country whose government is involved in some way in the conflict. In order to counter this strategy, NGOs should strive for "independence."
- CARE applies several criteria in determining whether to continue to operate or to withdraw: (1) presence (whether there is a baseline or infrastructure in-country to build on), (2) who else is continuing to work in that country, and (3) the ability of staff to communicate with each other and across the entire spectrum. However, these decisions are often strongly influenced by emotional responses, not technical criteria.
- In the field, *in extremis*, pragmatism tends to prevail and civil-military relations always work out. In a conflict environment, working together is an absolute requirement for people seeking to accomplish their respective missions. In the last ten years, NGOs and the military have begun to truly understand each other's needs.

Kevin M. Kennedy

- With respect to conflict transformation operations, the United Nations has been operating in a post–August 19, 2003, world—the date of the deadly bombing of the UN mission headquarters in Baghdad. This event has produced seismic changes. We are now committed to better information collection, more staff in the field, and closer collaboration with NGOs in operational theaters.
- Like the NGOs and ICRC, the United Nations is determined to continue to provide humanitarian assistance. Regrettably, in terms of the security environment in which these activities are conducted, Afghanistan and Iraq are not anomalies. Somalia and Chechnya are but two examples. It is not clear what the ICRC and other NGOs can do to dramatically reduce the security risks.
- With respect to the working relationship in the "civil-military humanitarian industry," perhaps we should not seek to turn art into science. With strong and effective interpersonal skills and the overarching objective of saving lives in focus, much can be accomplished together. It is also important to keep in mind that the

military is best suited to tackling security, while NGOs should take the lead in designing programs and delivering assistance.

Question-and-Answer Period

• Do private security companies have the potential to be effective peacekeepers? Kennedy said they have neither the legitimacy nor the mandate to play such a role. It is hard to conceive of the United Nations chartering any of them to conduct these operations.

• What happens when the military does not have the capacity to assist in complex emergencies? Williams responded that there should not be any surprises in this business. In-country resources are there, but roadblocks hamper activating them.

• Should NGOs deal with "extrasystemic" belligerents at all? According to Loane, impartiality means responding to victims irrespective of what they look like and who they are. There is a risk that in a refugee camp, for example, NGO staff might be susceptible to politically motivated charges of taking sides simply by discharging their responsibilities to help save lives. For the ICRC emblem to be respected, the belligerents have to perceive that the staff is helping all victims of conflict.

Analysis

Roy Williams was an excellent moderator, identifying themes of agreement and developing the nuances of provocative disagreement among the panelists. The panelists declined to confront directly a contradiction in their collective position that the humanitarian imperative (commitment to improving the lives of victims) takes priority over the principles of neutrality (treating all victims, regardless of side or belligerent status) or independence (autonomous operation, free from host government or security forces control or authority—or the perception of that control). Two separate questioners from the audience offered representative examples where actions taken by NGOs and the International Red Cross (IRC) appear to disprove the asserted dominance of the humanitarian imperative in decision making. The stunning observation was not a matter of the dominance or compromise of the humanitarian principle, but of the panelists' apparent inability to see the contradiction between their organizations' assertions and actions.

Agreement

The panelists agreed that effective security is a foundational requirement for conducting effective humanitarian assistance (HA) and development operations. There was also nearly unanimous agreement that the military's primary mission in HA operations is establishing a security environment in which the HA organizations can operate independently. The panel strongly defended the need for interagency architectures that stress host governments' and militaries' security roles, and for recognized NGOs and international HA organizations as being the most effective at delivering assistance and designing nation-building programs. An audience inquiry regarding the acceptability and suitability of contracting private armed security forces to provide some level of protection to NGOs and to ensure HA worker safety was rejected by the panel unless no other alternative was available.

The panelists observed that in response to the increased need, both the size and number of HA organizations involved in immediate recovery and longer-term reconstruction missions are increasing. Despite this growth, or perhaps exacerbated by it, civilian HA organizations are not adequately resourced for the task. The panelists refuted a perceived need to create a national organization along the National Guard model to build required HA capacity in favor of investing in existing civilian organizations. One panelist observed that the current model involves the military filling the void to "consolidate security," then gets stuck with the HA mission because civilian capacity is not resourced.

A consistent theme throughout the dialogue was a recognition that both military and HA organizations need to develop better understanding of each other, beyond accessing capabilities. A sophisticated awareness of the political pressures that influence decision making within respective organizational cultures is needed. While he specifically addressed the military, Kevin Kennedy offered three imperatives that would help achieve better understanding between the various operators in an HA mission. First, be better listeners. NGOs are normally on the ground before the military arrives and remain after the military departs. They have wisdom to share and a longer-vision horizon when measuring success. Second, develop liaison capacity. This is a face-to-face relationship business. Robust liaison capacity is critical to success. Finally, being open to ideas and suggestions from others working the mission goes a long way to fostering understanding and cooperation. This sound wisdom came from a person who has frequently succeeded in these environments.

Provocative disagreement

The panelists did not share a commonly held belief that the new security environment constitutes a new HA environment. Consensus is growing that the security environment may be new, and that current operations like Iraq and Afghanistan are not anomalies. From an HA perspective, Robert MacPherson made a compelling argument that in this new environment, HA worker deaths are no longer random, "wrong place, wrong time" events: they are part of an opponent's strategy. Attacks on unarmed HA organizations disrupt and discredit host government efforts at reconstruction and are a symptom of a changing HA environment.

The implication is that the historic view of HA worker security is changing. Organizations no longer can rely on community acceptance for security and a reprieve from belligerent interference through neutrality. The new environment renders humanitarian organizations vulnerable to targeting and attack by the belligerents, precisely because of the notable value and visibility associated with humanitarian action in communities.

The contrary view is that, from an HA mission perspective, Iraq and Afghanistan are not "new environments," but exceptions. They are unique because they represent collapsed states that generated enough world interest for other states to intervene with their militaries. This is not the historic environment in which NGOs and other HA organizations find themselves and, in fact, may not be the predominant HA environment of the future. HA operational environments traditionally have been characterized by international apathy and isolation. Even in today's world (of global information networks and economies), the predominant HA intervention environment looks more like the past than Iraq. Under this view of the future, HA organizations must rally around the traditional values of independence and neutrality to ensure relevance and acceptance when operating in the world's backwaters.

The view that current operations in Afghanistan and Iraq are unique from an HA operational perspective is compelling. While the security environment has changed from a military perspective, the historic condition in which HA organizations operate, with little or no international security force footprint, is likely to persist. The conclusion that the HA organizations should cling to the traditional value of independence in Iraq to maintain their security in another theater, however, appears flawed. Afghanistan and Iraq are unique. They should be viewed differently by HA organizations, and the methods employed to provide assistance should be tailored to the theater.

Contradiction and flawed logic

The panel failed to convincingly defend the assertion that the humanitarian principle takes precedence over the neutrality or independence principle when choices for action bring the principles in conflict. Although the panelists all agreed that the humanitarian principle is the controlling imperative, their other assertions and their respective organizations' actions when assessing risk in insecure environments often contradicted the humanitarian principle.

One can draw this conclusion by comparing two apparently contradictory statements made by one panelist. First Geoff Loane asserted, "The ICRC mandate is to be present and provide services to meet humanitarian needs generated by armed conflict." Then he stated, "Security guarantees from arms carriers are a precondition to effective humanitarian action." This security precondition for HA operations was echoed by Nancy Lindborg when she said, "There are going to be times and instances and environments in which NGOs are not able to operate because the insecurity is so great...." These statements, while factual, were made in the context of a dialogue involving the need to maintain independence from military security forces and preserve perceptions of neutrality among the belligerents. These assertions seem to lack internal consistency with a humanitarian imperative worldview. They appear to prioritize independence from security forces and neutrality vis-à-vis all belligerents, even while maintaining that independence and neutrality will undermine the security precondition necessary to providing HA.

The panelists did not address the examples proffered by two members of the audience regarding the apparent contradictions between the imperative of the humanitarian principle and observed action. Three sets of behaviors demonstrated by HA organizations appear to contradict the dominance of the humanitarian principle: access to reciprocal capacity, retreat from the field, and reluctance to cooperate directly with the security mission.

Nancy Lindborg attempted to frame the apparent contradiction as a matter of semantics when she indicated that the term "neutrality," used by the questioner to juxtapose the neutrality principle with the humanitarian principle, addresses the HA organizations' willingness to care for victims' humanitarian needs, regardless of their political affiliation or belligerent status. The confusion surrounding the proper context in which to consider the principle of neutrality seemed to be shared by members of the panel as well as the audience. This semantic clarification may well ameliorate the definitional confusion. But it did not adequately address the real issue: when the principle of independence conflicts with the humanitarian principle, which takes precedence (e.g., when only one side is willing to provide needed security)?

Reciprocal use of capacity

When questioned about the reciprocal use of capacity (the military using NGO/ICRC capacity), particularly in those situations where the military or UN security force footprint is small relative to the humanitarian organization footprint, the panelists agreed that the humanitarian imperative trumps other considerations. In other words, to meet the humanitarian need and prevent the further suffering of victims, the panelists believed that their HA organizations would provide security forces with the necessary capability to intervene on the victims' behalf. However, reciprocal use was not the experience of the questioner (an Australian brigadier). He related a story where he perceived that the denial of reciprocal use resulted indirectly in a significant loss of life at a refugee camp.

Leave the field

Another member of the audience cited an example where the IRC and other HA organizations left the field rather than compromise their principle of independence. The panelists did not contest the validity of the observation or declared motivation. Rather, a dialogue ensued regarding how the decision to cooperate or withdraw is complicated by the presence of third-party belligerents and security forces (nonstate, ideological terrorists; "impartial" U.S. or international security forces). The contradiction between the dominance of the humanitarian principle and the observed action was not directly addressed.

Cooperate with military or host government

Perhaps the most difficult question centered on the reluctance of HA organizations to frustrate insurgent terrorist activities by cooperating with security forces and the host nation government, despite the perception there would be an aggregate long-term humanitarian benefit. The questioner expressed a growing perception that HA and development activities contribute to establishing a secure environment. Panelists conceded that operations like Afghanistan and Iraq would entail increased military involvement in HA and development operations to establish a secure environment. Even so, the panel was reluctant to accept the notion that direct cooperation with a security force to achieve a stable and secure environment was in their interest. Problematically, when an insurgent or terrorist belligerent targets an NGO or international HA organization to undermine and discredit the government's effectiveness, the NGO must either accept its perceived partisan position or abandon the humanitarian imperative.

Through the skilled facilitation of the moderator, candid presentations of the panelists, and engaged participation of the audience, this panel dealt with some of the most demanding questions associated with NGO and HA organizations in the new security environment. Whether Iraq and Afghanistan are anomalies or an example of the future environment, we must continue this dialogue and confront the contradictions of our most fundamental cultural values and historical bias to maintain relevance.

Transcript

ANNOUNCER: Ladies and gentlemen, please welcome our moderator for our second panel discussion, president and chief executive officer of the Center for Humanitarian Cooperation, Mr. Roy Williams.

ROY WILLIAMS: Good afternoon, and thank you very much for your interest in this very important and obviously very evolving subject. I'd like to make a few observations before introducing the panel and letting them give you their perspectives on these issues. I think we can safely all recall a time when humanitarian work was seen against the backdrop of the dedicated people who were performing it—their energy and their willingness. The interesting part about that is that this perception was common to virtually everyone, including the beneficiaries. We're now looking at a very different world. It is a world in which, increasingly, no good deed goes unquestioned, and actions with humanitarian intent are almost certain to become the basis for a political reaction. This may well be the time of what has been referred to as a "terrible honesty," and I put that in quotes. It is an honesty stripped of emotion or assumption. For example, we heard humanitarian work referred to as a national security imperative. Yes, but how does that conclusion translate in the eyes of someone not part of our society? Does that make humanitarians a clear part of someone else's political process, leading us to the question of security? Unfortunately, we must conclude that humanitarian workers increasingly do their work within the framework of incredibly polarized groups and societies.

Roy Williams

And our work is no longer the exclusive province of the caring. The humanitarian world has become folded into the currency of political dialogue. It may be, therefore, as seen from the eyes of those looking at us, part of an unwanted outside political presence. In addition, there are new actors involved in the provision of assistance. The role of the military in the private sector and its influence in the overall perception of the humanitarian arena must be acknowledged. Where does this leave the humanitarian actors and their concerns about humanitarian space and issues of neutrality? In sum, I think we would all agree that humanitarian work is sorely needed, and our panelists will address the impact of these recent changes from the point of view of their own experiences and the experiences of their organizations.

Just a word about format… I will introduce the panelists, tell you something about them, as they speak. I would ask that you hold your questions until the very end of the presentations, and I should also let you know that the panelists may question each other. There may be points on which they don't agree. Our first panelist is Nancy Lindborg, who is the president of Mercy Corps. Nancy joined the Washington, D.C.-based international relief and development organization in 1996. She leads Mercy Corps's strategic planning, policy, and program development and emergency response in areas such as Iraq, Afghanistan, the Balkans, North Korea, and Central Asia. I first met Nancy in 1998, and my first impression was, wow, is she stubborn! I never told you that.

NANCY LINDBORG: I never heard that before.

WILLIAMS: From 2000 to 2005, Nancy served on the Sphere Management Committee. Sphere is a very important word in the humanitarian community, because it was our first serious effort to set standards for operations in the field, because, I think, we all felt that what we'd seen and done in Rwanda was rather, well, to put it pointedly, a dismal failure. Nancy.

LINDBORG: Thank you, Roy. I certainly didn't realize I had a reputation for being stubborn, but…

WILLIAMS: Oh, my personal perception.

LINDBORG: Anyway, it's great to be here, and thank you all for coming to this panel. We did have a very lively conversation over lunch, and so I think we may have further questions for each other as well. The title of the panel that we're here for is Operating in the New Security Environment. I would like to spend my remarks looking a little bit at the questions and maybe reframing the debate a little bit, because I think there is a question that a lot of us have, and—for those of you who saw the video—a lot of the issues that we have

Nancy E. Lindborg

struggled with now for a number of years were highlighted. But I think there is a legitimate question of how new is this security environment. How much does it really permeate the globe, or how much of it is an anomaly in a few places like Afghanistan and Iraq? And just as a quick illustration, my organization, Mercy Corps, is in about thirty countries around the world. We're twenty-five years old, and in our twenty-five-year history, we've had six of our workers killed. Five of them were in Afghanistan and in Eritrea, in a border incident, and I mean killed from being targeted, as opposed to the by-far-most-prevalent source of deaths among humanitarian workers, which is road accidents.

So I think that is an important question, because we deal in many, many insecure environments around the world, places like Liberia, the Sudan, Haiti, DRC [Democratic Republic of the Congo], Eritrea, Ethiopia—the list goes on. And all of our organizations represented here are in all of those places. But I don't know that it's fundamentally different in security than we've been dealing with through the years. As a result, all of our organizations have put substantial investment into better understanding how to operate in insecure environments—everything from training our people; having more dedicated security staff; also investing heavily in what we call the community acceptance strategy of helping the communities to really understand what we are there to do, what our mission is, and that we look to them to help give us the kind of information we need to ensure that we can appropriately navigate some of these confusing environments.

The reason that Iraq and Afghanistan, I think, have become additional lightning rods for part of this discussion and cause us to wonder whether we're in a new security environment or not, is how much they embody what has become an important point of discussion, which is the difference between emergency relief and development. And I think that ambiguity over the endeavor in which we're involved is a very important pivot point for this discussion, because many of our organizations do emergency life-saving relief, but many of us—not all of us, and there's a whole spectrum of mandates, even represented here in the panel—but many of us realize at some point in our organizational evolution that you can do band-aid after band-aid, and that's important and that saves lives, but at some point you want to start addressing more of the root causes and move very quickly into activities that become more developmental in nature. In my organizational approach, for example, by day 10 at the tsunami response, we were already doing more developmental activities. There're words that have evolved over the last ten years to describe that developmental relief, for example, and there's been a lot of energy to try to do that because it more quickly promotes the recovery. However, it becomes more difficult in environments where you've got a mixture of actors and you've got an ongoing insecurity that makes it extraordinarily difficult to determine who is really working on what part of the problem. In Afghanistan and Iraq, for example, I would argue that we're working in a complex development environment that has very different challenges than many of the other places in which we work. And the fundamental problem, which is the new security environment, is that we don't have any stability with which to work.

I participated in a panel that was convened by the AUSA [Association of the United States Army] and CSIS [Center for Strategic and International Studies] some years back that looked at what is this paradigm of state building that many of us are engaged in. The one thing that everybody around the table agreed on—and it was former government, military, NGO, academic, UN actors—is that the very first thing you needed for development was stability. Without stability, you couldn't really move forward on the enterprise of development. Those of you who heard Mr. de Soto, over lunch, he described, I think, very articulately some of the critical factors that go into that longer-term development. And you can't get that kind of investment into some things when there isn't any rule of law, and there has been, I think, a continual underinvestment in those capacities, both in this country and internationally, to move forward the ability to quickly begin establishing those institutions that bring forward more stability.

Therefore, when we get into discussions about humanitarianism and we do so in the context of Iraq and Afghanistan, it becomes quickly a very confusing conversation. And I think that different actors use many of these terms differently: humanitarianism being one, neutrality being another, and you heard this on the video. And what is the good thing, in terms of moving a country forward on the pathway to stability that is moving quickly into development, is a confusing thing if you're talking about humanitarianism in a very strict sense and division of roles. Neutrality should never be a prerequisite if you're trying to move toward stability. I think most of us who're engaged in more development approaches do not claim neutrality, and neutrality, in fact, is not a part of the code of conduct that many NGOs have been signatory to. There're NGOs that are neutral—and you'll probably hear from our colleagues from the ICRC [International Committee of the Red Cross] about who maintains strict neutrality—but I think it becomes confusing. So you have complex development environments, where you necessarily are trying to move forward from the strict humanitarian to a development agenda. And so the question really becomes, in my mind, not how do we operate in an insecure environment, but how do we, as a collection of global actors interested in bringing these countries forward to stability, how do we get that job done in these utterly collapsed states, where you do have the interests of the world enough to send military actors, which is not the case in many of the countries in which we work? And how do you construct the architecture to accomplish that in a way that respects and encourages and enables the value that each of those actors bring? The debate that has raged within some of these venues is the relationship between the military and the NGOs, and I think that's the wrong question. I really think the question is, what's the architecture for enabling both to do what they have to do in environments that may be anomalous or not, but that respects what the NGOs contribute and what only the military can do, which is securing peace?

I was at a conference yesterday where Senator [Chuck] Hagel was speaking to a number of Chinese NGOs about the development of Chinese NGOs in civil society. And it's really that critical piece of the sector that Mr. de Soto was talking about, without naming it: that group that's the constituency for reform and for stability, it's all of those individuals who are neither government nor business who have the power, when they come together, to advocate and to support change. What NGOs do is link up at that community level—and they can do so in the early stages of an emergency, and they can do so as you move forward the development piece, and they can relate to communities in a way that connects up to the larger endeavor. But they cannot do so, I think, in the value that we bring, if they're so tightly bound up into a governmental structure that they're seen as one and the same. The value that the NGOs bring is the independence that we represent, the civil society that we represent in each of the countries, which is really a hallmark of Western democracies, of global democracies, of countries that enable a lot of the structures to flourish, that contribute to stability. And there are going to be, I think, times and instances and environments in which NGOs are not able to operate because the insecurity is so great that the only way that anybody can be present is behind armed guards, wearing flak jackets, and behind barbed wire. I would submit that once you're in that position, you cannot, as an NGO, bring the very certain value that we need. However, I would then say—this is really a critical piece to the discussion—that it's very important for us to understand what you accomplish with different actors, and a lot of what the military is able to do best, I think, is difficult to reconcile with some of the longer-term objectives and the longer-term development needs that need to have that community piece.

There're lots of good discussions on this and many excellent recommendations, and the dialogue is quite robust with a long history of how all of those pieces can fit together. We're additionally challenged in the context of Iraq and Afghanistan, but I'm not sure that it's going to be the new global model. There're so many other countries in which we are working well together, despite the onset of disasters like the tsunami and now [Hurricane] Katrina, where I think you do find an excellent and complimentary working relationship between all of the different actors who have to come to play. I know there will be lots of good questions and further discussions, and I thank you.

WILLIAMS: Thank you, Nancy. I think implicit in some of the observations are what we have referred to as forgotten emergencies, where there is no political investment on the part of any of the major powers, and the economic support that is necessary for NGOs to actually go in and do something is typically lacking because of that. One thing I might have said earlier, and that you may have already observed, is that our panel is composed of the many sides of the humanitarian enterprise. We have the NGOs, we have the UN organizations, and we have the International Committee of the Red Cross, which, of course, is the guardian of the Geneva Conventions.

Our next speaker will be from the ICRC, Geoff Loane. He heads the regional delegation for the United States and Canada to the ICRC here in Washington. He previously headed the ICRC delegation to Serbia and Montenegro in Belgrade, Serbia, and Nairobi in East Africa. Mr. Loane served as regional relief coordinator in Nairobi, where he initiated and led ICRC relief operations in Sudan from 1989 to 1991 and Somalia during that historic period from 1991 to 1993. The Somalian relief effort involved more than 3,000 staff distributing 20,000 tons of food monthly to a million people. I would have to say that—again, throwing in a personal observation—my impression of ICRC staff in the field and many places around the world has always been extremely credible. It's an institution that takes its work extremely seriously and has the good insight and intelligence, I think, to train its staff well. Geoff.

GEOFF LOANE: Thank you, Roy, and thank you very much for the opportunity to be here this afternoon and to share some very general perspectives, I think, on this very topical and important subject. I would like to address this challenging question for all of us and by all of us who are working in the field of international relations—whether that be humanitarian assistance, development, diplomacy, commercial, or indeed armed intervention—from three different perspectives. First of all, I would like to share a few remarks on the view of the ICRC and some of the assumptions that we make about working in these contexts; Second, to provide you with some degree of historical perspective, which I think is important to place the current debate; and third, with what undoubtedly are the challenges in the future.

It goes, of course, without saying that security guarantees from arms carriers are a precondition to effective humanitarian action. This is the starting point for those of us who work in operations; and without those security guarantees, as we know, not only is it a restriction on our work, but the humanitarian consequences of the conflict simply rise sometimes unacceptably. The ICRC is arguably well placed to opine on this major challenge. We're an organization that has developed a huge experience in dealing with situations of both armed conflict and violence and have undoubtedly built up a vast reservoir of experience in working in insecure environments. At the same time, the ICRC has long pioneered the values of independence, neutrality, and impartiality. These values underpin the ICRC view that security guarantees are the responsibility and obligation of the belligerents to a conflict—whether those belligerents are governments or not governments, whether they're state actors or nonstate actors. Without those guarantees, we simply cannot work, and this is the basis for our work.

Geoff Loane

As an operation preamble, I would like to clarify two working assumptions of the ICRC, both of which, I feel, are particularly relevant. The first is that when it comes to work in situations of violence or armed conflict, as an organization the ICRC is obliged, in relation to its mandate, to be present, is obliged to offer its services. We don't have the choice or the option not to be present because of our legal obligations. This, of course, is not new, but I think what is—and this is one of the questions I will throw out—is the current relationship between armed conflict, insecurity, or an insecure environment and humanitarian assistance. This is not a well-developed or well-understood field, as much as we all work and live in it. And the second assumption that I would like to mention is that the ICRC considers that its operational role is primarily to *assess* the humanitarian needs generated by situations of armed conflict. Of course, that's not new in itself, but I think what is important in saying that is that the responsibility for *addressing* those needs does not lie with the ICRC, does not lie with the humanitarian community. The first responsibility lies with the authorities in place—the state or those who control the territory where the needs are—and I think it's important to remind all of us that that is a legal responsibility, that it is not the humanitarian community or those who practice humanitarianism who have that responsibility.

The assumption of the state's or the belligerents' responsibility is equally challenged by the new security environment, where some of the belligerents now, as indeed in many wars, choose to ignore those needs. I would hypothesize that the humanitarian community at large needs to examine both of those assumptions in relation to the current environment, and to address more effectively the strategies that can be employed to responsibilize or to persuade authorities, again with a state or nonstate, to assume greater responsibility for the consequences of armed conflict. It is through the responsibilization of the authorities that humanitarian needs are met, and I think all of us will certainly share the view that the greatest interventions are those provided by local people and their communities, who, in fact, are an extension of the state itself.

The second area I would like to touch upon is the changes to the humanitarian environment in the post–Cold War and specifically post-9/11 environment. In the space of not more than about fifteen years, because of significant and important shifts in international relations and in the way in which we do business, the humanitarian community is facing different challenges. Let's just look at a couple of those. During the Cold War, humanitarianism operated on some different premises. The practice of conflict by proxy carried as a partial consequence the nonaccess and, to some degree, the nonrecognition of humanitarian initiatives. As challenging as it is today, as recently as the 1980s, many humanitarian operations took place in a context where the origin of those operations—in other words, armed conflict—was denied by the belligerents. I'm certainly thinking of Eastern Africa, Southern Africa, in those days when political conflict did not exist, only famines. It goes without saying that vast strides have been taken in humanitarian interventions since those rather dark days when we were not able to confront states and nonstates in the same way. More recently, of course, the growth of transnational terrorism against both current and previous global powers has altered the form whereby political disagreements are converted into armed violence. Both the form and the content of violence contain new features, including—as there are many, I'll just mention one—including the idea that nonstate actors or terrorists do not aspire to or control physical space. The implication there is that their leadership is largely inaccessible and does not respect the international humanitarian and legal frameworks that have carefully been put into place over many years.

I would also like to take the opportunity to refer to the comments of Mr. de Soto, who argued recently at our lunch that 80 percent of the world is operating outside the legal frameworks, and I think this is the huge challenge for us.

What has changed for us in this new environment? How do we deal with this new environment? First of all, humanitarians are facilitated in and can negotiate much greater access to situations of active conflict. These are also the areas where humanitarian needs are greatest and where the greatest impact in terms of our intervention can be had. These are also the areas of greatest danger and insecurity. This is arguably the greatest development in the last fifty years and has guaranteed in virtually all contexts that humanitarian interventions can reach the needy. This year we had the twentieth anniversary of Band Aid. I think the classic African famine—in as much as there continues to be needs generated by conflict—I hope that the number of famine victims as a result of conflict has certainly decreased enormously. I think this is a major development.

Secondly, and in part as an extension of this, humanitarian organizations have, whether they like it or not, become very active stakeholders. Any actor who is present or in or near a situation of conflict is one who potentially has a stake in that conflict, as perceived by the belligerents and as perceived by their political masters, and I think this is largely a truism in most, if not all, conflicts. The price paid by civilians—including women and children, journalists and aid workers, and others—is an absolute testimony to the fact that they are considered to be stakeholders and to have a political interest. This has given rise to two of the greatest threats, in my view. Firstly, that of instrumentalization of humanitarian work by actors or other stakeholders for political purposes, and secondly, rejection of humanitarian work on ideological or other grounds. Instrumentalization, of course, is nothing more than the perception by one or other parties to the conflict that a humanitarian organization is being manipulated by the other for its political advantage. Thus, for example, in some countries the ICRC visits to detainees are invoked as meaning that if ICRC visits detainees in country X or Y, that the detainees or the prisons are in good condition. Rejection is the new security environment: those who we don't know, those who don't know us, and those who would quite happily do without us—and we have seen this in certain places and will continue to see this. Maybe at this point, a health warning can be a value. Most humanitarian operations—and indeed Nancy referred to this, too—do continue to unfold in contexts where there's generally very wide respect for humanitarian interventions by both civil society and the political and military leaders. It remains an isolated few contexts where challenges have become so extreme so as to limit direct access for humanitarians. We are able to continue our work and, I think, share and enjoy the support of civil society, which is extremely important.

A third feature of today's environment concerns the humanitarian industry itself. It has grown enormously. It has diversified enormously and, more than ever, it involves the use of military resources in some situations. While it is simply inappropriate to consider that military resources should not be used for humanitarian contexts, we need to be mindful of the implications if those same military units are belligerents in the same context. On a wider scale, not only do we have a multitude of humanitarian organizations, but they are largely, we hope, better organized, better prepared, better resourced, and more professional today. They equally operate on sometimes very different value systems. Whilst there is no doubt in the axiom that there is strength in diversity, it does raise the challenge for other stakeholders to understand what is the industry line, what are the humanitarians saying, and how many humanitarian voices are there? And this certainly is an area of enormous challenge. At best, it can be confusing, and at worst, it may, in some situations, generate suspicion amongst those engaged in violence. This is not a plea for humanitarian consensus, rather a presentation of what can generate challenges in today's conflicts.

Fourthly and finally, we all live in an environment of much greater accountability than we did twenty years ago or, indeed, even fifteen years ago. This is welcomed, but it comes with a price tag. Whilst accountability demands that the decision-making process is transparent and is clear, it also facilitates the lesson learning, which is so important in responding to new emergencies. That being said, it limits the freedom of movement of field actors who live and work in very dangerous environments. Most of us, if not all of us, have been in those environments and know the value of flexibility and being able to take decisions on the ground. Put very simply and put very crudely, the ICRC probably would not be in a position today to replicate some of the operations where I had the pleasure to work with some of my colleagues on the panel, such as Somalia, precisely because of those higher needs of accountability.

The last area I would like to point to are future trends in relations. Where do we go to from here? But first, in overall terms it needs to be repeated and recalled, that the inevitability of humanitarian crises is guaranteed, even if there is better access, and the extremes of that crisis can be dealt with. The year 2005 has certainly seen the domination of natural disasters, as in the tsunami and in Hurricane Katrina, and the global response will nonetheless remain to address the problem of insecurity. Second is the overwhelming power and authority of the military, and particularly the U.S. military, in some of today's humanitarian contexts. The military not only has huge resources, but is ready to mobilize them for humanitarian purposes. It is important for the humanitarian community to be closely engaged in this development, as indeed it is at the moment. Future emergencies will see greater humanitarian and military cooperation, and both groups have a great deal to learn from each other. I think the sheer size of the military and military response is something so important in humanitarian emergencies that it's important to have this dialogue. Of specific concern, and as mentioned earlier, are the threats of instrumentalization and rejection. It is not in the interests of the many stakeholders to reinforce these threats, as doing so will ultimately and negatively impact the essential provision of protection to mainly civilian victims.

And it's important to steer through the importance of what we call neutrality. Here I would argue that as humanitarians, as humanitarian organizations, we are not neutral. We have clear responsibilities toward the victims of conflict under very precise procedures and under very precise legal frameworks. They do not involve taking a legally neutral stand; they concern us providing assistance and providing protection. Where we are and where we must remain neutral, however, is in relation to the processes we use to negotiate humanitarian access on behalf of victims. It is not for humanitarians to classify, recognize, or provide legitimacy to the use or the abuse of political power. But faced with the need to ensure effective humanitarian intervention, negotiations with the parties to a conflict—with those fighting, with those involved in violence—must be based on the power, threats, or risks that the belligerents represent in addition to their internationally recognized status. It goes without saying, again, that a major challenge is the acceptance of humanitarian interventions as being exclusively in the interests of humanitarian need and not political goals, and therein maybe does lie one of the major dilemmas for us. The ICRC needs to talk to those who're carrying out acts of violence, and we need to not only try to persuade and responsibilize them for what they're legally obliged to do, but also to ensure that the security guarantees can be delivered. I think there is a major dilemma for that.

Finally, we need to foster an environment where, through dialogue, through humanitarian action, a greater recognition of the rights of civilian and military victims is understood and where the obligations of the belligerents are better respected. Humanitarianism has developed enormously in the last decades and needs to maintain its momentum as a collective exercise in order to rise to the current challenges. Thank you.

WILLIAMS: Thank you, Geoff. Our next speaker is Robert MacPherson. He is the director of the Security Unit of CARE. That title really evokes some unpleasant feelings in my mind, because I well remember when in the world of the NGOs, you did not have any such thing as a Security Unit because it was

Robert MacPherson

assumed that your mere presence in an environment was virtually a guarantee of security for the people around you. No one wanted witnesses, in other words. Obviously that world has changed dramatically. Bob joined CARE in 1994 to organize and implement emergency response activities in humanitarian crisis situations. In addition, he coordinated all CARE land mine action programs worldwide. Since 1994, he has helped CARE respond to emergencies in Albania, Bosnia, the Democratic Republic of the Congo, Kosovo, Rwanda, Somalia, Sudan, East Timor, Afghanistan, and Iraq. As part of the United Nations' Operation Restore Hope in Somalia beginning in late 1992, MacPherson served as deputy director for Civil and Military Operations, prioritizing and coordinating multinational relief efforts. MacPherson is a retired U.S. Marine Corps colonel with twenty-five years of service, including Vietnam, Operation DESERT STORM, and Somalia. After completing active service with the Marines, he founded Enable, a humanitarian relief organization dedicated to assisting the survivors of land mines and war. Enable is a co-recipient of the Nobel Peace Prize. Bob.

ROBERT MacPHERSON: Thank you. I'm really thankful that the word "deputy director" for the Somalia episode was in there, because Kevin was the director at that time and I wanted to make darn sure that that was kept correct. I appreciate that introduction, and the advantage of going third here is I can completely redesign everything, based on my predecessors. I liked one thing that Nancy started with, and I'll go back to that bio. When I came to CARE from 1994 to the year 2000, I did mine action and emergency response. Security was something, as Roy said, that we had to deal with, but at a just finite level. I can remember one of the first job descriptions that I had, security was in there for 10 percent. I'm moving back to Atlanta from Washington, D.C., on Friday with a security staff in CARE now of six people. CARE is an organization with thirteen thousand people in seventy-two locations, and I can follow through on what Nancy said in a different context. Since the beginning of CARE, we probably had just shy of two hundred people killed in service with CARE, but until about 2000, the majority of those people died as a result of accidents or natural disasters. That certainly has changed, at least in our organization, in the last five years. And I want to speak to that.

One of the dilemmas about coming here today, and maybe a gratifying element, is the fact that I see a lot of uniforms out there. You know, I feel much like a company commander engaged in a firefight, and somebody is asking me to help design the campaign at the army or the division level. The things that we're dealing with today in this organization, at least my own, are so much at the tactical and operational level, you can hardly get your head up to think about some of the broader issues here. We had a kidnapping in Afghanistan in May. During that kidnapping, I had a conversation with somebody and it was in a good sense, to remind ourselves that security is not the core business of CARE or humanitarian organizations. But we have reached a point where it is a critical element for everything we do. And that is a quantum leap over the past decade, and it is quite a steep learning curve at times for humanitarian organizations. The deaths that we incur now are no longer random—wrong time, wrong place; they're directed and, in many cases, there is a method or thought process behind it.

I'll give you a couple of examples of what humanitarians are up against. Imagine a country that's in chaos—it's just followed a war—and that a humanitarian organization is involved with things, as normal to a humanitarian as anything: water and sanitation, the organization is prominent in laying pipes in streets, helping with sanitation plants; on the health side, redoing hospitals. What do you do if you want to disrupt that reconstruction? What is one of the easiest things to attack? Attack that organization, have it shut down; force it to pull out and it disrupts the entire reconstruction process. It's a soft target; it makes sense if you are in that business of terrorism or trying to disrupt the government.

As I heard my two predecessors and especially my colleague from the ICRC say, we talk about what I call core issues, and one of the bullets here is, is it realistic to expect protection based on neutrality? And I really appreciated Geoff's remarks because I have found over the years—in fact, if you go to *Webster's Dictionary* and look up the term "neutrality," it's going to tell you it's impartiality. If you look up "impartiality," it's going to tell you it's neutrality. I've never gotten my arms around those two words, but I think, in the strongest sense, what the NGO community has to work toward is independence, and that is where we bump into a lot of issues that bring us together today. It is very easy for a terrorist organization or any organization that wants to undermine an NGO's credibility in a society to say, and we'll be candid here, well, that organization is taking money from the U.S. government and the U.S. government is a belligerent and is our enemy. Consequently, the NGO is our enemy. And how do we get around that? What do we do as a community and as individual members in that community to try and use the resources that are required to follow the humanitarian mandate and still project ourselves in a fashion that says, "Look, we do not take sides, let's just get right to it. We're an independent organization trying to assist people across the entire spectrum." It's an enormous challenge.

We in the humanitarian community generally don't use the word "protection"; within the UN we call it "acceptance." It's a model of security built on the fact that if the community accepts your presence by the benefits, by the fact of whatever value, candidly, that you bring into the community, that generally is the mantle of protection for humanitarians. The dilemma now has become that the exact reverse happens. It makes you notable. It brings you to the attention of people who would like to disrupt the process. In addition, what is the first thing that happens when CARE has an international staff member kidnapped in Afghanistan? It is not as notable on CNN, but it is notable on the BBC and in Italy and other places. Consequently, if you're an organization that wants to gain international attention, go for the soft target, go for the NGO, and you'll get all the publicity you need around the world. I'm not saying that that's right or wrong, just saying that's another element in the formula that we're trying to work our way through.

What is the context that, at least for CARE, allows us to operate or to continue to operate or forces us to withdraw and shut down? And withdraw and shut down is something that is anathema to the organizations, virtually all of them sitting here. It's not something that comes easily at all. In our case, and I would say for all of us, we look at presence. We're fortunate to be in seventy-two locations, as I said earlier. Consequently, many times when there is an emergency, CARE already has a presence in that country, which gives us a baseline, an infrastructure to build on, much like the UN in many cases and other NGOs. We take a critical look at who else is there. Is the UN there? Is the ICRC there? Is Mercy Corps there? What is the context of the situation? Capacity—this is a dilemma beyond description at times. Many of you in a uniform, and in fact I wore one, expected certain standards of capacity and realized just how fortunate we are in other places. Things like basic communications—the ability for your people in the field to communicate with one another or to communicate outside of the environment takes a tremendous amount of effort, simply because if we're involved with the military, in many cases they're using most of the frequencies and most of the nets. It becomes competition to try and at least build our own infrastructure, which is a guarantee for our safety, to communicate with each other and across the entire spectrum.

I can't believe I'm almost out of time here. Also, Nancy did a nice job of this. She brought up, and I want to get into a little more depth here—I call it the intensity of the emergency requirement. We have a mandate, and that mandate is that in places like Darfur, where there is a high risk, a high threat to the NGO community, you will find the NGOs are willing to take that risk. More and more, we're confronted with the fact of a place, let's just say like Iraq, where it's not a great humanitarian emergency. The NGO community continued to operate and the threat was skyrocketing. So at what level do we say, enough of this? Trying to determine the threshold for how long and what we're going to sustain becomes very, very difficult because there is no formula for it. And underneath it all is this interesting discussion we had at lunch today, amongst the six of us, that no matter how you cut it, people who are engaged in this work are engaged with one of the critical elements in an emotional response. Many times it is not technical; it's a fact that this is not a business. You might say it is, but let me tell you, when you meet the people in the field conducting humanitarian assistance, it is an emotional response. And as such, it becomes quite difficult to build these thresholds.

The last thing is the relationship between the NGO community and the military. I'm reminded of a statement, and I'll paraphrase it, which I heard someone say from New Orleans a couple of weeks ago, and that is, "For goodness sake, stop talking and do something." I have been at this since I left the Marines, and civil-military dialogue and interaction has become almost a business. Let me just tell you one person's observations. On the ground *in extremis*, the relations between the military and the humanitarian community and the ICRC always work out. They always work out. It is after the fact that, at many times, there is a lot of angst involved in it and people trying to determine what level of engagement, how to maintain independence, and the rest of it. But what this requires is absolute pragmatism. Kevin and I sat at one time, as Marine officers, with CH-53 helicopters that had the capacity to carry a measles vaccine through a desperate site for 5,000 people within 45 minutes. The NGO community, unfortunately, would have had to take several days. You can solve those things just like that, and I have gotten to the point where we continue to talk and talk about civil-military relations. They generally work. It becomes an absolute requirement for both sides to understand each other, and I think that has happened in ten years—much, much more so—but for people to be absolutely pragmatic in how we associate with each other and to set a lot of the emotions aside on all sides, and just get on with it.

WILLIAMS: Thank you, Bob. Our final speaker will be Kevin Kennedy from the UN Office for the Coordination of Humanitarian Affairs. Kevin is the director of the Coordination and Response Division in New York. Previous assignments include duty in Geneva with the Complex Emergency Support Unit and in New York as chief, African Division, and chief of the Office of the Undersecretary-General for Humanitarian Affairs. Kevin has also held UN field assignments in Somalia, Haiti, the Balkans, and East Timor, as well as numerous missions to Africa and Asia. I can never get him on the phones so that's just. . . . In 2003, Kevin was the deputy humanitarian coordinator for Iraq and then the officer-in-charge of the UN Assistance Mission for Iraq. He most recently served as the acting resident/humanitarian coordinator for the Sudan. You know that he was in the Marines, so I won't give you that information again. Kevin.

KEVIN KENNEDY: Thank you, Roy. Thank you very much. Thank you for inviting me this afternoon to speak with you all. I actually pretty much agree with my fellow colleagues on the panel, Roy, I think in the main, but with one or two exceptions I'd like to bring up during the course of the presentation. I may be speaking just from the UN perspective, though we share with the NGOs, with the ICRC, many of the same interests and concerns and approaches.

For us, it's not really so much a post-9/11 world as it's a post-19 August 2003 world, and this, as many of you would know, was when the UN headquarters in Baghdad was bombed. We lost 22 killed and 250 wounded. Now the UN has been operating, like the ICRC, like NGOs, in difficult locations

Kevin M. Kennedy

for many a year. I have lost many people. I have a very small office at the UN, OCHA, and we've had 12 killed and 20 wounded in the last twelve years of our existence, which is quite a few out of a staff of maybe 200 people, quite a few. But really 19 August 2003 created a seismic effect within the UN that I think, frankly, we're still grappling with. We've made many changes and many changes are underway, and again there's many people in New Orleans in uniform, and we're now doing things that you all might have thought would have come naturally or automatically. Such things as threat analysis, better information collection, dissemination, more staff in the fields. We've had many countries where we've had literally hundreds of UN staff deployed in conflict situations. I had only one or two security officers to staff the entire operation—simply inadequate. We work closely as well with NGOs in the field and with the ICRC, in a special relationship, and try to look after their security needs. So, at the operational level within the UN there are many changes, many reforms underway, all aimed at strengthening our ability to operate, to continue to operate in difficult countries. Like the Red Cross, like the NGOs, we intend to remain in these places. And I'm glad to see that the philosophical approach taken by the United Nations for security is that of creating an enabling security regime, that is, our program requirements, mission objectives that have to be accomplished.

How best can one accomplish these tasks in a difficult situation? We—particularly on the humanitarian side of the UN, certainly my department—we only work in conflict countries and natural disasters. So it's something we put up with all the time. So at the operational level, it's improving. Now, where I have some problems—maybe Nancy touched on this business, too—with this new security environment, which is the topic of this panel, is, how has it changed? I would say that Iraq and Afghanistan, though acute examples, are not anomalies and are more and more what we see. I think of, for instance, Somalia, a very difficult place, little known; last year in Mogadishu five humanitarian workers were killed in what was perceived to be the safest place in Somalia. We've had terrible things happen in Burundi with the ICRC, in Chechnya with the ICRC, and in many other places and increasingly for all kinds of reasons. Is it a lack of ideology of the belligerents? Is it an ideology aimed against you? Is it too many weapons out there, which I think is a big contributing factor? But people continue to be targets, and pretty much in most countries that we work with, and we've had to adjust to this. I think it has impacted negatively the ability of humanitarian organizations to reach out and deliver assistance. It certainly has increased our cost—and probably not enough, because we're still, in many ways, woefully ill prepared and untrained to deal in these environments.

As Bob indicated, there is a steep learning curve, if I could broadly speak, within the humanitarian community because most of the people working at that really don't come from a security background or a security-conscious background, and it's often taken some hard lessons to get there. I credit this to a sense of duty. There is a certain numbness. All these organizations lose people on a regular basis, but people carry on. Where I get concerned is, I don't see, either inside the humanitarian world or outside, in particular among governments, some of the sustained indignation that's required to put an end to things, or to seek justice, or to end the impunity of those people who have killed humanitarian workers. We know, in the UN, several places in the world who the killers of staff—of our staff and staff of other NGOs and the Red Cross—are. But no action was taken, and no continuous pressure is put on these governments to bring these people to justice. That's a problem. I think it was touched on by Bob or by Geoff, the whole issue of accountability, which is a common word, I think, certainly in the UN. With the NGOs we discussed over lunch, accountability has become the watchword in our world. Again, for those of you in the military, you're used to what accountability is. It comes with the job, it comes with the task, but it is becoming a bigger thing in terms of our accountability, particularly for security matters. It's serious business when you have people getting killed and people being put—I don't use the expression "in harm's way;" it's overused—but put in difficult situations. It's serious business if you're the boss and you have to be equipped and prepared to deal with this, when you make those kinds of decisions. We, like others, don't want to leave these countries in which crises stand, as long as possible and hard as we can. I was the officer in charge in Iraq. I left Iraq just before the bombing. I went back the day of the bombing. I volunteered to return and eventually become the officer in charge of all the UN operations in Iraq— quite an interesting assignment! And eventually, at the end of October 2003, we finally decided to pull out our remaining staff because conditions had just become so untenable; you just could not work. In that it was not a humanitarian emergency, it gave you less reason to stay, though I will note that we have since returned in rather large numbers, under very constrained conditions.

I know that time is running short; let me just touch on this civil-military thing. I very much agree with my colleague Bob. In the civil-military industry, people try to turn what is an art into a science. In my experience—I've been working with the ICRC, it's a perfect example, but also NGOs—a good operator, a person with decent interpersonal skills and who also has done a good job, whether he or she be civilian or military, can work just fine with others in a workshop or in the field. I find the differences more back in the United States or in Brussels or in Geneva, where it's on a more theological, philosophical level. I will say, however—and Nancy made this point, and I very much agree with it—in terms of who does what. What jobs are we supposed to do? The military's biggest contribution to humanitarian assistance is security; that is your primary thing. I think of Sierra Leone as a perfect example, a very insecure country, a place where I've worked in the past in very bad conditions. When the peacekeepers arrived, and particularly when the British forces arrived, that changed the whole equation. Suddenly NGOs, UN agencies could move about the country, deliver assistance. And that environment would not have been created without the presence of military. When it comes to delivering assistance, designing programs, water or sanitation, health, and education, frankly, the NGOs, the Red Cross, and the agencies tend to be better at it and tend to be on the scene for years to come, not just in and out on the two- or three-month mission; and I would recommend that they take the lead.

I would close with this: the guidance in terms of using military assets has really three components—as a last resort, as timely, and as unique capabilities. I, like others on the panel, was deeply involved in the tsunami. We could not have responded to the tsunami victims, with those governments, had it not been for the United States and the thirty-five other militaries—I think India was the second largest presence—without them there. They had timely and unique capacities that we did not have. So that's a good example. If you look at Goma in 1994, the help of United States, Japan, many other countries, France, Germany was massive; we needed that. In the Goma exodus of June '94, at one point too many people in a week went across the border, and we called in the military. What people forget is six weeks before, on Easter weekend in April of '94, we had 500,000 people go out of Rwanda into Tanzania, in the opposite direction into Angara, which was probably not seen too much by the world. It was the largest movement of people in a short time in recent history and was handled entirely by NGOs, the ICRC—I think Geoff was there actually—and UN agencies. It was only when our capacities were basically ended that we had to turn, as a last resort, to the military. I think that's probably the best way to do business. Well, I'll stop there. Thank you.

WILLIAMS: Thank you, Kevin. And thanks to the panel as a whole. I think we'll open the floor up to questions. I'd like to make one observation that I think has been implicit in some of the things that the panel has said. The humanitarian imperative is very much the function of individual initiatives, motivation, and desire, but individuals have to work within the framework of organizations. And one of the things that we found very difficult to translate is making that connection between that individual motivation and the way organizations function. Unfortunately, looked at from the outside, it's the organizations that the people with bad intentions, if you will, that's what they see. They don't see the individuals except through the rubric of the organizations. So we're sort of caught between a rock and a hard place. On questions, would you please identify yourself, and if there's a particular person on the panel to whom you would like to direct the question, that would be fine. Sir.

AUDIENCE - ERIC WASHABAUGH: My name's Eric Washabaugh, from the Matthew Ridgway Center. I had a question just for the general panel, maybe directed more toward Mr. Kennedy. A few years back, Kofi Annan was asked if private security companies could be used for peacekeeping and humanitarian operations. And I'm paraphrasing a bit here, he said, "The world's not ready for a private army." My question to you is, given proper regulation oversight—and that's a big if—do you see private military companies or private security companies as a possible viable alternative for security or logistical support on handling peacekeeping humanitarian operations?

KENNEDY: I would say in most cases, no. A private security company does not have the legitimacy or the mandate that's bestowed on a peacekeeping force, whether that be a UN peacekeeping force or a bilateral peacekeeping force that is sanctioned by the Security Council and the member states of the United Nations. I think it'll be hard to foresee a private company being chartered or commissioned by the UN to serve as its military peacekeeping element. I think it'll be a pretty sad turn of events if that's what it can turn to. I don't doubt that private security companies have a role in providing security, that is, point security or that type of thing, and they do and we certainly see it in Afghanistan and Iraq, we certainly do. But I suspect the role has been led to that. I would say, well, there have been similar writings on this and some work done in London a few years ago, particularly the case of Sierra Leone, which is quite interesting. Before the 2000 crisis, in the 1997–1998 crisis, after one bad experience the country had with a private security company, one came in that was actually quite effective. Now how that will work and what their connections were, I don't know. But I have to acknowledge that they were important in restoring stability for at least part of that country. So there may be a role, but I would offer a very small role.

WILLIAMS: Ma'am....

AUDIENCE - THEA HARVEY: Hi, my name is Thea Harvey, from Economists for Peace and Security. I have two questions actually, I think both for Colonel Kennedy. Following up on that, we saw in the Katrina aftermath that there is a conflict between the primary mission of the National Guard, which is to stand by to help the permanent active duty military in emergencies, and its secondary mission, to be available for humanitarian aid. I wondered whether it makes sense … you talked about the unique capacity of the military to be able to assist quickly and organize people in emergency situations. I've wondered if it isn't possible to build that capacity in organizations that don't have a primary mission elsewhere. And my second question is on the issue of sovereignty. We talked this morning about when it is appropriate to interfere in a nation where there's a humanitarian emergency going on. And I wonder, from the panel's point of view, as the people who have to deal with these emergencies on the ground, if you have comments on what's going on at the UN in terms of finally discussing a moderation of these sovereign rights.

KENNEDY: I'll start with the second question. I'm being advised here by my colleague on sovereignty. Obviously we respect the sovereignty of the member states of the United Nations; we have to. At the same time, there are obligations under international law, international humanitarian law, that often require a humanitarian response. And each situation is somewhat different and unique, which is a simple thing to say, but it's true. And I think in most cases, not every case, we're able to release—and I say "we," again, the collective we, the Red Cross, NGOs, the United Nations—are able to put people on the ground and to provide at least the immediate humanitarian assistance. I would say, certainly in some countries, we are greatly hampered by the governments or by rebel militants, as the case might be. You can look at Sudan particularly. Last year I was the coordinator in Sudan during the Darfur crisis, and it was quite difficult in large part, not entirely, but in large part, due to the restrictions imposed on us by the government in Khartoum and the Darfur provinces. You work through these things; you negotiate. Like the ICRC, we also try to specialize in negotiating humanitarian access: it requires lots of discussions at the capital level, in the field level, with various rebel leaders in order to make things work, and we do that. I don't know that you'll see going back—and I'm probably not in the position to speak too well to this—any change in terms of how sovereignty is respected, but certainly in the wake of Rwanda '94, in the wake of other events since then, people are certainly more willing to operate, Darfur is willing to operate under international humanitarian law as the primary entree to these types of situations. I don't know, Bob, if you want to mention about the National Guard or....

MacPHERSON: I thought I followed you where you talked about regular forces and National Guard, and then I thought you said building capacity elsewhere. I didn't pull that together. What was your meaning there?

HARVEY: What I was wondering was, since the National Guard's primary mission is to be available militarily, whether it would make sense to develop other organizations that had the capacity to quickly move personnel and materials and had the type of organizational capacity that the military has, but didn't have other ties.

MacPHERSON: Okay. Speaking for myself on this, I have some very strong views on this. When I have the opportunity around the world to engage with a military force, there are several things I expect of it. And one of the primary things I expect is an organization with good order and discipline and a chain of command that holds people accountable throughout that entire organization. What I bumped into, frankly, during the kidnapping of Margaret Hassan in Baghdad, when I spent about three months out there, is that if you build that capacity someplace else, as in private security companies, you have some private security companies that frankly rival the professionalism of the Armed Forces of the United States. They're not equal, but they're pretty good. You have a number of them that really have trouble. And I, just intuitively, don't feel that that's something—if you want to speak just within United States—that's something we want to give up, if that's what you're implying there. On the other hand, we discussed this earlier today, because the next question is going to be what one of us thinks about the initiative in the past twenty-four hours about turning, if you will, some emergency response in the United States over to the military. It'll be interesting to hear what the military has to say about that. But, I also think that that is something that we have to look very, very closely at. So, I hope I got it all, at least my understanding of what you're asking.

WILLIAMS: Right, Nancy.

LINDBORG: I would just add a slightly additional dimension to the discussion, and that is, in the context of international endeavors, not just in the U.S., I think there is a need, certainly within the United States, to put additional investment into our civilian capacity to engage around the world, without question. What I see personally is, in many environments, where the U.S. military is present around the world, they end up filling voids. And those voids are there because there isn't the civilian capacity to come in quickly enough, once the fighting stops. You've got that critical window to begin setting up the very early stages of institutions and all of the ways in which you begin to consolidate security and build on it. There just isn't anyone there, and so the military ends up doing it, and you end up tying up a lot of that capacity on those issues. So, I think a huge and important and vital thing that we need to do as a country is invest more in that civilian capacity.

WILLIAMS: Geoff?

LOANE: Yes. I'll go back, if I'm not confusing this debate, to sovereignty and give you the ICRC take on this is. Sovereignty is a political matter. This is outside the realm of the confidence of humanitarians to deal with. We don't, we can't deal with the issue of sovereignty per se; what we can deal with as humanitarian organizations, or at least as the ICRC, are two things. Number one, what does the law say? International humanitarian law is extremely explicit on the responsibilities of states, of the occupying authorities, on how to deal with and relations to operations when it comes to having access, as a point of principle. And it's more difficult today to apply it universally, for obvious reasons that you will fully understand. But as a point of principle, to operate in any part of any country requires the agreement of all the belligerents for security reasons. We operate in Darfur—Kevin's going to Sudan tonight. Not only do we negotiate with the Janjaweed, but we also provide some assistance to the Janjaweed victims of a conflict out there. That's not to say that they're the main victims, but it is a conflict and generally everybody is affected. But we need a buy-in of all the stakeholders—whoever those stakeholders are, if they control political power, military power—and we will discuss with them, if for nothing else but reasons of transparency and for reasons of the process of neutrality. But this does not mean that we treat the context in a neutral way.

WILLIAMS: Yes? A question, we have a question here…yes?

AUDIENCE - BRIGADIER GENERAL DAMIAN ROCHE: My name's Brigadier Damian Roche, from the Australian Army. By way of background, I served seven months in Rwanda in 1995. And listening to the comments from the panel in general this afternoon, something's obviously changed. Certainly my experience, based on comments about finding reasonable people making pragmatic decisions, is somewhat different from what I've heard this afternoon, is somewhat different from my experience in Rwanda in '95. Now there's also the comment about when the NGO or the UN runs out of capacity, it's only then they turn to the military. What happens when the military doesn't have the capacity and the NGOs and the UN organizations do, but don't pass it over?

WILLIAMS: Well, let me take a stab at that one because the perception of how you use your capacity turns upon, I think, one thing: not what is happening in the immediate circumstances, but what has happened before. And every operation I've been in since 1975, one of the consistent failures has been that people come up with unexpected demands. But those demands or needs should have been expected, if they'd had conversations prior. And I know that, for example, when I was working in Washington with the Office of Foreign Disaster Assistance, one of the things we tried to do was to solicit exactly that kind of conversation before disaster, so that the unexpected was not the unexpected; it was simply a matter of accommodating to what was known. I trust that speaks directly to your point, because there shouldn't be any surprises to this business, there really shouldn't be. We know what's going to happen; we know what our respective resources are. I was just involved in a humanitarian response review for the United Nations, and one of the most interesting things we uncovered in that review was that one part of an organization would say they have the capacity, and the other part of the same organization would question their ability to have that capacity. So even within organizations, there is a breakdown in knowledge as to what is real and what is not real, and I think that really permeates our entire response system.

ROCHE: Just to clarify my point, the request for capacity took place during operations, so it wasn't prior to the planning and deployment of military. It was a request for transport capacity from the organization to the military at that time, but because of their charter, they could not provide the capacity we needed to evacuate people out of the camps. It was against their charter. So it wasn't as if it there was a preplanning situation or a breakdown in the communications. There was a situation where we didn't have the resource or the UN organization didn't have the resource, but certainly the NGOs and even UNHCR in the country had resources that we could use to alleviate a situation. But those resources weren't given to us because it was not within the charter of those particular organizations.

WILLIAMS: Well, again, I think I take your point, because I can remember exactly the same situation happening in northern Iraq, where we NGOs couldn't get around in the mountains. We could see the refugees, but they were too far away. We asked the military, which had helicopters galore, and initially they could not fly us because of various insurance issues and whatever. It took three or four weeks before that was cleared. Now the point here, if I understand where we need to go on this, is that none of these situations are so singular as to be unpredictable. In other words, if the military is going to work—and this gets back to the question that I believe was asked over here in conjunction with other organizations—then the respective systems and capabilities of those organizations have to be meshed and discussed well beforehand. There are no surprises, there really aren't; at least in twenty-five years' experience, I haven't seen any.

LINDBORG: I would just add two quick points—one is that I am not aware of any organization involved in the humanitarian response world that doesn't have a humanitarian imperative that overrides whatever else might inform their charters, and that is that the most important of all is to save human lives, especially if you've got—and I want to go back to what my colleague just said—you've got pragmatic, dedicated people in the field who are going to look first and foremost to solving problems. That's an unfortunate example. The other issue is there has been, I think, an important evolution among the NGOs since '95, in terms of understanding, as a result of that crisis, that we needed to have additional standards and levels and methods of accountability to each other and the ability to communicate. There was, as Roy mentioned, a very broad-spread effort, called the Sphere Project, to jointly consolidate the standards by which all of us agreed to operate, to make the language more common so that we could coordinate more effectively, and that we were very clear about what we were trying to achieve, to what standard, in these environments. That was developed, and many of us trained to that and use it to communicate across NGOs and with the UN. So, there has been a lot of evolution in the past ten years.

LOANE: I'll just address the first part of the remark, which was, are people more reasonable these days in terms of humanitarian negotiations? If I understood it correctly, are there more reasonable people out there since Rwanda '95? Do you mean those who are deciding on behalf of the political authorities?

ROCHE: The case in point was back in 1995, the forced closure of the camp by the Rwandans, and the only organized transport in the country at the time was the UNHCR and ICRC. Both organizations did not provide the transport that was requested to try to get people out of the camp, which then resulted—not directly, obviously, but indirectly—in the massacre of about eight thousand people three days later. Now all I'm saying is, we're hearing things about finding pragmatic people making pragmatic decisions. Unfortunately, sometimes you're not going to find those people to make the decisions in time for those sorts of responses to be activated. We keep talking about Afghanistan and Iraq, where there is a massive military presence. But when there is a small UN military presence and there is a much larger NGO-UN civilian presence, it's often the case where the military is relying on those organizations for support, as opposed to vice versa, and sometimes that doesn't happen.

LOANE: Yes, I think there are certain conditions where that kind of mutual support won't work. And Kibeho [internally displaced persons (IDP) camp] maybe was an example. I recall it, in as much as the state authority decides to do something with its own population, it has to assume some responsibilities. I'm not sure that I agree that humanitarians are there under all circumstances to address, to implement governmental decisions. I know that's not specifically what you're saying, but there is an element there.

MacPHERSON: May I add something to that? I think that it's interesting, because the strength of the NGO community is centralized control and decentralized execution, to a degree that most of the military people here just really could not imagine the decentralized execution. And what is incumbent on the community, which has happened in the last ten years, is to build that flexibility into a situation—I don't know anything about this situation—but to empower that NGO representative, at least in my community on the ground, to be able to make those hard and fast pragmatic decisions and—although I don't know anything about that decision, coming out of places like Bosnia and Herzegovina—cut right through. We have a history of the last ten or fifteen years of distrust; there's not been a knowledge base, at least in the NGO community, on what the military stands for and represents, and that has impacted on things like that. And I will say that during the course of events, not to placate that, but from my time within at least this community, the scene has developed quite a bit where there is the ability for an NGO to say "we need to do something and this is"—as Nancy said—"the humanitarian imperative is the humanitarian imperative." That's what they're here for. I can't say much more on that except that I have seen an evolution: maybe not trust, but more understanding on both sides of the issues.

WILLIAMS: One final observation on that point. I think that implicit in the question is a matter of expectations and assumptions. And I also think that this speaks to what Bob was just saying: we don't know enough about each other to properly understand all the time what those expectations and assumptions reasonably can be. Question here.

AUDIENCE - LIEUTENANT COLONEL RICHARD LACQUEMENT: LTC Lacquement, U.S. Army. I guess this is a good take-away to the last question, but in particular for Colonels MacPherson and Kennedy. I was thinking of coming to his current military relations piece, and what I heard at the tail end of the last question was that the NGO communities were coming to grips a little better with the pragmatic aspects of dealing with the military. I guess maybe things are being done well due to a pragmatic common sense to get the job right on the ground, but are there things that we in the military should be doing better to prepare for dealing with NGOs? Rather than saying it's a civilian-military relations issue, maybe, as the moderator suggested, it's a cultural awareness issue of the NGOs and military communities understanding each other. What can we in the military do to better understand the NGO community, to improve our dealing with them? Thank you.

KENNEDY: I'll take it first. Thank you very much, Colonel, for the question. Not to stereotype anything, but I think this particularly refers to the U.S. forces, maybe militaries in a number of countries. One is to be a bit better listeners. I know this sounds like a rather nice kind of advice, but it's true. As Nancy mentioned, in most of these countries, in fact in just about all situations I can think of, the NGOs, agencies, ICRC are all on the ground long before the military comes, and on the ground long after the military leaves. Not that they're the experts from a particular country—they're expatriates themselves—but they have a lot more insight and wisdom, perhaps, and experience than newly arriving people coming off the ship or off the plane. I've seen a number of instances where the military charges in, trying to do a good job, trying to get established, trying to get things going quickly under those pressures that we all understand, but fail to take into account, to listen, to some people who might be able to help them out a little bit. Bob and I both worked for General Tony Zinni, who was quite skilled at these things. I remember being in Haiti in '94 and taking some NGOs into the headquarters—I think it was the Tenth Mountain Division. I went to some huge warehouse building down the street. There probably were about 800 people in camouflage uniform, just as far as I could see. And one fellow said, "Oh, my God!" when he saw this, because we were just so big. One way to get around that and one way, I think, to improve listening is to do some things as Zinni did: he formed advice cells. So this whole business of the J-3, G-3, G-4, and all that structure and layers that this military has like no one else does—he was able to go around that. He put two NGOs, a local scholar, an officer or two, an ICRC person together just to tackle one particular issue and be able to write direct advice to him as the operations officer. That was the way. I think that the second thing people should prepare for in an operational sense, and I think many would understand this, is the capacity to have a liaison. Now sometimes your liaisons may not be accepted. But in doing the force planning and cooperation, you have to have lots of liaison officers, lots of people available to do that, to represent the command. And lastly, I'd say a little humility goes a long way. There are the people who actually do the job quite well, and, I think, sometimes having a bit of rhino skin, as we say, and a little humility, will really sort of bring people on board with you better than other approaches.

WILLIAMS: I would like to turn your question and say yet again, I would like to see the NGOs more interested in learning more about the military as a routine, because we tend to be rather secretive in our own behavior. But one of the difficulties is I've noticed is that the military and the NGOs have a lot more in common than they realize, and that is part of the problem: both groups are very objective oriented. The problem is that the NGOs want to do it their way, and the military wants to do it its way; but that's the beginning of some of their failure of discussion.

LINDBORG: Well, I appreciate both the question and your response, and I think, obviously, there's a lot that can still be done to facilitate mutual understanding and respect, and actually quite a bit has been done. And I think there've been lots of exercises with references to the cottage industry. From what we can tell from our perspective of an operational NGO, there's such fast rotation in the field. You know, every six months, we are dealing with a new crop of folks, and so it seems like it needs to get in at some policy level. From an NGO perspective, that sounds like the Holy Grail that we're trying to figure out. And just like the military probably feels like they're swimming through an alphabet soup of acronyms of all these NGOs—you know, ICRC, IRC—it gets very bewildering. Similarly, it's very difficult for an NGO to navigate what military channels really make things happen. So I think that's a place that we can't stop doing, even though it seems like a cottage industry because of the turnover. There needs to be a continual facilitation of that understanding and dialogue and then just respect at the field level, respect for understanding why an NGO may not want to have armed personnel coming on to their premises when they have a no-weapons policy. And vice versa, an NGO can't understand why the military folks are confused at the lack of a command and control culture. I think that we're further than we think for the most part, and it will be an ongoing effort.

MacPHERSON: I just wanted to add to that it's a dilemma, because it's one of these times where you're going to offer a problem or state a problem, and really, the solution is beyond this person. The dilemma is more fundamental. The military takes on an objective, and in a truer sense, it is going to shape the battlefield. That's how the military looks at the process. And everything in that battlefield or on that plane or within that realm from the enemy, a civilian population, host nation, government, and NGOs are simply components to victory or to whatever success is designated as. What Kevin and Nancy alluded to a moment ago is that the NGO community was there long before and will be there long after. And in this complex situation and in most cases, the amount of hostility and violence, you've got the ICRC and the NGO community trying to stand back as far as possible to eliminate associations with belligerents. But then you have a force—let's just be candid—you have a force of the size and the capability of what the U.S. can project on to a battlefield, it sees the NGO community as just another component. That's not bad! Trust me, if my son was out there, that's exactly the way I'd want them to look at a situation. But it's a dilemma, and this person and the rest of us are probably trying to get our arms around that, through both sides, because in the end, it has happened to us in Somalia when Kevin and I were there. We virtually adopted an orphanage—excuse me, an IDP center that had an orphanage—and component feeding centers taking care of five thousand people. The Marines fell in love with that place, they fell in love with it, took President Bush, the elder, out there; showed him the Somali effort to develop their only capacity. We went home. I went back there three years later, and Doctor Hawa, who was a very small, very petite, very quiet physician who ran that place in that period of time, she'd become so associated with the U.S. government that both her son and her husband had been killed, ostensibly because they were CIA agents, which was not true. The people who wanted to find some reason to disrupt something she was involved in used that as an excuse. And that's the lesson that we learned. To go back to our colleague from Australia, this is a long and hard process, and not to make excuses, but the Kevin Kennedy and Bob MacPherson who landed in Somalia in 1992 are quite different, from those hard lessons learned over the years. It is difficult to look at both sides of this dilemma, but in the end, the UN and all of us up here will stay the course. That's not out of bravado; that's just out of reality. And how we associate, how we maneuver through this, is really difficult.

WILLIAMS: You have a question here?

AUDIENCE - DEAN ERWIN: My name is Dean Erwin, from the U.S. Military Academy. Mr. Loane, if you and your colleagues could help me at least understand where the neutrality principle and humanitarian principle intersect for NGOs. What I'm gleaning here, as I listen, is that pretty much, you have two different environments in which you all work. One where, say, two belligerents interact antagonistically within a legal system, within a legal framework—whether that be a Westphalia system, whether that be an international law, whether it be a common law—and in that instance, at least to me as a layperson, it makes a lot of sense why neutrality is important. But in a more contemporary and probably more relevant system for what we're talking about in this conference, there seems to be a second environment where one or more of the belligerents is almost extrasystemic, that is they operate outside of, in fact they often renounce, legal systems that one or more of the other belligerents may, in fact, operate within. Now, sir, you may not agree with the politics of a given party, but clearly, at least they are operating within the legal system that you agree with. So I don't understand why, within the humanitarian principle, you would still try to work for neutrality where, at least tactically for you, partiality would guarantee your mission and your security. Strategically it would guarantee you diplomatic support at a minimum; it might also include resourcing, tax breaks, etc. But yet, at the same time, the extrasystemic belligerent not only cannot guarantee you your security, but at times, as we've heard several examples, clearly will work proactively and very aggressively to interdict your mission and your personal security. So if you could help me understand where these two principles intersect, I'd be very grateful. Thanks.

LOANE: Your question points very specifically to a part of the context that we have to deal with as an operational agency. Impartiality for us means the response to victims, irrespective of where they're coming from or what they look like or who they are supporting or not supporting. For us means impartiality simply means those who are affected by conflict and who require either protection or assistance that they receive from whoever is the authority or, in another situation, from indeed the ICRC. The neutrality is complex. Let me try to rephrase a little bit how we approach it and maybe I'll use the example of Kibeho, which was mentioned earlier. There are many reasons why the ICRC did not get involved in the evacuation of a refugee camp in Rwanda in 1995, really quite a lot. But one of the reasons is that there is a risk that inside a refugee camp—I'm not saying this was the case, others can judge—that you have inside a refugee camp politically motivated groups and factions that have an interest, a political stake in remaining there or in going home. Your involvement with them as a strictly humanitarian organization can be misinterpreted as politically motivated; it goes that far. Now the only thing we have going for us is the fact that everybody out there who has power, who has authority, respects what the emblem is. Now we have reason to believe that those are the glory days, and those days don't exist in the same way anymore. That's true, and in some places, we don't use our emblem because it's not respected. But for that emblem to be respected means that the types of decisions we take have to be perceived by the belligerents to the conflict as not favoring one or the other, but favoring the victim. So when we look at the very difficult context—and the very difficult contexts are the same for us as for everybody else—it is where you have this form of transnational terrorism. Your difficulty applying the body of law—and the lawyers there can explain that in detail—but from our point, from another point of view, which is an operational point of view, on one side you need to have the confidence and the respect of the people undertaking the conflict in order to be able to do your job. In other words, if we want to work in Somalia, in Baghdad, in parts of Afghanistan, and in Chechnya, there's a number on the list. It's not a huge list, but there is a number on the list; we need to have that level of confidence, that level of respect for everybody. That means that they have to perceive and understand that what we do, we do purely, simply, and exclusively on the basis of humanitarian need. We have no interest, per se, operationally in what the conflict is about. Of course, that's what I mean by "we're not neutral at all." Of course we have an interest, but in terms of our responsibility and our mandate, our obligation is to in someway do that. Now I think historically we have managed, historically we have managed, I think, in 2005. Have we managed in, for example, in Iraq? No, we have certainly not managed. Absolutely not, and that's why we don't have an operation—or we have a very limited operation—in Iraq. That's why we don't have a presence in Iraq, because we are rejected by one of the parties, to put it very bluntly and crudely.

ERWIN: Yes, sir, and I appreciate your patience, but perhaps I don't understand. So you're saying to me that this neutrality, at least in your opinion, is more important than humanitarian efforts? Because clearly, if you're there to help the people and one of the belligerent parties has not only rejected the system within which the rest of the world operates, but in particular has rejected you, you'd much rather abandon the people in need of help rather than appear partial and actually assist the people of the systemic parties where the UN resolution or whatnot is there to provide the solution. I'm just trying to see, because I envision these poor people going unfed or continue to be starved because you're concerned your partiality affects your operation somehow, and I see a contradiction there.

LOANE: Let the others comment. I'll just give my one remark. For us, of course humanity comes first. We operate on the basis of the humanitarian principle. But if our security is compromised because there are belligerents who are going to destroy and undermine our resources, then there's nothing we can do. We will not operate, we are not responsible to go in alone and operate totally independently. We are there because the authorities provide us the support at the political level, the military level, and the community level.

WILLIAMS: Well, let me give you a situation that actually happened, and then you can tell me how it speaks to this issue. After the Rwanda genocide, the one and a half million people that Kevin spoke about went into Zaire; they ended up in this place called Goma. Now the camp ended up being run basically by the genocideers. They prevented people who wanted to repatriate. They were running the camp pretty much on their own terms. The UN tried to intercede, but its forces or its ability to do so were limited. The NGOs working there found themselves actually supporting a systemic situation, to use your term, which was working against the interests not only of the refugees in the camp, but against their own humanitarian principles. In other words, a small group of people who learned to turn humanitarian principles to their account were keeping the NGOs basically hostage. The NGOs signed a document, which was intended to be public to the world, saying that unless the UN did something to correct this situation, namely impose arms control of the camp, that they were going to leave. The UN did the best it could, but its attempt to do so were not exactly up to what the NGOs expected. So some of the NGOs left, something they had never done in their entire history, which in the case of one was over 50 years and it had survived many wars. Now I'm throwing the question back to you: how would you interpret that act, basically?

ERWIN: Again, sir, maybe it's a cultural difference. But to me, if you are arguing that the humanitarian principle overrides, then clearly you have to collaborate, and maybe it's just because you have access to particular information that military authorities in this particular case—not necessarily in this particular case—but military authorities could use to interdict threats. But if you refuse to be partial, you refuse to provide resources or information or assistance to a particular party, then the situation only worsens. And in this particular case, the decision was made to be neutral; they pulled out and ultimately all the holes in the Swiss cheese lined up and we had a terrible crisis in Rwanda. But there are plenty of instances where you could see that by not taking a side, when at least the end states agree that, whether it's an insurgent, terrorist insurgent, or a terrorist—to me, at least, all these three are different—theNGO community, the military, the systemic governments all agree that at least the one belligerent party needs to be eradicated, whether you need to accomplish your mission or we need to accomplish our mission. But if you don't work toward partiality, then you leave and that makes our job harder and that makes your job impossible. So I'm just trying to see how we work through that, at least from my layperson's perspective.

WILLIAMS: Nancy?

LINDBORG: I feel like there's some confusion in some of the terms in the examples and also the roles of various actors. I would strongly suggest that most of the humanitarian community would not say that humanitarian principle trumps the humanitarian imperative, which is saving lives, which is number one. Number two, the impartiality is about impartiality toward working with people who are victims, regardless of where they're coming from. And so that's what the meaning of the impartiality is. And as we've discussed earlier, I don't think that neutrality is something that most of us hold toward. We recognize that by virtue of being present in these conflict environments, we are automatically a stakeholder in the outcome, and the outcome is to move toward a situation in which fewer people are suffering. The complications, which always arise, but were particularly difficult in the example that you all are talking about, is how you interpret the impact of your actions in that particular complicated political environment: whether you're going to serve a greater good by withdrawing versus staying on and potentially supporting a systemic problem that could have led to greater suffering. So the example that you're talking about, I think, was one in which judgment was exercised. You can disagree with the judgment and the analysis. But it's really a different set of issues than the concepts of humanitarian principles, neutrality, and impartiality, so I think it just might be useful to disentangle that a little bit. The final word I would say is, as a number of us have mentioned, the concept of independence is really an important one as well. I think it's often misunderstood as some sense of unruliness or not wanting to play ball with other actors who are in the field. In fact, as we've discussed, NGOs are often there before and often stay later, and being independent from some particularly belligerent forces that come in enables that group—the NGOs and the UN actors—to continue that effort long past when a military force might depart. And so what I see as the challenge, and what I think we've quite appropriately grappled with together, is, how can you work together and how can you move toward the same overall objective, respecting that we come at it with different strengths and we play different kinds of roles? And I think, just from the NGO perspective, you want us to be independent, we're the arms and legs, we go out in places that hardly anyone else can go often, and we're able to do so because—and I understand and agree that it's changing in certain environments—but we're accepted, that we're there to facilitate and support the communities and the individuals in what they're trying to do to survive or rebuild their lives. So it's a tactical advantage to have an independent group out there, able to do the things that the NGOs do. So just to disentangle some of these concepts and approaches helps us understand how better to work together in the future.

WILLIAMS: I think I'd like to continue that discussion with this gentleman from West Point after the meeting. You've touched upon a difficult subject, but I think maybe it can be untangled a bit. One final question and then I'd like to ask the panel if they have any observations before we have to close. Sir.

AUDIENCE - MAJOR GENERAL KENNETH J. QUINLAN, JR.: Now if I can look at my notes. I'm Major General Kenneth J. Quinlan, commandant of the Joint Forces Staff College. I would like to offer an educational opportunity for NGOs, for yourselves and your colleagues, as well as my student population, which is a joint community. It includes coalition partners, and we have four ten-week courses every year. I'd be more than glad to have a half a dozen or eight to ten NGOs in every single class, so that we could develop what we would call a joint coalition doctrine of how we're going to operate. Because I have difficulty with saying you're independent, but then you want to coordinate and you want to have support from us or us from you; it seems to be a contradiction. So I think if we really are going to move forward on this in a meaningful way, it seems to me that we should train together and educate ourselves together so we can understand each other's cultures and come together and have a better meeting of minds. That way, when we go on these battlefields in these complex environments, we already have personal and professional relationships and a better understanding of how we're going to oper-ate, rather than an ad hoc approach to every situation we face. So I would offer that up to you, if that is of any use. Thank you.

WILLIAMS: Well, thank you very much indeed. One of the constant recom-mendations is that we need to have a common terminology even before we can begin relating. And I think that's pretty clear. I'll ask my colleagues for any final comments.

LOANE: Well, thanks. Actually we enjoyed it very much. Thank you, I'll make it easy for you.

AUDIENCE - LARRY WOODS: I'd like to do a quick follow-on to the last question. Larry Woods, headquarters of the Army, G-3. This education is very important. There are a couple of ex-military folks here; I'm certain you work in terms of lessons learned, and I'm certain you've captured some. You mentioned a sphere of operations perhaps that you've cochaired, and hopefully there are some lessons learned. Maybe you produced a document, a manual, something that would cut across the grain of all the NGOs and such. If you haven't, you might want to consider producing such a document or capturing those pertinent lessons learned. And then lastly, in conjunction with the invitation that you've just had, there's a thing called the Joint Electronic Library, which is accessible, that is, nonsecure, that you can get on the Internet. The military is constantly groping with these issues as a single surface and in a joint and allied context. You will find there the latest in terms of military thinking for our combatant commanders, how to operate. Joint doctrine 3.0 is just about to be finalized this fall, which is the overriding operational doctrine that provides the premise. There are more detailed documents, and they would be a great reference point for you in terms of your field operations. They would also be of great use to you in any training that you might do. So I just offer that for your consideration as well. Thank you.

WILLIAMS: Thank you. Kevin.

KENNEDY: Well, I will take that last comment after all. One thank you to the General and to you, sir, for this offer. And just as a matter of information, my deputy is actually briefing the Army War College today, the students and visiting the UN in New York. We also do a lot of lessons-learned exercises in the UN and, I suspect, elsewhere as well. And I would commend you to www.reliefweb.int; it's the website run by my department. I've nothing to do with it. It's the most visited UN website on the Internet, and you'll find on that every SITREP [situation report], every fund-raising document, every lessons-learned exercise, every humanitarian map that you could possibly want to get your hands on. Thank you.

LOANE: I think I'll just also respond with thanks for that appreciation, for the need to develop this style. I want to make two remarks. The first remark: from our point of view, we believe that the military is going to become much more engaged in humanitarian intervention, and that's our perception, that's how we see it. We see an increasing dialogue, an increasing role, and if we take the very safe examples like the tsunami, this is not as valuable, but this is essential in terms of saving lives. And I don't think any of us would dispute that. I just throw out one of the major constraints, and I don't know how this is ever solved. One of the major constraints is one of proportionality. When the military starts to become involved in something—in this case, humanitarian affairs—the sheer size of what you bring, the waves, the force, we are completely disproportionate-alized because what we probably have to offer the humanitarian community in terms of numbers is much smaller and there is a risk. It's a risk for all of us. It's not a threat; I think it's a risk that we need to take into consideration, that humanitarian intervention does not become overwhelmed because of the sheer force and size of the capacity of the military. And I think there many opportunities where we can provide our view and our take on what is a very, as you all well know, a sophisticated, complex and unfortunately, insecure environment.

WILLIAMS: Well, thank you very much, and I would just like to end with one final observation. The title of this panel was Nongovernmental and Humanitarian Organizations in the New Security Environment. We certainly talked about the elements that are impinging more and more upon the security of the people in the field, and unfortunately, we've heard a good deal about how many more people have been put in jeopardy over the last decade. But inadvertently, perhaps, I think we also touched upon something else in recent questions and from over here and in the back. There is confusion, in my mind, of language and understanding as to sometimes what it is we're fundamentally all about. And that, I think, applies to both sides. And from our side, I think that that confusion is based upon—I'll admit it—we've struggled along or gotten along for decades only with a high degree of arrogance. We occupied the moral high ground, and what we did was never threatened, never challenged. We always felt that we knew exactly why we were doing what we were doing. Over the last decade, that illusion began to slip. I think it began to slip in Bosnia, where suddenly we found ourselves working, crossing check-points from where, from one moment to the next, we were on the other side of a conflict. And getting back to the question of neutrality and impartiality, Charlie sees you as neutral and impartial, you cross over, and Joe sees you as his hated enemy because you helped Charlie. We were not used to that, and it began to, I think, sort of shake the foundations of our assumptions. And it went on through Rwanda, it went on through Kosovo, and so forth. And to be perfectly honest—and I'll take the liberty of saying this and I don't even ask my colleagues to agree—we've got to do a lot of soul-searching ourselves in terms of understanding our own terms of reference. For example, all my life, professionally I've been using the term "humanitarian." I'm not even sure what I mean by that. And I think if I were to ask a lot of my colleagues, they'd say the same thing. I know intuitively what I mean by that, but beyond that, what do I mean by that? So it really can come down to that simple a level. Enough of this! Thank you very much for your interest and for your questions, and we certainly will get back to you and your offer, sir. Thank you.

KEYNOTE ADDRESS

WHERE DOES AMERICA FIT IN THE NEW WORLD?

Eliot Cohen, Ph.D., Professor, Johns Hopkins University
Introduction by: General Richard A. Cody, Vice Chief of Staff, United
      States Army

Summary

Eliot Cohen, Ph.D.

- How do Americans—indeed, how should Americans think about fitting into the world in which they live? During Dwight Eisenhower's tenure as president, his world, like ours, had contradictory elements. It is important to reflect on the tensions and contradictions in the world and in our own country that prevailed then, and that prevail today. Neat categories of thought do not work. Lumping political leaders into one camp or another is a wasteful exercise.

- The realist school of international relations rests on certain fundamental assumptions. One is that states act in a drive to maximize their power or to check the power of others. Another is that it is folly to introduce the values of domestic politics into foreign policy. Idealists, a more diverse group than their realist counterparts, are generally associated with the notion of change—that international behavior can be modified and moderated. They might, of course, disagree among themselves about the exact role of international institutions or law in producing such change.

- The distinction between realism and idealism in foreign policy is, for the most part, phony. This is because neither realism nor idealism in its purest form is tenable. Over the years, American statesmen have exhibited a little bit of both. John Quincy Adams is often depicted as the quintessential prudent realist, and often quoted for counseling that the wise statesman "goes not abroad in search of monsters...." But the speech from which this quotation is excerpted also contains references to the Declaration of Independence as the solemn and sole "beacon on the summit of the mountain." U.S. foreign policy is always moving on an uneasy path between realism and idealism. Classifying presidents and their advisors as one or the other is difficult. Ronald Reagan labeled the Soviet Union "the Evil Empire" yet negotiated with Soviet leaders. George W. Bush has declared that supporting democracy in the Middle East is of the highest priority to the United States, yet the Bush administration applies relatively light pressure on Russia to reform.

• Anyone who suggests that policy is based on great principles invariably comes to grief. All political leaders find themselves in situations where they must compromise their principles. Consistency may or may not be a virtue, but it is unsustainable in the long term.

• Realists have a ready diagnosis and prescription for a rising China. They are not surprised by greed, avarice, violence, and the drive for power. They are not surprised to find that most South Koreans want U.S. troops withdrawn from the Korean Peninsula. Realists assert that the balance of power tells us which countries will align with the United States and which will not. And they believe in the predominance of the state system and that states are resilient.

• The idealist temperament—rooted in the values of the Enlightenment—is not that unrealistic and has much to commend it. Take, for example, the call for democratic change in the Middle East and North Africa. What alternatives are available to the United States? Should we rely on dictators to crush terrorists? Should we build a "Fortress America" in an effort to insulate ourselves from terrorism? Should we opt for appeasement? Whether the U.S. policy of supporting democratic change has hitherto been wisely and effectively executed is, of course, another matter. But adopting such a policy is who we are. Reading this country's founding documents, one might be struck, even distressed, by their universality. What is America? America is an idea, or at any rate, a nation born of an idea. The idea of America is still alluring to others. Clearly, this is a dark, dangerous world. But it is also a world in which American ideals have done much good and retain their power.

• In conducting foreign policy, American statesmen always have, and still do, navigate through a middle ground. Ideas and interests can walk hand in hand.

Analysis

In asking where, not whether, America fits in the new world, Dr. Cohen took to task a timeworn category of political and strategic analysis, namely, that strategic approaches, particularly American ones, fall neatly into either the realist or idealist schools of thought. Defined simply, the former school sees international relations as a struggle for power, the conscious protection and advancement of one's interests. The latter, in contrast, views international relations as an opportunity for advancing ideals, especially broad Enlightenment-based principles aimed at making the world a better place.

Such categories, Dr. Cohen noted, ultimately fail us: they add little to the understanding of our strategic past and offer little in the way of guidance for the future. Historically, neither approach has been pure; nor is either theory, in its pure form, a tenable way of viewing the world. Just as our strategic past has been a mixture of realism and idealism, so must our strategic future be. It is impossible to base policy on general principles, regardless of their origin. Specific circumstances always demand consideration, which in turn ultimately means a compromise of some sort.

Rather than useful categories of analysis, Dr. Cohen suggested that these two schools actually reflect the two broader tempers that characterize the current debates over U.S. policy and strategy. Both can teach and learn from the other. At times America will have to compromise its ideals to protect its interests, and at other times it will have to subordinate its interests to its ideals. Indeed, in many cases in America's history, its ideals have been indistinguishable from its interests. Who can really tell the difference? More important, does it matter? The learning, the exchange of views in the course of the debate, seems to be more important.

Dr. Cohen's attack on the conventional categories of strategic and political analysis was, in part, an attack on the seemingly intractable state of the current debate over the direction of U.S. policy. Some elements of that debate have become polemical. Consider the ongoing disputes over the merits of multilateralism versus unilateralism, neoconservatisim, and whether America is a twenty-first century empire (whether it wants to be or not) and what, if anything, that means. Opposing views are firmly entrenched. And a compromise, at least in the strategic literature, appears as unlikely as a clear winner. In the meantime, decisions of strategic import have to be made. The war in Iraq is entering perhaps its most critical phase, and the larger war on terror requires ever more attention. In fact, Dr. Cohen's attack on the timeworn categories of realism and idealism did not go beyond what students are taught in Political Science 101: that such categories are inadequate and always have been, and that the differences between the two schools of thought are as obvious as they are academic. But perhaps this basic message is more important than it seems at first blush. Perhaps it is a genuine call for both sides of the debate to acknowledge the obvious and move forward.

Transcript

ANNOUNCER: Ladies and gentlemen, please welcome tonight's master of ceremonies, Major General Keith W. Dayton.

MAJOR GENERAL KEITH W. DAYTON: Okay, folks, if you can hear me, we're going to go ahead and keep the program running. You know, one of the goals of this conference has been to provide a broad and diverse forum for discussing national security issues. And for those of you who were here earlier today, you know we had Prince [El] Hassan [bin Talal] of Jordan this morning as our opening address. We had a panel that dealt with sovereignty and national power. Then at lunchtime we had Hernando de Soto from Peru, who came in and talked to us about some pretty interesting economic ideas that underlie national security. And then we had a panel just before we broke to come here to dinner that dealt with NGOs and humanitarian organizations and how they fit into the emerging pattern of national security. What we'd like to do tonight is continue that discussion. Our guest speaker, who will be introduced in a minute, has graciously agreed to answer some questions at the end of his presentation. My job is actually to introduce the guy that's going to introduce the guest speaker. And that is our Vice Chief of Staff of the Army, General Richard Cody. He asked me to be short, so I'll be short. He'd want me to tell you he's a master aviator with over 5,000 hours of aviation flight time. He's been in a variety of command and staff assignments, commanding general of the 101st Airborne Division. He was deputy commander—yeah, all of you hooah guys out there for the 101st—deputy commanding general of Task Force

Richard A. Cody

Hawk. He has been in Albania. He has been the commander of the 160th Special Operations Regiment. And to those of us who remember more recent days, he was the Army's G-3 chief operations officer during Operation IRAQI FREEDOM and Operation ENDURING FREEDOM. So, with no further ado, ladies and gentlemen, the thirty-first vice Chief of Staff of the Army, General Dick Cody. Sir, all yours.

GENERAL RICHARD A. CODY: You left out an important thing. I'm the guy who hired you.

DAYTON: And I'll never forgive you.

CODY: Well, good evening, everybody. Secretary [Francis J.] Harvey, good to see you, sir. Mr. [Raymond F.] Dubois, fellow general officers, distinguished guests, civilians, service members, on behalf of our Army's Chief of Staff Peter J. Schoomaker, welcome to this 2005 Eisenhower National Security Conference dinner. It's a distinct pleasure to be here among you. I'm honored to be able to introduce one of our nation's most distinguished scholars, Dr. Eliot Cohen. A leading voice on a wide variety of diplomatic and security issues, Dr. Cohen's expertise is widely sought by senior government and national defense policy decision makers, especially during this global war on terrorism. A little bit about him: After earning his doctorate in political science from Harvard [University] in 1982—somehow he missed the recruiting effort we had there; they're back, and we did get his son—and serving as assistant professor of government and assistant dean of Harvard College, he became a member of the Strategic Department of the United States Naval War College in 1985. Subsequently, he directed the Gulf War Air Power Survey, a project that showed the United States Army was very dominant in that war, for which he received the Air Force's Declaration for Exceptional Civilian Service. You don't remember that part, sir. We were right in the middle of QDR. Dr. Cohen is the founding director of the Philip Merrill Center for Strategic Studies. In 2004 he was named to the Robert E. Osgood Chair at Johns Hopkins University. Most of you in this audience are no doubt familiar with Professor Cohen through his important and award-winning writing, such as *War Over Kosovo [Politics and Strategy in a Global Age]* and *Supreme Command [Soldiers, Statesmen and Leadership in Wartime]*. But I feel bound to mention that Eliot Cohen has not only contributed to our nation as a thinker and as a teacher, he is also a father of a U.S. Army soldier. Lieutenant Rafi Cohen, Ranger Airborne Infantry, is serving today, and tonight as we speak, with our Brigade of the 10th Mountain Division over there in Iraq, and we're very proud of him.

So I know tonight when Dr. Cohen shares his convictions about America's place in the new world, he speaks from both his mind and his heart. And as each of us grapples with the issues of national power and an international war, we are fortunate to have Professor Cohen's words to inform our endeavor. So it's a great pleasure for me to present to you Dr. Eliot Cohen.

ELIOT A. COHEN, PH.D.: Well, General Cody, thank you for those kind words. Let me begin by doing what we academics do best, and that's of course quibbling. About escaping Harvard without being hit by your recruiting effort—not entirely true, since the day before I got my doctorate I was sworn in as a second lieutenant in the United States Army Reserve, where I had a brief and admittedly entirely undistinguished career. The other point I have to make, just to clarify the Air Force's somewhat mixed view of the Gulf War Air Power Survey, I think the most striking comment that came in directly to my ears from an Air Force three star was, "I only want to read that man's name in an obituary." So, there were somewhat mixed reactions.

It's always a great honor to be associated with the United States Army and to have an opportunity, first and foremost, to express my appreciation for all that you folks do and have done for our country. And that, as you know, comes from the heart. It's an honor in particular to speak to this conference, which commemorates a great soldier and great statesman, Dwight D. Eisenhower. Now, Eisenhower wasn't a scholar, and I don't think he would have called himself an intellectual. But he was a thoughtful warrior, a man who read more widely than he led on and believed in the value to Soldiers of what I believe to be the greatest of all intellectual virtues, reverence for the unvarnished truth. In 1947 as chief of staff of the Army, Eisenhower issued a directive for the writing of the official history of World War II, which contained these lines: "The Army possesses no inherent right to conceal the history of its affairs behind a cloak of secrecy, nor is such conduct conducive to a sound and healthy approach to the day-to-day performance of its duties. The foregoing directive will be interpreted in the most liberal sense, with no reservations as to whether or not the evidence of history places the Army in a favorable light." That's really a remarkable statement, and it speaks volumes about Ike's integrity and of his understanding of the importance to the Army of that old dictum, which I'm happy to say is also the motto of my university, Johns Hopkins University, *Veritas vos liberabit*, the truth will make you free.

Eliot A. Cohen

Well, the topic that you gave me is "Where Does America Fit in the New World?" And I'm going to avail myself of the second privilege of academics, and that is to beg the question and talk about something a little bit different because the truth is, if you really want a professor to talk about that topic, you're going to get a stream of platitudes or megalomania, and it's going to go on for two hours, which I don't think you want. So instead I'm going to rephrase the question a little bit, which is, how do Americans—and perhaps how *should* Americans—think about how they fit themselves into the world? Or to hark back to another old dictum from the Greeks, know thyself.

Let me begin to address that by going back to Eisenhower. Eisenhower's tenure as president at the very outset of the Cold War was marked by some very contradictory elements: a hard, ideologically driven, anticommunism, which was coupled with a willingness to come down equally hard on our British and French allies at Suez; the strange spectacle of America's leading Soldier at war with his own service, the Army, over whether we really needed large conventional ground forces; appalling racial tensions in a country that was still segregated; and the first tentative moves toward equal voting rights and educational opportunities for all of America's citizens. I think it's worth reflecting on that tension and on those contradictions because they capture a reality that most commentators on foreign affairs often avoid, namely, that neat categories of thought, particularly those built on easy dichotomies, don't work. There's a certain appeal to what someone once called "minds that swing on hinges," in lumping politicians or political people into one camp or another. And what I want to do this evening is to look at one such distinction in American foreign policy—a very old one, but also one that is very contemporary and very much with us—and that's the supposed distinction between realists and idealists.

We Americans often reduce our history to simple narratives. And one of those simple narratives consists of a supposed swing between realism and idealism as the driving forces in American foreign policy. Realism is a school of political thought that draws on the classical European balance-of-power system and the writing of historians as far back as Thucydides over two millennia ago, which takes as its point of departure some very fundamental assumptions: that the world is an anarchic place composed of states; that although one can speak of justice in internal politics, it has little or no meaning in international relations; that states act upon either a drive for power or the fear of the power of others; that these motivations and the policies they produce have nothing to do with the internal construction or ordering of states; and that, more important, it's folly to introduce the values of domestic politics into international relations. [Former president] Richard Nixon and his secretary of state, Henry Kissinger, perhaps most closely fit this school of thought, but in a toned-down way. So, too, did many others, from Colin Powell in our own time to Henry Cabot Lodge a century ago. The idealists are a more diverse group, but I think we can characterize them as the politicians and thinkers whom we associate with efforts to Americanize the world, who believe in the universality of American values and the possibility of spreading them. There are idealists at both left and right, ranging from Woodrow Wilson to Ronald Reagan in the last century. They might disagree amongst themselves about, say, the role that international institutions or international law should play in the world, but in changing the world they most certainly believe, and in changing it in the direction of American understandings of political justice, limited government, independent courts, widespread suffrage, freedom of religion, freedom of speech and assembly, and property.

We are living in a time when many are inclined to suspect that the idealists have had their shot and it's time for the realists to return, or as the managing editor of *Foreign Affairs* recently put it, "For more than half a century, overenthusiastic idealists of one variety or another have gotten themselves and the country into trouble abroad and had to be bailed out by prudent successors brought in to clean up the mess." He called realism "the perennial hangover cure of American foreign policy." As Americans look at the tangled mess that is Iraq, the recriminations have begun, the realists saying, we never would have done this, and the idealists saying, well, this isn't what we argued for. Like most recriminations, they won't be terribly helpful. They won't be helpful because there were realist as well as idealist arguments for and against going to war in Iraq. They won't be terribly helpful because execution is as important as the decision for war itself, and perhaps more so, and most of all, because we really don't know how Iraq is going to turn out. Here instead is the thesis I want to put to you tonight: that the distinction between realists and idealists or between realism and idealism in American foreign policy is for the most part phony, perhaps even dangerous, because in their purer forms—and their advocates will always try to make these things pure—neither school is tenable. And in the real world, American statesmen, Eisenhower among them, have been more than a bit of both.

Let's take one of those heroes of American realism, John Quincy Adams, a highly successful secretary of state and a pretty unhappy president. How often have we heard quoted his famous lines, "The United States goes not abroad in search of monsters to destroy. She is the well-wisher to the freedom and independence of all, she is the champion and vindicator only of her own." Prudent realism. Well, maybe, until you read the rest of the speech, a July 4th address delivered in 1820 that could only have been written by a wild-eyed idealist. John Quincy Adams, in that speech, described the Declaration of Independence as "the first solemn declaration by a nation of the only legitimate foundation of civil government. It was the cornerstone of a new fabric destined to cover the surface of the globe. It stands and must forever stand alone, a beacon on the summit of the mountain to which all the inhabitants of the earth may turn their eyes for a genial and saving light 'til time shall be lost in eternity and this globe itself dissolve nor leave a wreck behind." Now, maybe that sounds like Henry Kissinger to you, but it sure doesn't sound like Henry Kissinger to me.

The truth is that American foreign policy has always found itself moving in an uneasy middle path. We have lived in a world of states for the most part and played by those rules. Yet, in our greatest war, which was a civil war, the greatest of our presidents after Washington said that that terrible conflict was a test not just of whether our nation would survive, but whether "any nation so conceived and so dedicated could long endure." The success of America had, Lincoln believed, a significance that went far beyond the question of how many states would occupy the North American continent.

Classifying presidents and their advisors as realists and idealists is a lot harder than one might think. Was Franklin Roosevelt an idealist when he cut deals with Stalin in order to maintain the coalition against Hitler? Was he a realist when he proclaimed the Four Freedoms? Was Ronald Reagan a realist when he called the Soviet Union an evil empire and challenged its leaders to tear down the Berlin Wall? Was he an idealist when he made deals with communist China or Islamic fundamentalists to contain and roll back Soviet power? Is George W. Bush a realist when he proclaims the universal aspiration of men and women to rule themselves, including in the Middle East? Is he an idealist when he refrains from criticizing too harshly the brutal means used by Russia to suppress the insurgency in Chechnya? Even these admittedly crude examples suggest that trying to lump policymakers into one camp or another is unproductive. Political judgment, as the British political philosopher, Isaiah Berlin, put it, is not general, but particular. He describes it as "an acute sense of what fits with what, what springs from what, what leads to what." And someone who tries to prescribe policy based on general principles will find themselves making absurd decisions. Doctrinaire politicians, realists or idealists, who treat the world as if it were a great political science field experiment invariably come to grief. Put differently, sooner or later all politicians find themselves compromising their principles of whatever kind, acting in the name of the balance of power when they would really like to strengthen international law, or denouncing tyranny and oppression when what they would really much prefer to do is sign another arms control agreement. Consistency in politics may or may not be a virtue. What's important in the long run is that it's unsustainable. Labeling people or positions is laziness masquerading as taxonomy.

But the substance of realism and idealism, that's a different matter. Undoubtedly, there is a realist temper and an idealist temper. There are attitudes and predispositions to be understood and discussed, insights and understandings to be gleaned from both camps. What might some of those insights be? Let's start with the realists. They tend to believe, rightly I think, that there is a certain logic in international politics that's very difficult to overcome. A good example is the rise of China, an emerging power that, like most emerging powers, will be inclined to contest the dominance of the previous leading power in the system, namely, us. A realistic perspective would expect tension between the United States and China, now and for the foreseeable future. Note that realism gives a diagnosis but no prescription. It's as logical from a realist's point of view to say that we should balance China by allying with Japan and India, which is, of course, what we are doing, as it is to say that we should appease China by, say, acceding to its wishes over Taiwan. Realists tend not to see much that's good in human nature. They are not surprised by ingratitude, infidelity, cowardice, avarice, and above all, the drive for power. It would not surprise them, for example, that most South Koreans, if you believe the public opinion polls, are quite prepared to dispense with the presence of the American forces that have protected that country for half a century, and that those same folks think of us as more of a threat than the crazed dictatorship within artillery range of their capital city. Believing, like Charles de Gaulle, that states are cold beasts, those who are of a realist cast of mind are not anguished by the ingratitude of Franco-German efforts to counterbalance Anglo-American influence in Europe. Their belief in the predominance of state interests narrowly defined helps us to understand—to continue the China example—which states will line up with us and, perhaps more important, which states will try to wriggle out of any confrontation between the two giants, no matter how close their ties with us have been. Finally, realists believe in the predominance of the state system, no matter what the status of international organizations, including terrorist networks. And they are apparently right in thinking that states are extremely resilient instruments of government and that there are not any substitutes for them. The failures of international organizations—of, say, the UN and the Oil for Food scandal or even, alas, of NATO and fighting the Taliban—remind us that in the end, it is states that wield power in international affairs. The realist temperament has the appeal of looking like wisdom because it is so often cynical. That's why a certain kind of graduate student likes it so much.

But when one descends from the lofty heights of foreign policy ruminations, one finds that the idealist temperament has much to be said for it, as well. It affirms the values that we really do hold dear: moderate politics, religious tolerance, equality before the law, and all the rest. Those are the values of the Enlightenment. It's well to remind ourselves periodically of the sacrifices that it required to realize them and what happens when they are cast aside. When a thoroughgoing realist looks at machete-hewn bodies in Rwanda or burning villages in Darfur or rape camps and mass graves in Yugoslavia, he shrugs his shoulders, says, it's not my problem, and goes back to his coffee and donuts. And that's why ultimately most of us, if we are honest with ourselves, can't be thoroughgoing realists. Idealism captures another truth about international politics, which is that the domestic and the international have never been quite as separate as the realists would like to believe. Hitler wasn't merely Bismarck with bad manners, nor was Stalin merely a Georgian seminarian playing at being Czar Nicholas I. They were qualitatively different actors in the international system because of their beliefs, which emerged from domestic politics. Furthermore, in an age of global communications, of the Internet, of increasingly easy international travel, and certainly of an ever-more-tightly linked international economy, those distinctions between external politics and internal politics are diminishing fast.

Beyond this, I'm not at all certain that idealism is so unrealistic. Let's take the president's much-derided aspirations for a liberalized Middle East, which is a reaction chiefly to the events of September 11th and the threat of a radicalized Islam largely emanating from that region. What were the alternatives available to the United States? To rely on dictators to crush the Islamists? Experience suggests that such repression was as likely to breed terrorists as to suppress them. To build a Great Wall of China around the United States? Hard to do if we were to remain accessible to an international economy upon which we depend. Appeasement? Our enemies are unappeasable. Whether the president's initiative has been executed wisely and effectively, that's another matter. But I submit that any president would have found himself embarked on some kind of policy of this type.

There is one final aspect of the idealist temperament, and in some ways the most important one from the point of view of American foreign policy. It is who we are. When foreigners read the founding documents of American politics—the Declaration of Independence and the Gettysburg Address, to name just two—they are struck, and in my experience often distressed, by their universality. But that's what America is: not just a nation, but an idea, or rather a nation born of an idea. In 1790 George Washington wrote to the leader of the synagogue in Newport, Rhode Island, the following words: "It is now no more that toleration is spoken of as if it was by the indulgence of one class of people that another enjoyed the exercise of their inherent natural rights. For, happily, the government of the United States, which gives to bigotry no sanction, to persecution no assistance, requires only that those who live under its protection should demean themselves as good citizens in giving it on all occasions their effectual support." That was an astounding notion at the time. I still think it's astounding, and that it's an idea that is valid not only for Americans. It's one of those ideas that still lure people to this country and that make us loved by some and hated by others. We can't escape it. It is who we are. It's a dark, dangerous old world out there. It is still driven, as Thucydides taught nearly two and a half millennia ago, by states operating under the impulse of fear, honor, and interest. But it's also a world in which American ideals have done much good and retain their power. It's a world in which we remain the noisy, gaudily dressed tourists who fall silent and tear up at the Lincoln Memorial and who send our sons and daughters to fight for the freedom of distant peoples.

What this means, then, is that we must navigate through a murky middle ground, sometimes compromising our ideals to serve our interests, sometimes redefining our interests in terms of our ideals. Our ideals and our interests will often be at odds with one another, and we have to recognize that. But not always. Indeed, on more occasions than we might suspect, ideals and interests may walk hand-in-hand.

Let me conclude by returning to General Eisenhower. Many of you, I'm sure, are familiar with his inspiring message of the day on June 6th, 1944, D-day. You may not know that accompanying that message and distributed equally to all the troops in the expeditionary force was a second message describing what General Eisenhower expected of those troops in their dealings with the population of liberated Europe. The last paragraph of that message read as follows: "I urge each of you to bear constantly in mind that by your actions, not only you as an individual but your country as well will be judged. By establishing a relationship with the liberated peoples based on mutual understanding and respect, we shall enlist their wholehearted assistance in the defeat of our common enemy. Thus, we shall lay the foundations for a lasting peace, without which our great effort will have been in vain." Who was speaking here? General Eisenhower, the hard-headed Soldier and practical realist who wanted undisturbed lines of communication as his armies advanced across chaotic, war-torn countries? Or Ike, the idealistic average American from Abilene, Kansas, who described the Normandy invasion as the great crusade and wanted his fellow citizens to embody the virtues of the small town America of his time? Who can tell? More important, what does it matter? Thank you very much.

General Dayton offered to take the questions for me, but I told him I've done it once or twice before myself, so I'll do it again. I'd be happy to take any questions or comments you might have. Sir?

AUDIENCE - MIKE PELISH: Mike Pelish, National Guard Bureau. Can we still say the only thing we have to fear is fear itself? And how can security protect freedom without diminishing freedom?

COHEN: It's a wonderful line of that extremely cunning politician, Franklin Delano Roosevelt, who knew how to inspire a country. Remember, when he said we have nothing to fear but fear itself, he was talking about the Depression. He wasn't talking about World War II. And that's a big difference. I think he was in large measure right, talking about an economy that was suffering the way it was. But I think there is no question in the world there are real things to fear. My wife and I have figured out what the evacuation plan is for how we get the heck out of Washington when somebody lights a nuke off downtown. So there is clearly a great deal to fear. To your second question, that doesn't mean you should be paralyzed by it or on your knees. It just means one should be realistic. And that's one of the things Soldiers are very good at being. I think your second question is very much to the point, and it's one where I wish our leaders were more open in addressing the problem of the trade-offs between our security and our liberties. Personally, I'm very disturbed at the idea that American citizens can be held without trial or trial by jury. That troubles me greatly. In all of our wars, we have made trade-offs. In the past, the way it was dealt with was the Supreme Court kind of looked the other way during the war—whether it was the Civil War or World War II—and then afterward told the federal government, you really should not have done that, but with an understanding that, okay, for the duration of an emergency you can do things like that. The difficulty with the war that we're in now is this is going to go on, I believe, for decades, possibly for generations. And we're going to be making trade-offs. We are already making some trade-offs. And what we need is a very, very explicit discussion of what those trade-offs are and what risks. Ultimately what that boils down to is, what risks are we really willing to accept in order to remain who we are? Because in this respect, the United States is very different from France. You know, France is France, whether it's ruled by Jacques Chirac or Louis XIV or Napoleon or Marshal Petain. I have some preferences among those—not quite as extensive as you might think. But France will be France. The United States ceases to be the United States if the values embodied in the Declaration and the Bill of Rights and all the things we treasure about this country somehow go away. So for us, in some level, the stakes are greater. Sir?

AUDIENCE - GEORGE SCHWAB, PH.D.: George Schwab, National Committee on American Foreign Policy. Thank you for your remarks. I wonder whether you would care to comment on where the neocons combine realism with idealism. There's been a lot of discussion, as you know, in the neocon literature.

COHEN: Ah, the neocons. I have a problem with that because there are people who are convinced that I am a neocon. If I say I really don't like that term, that just shows that I'm undercover or—I am not actually, I mean, the whole point of my talk was to say that I think most of these labels are not useful. I am not sure that there is a distinctive neocon school of American foreign policy. I think rather that the people who identify themselves as such represent part of what has been in many ways the great middle ground of thinking about American foreign policy, which you would have found in Teddy Roosevelt or in Scoop Jackson, in some ways I suppose in [Ronald] Reagan, in some ways in Franklin Delano Roosevelt. And the problem is trying to figure out what makes sense in that murky middle ground. One of the reasons why I reject that label for myself is, first, I hate being labeled anything. But also, I think it distracts us from the real problems of the world around us. As you know, I'm on the record as saying that I thought the war in Iraq was the right thing to do. I am also on the record as saying reasonable people could disagree with that position. And I cannot tell you honestly that I'm 100 percent sure that I was right. That being the case, it seems to me it's more useful to get into the particulars of the case, rather than worrying about what this school of thought is up to. Janne?

AUDIENCE - JANNE E. NOLAN, PH.D. : Eliot, I'm sure you and many other people in this room know that General [Eric] Shinseki [former Army chief of staff] was the inspiration for the Eisenhower series. And in that spirit and that of all of the great leaders who have sustained the attention to this series and support it, I wonder if you, in the context of the Bill of Rights and the open discussion we are having today, if you think that all the options for the future of Iraq are being discussed as openly and in as much detail and pragmatism and idealism as they deserve to be discussed? Thank you.

COHEN: Most of what I know about Iraq is from two sources: what I read in the newspapers, and the e-mails I get from friends and former students and now periodically my son—but he's just an angry second lieutenant, so what the heck does he know—who are over there. I get occasional windows into the policy world, but I'm very much aware that they are only windows, they're glimpses, they're nothing more than that. I think it's in the nature of any government, any administration, in very short order to feel that you're in the bunker, that people are taking completely unfair shots at you, that you're surrounded by enemies. And we're just talking about the people across the river. Forget the Chinese and jihadis and [Abu Musab] al-Zarkawi and all the rest. You're under the tremendous pressure of responsibility that people have when they have a sense that they're close to great events, and particularly when they know that people's lives are quite literally at stake. I think the natural tendency in all administrations as a result of that is, over time, for the sense of reality to diminish. There are all kinds of psychological mechanisms, and as a kind of a pained external observer, I'm interested in them. One thing is, you keep on saying some things in public. I think people find it much harder to be two-faced than we often think. And it's much harder for them to say one thing in public and then to turn around and have a completely candid discussion that is utterly and totally the other way internally. Maybe there are some people who do that, but I actually think that's pretty rare. So you begin to believe the things that you say—and in politics you can't say the things you believe. That's irresponsible. People like academics get to do that. Responsible people can't do that. That said, I don't think the administration now is delusional about what's going on in Iraq. But I think they find themselves in a situation where, in part, they're the prisoner of decisions that were made very early on or decisions that weren't made very early on, and in particular of failures in the initial planning and in the initial phase of occupation. And we will never get that year or eighteen months back. And I guess if you were to ask me what my bottom line is, I think Iraq was always bound to be very tough, but I don't think it had to be nearly as tough as we have allowed it to be. Yes?

AUDIENCE - PETER J. SHARFMAN: Peter Sharfman. Would you talk a little bit about the conflicting schools of thought on the extent to which the United States ought to pay attention to other countries' views as we formulate our own policies?

COHEN: Again, I think there are a few die-hard, real unilateralists out there, but they're kind of limited in number because certainly, as you just begin looking at the practicalities of moving planes and people and ships and so on, it turns out you need bases, you need overflight rights. And, more broadly, I think people want to have the reassurance of having allies. So even this supposedly very unilateral administration is clinging for dear life to the Salvadoran contingent and the Lithuanians and all the others in Iraq. And it's interesting, one of the things they're getting criticized for is being excessively multilateral when it comes to North Korea, as opposed to being more unilateral. So I think all administrations sooner or later realize that you need allies. There are two qualifications, though, I would say to that. First, in this tremendously networked age of ours, it's much easier than it ever was in the past for a presidential speech or even an offhand remark at a press conference to rocket around the world, and for people to get impressions of who our leaders are and to form sometimes very negative impressions very, very fast. If you're careless with the words you use, there can be repercussions in terms of how you're viewed, which take a long while to walk back. The second thing is that more narrowly, if you think particularly about American relations with Europe, the real part of what has happened—not just in this administration, but in the previous administration and I think its succeeding administrations—is they are finding that although there are some areas where you can work very closely and productively with the Europeans, when it comes to the use of power and to confronting hard things, whether it's a nuclear Iran or the need to chase down the Taliban in Afghanistan, there is not much they can do, or not much that they're willing to do. And what's in some ways more significant than the sort of overt comments and speeches and so on—what I detect in a broader foreign policy establishment, Democrats as well as Republicans and Independents like myself—is just kind of, I wouldn't say disgust, but a sort of dismissiveness about the Europeans. That's not what one sees about people dealing with the Indians and the Japanese. And sometimes what we've done is, we've talked about relations with allies as if the only allies in the world are the Europeans. And for the future, our relationships with India and Japan in particular and with smaller countries like Australia or Singapore are going to loom as large and, in fact, larger than the relationship with Europe. And there we have a very different style. The last thing I'll say on this topic is just as an observation about the administration. I think, although they would never say this, they looked at the first term and said, we don't want to do this again, and so the first foreign policy things that the administration did in the second term were visits to Europe, lots of friendly talk, extending themselves in a variety of ways, and that smoothed things over on the surface. But most of it's superficial. And that has something to do with the United States, but it has a lot to do with Europe.

AUDIENCE - RANDALL FOFI: Randy Fofi, Corps of Engineers. You mentioned in your talk that going back to "Fortress America" isn't really an option. But what is the downside of taking the model of Notre Dame, becoming a major independent?

COHEN: I'm sorry. Could you repeat that.

FOFI: Going the way of Notre Dame to become a major independent, to take an observer status in the UN, an observer status in NATO, to take a step back to force the European Union, to force the Chinese, to force the Russians to play a larger role in the world, because right now they sit back and say, why should we do anything? The Americans will take care of it. But not completely sign out of the international scene. Like Notre Dame—everybody has to come to Notre Dame to get the big audience, to get the big payoff. People know who America is. People would still have to come to us. But as long as we play the role we play today, and as mentioned in your last question, Europe will continue to depend on America to take on the hard problems and won't make the hard decisions.

COHEN: I think there will always be a temptation for some Americans. I think at the end of the day, it's a prescription for disaster for us to try to withdraw from the world, and it won't work. We have been engaged in the world's affairs, not since World War II—that's part of the way in which we've mistaught our history—but going back to the colonial period. You know, World War I and World War II were not the first world wars. The first world wars that really happened were in the 18th century. And you know what? The United States or the American colonies were deeply enmeshed in every single one of those wars: the Seven Years War and the wars of the French Revolution and Empire. We are part of that wide world. And not to be sly about it, but I'd say part of the lesson of September 11th is, if you're not prepared to go visit those places, those places will come to visit you. And that's what happened. One way to understand September 11th is, we pursued a policy of neglect. Where did the hijackers come from? They came from our allies. Were those places where we had been beating up on them to change the kinds of regime? No, we were perfectly happy with the House of Saud being what the House of Saud is, and with the Egyptian government being what the Egyptian government is. It was very much a hands-off relationship. And it brought us what it brought us. Yes?

AUDIENCE - LARRY WOOD: Larry Wood, headquarters, DA, G-3. If, it is a fact, as you've kind of stated as a start point for many of your remarks tonight, that in the world in which we live today, the threat is dramatically different than it was during the Eisenhower presidency, the role of the military must change and adapt. There's got to be a new paradigm. Limited resources, all the constraints, a threat that's not clearly defined, highly adaptive, as we see every day. How do you perceive the role of the military in the future?

COHEN: Well, I guess the first thing I would say is, some of the challenges are quite new. Some of them are not new at all. Thinking strategically about it, there are two big issues that are going to be on our plate for the next three or four decades. One is the "global war on terror"—I don't like the term, but I'll use that as shorthand. And the other is the rise of China. The rise of China is a very traditional kind of great-power issue to be managed, hopefully not to go to violence, but we'd be foolish to think that there isn't potential for that. Either the good news or the bad news, from the Army's point of view, is that the Army is not going to play a very large role in that. It has some role, but less of a role than, say, it did during the Cold War. The other conflict is this much more elusive one, and I think it's fair to say that, particularly in the case of the Army, what we're going to be looking at is an Army that's going to be doing more of these messy, irregular, unconventional wars. I guess what that suggests to me is —I'll go back to Dwight D. Eisenhower—we really need some Soldier scholars, a few. We need some Soldier statesmen, a few. But above all, what we need is thoughtful warriors, because the truth is nobody can anticipate everything that we're going to need. And what's most important is, how do all the services prepare their leaders to adapt to a world that's going to be very, very fluid, perhaps more fluid than any of the international systems that we've lived in in the past? Because the truth is that nobody can really anticipate exactly what the world's going to look like ten, fifteen, twenty years out. And the critical question is, how good are we at adapting? Yes, ma'am? They're about to bring you a mic, I think.

AUDIENCE - CAMILLE CAESAR: Hi. Camille Caesar. Three things quickly. First thing is, God bless your son and may the wind stay at his back. Second thing is, I have to confess that twenty-something years ago, as a Harvard undergraduate, I never took your class because everyone said you were a neocon, so I feel so chagrined now, learning that I was ever so terribly mistaken and probably missed out. So thanks for your remarks tonight. The third thing is my question finally, and that is, and what about China?

COHEN: Well, first, thanks for the thoughts about my son, the irritable second lieutenant. Thanks—I didn't even know neocons existed twenty-seven years ago, and I will not thank you for giving things that would suggest my age to this group. What about China? China is clearly a different kind of problem for us than the Soviet Union was. It's not an ideological threat, clearly. It's a rising power with its own particular history of grievances, with its own objectives, and we are already bumping into each other throughout East Asia. What's different is that they are economically dynamic, and everybody looks at them and wants to do business with them. And there's also a sense that they're kind of the coming force that's out there. Now it's also possible that they may be domestically more troubled than we currently think. That would be one thought that I would put out there. What troubles me is, the Chinese have in the past made large miscalculations. I mean, miscalculation is part of what international politics is all about. And I can imagine us getting into a shooting war with them. I don't think it's likely, but I certainly think it's a possibility. And even if we don't, there will be a strategic relationship that will not be a friendly one, I think, throughout much of Asia. And, by the way, an important point to remember is, we are not the only ones who have a say in this. If you talk to the Japanese about the Chinese military, or if you talk to the Indian military about the Chinese military, or if you have offline conversations with some Indonesians and others, they're thinking about this too. Asia is a world in which, in many respects, old-fashioned power politics are alive and well. Sir?

AUDIENCE - TIMOTHY REESE: Tim Reese from the Combined Arms Center at Fort Leavenworth. Could you comment on any dangers that you perceive about using the Army as a primary instrument of American foreign policy, and even now, after the hurricanes, as the primary instrument of domestic emergency response.

COHEN: There is an argument out there—which I think I have more sympathy with than I used to—that there can be this tendency to turn to the military too readily. My friend, with whom I often disagree, Andy Bacevitch [Andrew J. Bacevitch], has written a couple of books on this subject, arguing that it's really militarized American foreign policy. I think that goes way too far. I also think that when it comes down to it, political leaders are, in fact, quite reluctant to put American Soldiers in harm's way. I can't think of any political leader who's cavalier about that. But, we are operating in a violent world where all American leaders after George Bush are going to have this sense that if they miss something, something really awful could happen in an American city. And believing that in their gut, as opposed to their head, means that there will be a predisposition to—where there's a calculus, as there always is, there's probably going to be more of an instinct to use force rather than not use force, and that's because of a change in the viscera, not in the cerebrum. In terms of disaster relief, I think there is no one else but the United States Army—ably assisted by the Navy, Air Force, Marine Corps, and Coast Guard—to deal with that scale of disaster relief. I don't see how you're going to turn FEMA [Federal Emergency Management Agency] into an outfit that can really do the things on the scale that need to be done. And I think one of the sad things about Katrina—but it's worth something we've got to take onboard—was the complete breakdown in law and order. And there's not going to be any substitute for the National Guard or even active duty forces in coping with that. So I think that the United States Army does accept that that's part of its mission, and it's going to have to accept that part of its mission is going to be responding to major catastrophes in American cities. And the only question is whether you do a really good job at it or a less good job at it. I think we have time for one more. Yes, ma'am?

AUDIENCE - KATE TURNER: Kate Turner. I'm a graduate student at SAIS [School of Advanced International Studies] and I hope to take your course next fall, if I can get into it.

COHEN: Forget the neocon stuff. The real problem is my grading standards.

TURNER: I've heard about that, too. But he does give as entertaining lectures as he has tonight. My question is that your talk somewhat aligns state interests with realists, and the idea of world government, for want of a better term, with idealists. And in light of the fact of an increasing integration and interdependence in our world, which you explicitly state in your talk, do you see a point at which realism will begin to engage in a different reality on the ground and say, we do need more, stronger international structures? And what do you think that would look like?

COHEN: Well, between you and me, some of my academic colleagues—not at SAIS, but elsewhere—are hopeless on this point. They're in the grips of a belief about how the world works, which is driven by the assumption that it's just states. And that's clearly not true. There's a reason why I tell all my students to go take courses on international law, because it's for real. And the military knows that, I think, more than anybody else, because you have JAGs [judge advocates general] all over you telling you what you can and can't do. And I'm sure you appreciate everything they have to tell you. But I think the realists—people of that predisposition—do in fact have to make some accommodations. And they tend not to see change all that much. If people are dismissive of the UN, they'll just stay dismissive of the UN until their dying days. On the other hand, the very basic facts, I think, remain. And, for me actually, the most sobering thing has been watching our efforts to get Europeans, who at least on paper have been completely behind us on Afghanistan, to really engage in counterinsurgency operations against the Taliban. That's NATO, and you know what a wonderful alliance NATO has been, and absolutely you know, when push really comes to shove—that is to say, sending people into harm's way—not really. Not really. So I think there's a kind of a residual truth there. Part of what I'm arguing against is the idea that there are predetermined trends in how the world is going to go. And I'll end with this. I have a colleague for whom I have enormous admiration, Francis Fukayama, who wrote this wonderful article, "The End of History." The title makes it sound silly, but basically, he was making the argument that there is really sort of one direction in which history is going. And I fundamentally don't believe that. I fundamentally believe the future is indeterminate. It can go in either direction. And I can imagine my children inheriting a world in which you have very strong international institutions and regimes and in which many countries have given away a lot of their sovereignty and it's maybe a peaceful sort of place. I can imagine a world where people have tried that, and we've got anarchy and disaster and cities being blown up. I can imagine a number of different possible worlds. And let me just conclude with that. I think part of—again, going back to Eisenhower—what it means to be thoughtful, whether you're a warrior or not, is having enough imagination to realize that there are multiple possibilities out there, and a lot of what that world will be depends on what folks like you do. Thank you very much.

DAYTON: You know, Eliot, as I sit here and listen to you, I'm always impressed at what a marvelous thing it is that this country can generate scholars and thinkers like you, and how equally marvelous it is that an organization like the Department of the Army would invite you in our midst to share these thoughts. Today we have focused pretty much on where we are and what we have in the world. Tomorrow we're going to shift gears a little bit, and we're going to focus on what should be or what we think should be. Tonight you have given us a tremendous bridge to get to that point, and I want to thank you very much. And if you join me once more in thanking Dr. Cohen.

Okay, folks, this is kind of it for this evening. We're going to start tomorrow at 8:20 a.m. Our first speaker, for those of you who do not know him, is Ambassador Carlos Pascual, who is the State Department's—and you could say the nation's—director for Stability and Reconstruction Operations. And this is indeed a futuristic thing. We'll talk tomorrow about intelligence. We'll talk tomorrow about proliferation and terrorism. And we'll finish the day with Congressman Ike Skelton talking to us about his vision of the future in building a national security cadre for the future. So if you can join us tomorrow, I encourage you to do so. I think we had a pretty good day on day one. Mr. Secretary and Mr. Vice, we appreciate you being here tonight. And Dr. Cohen, again, thank you for kicking us off for a good day tomorrow. And, folks, it starts at 8:20. So thank you very much.

MORNING ADDRESS

STABILITY AND RECONSTRUCTION CHALLENGES

Ambassador Carlos Pascual, Coordinator, Office of Reconstruction and
Stabilization, Department of State
Introduction by: Thomas Lynch, Minister-Counselor, U.S. Foreign
Service, and Political Advisor to the Chief of Staff of the Army

Summary

Ambassador Carlos Pascual

- The nature of security and of the foreign policy challenges we face have completely changed since the end of the twentieth century. The terminology and practical preoccupations of the Cold War era have given way to concerns about weak and failed states, particularly those states emerging from conflict. Through the experiences of the 1990s, we came to learn that unless peace is sustainable, there is no effective military exit strategy.

- We have had to take into account certain operational realities. We are equipped to handle just two or three significant postconflict enterprises at any given time, and these endeavors are likely to last at least five to ten years. History teaches that at least 50 percent of those countries emerging from conflict relapse within the first five years.

- The previously mentioned changing security environment, together with the operational realities of supporting the conflict transformation process, form the context within which the Office of the Coordinator for Reconstruction and Stabilization (S/CRS) was created and located in the U.S. Department of State in April 2004. The aim of establishing this office is to institutionalize and develop the U.S. capacity to understand and sustain over time the lessons that we have learned in reconstruction. "We must stress the importance of asking early on the questions of what is going to be necessary to put a state on a path of a sustained and marketable economy." Without this, we will continue to make mistakes in the short term, and these mistakes are extremely hard to correct.

- In postconflict reconstruction, joint operations are essential. Civilians and the military must work together to devise the most efficient and effective assistance that they can provide. So far, mechanisms have been created to link early-warning capabilities with the military and regional organizations working on the ground to garner early success.

- The challenge that the United States faces today is "moving from developing policies of conflict prevention [to] actually moving forward into implementing them."

- It is important to recognize that conflict prevention is "the hardest thing for us to do." Through our past experiences in postconflict settings, we have learned that investing in the local economies, ensuring that adequate health care is available, and establishing an education system are the areas that are essential for a failed or weak state to make the leap to a successful and functioning one.

- Local credibility and local ownership of the conflict transformation process are critical to its success. We cannot simply throw resources at these regions without working with local authorities and properly implementing these resources. We must "move conflict prevention from a simple process to a mainstream policy."

- There are four concurrent phases of conflict transformation: (1) stabilization (beginning the political process of transferring ownership), (2) dealing with the root causes of conflict, (3) creating a supply side of governance (through establishing the basic laws and institutions of a market economy), and (4) addressing the demand side of politics (nurturing civil society so as to hold governments accountable).

- There is a growing body of lessons learned that should be incorporated into our approach to conflict transformation. First, it takes time to put countries on a path to sustainable peace. Second, it is necessary not only to employ a variety of tools for the transformation process, but also to know (as in the case of food aid) when to apply and when to cease applying them. Third, outsiders can play a catalytic role at the beginning, but if the society does not have the capacity to carry out basic functions of security and run its economy, peace cannot be sustained. Fourth, it takes time for local leaders to develop consensus and capacity to achieve the kind of changes they want for themselves. Paradoxically, the early stage is when it is easiest for external actors to mobilize and deliver resources to support the process.

- The S/CRS is working to develop ten tools that can strengthen the U.S. capacity to help prevent and resolve conflicts: (1) an early-warning system (a management tool produced every six months by the National Intelligence Council that identifies at-risk countries); (2) a common planning framework (a planning tool, consisting of a common vocabulary and common doctrine that could then be injected into training programs); (3) agreement in principle to dispatch civilian interagency teams embedded with combatant commands; (4) advance civilian teams (or ACTs, an active response corps with diplomatic skills married to technical capabilities, able to deploy quickly); (5) new interagency mechanisms to guide Washington management; (6) development, preparation, and pre-positioning of technical capabilities; (7) a complement of specialists and contractors on retainer, along with a database of precompeted contracts, to deliver assistance; (8) improved coordination of international responses by engaging the United Nations and bilateral partners, which are, themselves, trying to develop stronger interoperability; (9) a common agenda across key bodies (to help assess lessons that can be extracted from postconflict experiences); and (10) development of a conflict response fund of about $100 million (sufficient resources to plug in up front to target a particular sector, while additional resources are sought to support the full range of needs).

• Two decades ago, we would have sympathized with societies in conflict, but we would not have intervened. Nor would we have tried to reconstruct these societies. At the time, tasks such as these were not perceived to be in our national interest. Now we have seen that even the poorest countries in the world can be a threat to our national security. "We have an opportunity to make these societies more peaceful, and that would be better for them as well as better for us."

Question-and-Answer Period

• Regarding possible similarities between this thinking and that of Hernando de Soto, we must work not just at the strategic level, but also at the tactical level. De Soto appropriately targets business ownership and other aspects. An "essential task framework" in the economic sector would include tackling the kinds of problems identified by de Soto.

• Is Albania a failed state, or perhaps on the brink of state failure? The S/CRS is not working on Albania today. However, it is important to note that many countries merit attention in terms of conflict prevention or transitioning. A key challenge in the case of Albania and many other countries is establishing the rule of law. In terms of U.S. response capacity, S/CRS must work to ensure that conflict prevention becomes a mainstream part of the policy process.

• What synergy is there, or might there be, between S/CRS and the Federal Emergency Management Agency (FEMA)? While the two offices do not work hand in hand, their respective officials do consult each other. One of the lessons learned from this dialogue is that to operate effectively, we must be able to act with a national response team.

Analysis

Ambassador Carlos Pascual's remarks on the American response to state failure and postconflict instability are noteworthy, as they underscore a substantial philosophical shift among many within the American strategy and policy elite. Since the attacks of 9/11, national security decision makers have become acutely interested in the authoritative, responsible control of states and their people. Indeed, state weakness and failure represent key examples of the "irregular challenges" outlined in the 2005 National Defense Strategy.

The near-complete collapse of the Iraqi state in the aftermath of the American-led invasion is instructive. Indeed, the complex, state-building enterprise in Iraq is likely emblematic of the types of challenges that will dominate the security agenda of American policymakers for the foreseeable future. Iraq's precipitous collapse indicates that authoritative control of any number of strategically significant states may, in fact, be more fragile than many believe. Thus, the United States and its partners must anticipate and prevent catastrophic state failure while, at the same time, preparing to rapidly establish conditions necessary to a self-sustaining recovery should collapse occur.

Pascual's key focus areas—among them, early warning, conflict prevention, and durable conflict resolution—represent essential components of an integrated response to state weakness and failure. Yet, a more thorough strategic assessment of the challenge leads to a recognition that some instances of weakness and failure matter more. Pascual avoided this point, failing to consider, in any meaningful way, the idea of calculated strategic prioritization.

While the failure of any state is tragic, the failure of some specific states could promise strategic catastrophes. Distinguishing between the two and accounting for their differences in strategy formulation and contingency planning is now more critical than ever. Crises of state weakness and failure presenting obvious, compelling national and international security challenges must necessarily trump crises that entail great human costs but that are of limited strategic significance to the United States.

If American strategists are to account properly for those prospective incidents of weakness and failure of real strategic importance, a number of key issues must be addressed. The most urgent involves the deliberate identification of vulnerable states or types of states that matter most, as these also will present the United States with its most complicated and resource-intensive state-building challenges.

A number of prospective instances of state weakness and failure are unmistakably important. Further, deliberate "regime change" should always be expected to precipitate state collapse. Wise counsel would recognize that unsuccessful state building could be as disastrous as inaction. Therefore, detailed early planning should emphasize the establishment of minimum essential conditions at the expense of lower probability, but likely more ideal, outcomes. Finally, extended commitment in one theater could prevent an American response to even more compelling requirements for intervention elsewhere. Thus, detailed risk assessment and cost-benefit analysis are key preconditions to effective crisis decision making.

Ambassador Pascual's remarks outlined important first steps in a new, more sophisticated view of conflict and conflict resolution. The prospective dissolution of responsible state authority in nations of enormous strategic significance threatens enduring American interests fundamentally. Pascual rightly recognized this, arguing implicitly that a national security apparatus focused exclusively on countering irresponsible state behavior is no longer sufficient.

Transcript

MAJOR GENERAL KEITH DAYTON: Hi, folks. I see we are still kind of getting a quorum here, but we are going to go ahead and get started. Just kind of a recap. You all know what we did yesterday, if you were here. I think we had some pretty good discussions. Today, we are going to lead off with Ambassador Carlos Pascual, and he will be introduced appropriately in just a second. We will follow that with a panel on intelligence operations. We will follow that with a panel during the lunch hour. This will actually be where you will have lunch and the panel talks at the same time. We will follow that with a panel on proliferation and terrorism this afternoon, to be finished off with Congressman Ike Skelton, as he kind of gives his vision of where we ought to be going in the future as far as building a security cadre. He has some pretty strong ideas and that ought to be very interesting.

As we get started this morning, I am going to introduce the introducer, who is Mr. Tom Lynch. Tom Lynch is what we call the political advisor to the chief of staff of the Army. Tom carries the rank of minister-counselor within the Foreign Service, and he has done a variety of works with the military over his career, most recently with the Combined Forces Command in Afghanistan. Thomas worked with Joint Forces Command. He has worked with NATO, and he has worked with the Stabilization Force in Bosnia. You will not find a more prescient guy who understands things, or how they work throughout the interagency, and how the State Department's influence can permeate what we do. If you have a chance to talk to Tom Lynch afterwards, I guarantee you any discussion with him is time well spent. And I go back with Tom, back when he was the counsel general in St. Petersburg, Russia, where he was one of our foremost specialists in Russia. Anyway, with no further ado, let me introduce to you Mr. Tom Lynch.

THOMAS LYNCH: Good morning. It is early and my ears are burning already. Thank you, Keith. That was very gracious. I am just here this morning to spare Ambassador Carlos Pascual from having to talk about himself. I have known him for about a dozen years now. I was frankly elated when I was in Kabul fifteen months ago and I heard that he had agreed to take on the new job of coordinator for the Office of Reconstruction and Stabilization. My reaction was "right person for a very tough and very necessary assignment." I had known him over the years in a series of situations where he was a force with energy, who represented clarity and organization—and this was a series of situations where there were people and an environment, or a set of them, that were not given to clarity and order. This was when he was working with assistance to the newly independent states, when he was in the National Security Council as director for Eurasian Affairs, and when he was our ambassador in Kiev. He came out of the AID [U.S. Agency for International Development] world and I should say, particularly to the military in the audience, that this says something to me. This is different from the State Department, perhaps in the way that the Marines are different from the Navy, but this is a different and special culture, which Ambassador Pascual honed in a lot of tough places, like Sudan and Mozambique and South Africa.

So I would like to say a couple of words about reconstruction and stabilization, our topic for the next hour. This is all basically about two things. There is an "us" and there is a "them." The "us" is the "we" who would do the reconstructing and stabilizing, and the "them" would be the objects of attention who would have interaction with us. "Us" is something with infinitely variable geometry. It is the U.S. government, the U.S. government including the military, NGOs, regional organizations, international organizations, and so on. But I would just like to say, because this is a diverse audience today, that if we tend to hear a lot and talk a lot in the next hour about "us," and if it seems to be a bit U.S.-government centric, this is not out

Thomas Lynch

of a sense of unilateralism or egotism or anything like that. It is, rather, a sense that we have not been very good at doing stability operations and reconstruction over the past dozen years. And Ambassador Pascual's office is an important undertaking, aimed at putting our house in order, at finding a better way to do things, getting away from extemporizing, failing to learn lessons from one endeavor to the other, and seemingly always to go to the U.S. military as a default capability—which is a very expensive one and not always the most effective one.

Before handing over, I want to put out sort of three questions for all of you. In Washington, the difference is, this is about civilians and military. The differences in Washington are very distinct. There are people in uniform and people not in uniform. There are civilian agencies of the government and there is DoD. When you are at the sort of cutting edge in Afghanistan or the Balkans or wherever, it is all a bit more blurred, and I think we need to reflect on this disparity of a clear distinction in Washington and a bit more blurred situation in the field. How do we put the two closer together in Washington? About the EU and sovereignty. Yesterday, some of our speakers talked about the EU nations' success in managing limits to their national sovereignty in order to pool sovereignty and get the job done. Question: can the U.S. government manage to do that among its competing sovereign entities? All of this is going to take time and money and congressional support, and these are scarce and perhaps elusive commodities. So what are we going to do in the meantime, in the near term, as we confront the problem with stability operations and reconstruction, when we do not yet have new structures in place? Ambassador Pascual.

AMBASSADOR CARLOS PASCU-
AL: Tom, thank you very much for that
introduction, both the personal introduction and for laying out the issues so
well, because what you really highlight
is the importance of the challenges that
we face today and the nature of the
difficulty of some of those challenges.
I want to thank General Schoomaker
for the invitation to participate today
and, in particular, the support that
we have gotten from the U.S. Army in
developing these capabilities in serving
as a counterpart, especially at looking
at issues of transitional security. In
particular we have gotten special help
from the [U.S. Army] Peacekeeping and
Stability Operations Institute at Carlisle.
Just a tremendous organization, which
is headed up by Colonel John Agoglia,
who has been a tremendous partner to

Carlos Pascual

us. General Dayton, thank you for the opportunity to participate today and for
the partnership that you have had with us as a principal counterpart on the Army
staff. And mostly, let me thank the military and the civilians who are in this audience, many of whom have risked their lives to be able to help others achieve a
sustainable peace.

We have seen so much of those efforts recently in Iraq and Afghanistan, but it
is not just Iraq and Afghanistan if we look over the history of the last ten to fifteen
years. It has also been Haiti, Somalia, Kosovo, and Bosnia, and then other places
where the U.S. has not been as directly involved, such as East Timor. It has become
indicative of the nature of the foreign policy and security challenges that we face
today. And indeed, what I would suggest is that today, the nature of the security
and foreign policy challenges that we face have completely changed from the last
half the twentieth century.

If we think of that period of time in the very words and vocabulary that
we used on security issues—words like détente, containment, and balance of
power—our focus was on the relationship between power states and nation-states,
and how those nation-states interrelated with one another, and how the scrutiny
among nation-states as rational actors would avoid egregious behavior. And then
we had September 11th, and it would begin to underscore to us in a very powerful and tragic way, that weak and failed states, when there are voids of power in
the ability to direct the country, can be filled with forces such as terrorism and
organized crime and trafficking in people, which can create a direct threat to our
national security. Indeed, the most significant strike against the United States on

our territory was coordinated from one of the poorest countries in the world, and it forced us to recognize the danger of those voids in governance and the dangers of state failure. And it forced us to recognize that in fact, one of those areas that may have the greatest potential for state failure is immediately in the transition after conflict, when state systems have collapsed and new ones have not been put in place again. And over time, what we have to come to learn is that unless we deal with an effective transition to state governance capacity and to a sustainable peace, that we do not have an effective exit strategy for our military operations and our peacekeeping operations.

As these strategic realities have honed in on us, it has also forced us to take into account certain operational realities. In particular, we have to come to see that we need to be able to prepare ourselves to handle two or three significant stabilization and reconstruction operations around the world at any given time. We also need to think about these as operations that have to last at least five to ten years. If we look at the history of postconflict stabilization and reconstruction, 50 percent of countries that have been through conflict have lapsed back into conflict after five years, which sends a warning sign that if we are not prepared to be able to stay with this for the long haul, we will not achieve success. It is in this context that this Office for Reconstruction and Stabilization was created in the U.S. government and was specifically located in the State Department. The office was established after a meeting by National Security Council principals in April of 2004. We had an opportunity to go back and present our strategy and rationale to the principals in December of 2004 and get their complete, unanimous endorsement to move ahead with the types of approaches that I'll outline for you today. The president underscored the importance of this initiative in his budget request to the Congress in February of 2005, and then again in May of 2005 in a speech that he gave to the International Republican Institute, underscored the need to have this type of capability in order to address today's challenges of transformational diplomacy. And the mandate that we were given was to be able to lead, coordinate, and institutionalize—and I underscore the word "institutionalize"—U.S. government capabilities, so we are not just responding on an ad hoc basis, but we have the capacity to actually sustain over time the lessons that have been learned on stabilization and reconstruction and apply them into the future.

The mandate we have been given also calls for us to look at prevention and preparation for conflict, because if we do not work at the front end, we are not going to be able to do what is necessary to respond quickly to help stabilize and reconstruct societies that are in transition from conflict and civil strife. But just as important as this, we have stressed the importance of asking early on the questions about what is going to be necessary to put a country on a sustainable path toward peace, democracy, and a market economy. Because if we do not ask those long-term questions up front and do not have a clear understanding of how to help a country get onto that path, then we will make mistakes in the short term, and it becomes it much more difficult to correct course later on, after a country has been on a certain vector for a period of time. In a phrase, what I would say is that we have been given a mandate to help establish the capacity for joint operations in stabilization and reconstruction, and I think that the analogy to the role the joint staff plays generally is appropriate and useful.

We are a coordinating entity, and our job is to help ensure that individual agencies such as the State Department, USAID, Treasury, the Department of Justice, the Department of Defense, and the different elements of the Department of Defense, have the capacity to work together in an interoperable way to achieve a unified strategy within a given theatre. And just as within the military, having joint operations does not mean that you do not need an Army, a Navy, an Air Force, and a Marines. You absolutely need every single one of those capabilities, but they have to operate together in a unified way within a given theatre. So we have to create a similar capability within the civilian world, and between the civilian world and the military world, on stabilization and reconstruction.

A few words on where the office stands right now. Even though we are located in the State Department, we are an interagency office that currently has over fifty staff from the State Department, AID, the Office of the Secretary of Defense, the Joint Staff, the Army Corps of Engineers, Joint Forces Command, the Army, the CIA, Treasury, the Department of Justice, and the Department of Labor. I think it is one of the most unique places to work in the U.S. government. It actually has this range of capabilities embedded within it, strengthening the skills that we have to apply to any given problem, and also strengthening our ability to reach back to individual agencies and get their support. Thus far, I think we have been able to create and introduce more effective coordinating mechanisms for stabilization and reconstruction policies. We have been able to work on creating mechanisms for early warning and linking early warning to early response. We have had considerable success in working on developing international partners with the UN, the EU, individual countries such as the UK, Canada, France, Germany, the Nordic countries, and we are working to strengthen relationships with regional organizations such as the African Union. And, of course, we have made, I think, significant strides in building a strong partnership with our military counterparts. In particular, I want to thank Joint Forces Command, especially when they were under the leadership of Admiral [Edmund P.] Giambastiani, Jr., for the tremendous support, material support that was provided by Joint Forces Command and intellectual leadership that they showed as we were launching our planning processes. I would say that to date, we have developed a strong capability as a Washington-based management body, and the challenge that we face today is to achieve or to get the resources that are necessary to be able to move from conflict prevention and developing the policies on conflict prevention, to actually implement the activities that are necessary to sustain it and to have the kind of strong response capability on the ground that is necessary to affect the dynamic of a conflict. And the key factor affecting that obviously will be the budget that we are able to obtain in the next six weeks or so from the U.S. Congress.

What I would like to do in my remaining time today is to spend some time first on some of the conceptual issues that affect the way that we think about prevention, and the transformation from conflict to a sustainable peace, and then some of the tools that we have put in place, or are in the process of putting in place, in order to be able to achieve that. Let me start with conflict prevention. When I first took this job and had my first discussion with Secretary Powell about the work that we needed to do, one of the things he underscored was, if you can ever prevent a conflict and avoid having to go in and clean up after a military operation, obviously that is preferable to the investment that has to be made [in engaging in conflict], particularly if there are lives that are going to be lost and the resources that have to be used. But what is also important to recognize is that conflict prevention is one of the most difficult things for us to do. It is important for us to understand, as well, that there is a difference between prevention in a long-term sense and prevention when you have two parties that are ready to go to war. In the long term, what we have come to recognize is that investments in stronger economies, in the private sector, in a more prosperous society, in a more open political system, in health care, and in education, that these are the kinds of things that will help a society prosper and can serve as a preventive force against conflict. But in order to achieve in those areas, we have learned that what is necessary is to have local strategies, local leadership, local ownership, and local credibility of the approach. And when two parties are about to go to war, that is exactly what is absent, making it all the more difficult to achieve success in that environment. What that begins to tell us is that simply dumping resources in that environment is not going to be successful if we do not understand how to target those resources, whether they be diplomatic or financial, and use them effectively to promote change. What we have also seen over time is that we understand a great deal about what some of the situational drivers are that might promote conflict, but we do not always know what some of the triggers might be. And so in a sense, what we might be able to do is to understand when there are a lot of leaves on the ground in the forest in the fall, but we do not necessarily know who is going to throw that match, which at times makes it very difficult to move from early warning to early response.

What has also made conflict prevention difficult and a challenge is the risk of failure. If you think about what is involved, you have two parties with constituencies behind them, who generally want to go to war, and an outside party comes in and says, you know, you should rethink that and perhaps actually look at a peaceful way to resolve your differences. They are not going to do that simply on the basis of personality. They are going to do it if they think that a country and an organization and the international system is behind it, and that resources can be mobilized, and that they can actually have a better life as a result of a compromise. And the only way that you do that is to actually commit your countries and your organizations to this process of conflict resolution, which indeed involves risk and which we have sometimes had a difficult time bearing. And so it requires us to rethink the nature of the risk of failure and conflict prevention.

I think, in order to be able to achieve these things, one of the things that we are going to have to do is to be able to move conflict prevention from a simple crisis response of moving in when there is a critical situation on the ground, to a mainstream part of our policy. I will come back to that in a couple of minutes and discuss how we are seeking to do that. As much as we do to try to prevent conflict, what we have also learned over time is that conflicts will occur, and it is important for us to understand the nature of the transition from conflict to sustainable peace if we are going to be able to respond to it effectively and help put countries on a path toward sustainable peace. Now, in the military, a great deal of attention has been given to focusing on Phase IV. And one of the things that I would hope to encourage you to think about is to actually wipe Phase IV out of your vocabulary or think about it completely differently. For one reason, there is usually a tremendous amount of ambiguity of when you end military operations and move into a situation of postconflict operations. What we have seen over time is that you generally have a mixture of the two. But in addition to that, the whole process of postconflict transformation or transformation to a sustainable peace, I would offer, in and of itself has to have a number of different phases. The hypothesis that I would put out to you is that there are four stages of postconflict transformation, and that these stages can actually proceed concurrently: some might move forward, some might move backward, but indeed, we have to move forward on all of these eventually if that peace is going to be sustainable.

The first of these is the one that we tend to hear about most, one of stabilization, which usually involves a focus of promoting order and peace and public safety, providing food, and needing basic services. It involves the beginning of a political transition process where the international community moves from being the principal doers to starting to think about how to transition that to local ownership and leadership. But simply doing stabilization, in and of itself, is not going to be sustainable; and simply doing that from the outside, as outsiders who are enablers or doers, is not going to be a successful operation. And hence, we need to think about a number of other pieces as well.

A second element is clearly the importance of dealing with some of the root causes of conflict, those elements of corruption or state failure, ethnic differences, or religious tension in a society that might have started the conflict to begin with. The irony that we have seen, however, is that as you start to tackle those very causes of conflict, that can be destabilizing in and of itself. And so we need to think about the kinds of safety nets that are necessary in order to help countries sustain those transitions. Think about a country like Iraq and the state economy that it inherited. If you started to tackle immediately the dismantlement of those state enterprises and the implications that would have for employment and unemployment, that, in and of itself, would be major destabilizing factor. Yet we know that if we cannot help Iraq move off of the economic dependence of those state entities, that it cannot be successful economically. And hence this dilemma, that at the very time that we are trying to promote stability, we have to tackle forces that, in and of themselves, can be destabilizing.

The third phase of transition to sustainable peace, I would offer, is the creation of the supply side of governance, the laws and the institutions of a market economy. Think of those things that we take for granted in our own economic and political systems: tax systems, banking systems, the ability of a government to collect revenue, of having a dependable budget, of having dependable regulatory policies, of having political parties, of parliament, the election of political leaders, of court systems that can actually implement the law in a civilian-controlled military and police force. In most of these countries, these have to be created from scratch. And if we put this into the context of what it means to promote order—and we think that we recognize that in many of these countries, they are coming from an authoritarian past—order was something that was imposed from the top and essentially pushed down to the society through force. What we are asking the societies to do is move to an environment where order is based on openness and competition and freedom, with laws that regulate the way that people interrelate with one another, and a court system to mediate the disputes, and a political system that is based on an election of leaders who are accountable to the population. That is not something that is just a change of laws that can be written overnight. It is a fundamental change in culture that will take time to be able to achieve and that will require local ownership of it, because it cannot be imposed from the outside.

And finally, I would offer that the fourth stage of this transition to sustainable peace is creating the demand side of politics: the development of a civil society, nongovernmental organizations, media that can hold leaders accountable, because if there are no checks and balances on those leaders outside of government, there is a tremendous risk of going back to the type of authoritarian roots that, in many cases, resulted in the creation of conflict to begin with.

Now, what are some of the lessons here? Very basic. First of all, it takes time to put a country on a path to sustainable peace. Often, elections have been seen as an endpoint. I would offer that in many cases, that is a mistake. Elections can be a benchmark for progress, but generally, they are not an endpoint that indicates, in and of themselves, that there is success. And if we do not make a commitment for the long term, the chances of a country relapsing into conflict are extraordinarily high. If we have these different stages of transition, it means that we need different tools for the stages, as appropriate. In some cases, we need to understand how to apply those different tools, and in some cases, we need to understand when we actually need to turn some of those tools off. And a good example of this is humanitarian aid. When do we actually stop that humanitarian assistance or food assistance because it runs a risk of destroying local agricultural markets and the development of an indigenous private sector? It is absolutely critical that from the outset, we begin thinking about the transition from outside leadership to local involvement and ownership. Outsiders can play a critical catalytic role at the beginning. We can help promote stability and order. But we have seen over time that if a society does not have the capacity for itself to define its future and implement that and carry out the basic functions of security and political process and run its economy, that an outsider cannot sustain that in a way that is successful over a period of time.

Finally, I just wanted to underscore the importance of thinking about absorptive capacity. It is a concept that sometimes seems technical but, in fact, is actually very practical and real. As you move from external leadership and outsiders doing to local involvement in ownership, what we tend to find is that there is a slowdown in the process of transition. It takes time for local actors to develop a consensus of how they want to move their country forward and change it. It takes time to develop the capacity for them to be able to move forward and achieve the kind of changes in their security and political and economic systems that they want to achieve for themselves. And usually, this is completely off schedule with the flow of resources that we have to apply to a process of transition. What we generally find is that early on in the process of change, we can actually mobilize resources because of an interest in the nature of the problem, and then we hit this wall where a society is beginning to actually decide for itself how it wants to transform itself, and there is a frustration that the resources do not actually flow. You start to move along and work with that society, and you get to a situation where, in fact, they are starting to achieve a consensus of how they want to move. They are starting to build the capacity, and what has happened? Those resources are generally moved to the next problem. And so, at that very critical time when you actually need the resources to be able to sustain change, we often do not have the money available that we need in order to support this process.

Based on this understanding of conflict prevention and postconflict transformation, we have begun the process of putting in place ten sets of tools that will help us respond more effectively to conflict. The first is an early warning system. We have begun working with the National Intelligence Council where every six months, they will produce for us, or for the interagency community, a list of countries that are at risk of instability. We bring that back to an interagency working group. We also bring it to the State Department, and the State Department will work it with the undersecretary for political affairs and the regional assistance secretaries. The purpose is not simply the early warning portion of this. There are a lot of early warning risks out there. But by having this as a management tool that we can use with the undersecretaries and with the assistant secretaries in the regional bureaus, we can review with them where there is a risk of instability and where there is a need for support, to undertake policy roundtables or gaming exercises, or look at conflict prevention programs that can be put in place in anticipation of a conflict to mitigate the chances that conflict might occur. It is a starting point to actually try to move from conflict prevention as simply a crisis action, set of activities, to conflict prevention as the mainstream part of our policy process.

Secondly, we have begun to put in place a common planning framework for the military and for the civilians for stabilization and reconstruction. The military is outstanding at planning, but generally planning for military operations and the immediate stability operations after that—not necessarily for transformation of the civilian types of forces that are necessary in a society in order to achieve sustainable peace. In the civilian world, USAID has had a culture of planning, but generally, the State Department and other agencies have not. And so what we have needed to do is to introduce a set of planning tools that will allow the military and civilians alike to have a common planning framework and a common vocabulary for the ways that we think about stabilization and reconstruction. We have now begun using this planning framework in Sudan and Haiti. We have been testing it for Cuba. We have been working with the military, which will issue it as an experimental pamphlet through Joint Forces Command to the regional combatant commanders so that it can be tested throughout the combatant commands. The intent of this is to build up the experience in both the civilian and the military worlds over the next year, so that we can then bring that back together and have a common doctrine for stabilization and reconstruction planning. That common doctrine can then be injected into training programs throughout the civilian and military worlds so that we have a common ability to plan and to act.

Once we have that stronger capacity to plan, it will strengthen the ability to undertake other types of operations, such as we indicate here in number three, which is an agreement in principle to deploy civilian stabilization and reconstruction teams to combatant commands when they have been asked to develop a war plan. And what it will give us the ability to do is actually have civilian interagency teams there, embedded with a combat and command, to work on stabilization and reconstruction planning from the outset. We just undertook the first such planning exercise with SOUTHCOM about two weeks ago, and I think we both found that we have tremendous skills that complement each other and we will be able to bring to bear on any given situation. We have been putting in place new mechanisms to strengthen coordination in Washington across the interagency, where we will create policy-coordinating-committee-level, or what we call assistant-secretary-level, policy groups, which will become the focal groups for coordinating policy recommendations to deputies and principals at the National Security Council on stabilization and reconstruction. And those groups, which we call country-reconstruction stabilization groups, will then have the responsibility for pushing the implementation of those decisions throughout the interagency system and reporting back to our deputies and principals on progress.

We have reached the agreement in principle, as well, for a very basic concept, which I think will have tremendous payoffs—the development of what we call "advanced civilian teams," which can embed with the military at a division or brigade level from the beginning of military operations. And the intent is to have civilians who can begin to work with the military from the outset on those things that are fundamental civilian functions: working with local ethnic groups and leaders to try to achieve a viable political situation in municipalities, looking at transitional security situations at a local level, of getting economic activity started again, of looking at when we can be able to pull in much bigger and broader interagency support teams and nongovernmental groups to rule out their operations on the ground. In the past, we have not had in the civilian world the capacity to be able to deploy like this with the military, and we are establishing that capacity for the first time.

In [slides] six and seven, what we have underscored is the importance of creating a stronger response capacity in a civilian world. Let me describe that division as follows. In [slide] six, what we are trying to get out is the importance of having a U.S. government capacity to exercise diplomatic and technical leadership on the ground. So we are creating advanced civilian teams or an active response corps of civilians who will be able to deploy up front and have a mix of political and economic and diplomatic security and administrative and communication skills that are linked together with technical capabilities, which we are seeking to develop with agencies such as USAID or the Department of Treasury or the Department of Justice. That way we can put on the ground those individuals who can provide the core diplomatic leadership, establish a diplomatic presence, and begin the development and design of programs that the U.S. government needs to be able to put on the ground to effect change. What we will try to get out in [slide] number seven is that beyond those U.S. government capabilities, there is a need for strong capabilities in the nongovernmental world—the private sector, think tanks, universities, individuals with specific skills—who need to be able to be tapped to actually implement these programs. Things like civilian police or police trainers or rule of law specialists, or economic development specialists, private sector development specialists, those who can work on transitional security or on political governance and transition. And so we are in the process of working with the interagency community to put together a database that will help us get access to precompeted contracts, which will allow us to move much more quickly when we need to deploy them on the ground. And we are also at early stages of doing a feasibility study of a civilian reserve corps that would be akin to a military reserve, that would allow us to tap directly for U.S. government service specialized skills such as civilian police or police trainers or civil administrators. This is going to take some time to develop. It is going to require legislative change to be put in place. But we feel that it is critical to actually have this mix so you will have individuals who can directly be pulled into the U.S. government and can be deployed more quickly, with advance training already done ahead of time.

It has been absolutely crucial for us to be able to think about development of these operations, not just as the U.S. government, but as part of the international community. And indeed, what we have seen is that if we want to see successful transformation to a sustainable peace, we need to do this with our international partners. So from the outset, we have been working with the UN and have been heavily engaged, as the UN has been, working to create a peacebuilding commission and a peacebuilding support office for greater coordination among its bodies, like the Department of Peacekeeping Operations and the Department of Political Affairs and UNDP, so that they have a much stronger interoperable capability out of New York. We have been working with the EU as they develop their civilian response mechanisms. What is interesting to see is that most of our bilateral partners have now begun to create similar capabilities as well, reflecting their similar understanding of the security challenges that we face today, where we have seen that we have to have a coordinated international capability to be able to anticipate conflict and respond to conflict if we are going to protect national security and promote a more stable global environment. We are building a capacity to capture lessons learned, so that over time, we are not simply reconstructing operations over and over again—and perhaps not only trying to learn from the past, but perhaps avoid repeating some of the mistakes of the past. We do not need to do that. What we need to be able to do is have an institutional memory that works across the interagency community. So a key challenge over the coming year will be to develop a common agenda across key bodies across the interagency community that will help us assess lessons on issues such as how have the provincial reconstruction teams worked in Afghanistan, or what are some of the lessons that we can extract and learn on NGO and military operations. As we have seen, some of the exercises that we have recently conducted, most particularly an exercise that was sponsored by the Naval Postgraduate School in Monterey, helped us learn a great deal of how the NGO community and the military can work together. Because in the end, we have a similar set of goals, which is the transformation of a society in building an indigenous capacity to address the needs of the people and a country.

Finally, in order to make all of this work, it is going to require resources. And one of the things that we have sought from the Congress is the development of a conflict response fund. This conflict response fund would be about $100 million. As most of us know, that is not enough to completely address a full conflict transformation, but what it would give us sufficient resources to do is to plug in an initial $30, $40, or $50 million up front to target a key sector. For example, the development of indigenous police forces while we are deploying international civilian police and rule of law experts would get that process of change on transitional security moving up front, and give us then a greater opportunity to work with the Congress and across the interagency community to find where we can actually obtain the greater set of resources that is necessary to support the full stabilization and reconstruction operation. In addition to that, the administration has requested of the Congress, particularly underscored in a joint letter that was sent by Secretary [Donald] Rumsfeld and Secretary [Condoleezza] Rice to the chairman of the Defense Authorization Committee and the ranking minority member, the authority to allow the Department of Defense to transfer up to $200 million to the State Department for stabilization and reconstruction operations in cases where they determine it is an absolute emergency. What it would actually allow us to do for the first time is operate in a way that utilizes the resources of the State Department and the Department of Defense to apply a common set of civilian transformational objectives that are, in the end, going to have a fundamental impact on the ability of the military to achieve its objectives and withdraw successfully from a conflict environment and achieve a sustainable peace.

I just want to take a moment to look at how we transfer these concepts into specific capabilities. A key element of this is how we apply them to country situations. There are three types of responses that we are dealing with on individual countries. One is where we work with the regional bureau in comanagement of a postconflict response. This is the most labor-intensive set of activities that we might undertake, and at any given time the maximum number of activities that we will be able to address are two to three conflict transformations at any given time. Right now, the two countries that we are focusing on are Sudan and Haiti. Secondly, there are prevention activities, as I described before, where we will be able to work on a consultancy basis with our partners in regional bureaus to focus on how they might be able to improve their capacity in advance to be able to mitigate the prospects for conflict. A couple of examples of this are with the Democratic Republic of Congo, where we worked together with the Africa Bureau in simulating what the upcoming elections might look like; what could go wrong immediately after the elections; and on the basis of that, asking ourselves, what would we do differently today in order to prepare for those situations. We have done a similar exercise in Nepal. We are beginning to work on a similar set of activities in Bangladesh. These are the kinds of gaming and strategizing activities that the military has regularly done in the past, but generally have not been a mainstream part of the civilian policy process. Thirdly, we will engage in contingency planning, either for specific country exercises or, in some cases, for specific sectoral challenges. One of the areas of contingency planning that we have been involved with is Cuba. At some point, there will be a transition after Fidel [Castro]. There is, I think, common international agreement that what we would like to see as an international community is a Cuba that is democratic and run by the Cuban people. So it is up to us to begin thinking now about how we would respond to that situation so that we can be as effective in mobilizing and helping to mobilize a strong international response that gives a voice to the Cuban people in promoting a democratic future.

In addition to that, we have been applying our capabilities, as I indicated earlier, to military coordination, international coordination, and development of civilian response mechanisms. At this point, the way that I would characterize it is that we have a much stronger planning capability in the U.S. government. We have been able to do this with personnel who have been taken, to some extent, on an ad hoc basis throughout the interagency community. But when it comes to the point of actually deploying overseas, we are still dealing with the same pool of people that we have had in the past. When it comes to dealing with resources that are necessary for those deployments and for conflict transformation, we are still working from a reallocation of existing resources, which inevitably means that it is a slow process. Hence, in the second and third stages that we are proposing here—the second being in fiscal year 2006, contingent upon appropriations that we might be able to get from the Congress, and then finally in 2007—what we are looking at is a stronger capability to actually have the capacity to deploy staff to the ground; to have resources for immediate conflict responses that can help; and have an impact on the conflict situation early on in the process of change, where you can really affect the dynamic of a situation on the ground. Now, often we have, unfortunately, tended to characterize these kinds of investments as spending money rather than saving money and, most important, saving lives. But let us look at this from this perspective: If we look at the budget request that the administration has on the Hill right now for fiscal year 2006, we have requested $124 million in foreign operations and state operations money, $100 million for a conflict response fund, $24 million for the planning and exercise and staff capacities in my office and a more effective rapid response capability, and then the $200 million transfer authority that has been requested for the Department of Defense. And if we just take the hypothesis that by having this capacity to be able to more effectively deploy skills and capabilities early on in a conflict, it would allow us to simply withdraw one division from Iraq one month early, it would save us $1.2 billion. If we would look at what it would save us if we can withdraw an international peacekeeping mission six months early, generally, it would be on a scale of $400 million to $500 million. So this is not just simply saving resources or spending resources; it is an investment of resources to save money, save lives, and address our national security.

Twenty-five years ago, we might have been in a situation where we would have said that we might have empathized with the people of a country if they were undergoing conflict, but that in some cases, it just simply was not in the interest of the Unites States to become engaged and involved. Indeed, we cannot become engaged and involved in every circumstance. But what we have also seen is that even the poorest countries in the world, if they become a base for terrorist operations and organized crime, can become a threat to our national security. We have an opportunity today to actually invest the resources that protect our security and make an investment in the transformation of societies that will make them more stable and peaceful, and that would, in the end, be better for them and a better investment for the United States as well.

Thank you for your attention and I would be happy to answer your questions. Yes, over here. I am going to need your help on waving your arms because this light is so bright that I can see about three or four faces in the audience, but most of you I cannot see.

AUDIENCE - CAPTAIN DAVID BUFFALOE: Sir, I am Captain David Buffaloe. I am a Joint Staff intern going to Georgetown right now. Last week, at Georgetown, General Zinni gave a speech, and he identified the need that it seems you have addressed, and that is, for the interagencies of the federal government to work, to become engaged not just at the strategic level, but also at the operational tactical level. It seems like you have brought a blueprint for making that happen. As a young infantry captain responsible for bringing peace to a region in Afghanistan, I thank you for your efforts. It would have been a big help back then. But my question, however, addresses one of our speakers from yesterday. Mr. de Soto gave a very interesting and compelling argument that we cannot establish peace or establish a lasting development or stability or capitalism or democracy in basically 80 percent of the world without three specific things, and what those are is establishing a legal system within a country of property ownership, of incorporating businesses, and establishing a personal identification system. And I was just wondering, sir, do you see within the planning of your organization when you tackle how to establish peace, development, and reconstruction in a country, do you see yourself addressing these three goals?

PASCUAL: First of all, let me just comment very quickly on General Zinni and thank him, as well, for some of the help that he gave us early on as we were developing these operations. He was very generous with his time, sitting through with us and brainstorming some of these capabilities that we were seeking to develop. So if some of this actually seems to respond to the kind of operational and tactical requirements that Zinni was laying out for you in your course, it is probably not just happenstance; it is very much as a result of some of the direct input that we got from him. On your comment on Hernando de Soto—who has played a revolutionary role in the international development community and thinking about some of the prerequisites of helping informal societies and communities actually become legal, and as a result of that, become more prosperous—I think he very appropriately targets a few key questions on establishing a legal framework for businesses to operate in, particularly for the creation of property ownership, incorporation of businesses, and giving individuals a sense that they are a part of society and therefore legitimate. I think those are very much key elements. If you think back to the four stages of transformation or transition from conflict to sustainable peace that I talked about earlier, one of those, I indicated, was developing the laws and the institutions of a market economy. I do not want to say that there are the same laws in the institutions for every society, but there are some basics that we have learned over time that are particularly necessary to address. We have tried to capture some of those basic issues in what we call an essential task framework. That framework is based on work that was started by CSIS and the Association of the U.S. Army (AUSA). We brought it back to an interagency community, and what we did was we looked at five different areas of transitional security: humanitarian and social issues, economic development, transitional justice, and infrastructure. And in those areas, we looked at what are some of the things that are critical to do up front and immediately, what is necessary to be able to transform or move from international leadership to local leadership, and then finally, what is necessary for a long-term sustainability. In the economic sections of that piece, what you will find is a checklist of some of the key questions that need to be asked or addressed in being able to move toward a sustainable economic transformation. Actually, the slides are not up yet, but the slides will be handed out, and at the end of them, you will find our website, which is www.crs.state.gov. And on that website, you will be able to pull down that essential task list. I mention it because I think you will find on that, not only those issues that are highlighted or underscored there, but a range of others. The final point that I want to make on this is, it goes back to the point on joint operations that I made earlier. There is no way that one organization in the U.S. government—my office right now with 50 plus people; eventually, we hope to be able to get to 80 people—can actually do all of those things in any given environment. It means that we do have to bring in the capabilities of the individual responsible agencies. In this case, the most appropriate agency would be USAID. The challenge is to bring that together in the context of one overall U.S. government planning strategy rather than ad hoc pieces that are undertaken by each individual agency. So what we are seeking to do exactly is raise these kinds of questions as part of our overall strategic approach—identify who has the lead responsibility, where the resources are going to come from—and be able to tie that back into our long-term goals, rather than set the long-term goal of trying to do every single piece of this ourselves. Because if we try to do that out of one central agency, then we will relearn the lessons of communist authoritarianism, and we will see that it simply fails because it is impossible to carry out. It does require individual capabilities of different agencies. Yes.

AUDIENCE - GEORGE SCHWAB, Ph.D.: George Schwab, National Committee on American Foreign Policy. I wonder whether you would consider Albania a failed state, a state in the process of failing, and what you are doing about it. Thank you.

PASCUAL: It is probably not useful for me to put a label on whether Albania is or is not a failed state, because I am sure that, given the magic of international communications right now, that would provoke a debate in Albania on what the U.S. government policy is and whether we think they are a failed state today, as opposed to keeping the debate focused on the specific policy issues that need to be addressed in Albania. My office is not working on Albania today. One can argue that there are a whole range of countries throughout the world that can merit attention, either for conflict prevention purposes or for addressing some of the transitional challenges that exist after a society has gone through a major transformation, and obviously, Albania has gone through a very significant transformation. In my previous job, when I worked as the coordinator for assistance to Europe and Eurasia, I was very actively involved in Albania. In fact, the last time I was there was in December of 2004. I would underscore two things. One is the importance of the rule of law, and in Albania, one of the very strong challenges today has been to move from a society that is extraordinarily laissez-faire to one that can apply that kind of entrepreneurship in a context of rules for society and a court system that is broadly respected and respects the rights of individuals. And if that kind of transformation can be made, it can actually be a tremendous platform for building on the entrepreneurship that exists in Albanian society. The second point that I would make is the importance of what I had mentioned earlier, which is to ensure that conflict prevention and conflict response activities, but in particular conflict prevention, become a mainstream part of the policy process. Because if you think about the Balkans, if you think about Africa, if you think about different parts of Latin America or Southeast Asia, there are a tremendous number of countries that are potentially at risk of instability. You can look at the websites of the International Crisis Group or Human Rights Watch or International Alert and come up with a list in a few seconds, right? And if it is dependent on one part of the U.S. government, one organization of the U.S. government, to stimulate attention to those countries that are potentially at risk, it is not going to work. What needs to happen over time is that we need to have strong sensitivity to these long-term transitional issues and prevention issues in the mainstream part of our policy process to ensure that we can address them effectively. And so what we are trying to do is to be a catalyst for that process. We cannot ensure out of one office that we undertake all of the kinds of preventive activities that are necessary around the world. But what we are beginning to do is to put in place a policy process that will focus attention on those places that potentially could be unstable or where potentially conflict could arise, so that our colleagues in the regional bureaus are giving them greater attention and thinking more creatively about the steps that they might be able to take. Yes, back here.

AUDIENCE - JEFFREY J. CLARKE: Is this working? Yes. Jeff Clark. I am a chief historian of the Army, but also for many years, I have been a civil affairs officer and worked in DOMS, a director of military support. I understand everything you said about what you are trying to put together and what you are trying to do, and it all makes very, very good sense. Our problems really have always been, from the Army's point of view, of getting Treasury, Justice, INS [U.S. Immigration and Naturalization Service], and Interior to get involved with the planning and to encourage them to have the ability to put people on the ground as quickly as possible, and not in two, or three, or six months, but now. It has always been pretty tough to do. It strikes me, whether you're doing it domestically or abroad, that there is a lot of overlap between what you are trying to do that involves changing job descriptions, budget things, financial instruments, and everything, and what FEMA [Federal Emergency Management Agency] is trying to do. You have the same kind of problems regarding planning and deployment of, say, the other government agencies and working together in interagency group. Is there any synergy between you and FEMA? Do you work kind of closely with them, because it would seem to me you are both interested in the same sort of personnel and budget instruments that would enhance your ability to do things? You are very similar organizations, it would seem to me. Thanks.

PASCUAL: A few comments. First of all, I think it is important just to mention that we have been working with our civil affairs colleagues to look at how we can coordinate with the strong capabilities that they bring to bear on the ground. We have had several visits down to Fort Bragg. In December we will be running an exercise where we look at how civilian affairs officers and individuals in the advanced civilian teams that I mentioned would work together on the ground and be able to combine their skills and capabilities. As [Major] General [Herbert A.] Altshuler put it to me, in a sense the civil affairs folks are the paramedics. They can get on the ground quickly, they can apply a tourniquet to stop that bleeding; but unless they have partners who are there to work with them, who can take a longer-term perspective, they are not going to actually be able to fix that wound.

And so this is the sort of philosophy that we are working toward, and we are going to be running through an exercise that helps to start to run through some of
the nitty-gritty requirements to be able to work together effectively on the ground
starting in December. In terms of bringing together various agencies for planning,
getting the right people, being able to get them now, it is a big challenge, and we
need to be realistic. Again, when I started this job and was discussing this with
Secretary Powell, one of the things that we reflected on was that in the military,
after Goldwater-Nichols, where there were legislation, resources, and a history of
a hierarchical culture, it took the military a good fifteen years to really get good
at joint operations. What we are proposing here is to develop a joint operations
capability in the civilian world, with no comparable legislation. If you just simply
compare the foreign affairs budget of $30 million to $35 million between the State
Department budget and the AID budget, and the military budget of some plus or
minus $450 billion—obviously, a phenomenal difference in resources—this is
going to take time. It is going to be a challenge and we need to be realistic about
that, and we cannot let that keep disappointing us, but it means that we have to
be deliberate in our efforts. Now, part of being deliberate means that you have to
have a planning framework, you have to change a culture, you have to identify
individuals in advance, you have to have rosters that you can tap, you have to have
individual agencies that are identifying individuals who can be made available for
planning exercises and for deployment. That process is getting underway, and we
are starting to put those kinds of rosters in place.

Regarding your question about FEMA, early on we had discussions with FEMA
about how we might be able to learn from some of their experiences. We had some
staff who actually were embedded with FEMA for a few days during the response
to Hurricane Katrina to be able to help them with some of the issues that they
were dealing with, on responding to international offers of assistance. One of the
things that we learned is that for FEMA to be able to operate effectively, it has to
do it on the basis of the national response plan. And that national response plan is
based completely on reimbursement of resources. We are in a somewhat difficult
situation here because right now, we do not have an operational budget to reim-
burse resources; so it makes it difficult to operate quite through that mechanism.
What we also saw from the FEMA network was that they have the ability to tap
U.S. government agencies and then use the contracts in those agencies, so that
those contracts can be applied for domestic relief and reconstruction activities. In
some cases, we will have the capacity to actually tap those same kinds of contracts
through U.S. government agencies. In other cases, it may be more expeditious to
just go directly to the private sector directly. And in some cases, it may be necessary to have a direct civilian response capability in something like a civilian reserve
corps for things like international civilian police, because that actually does not
exist anywhere in the U.S. government right now. We have no national police force,
and so when we deploy international police to a foreign country, they are being
taken from all different parts of the United States without any common doctrine.
We can change that if we have some form of a civilian reserve. So we are trying to

learn from FEMA's experiences and the mechanisms FEMA has created. But what it has taught us and showed us is that when you apply FEMA's capabilities or the kinds of contractual mechanisms that they have to an international environment, that in some cases, we are just going to have to change the operating modes because it does not always tap the skills and resources that we need overseas.

DAYTON: Carlos, we can take one more question.

PASCUAL: Okay.

AUDIENCE - DAVE LOUDEN: Thank you, Ambassador Pascual, my name is Dave Louden. I am retired Navy and a government contractor now. So much of your last ten minutes keeps reminding me of the role that deliberate planning plays in some of your goals in the civil affairs side, and that deliberate planning seems to be something you could certainly take advantage of. My question is very short. In your concept of a crisis response fund, how would you approach that where the U.S. may be considered belligerent, or to have its own motivation in this? Do you conceive of the support of allies that would play that role? And the reason that comes to mind is, my former boss, Rear Admiral Windsor Whitton, said that it is amazing how much success we can achieve when we do not worry about who gets the credit for it. Thank you.

PASCUAL: I interpret your question as whether or not that conflict response fund can be used in support of international partners; is that correct?

LOUDEN: To resolve conflict.

PASCUAL: Okay, it is a good question, and I agree with you that one of the things that we need to do is be able to look at how the job gets done and not necessarily who obtains the credit for it. There are also going to be some practical realities that we need to address for the U.S. Congress on how we use those funds and the accountability for those funds. There are practical questions that we are going to need to address, as well, on how we use those funds to leverage the participation of others. I would not want to exclude that funding from being used to channel it through another international partner or a multilateral organization. In some cases the United Nations, particularly through UN Ops, has been establishing very broad contractual capability internationally that can be quite attractive to utilize. But what we also want to be able to do is to challenge our partners and say, if we have $50 million to put on the table tomorrow to get activities X, Y, and Z going, I want to be able to go back to the EU, to the French, to the Germans, and the Nordic countries and say, we need you to establish that same kind of capability so that you can get on the ground quickly as well. So, while I want to leave that open as a possibility, I want to use this as a tool that gets us the maximum impact with the most resources that we possibly can on the ground in any given situation.

DAYTON: Let me jump in here because we are going to have to move on in the schedule. But the overall theme that we have is shaping national security. And what you have heard this morning, if the United States government continues to sustain the vision and resources, what Ambassador Pascual is up to is one of the most profound reshaping of national security events that we have had probably since the end of the Second World War. What he is trying to do is truly cutting edge. It is truly the view of the future, I think. The Defense Science Board last year did a study that very much reinforced what Ambassador Pascual is doing. They are going to do more of that this year. The Quadrennial Defense Review [QDR] that the Department of Defense is finishing up now has stability operations at the center, as part of a new overall military strategy for the United States. So what you heard this morning is pretty profound stuff, and I hope all of you can take this away as something that you have not heard the last of. I have to admit that sometimes I think of Ambassador Pascual as sort of a modern day Rumpelstiltskin, who has been taken into a room and has been told to turn all of this straw into gold. And yet when he walked into the room, there was not even any straw there. This is a man who, I just have to say, has individually, and with his team, created something out of nothing. He has created what may be the first truly functioning interagency process on a national security issue that we have seen in a very, very long time. So Carlos, on behalf of the chief of staff of the Army, and I know I do speak for General Pete Schoomaker, we want to thank you for being here today, but also for everything you do everyday because what you are doing, I think, is key to the future of the national security of the United States. So thank you very much.

Panel III

The Intelligence Challenge: Understanding and Preventing Strategic Surprises

Co-sponsor: The Matthew B. Ridgway Center for International Security
Studies
Moderator: Janne E. Nolan, Ph.D., Matthew B. Ridgway Center for
International Security Studies, Graduate School of Public and
International Affairs, University of Pittsburgh
Admiral William J. Crowe, Jr., Former Chairman of the Joint Chiefs of
Staff and Chairman, Board of Advisors, Global Options
Carl W. Ford, Jr., Executive Vice President, Cassidy & Associates
Dennis M. Gormley, Senior Fellow, Center for Nonproliferation Studies,
Monterey Institute of International Studies
David A. Kay, Ph.D., Senior Research Fellow, Potomac Institute for
Policy Studies

Panel Charter

"The policy road between Washington and an embassy officer in Laos, a
military field commander in Germany, an information officer in Panama, a technical assistance worker in India, or a scientist in a top-secret weapons laboratory
is tortuous and long. Elaborate and complicated mechanisms and processes are
inevitably needed to translate the national will into coherent and effective plans
and programs."

—Interim Report to the Subcommittee on National Policy Machinery,
January 12, 1960

The publication of *The 9/11 Commission Report* in late 2004, followed
by several other official and private analyses of U.S. intelligence capabilities,
underscored the strong national consensus in favor of overhauling the intelligence community for its failure to anticipate the terrorist attacks on American
soil. There has been discussion, however, about the need for reforms within

Left to right: *Janne E. Nolan, William J. Crowe, Jr., Carl W. Ford, Dennis M. Gromley, and David A. Kay.*

the policy community to better prepare for rapidly changing international challenges.

Events commonly described as "strategic surprises" or "intelligence failures"—from the advent of the Soviet atomic bomb to the ascendance of the Islamic anti-Western radicals who masterminded the September 11 attacks—seem often to be neither especially surprising nor failures of intelligence gathering. As is the case with the events preceding September 11, such episodes can reveal systemic failures of decision makers to consider available information that could have informed more effective policy choices.

This panel analyzed the relative influence of intelligence and policy considerations in crafting key areas of national security decision making. The panel offered a variety of perspectives presented by seasoned practitioners and scholars in the field who have grappled with these issues from within both the intelligence and policy worlds.

Discussion Points

The panel discussed the following questions:

1. What are some examples of decisions commonly thought to be "intelligence failures" that, upon reflection, are as much or more the result of failures among policymakers to take new information into account?

2. Are there systemic challenges facing the U.S. government in adapting to a rapidly changing world and competing sources of information and intelligence?

3. Can we identify ways to promote a healthy "marketplace of ideas" in official discourse to ensure that policymakers can take advantage of the best possible information from all sources, and are fully informed of alternative implications?

What structural changes, procedural reforms, or new bureaucratic incentives might improve the quality of expertise flowing into the decision-making process?

Summary

Admiral William J. Crowe, Jr.

- If the republic is going to have a viable and healthy national intelligence establishment, it is imperative that the president himself be involved. He should believe in the value of intelligence. If he communicates his disinterest, has little interest in giving bottom-line guidance, and leaves it to his subordinates, he risks confusion. Above all, his disinterest will be contagious, and that can be fatal to a viable and successful establishment.

- The intelligence "customer" should always have a skeptical eye.

- Those who are charged with interpreting intelligence data are not decision makers. Their guidance should be fact-based and strictly analytical, and should not aim at influencing the decision itself.

- Political leaders should choose top intelligence officials with the utmost care. After all, these officials are called upon to manage high-caliber experts. The best managers are those who have a good grasp of both the possibilities and the limitations of intelligence work. They encourage out-of-the-box thinking. They are committed and capable of shielding their work and those who produce it from the spin artists. They ensure that the intelligence product is focused and precise, but at the same time they are nimble enough to assign priority and to think in the larger context.

- More thinking and more effort must be invested in counteracting the tendency within the intelligence community to see intelligence as the center of the universe. It is essential to rein in excesses, to ensure that intelligence requirements do not override all other imperatives, and especially to ensure that intelligence activities stay within the boundaries of the law.

- Intelligence must be geared toward wide opinion gathering. There are a number of ways to accomplish this, including the creation of "A" and "B" teams. But special emphasis should be placed on the infusion of new blood into the intelligence community. In addition, we must be vigilant in searching for crippling mind-sets and, when they are found, acting decisively against them.

- The U.S. government has a variety of intelligence organizations, but at times, they tend to be guarded about what they share, especially if it strengthens a competitor or threatens their own sovereign sphere. Sovereignty is a tough mistress, and in the intelligence business it can be a very harmful trait.

Carl W. Ford, Jr.

- The best work done by the U.S. intelligence community can be seen in the 2002 National Intelligence Estimate (NIE) with respect to Iraq's weapons of mass destruction (WMD) programs. But the problem is that we got it flat wrong.

Budget cuts are not the primary reason for this colossal intelligence failure; there were sufficient resources in place. Furthermore, the people assigned to the task were the best and brightest. In this case, we were well served by all the intelligence agencies. The caliber, training, and experience of those tasked with producing this assessment were top-notch. And, it is important to note, intelligence collection of all types was better than it had ever been.

- The Director of National Intelligence (DNI) system is a good first step to strengthen our intelligence community. Arguing for more budgetary and operational authority for the DNI is also potentially valuable. But organizational changes alone will not produce a magic solution.

- We must rebalance our intelligence efforts to focus much more on analysis. We can make dramatic improvements in this area relatively quickly. Today, about 90 percent of our analytical workforce is "reporting the news" when, history teaches, less than a third of our analytical force can provide as much information as anyone could read in a lifetime. Analysis is vital. Analysis starts from a different premise: what is the problem or question that the policymaker has? The analyst looks for trends, answers, and scenarios.

- Besides greater emphasis on analysis, we must adjust the way we do analysis. This will require a culture change. Analysts tend to observe the problem and, from their own experience, try to tell you what is going on. We must return to fundamentals and strive to create new knowledge.

Dennis M. Gormley

- The prospect of strategic surprises has been a constant. What is especially worrisome is that the strategic surprise of the future could be a catastrophic attack on the U.S. homeland. Besides the immediate destructive impact, such an attack would change fundamental assumptions about national security. It is likely to lead, among other things, to major abridgments of civil liberties.

- So-called "intelligence failures" are as much policy failures as failures of intelligence itself.

- Any quest to fix the intelligence problem through reorganizing the intelligence apparatus is futile in that it avoids the more critical issue of how to improve the quality of intelligence and of the analytic process. With respect to the quality of intelligence, we must acknowledge that we are prone to analytic error and susceptible to politicization. More and better quality case officers will only yield incremental improvement. We need to penetrate denied areas to build more predictability into our systems. With respect to improving analysis, our chief shortcoming is that our methodology is decidedly unscientific. Idiosyncratic approaches lend themselves to individual and institutional biases. We need more science and less art, or else our intelligence community will be nothing more than "classified CNN."

- Entrenched government bureaucracies supported by longtime congressional advocates with huge stakes in the present model are an obvious impediment to change. Although there are signs of a willingness to introduce more formalism into the analytic process, the revolution in analytic affairs requires change from below as well as above. The well-known outliers in the system need to play a more central role in fostering change, with much greater attention given to examining the benefits against the risks of network derangements for broad intelligence community collaboration, and much more training, education, and outreach with academia and nongovernmental organizations.

• The temptation of the intelligence community is to distance itself from the policymakers to avoid being blamed for policy failures. Yet, the idea that intelligence and policy are neatly divided is erroneous. Intelligence officials must be intimately aware of what the government is doing. The attack on the USS *Cole* in October 2000 is a classic illustration of the absence of the harmonization of intelligence and policymaking. Intelligence that such an attack could occur was ample, albeit ambiguous. Surely we should have known about the dangers of taking the vessel into those waters on ship visits. The only close coordination was between the U.S. Department of State and Central Command, but the former was pursuing closer counterterrorism cooperation with the Yemeni authority's cooperation, and the latter was seeking basing rights. Had the issue of security been elevated to the National Security Council (NSC) level, more thorough examination of the threat context would have, perhaps, resulted in sharper probing actions.

David A. Kay, Ph.D.

• There are five reasons why the intelligence community has such a tough time anticipating strategic surprises. First, the intelligence community generally finds it difficult to recognize sharp breaks with the past behavior of the adversary. Second, there are actors/situations with which we have little experience or coverage (e.g., the 1979 Iranian revolution or present-day North Korea). Third, there are actors that we think we understand but do not, as illustrated by the 1998 Indian nuclear test. Fourth, there are actors for which we have ruled out collection and analysis, such as Saudi Arabia and Israel. Finally, there is the challenge of operating in "an atmosphere of zero accountability" at the policy level, which, regrettably, appears to be the prevailing climate.

• The intelligence community faces several systemic challenges as well. The first is dealing with the rapidity of change. The second is the existence of multiple intelligence targets, ranging from rogue states to terrorist organizations. The third is competing for specialized personnel with academia and domestic and international corporations. The fourth is the intelligence community's loss of information dominance.

• We must use competition, not try to eliminate it. Open-source information is not the solution. Open analysis and competition of ideas are needed to improve analytical quality.

Question-and-Answer Period

• Isn't the intelligence community trapped in the dilemma that they cannot talk about their successes and about improvements that might have been made since 9/11? Ford and Kay concurred that not to recognize that the intelligence system is broken will keep it that way.

• Regarding the possibility of the failure of capitalism in the Russian Federation or the collapse of the House of Saud, Nolan said that the reluctance of U.S. officials to discuss instability in Saudi Arabia is misguided. Our degree of dependency on Saudi Arabia actually precludes our discussing this subject, even though thinking through such a contingency is vitally important.

• Regarding how to further improve the organizational structure, Ford suggested that we must organize around problems that need to be addressed, rather than use the existing organizational structure and relationships between them to address the problem. Gormley added that we must move toward a "networked organization" model. However, we will not be able to do so without revolutionary changes in collaborative methods. According to Kay, unless top policymakers (the customers) are dissatisfied with the product, there will be no fundamental organizational changes.

Analysis

The panel provided excellent insights for strengthening American intelligence processes. In particular, the recommendation to focus more resources on long-term intelligence analysis is apt. Most critical to avoiding strategic surprises and addressing security issues before they become full-blown crises, future administrations must improve the NSC decision-making and policymaking processes.

The essential problem facing decision makers is not the dearth of intelligence or the failure to act on intelligence. The trick is acting on the right intelligence. As Napoleon and Clausewitz duly noted, decision makers are forced to make decisions on a profusion of data and intelligence, which is often false, contradictory, and exaggerated. Quite often, connecting the dots is only possible in hindsight.

Fortunately, U.S. administrations have an effective foreign policy formulation process for reference. The Eisenhower administration created an NSC process that no other administration has equaled in effectiveness. Future administrations would be well served by adopting the Eisenhower NSC structure in terms of assessing intelligence and acting on it in a timely manner. Moreover, decision makers must establish an active dialogue with their intelligence analysts and advisors. Much to the chagrin and irritation of their generals and advisors, both President Abraham Lincoln and British Prime Minister Winston Churchill were never satisfied with initial assessments. They asked probing questions until they got the information they could work with or sent their advisors scurrying back to gather more information. Only in this way could Lincoln and Churchill identify intelligence gaps and dismiss assumptions dressed as facts.

Human intelligence is by far the weakest component of U.S. intelligence gathering. This revelation should come as no surprise because the United States relies on it less than it should. U.S. intelligence agencies must lay the cold, hard facts on the table regarding the proper approach to human intelligence. First, intelligence agencies can rarely (very rarely) penetrate the inner circle of the enemy leadership. Intelligence moles have the greatest chance of succeeding (and surviving), but they take years of investment against identified threats. Second, agent recruitment offers the most reliable way of penetrating the enemy organization. Recruitment is not a savory business and often involves unsavory characters. The Soviet recruitment model exploited human vices—greed, ideology, compromise, and ego. If the United States is serious about human intelligence, it needs to reconcile the morality of recruitment with the morality of suffering surprise attacks. Lastly, human intelligence is slow and often false for a variety of reasons. It requires confirmation using other sources, and even this may not provide the fidelity to prevent a surprise.

The United States has taken prudent measures to address intelligence failings, but it would be a mistake to conclude that with enough resources and money, intelligence failures will disappear. History reveals that savvy adversaries will achieve surprise from time to time. Naturally, intelligence agencies should strive for fidelity and timely intelligence, but U.S. political leadership must not vitiate the agencies

Transcript

ANNOUNCER: Ladies and gentlemen, please welcome the moderator of the third panel, professor at the Matthew B. Ridgway Center of the graduate school of Public and International Affairs at the University of Pittsburgh, Dr. Janne E. Nolan.

JANNE E. NOLAN, PH.D.: Good morning to our distinguished guests and sponsors. Welcome to the second day, first panel, of the Eisenhower National Security Conference. This is my third or perhaps fourth time appearing at this very exemplary conference organized by such dedicated people from the U.S. Army. It is by far the most forward-looking and progressive discourse that goes on in Washington, certainly and currently, and has been since the inception of the series. The unprecedented efforts to foster constructive, diverse dialogue, not only civil-military but across many disciplines and across, as we saw, certainly, from this morning's address by Ambassador [Carlos] Pascual, are an effort to really bring together the expertise, the instruments that we need for a strong national security. I really hand it to General [Peter] Schoomaker, General [Richard] Cody, General [Keith] Dayton, and all their very dedicated staff for having the vision to sustain this dialogue in such a marvelous way. We are all very grateful to you and hope that this goes on for many more years.

I think, particularly when we are at war as a country, that civilian experts and policymakers have a special responsibility to conduct their work in a very objec-

Janne E. Nolan

tive and sober manner, in a way that is supportive, insightful, and helps particularly with respect to the people who are currently facing risks in Iraq. And to show our partnership, it should be not unanimity of dialogue, but constructive dialogue—not the kind of dialogue that so often goes on in Washington, which is partisan or ideological or self-centered. This is the key issue of this panel. We are charged with looking at the challenges to the future of intelligence and to discuss the nature of strategic surprise and what has become now a buzzword, "intelligence failures." One aspect of this that I find particularly important, and that this panel will address, is the degree to which many of the episodes historically and recently of so-called intelligence failures appear, on further examination, to be at least as much policy failures. At a time when there is a consensus that there should be an overhaul of the intelligence community, very little has been said about what should be done to also modernize and reform the policy community, which is not just the recipient of intelligence but, as we have seen particularly in recent years, shapes intelligence in much more active and dynamic ways. It is the systemic failures—or reluctance—to adapt across our government that we are interested in redressing, and doing so in a very pragmatic way, again, without ideology or blaming people. And this is a particularly acute objective, given the changing nature of the international threat environment.

A key issue, I think, for a couple of the panelists is, how do you empower individuals and the system to truly allow for a marketplace of ideas? How do you empower individuals to speak up about unfamiliar security threats that challenge sometimes the basic assumptions of the core consensus? How do you, in fact, as the Robb-Silverman Commission [The Commission on the Intelligence Capabilities of the United States Regarding Weapons of Mass Destruction] recommended, foster imagination and give individuals and groups the courage to "speak truth to power," which was a key conclusion of the Robb-Silverman Commission? It is very difficult to do that in the current system, which has a tendency to, in a nutshell, shoot the messenger when the information is not popular or consistent with the current paradigm.

We have an excellent panel of distinguished practitioners and experts, and you have their bios. I am going to just touch on the highlights and introduce all four of them now so that we do not have to be getting up and down. My job from now on is to enforce ruthless time agreements. There is a trapdoor that I can activate from my seat here that makes the speakers disappear after fifteen minutes. We want to maximize the exchange of the audience and encourage you to all speak to these experts. And I suspect that there might be a little bit of provocative content here, but that remains to be seen. First, it is my great pleasure to introduce Admiral William Crowe. Admiral Crowe has one of those wonderful professional careers that saves him from having to have a ten-page resume full of deputy this, deputy that, and assistant this, because he can just say chairman of the Joint Chiefs, ambassador to the Court of St. James; there are a lot of other details, but that carries a little bit of weight. He does not have to puff up his bio—let's put it that way. I had the great privilege of working with Admiral Crowe when he chaired one of the first investigations into terrorism in 1998, after the embassy bombings in East Africa. Serving on the Accountability Review Board with Admiral Crowe was a lesson in the tremendous judiciousness and courage that this man has shown throughout his career. He currently teaches at the Naval Academy and at George Washington University and is a graduate of the Naval Academy, but even in an Army audience, that is a cool thing, so okay. Our next speaker is Carl Ford, who is currently the executive vice president of Cassidy and Associates, but is known to probably many of you as the true insider expert in the intelligence world who has also worked on Capitol Hill. He is an expert on East Asia, and he served previously as the assistant secretary for Intelligence and Research in the State Department during the Bush administration. He did two tours of duty in Vietnam. He served as a military intelligence officer and DIA [Defense Intelligence Agency] China expert. He was the national intelligence officer on the NIC [National Intelligence Council] for East Asia. I actually remember him when he worked in the Senate, and I wrote my first Senate report for him, but he does not remember that because I was only thirteen at that time. Our next speaker is Dennis Gormley, who is a senior fellow at the Center for Nonproliferation Studies at the Monterey Institute and the author most recently of an IISS [International Institute for Strategic Studies] article in *Survival* called "The Limits of Intelligence: Lessons of Iraq." I recommend it highly to all of you. He spent twenty years as the vice president of Pacific-Sierra, a research consulting firm. He has served on multiple advisor groups for the Pentagon, and he himself is also a true expert who does not show off. Finally, David Kay, who was himself a very modest and understated individual until he became a media star. He remains modest and understated despite the buzz that lasted for a long time and probably still lasts. I last saw him at the White House Correspondents Dinner, at the party afterwards, which was full of real celebrities, movie stars, models, and David Kay. He certainly is known as the leading expert on Iraqi weapons of mass destruction. His last assignment, appointed by the DCI [director of Central Intelligence], was to head up the Iraq survey group to determine that there were, in fact, no active WMD programs in Iraq. Prior to that, he served as the chief nuclear weapons inspector for the UN special commission. When we first went into Iraq, some of you may remember the film of David Kay confronting the Iraqi National Guard and really operating on his own instincts and extremely intelligent assessment of what to do, confronting the guards who were preventing legitimate access by the UN to the weapon sites. He is a pioneer in the huge area now of our national security, which is inclusive of onsite inspections as well as Iraq, and serves on many boards—a very distinguished expert. So please join me in welcoming these experts. First, we will hear from Admiral Crowe. Thank you very much.

William J. Crowe, Jr.

ADMIRAL WILLIAM J. CROWE, JR.: Should I proceed? Well, good morning. It is nice to see a sense of humor in the moderator—not all panels have that, although it is a rather irreverent jam. Thank you. I do not pretend to be an expert in the intelligence field. Certainly I used intelligence product for a number of years. I have just a few preliminary comments before this group discussion. I should warn you, these are based on my personal experience and are of a very general nature. There are some handicaps in retirement. I no longer have a staff to tell me what to think, and I really miss that, I must admit. I am not privy to the mainstream events of today particularly. I have often heard that advice is worth what you pay for it, so I should warn you that everything I advise this morning is free of charge.

I assume there will be little argument that intelligence is important, and, if properly used, it will be extremely helpful to decision makers. They understand that and should understand it. But seldom will intelligence furnish us a complete and flawless picture, particularly where major decisions are concerned. Consequently, the user should, in my judgment, always use a cynical eye and should be a skeptic to begin with. Above all, he should not expect too much, and he must always bear in mind it may be wrong. Most likely you will be dealing with probabilities, not precise data or information. Consequently, I would advise, anytime, for the user to use a jaundiced eye. He would appreciate it if he does.

Now let me get a little more specific. If the republic is going to have a viable and healthy national intelligence establishment, I believe it is imperative that the president himself be involved. He should believe in the value of intelligence and trying to clear himself, of course, with some of the failures and some of their challenges and some of the problems. But nevertheless, he should make his personal interest and encouragement known to his administration. It helps tremendously if he can lay out, in some specificity, what he expects, what he wants, but preferably he must do this. Preferably the product he asked for must be unvarnished by domestic political interest. Frankly, once the product is submitted, either the president or the White House will put the political content or spin into it. It should not come from the analysts. He does not expect his analysts to follow the public opinion polls. If he communicates his disinterest and has little interest in giving bottom-line guidance, and leaves it to his subordinates, I believe he risks confusion. He will push effort into directions that are not particularly profitable. It will be a great waste and of little concern to him. But above all, his disinterest will be contagious, and that can be fatal to a viable and successful establishment.

Sophie Tucker used to say that "I have been rich and I have been poor and believe me, being rich is better." Well, in my position as chairman [of the Joint Chiefs of Staff] and later as chairman of the PFIAB, the President's Foreign Intelligence Advisory Board, I have worked both with a president who was involved and a president who paid little attention to intelligence. Believe me, being involved is better. Intelligence gatherers or interpreters are not decision makers. They desperately need clear guidance of their own on the subjects that are being pursued, the information that the manager wants, and how he wants it to assist the policy process. At the same time, the policy guidance should not directly or indirectly influence the final answers. This, of course, is hard, very hard for a decision maker to do, much more difficult than it is to talk about. I had a boss once in my career who had a sign on his desk that said, "Every man is entitled to his own opinion, but not to his own facts." I often wished that that sign was reprinted in volume and distributed throughout the Pentagon.

Next, I would say that intelligence leaders, the top managers, should be chosen with great care. It is my opinion, my humble opinion, as John Wickham used to say, that they are often selected for the wrong reason. Actually, heading up a highly educated and skilled group of intelligence analysts or experts is probably the hardest job imaginable. To begin with, the manager must have a good grasp of the possibilities and the limitations of intelligence work. He should, of course, encourage creativity and thinking out of the box and protect his people from outside spin artists. At the same time, he is forced to look at it from a much broader perspective than his analysts. He must ensure that the production of intelligence is relatively accurate, is to the point, but that it is put into proper perspective and given the right priority. It is his job to do this and to think in the larger context. There is a strong tendency for talented experts to conclude that intelligence is the center of the universe and that it is imperative to the extent that it overrides all other considerations, even on occasion, U.S. law. It is the boss's job to reign in such excesses and to keep them in their proper boundaries and subjugated to U.S. law.

This, of course, leads to the fundamental problem of mindset. Every intelligence organization, to one degree or another, is faced with troublesome mindsets, recurring mindsets. I heard a wag describe a specialist as a man who knows more and more about less and less until he knows everything about nothing. I guess the opposite of that would be a general, who knows less and less about everything until he knows nothing about everything. But the point I am trying to make is that for an analyst who devotes months and years to a particular subject, the mindset disease often settles in. There are a variety of ways, of course, to combat this. Widen your opinion gathering, new blood, A and B teams, etc., etc. I personally subscribe to a continuous flow of new blood. I feel that it is extremely important. For example, our Russian specialists, when I was involved in that business, were not as sensitive as we would have preferred to liberal changes behind the [Iron] Curtain that preceded the fall of the wall. My point is that leaders must be constantly searching for signs of crippling mindset, and they must act decisively to overcome it.

Lastly, the issues of communication and sovereignty. The U.S. government has a variety of intelligence organizations, but at times, they tend to be guarded about what they share, especially if it strengthens a competitor or threatens their own sovereign sphere. I watched this phenomenon at close hand when Janne and I were working on the Accountability Review Boards for the bombings in Nairobi and Dar El Salaam. In particular, the FBI stiff-armed our boards, and I mean it literally. We were attempting to derive lessons for the future. We were established by statute. We had access, theoretically, to all the information that was available, but we could never get to what we wanted from the FBI. This carried little weight with them. I often thought, in the back of my mind, the organization that is responsible for enforcing the law sometimes is tempted to ignore it when their own interests are involved. What I am trying to say is that sovereignty is a tough mistress, and in the intelligence business it can be a very harmful trait. I hope that some of the structural changes that are being made will overcome this. I am not optimistic, but I think only time will really tell us. And that concludes my remarks. Thank you.

NOLAN: Thank you very much.

CARL W. FORD, JR.: Well, I had planned to begin my presentation this morning with a few introductory cautions. I have had to add one. They told me that I would not be able to see anybody out there for the bright lights. I didn't really believe them, but I really cannot see anything. So if anyone wants to throw anything, I would appreciate the courtesy of at least yelling out first so that I can duck when it gets up here. In my thirty-five years in and around the intelligence community, I have worn a number of hats, including humint [human intelligence] collector, intelligence manager. But I spent most of my time as an all-source analyst, and indeed, my comments and criticisms today come really from that experience. Second, if the problems of the intelligence community and the challenges that we face were straightforward and easily solved, somebody a lot smarter than me would have already figured it out and come up with some solutions. I certainly do not have any magic solutions. But unfortunately, like Admiral Crowe, I am not very optimistic. I have as you have, I am sure, lived through a number or profound intelligence failures over the last several decades, and I have been witness to excellent after-action studies by various commissions—the most recent being the Silverman-Robb Commission, which not only did a very thorough and commendable job, but came up with very excellent suggestions about where we go in the future. Unfortunately, if history is a guide, any improvements in the intelligence community will be by accident, not necessarily by malice aforethought.

Carl W. Ford

Well, if you could not tell from my introductory comments, let me set the record very straight from the beginning. I think that we in the intelligence community are badly underperforming, dangerously so, and that you, the consumers, if you accept as gospel what we tell you, you do it at your own risk. Indeed, my sense is in that until consumers demand better quality from us in the community and hold responsible those individuals who continue to label the crap that we turn out on a daily basis, then it is not going to get any better. Let me just briefly give you this point, a different cut of what I have just said. That is, if you want an example of the very best thing that we in the intelligence community have done in the last decade or so, read the now-unclassified key judgments of the November 2002 NIE [National Intelligence Estimate] on weapons of mass destruction in Iraq. That is clearly the best production that we are capable of. There is not a single problem that has received more time, command emphasis, money, or attention over the last decade than Iraq weapons of mass destruction. We saw that problem coming and we spared no expense in getting ready for it. The problem was that we got it flat wrong, and that if you think that this was a perfect storm or this was an exceptional case, I beg to differ. That is the best we can do, not the worst.

Now, in looking at the anatomy of the problem, I would urge you not to fall for the excuses that, well, we had budget cuts and there has not been enough collection. At least from my experience, do not fall for that. That is simply baloney. The people who are assigned to the intelligence community today are some of the best and the brightest that this country has to offer. You are well served by the people at CIA [Central Intelligence Agency], DIA, INR [Bureau of Intelligence and Research], NSA [National Security Agency]—I could go on to all the other ends. The fact is that the caliber and experience and training of these people is top notch. Collections of all types, whether you are talking about humint, photint [photographic intelligence], sigint [signals intelligence], masint [measurement and signatures intelligence], whatever "INT" you are talking about, the collection is better than it has ever been before. When I started off as an analyst thirty years ago, I would have killed for half of the collection that we have today. Could it be better? Of course. Would I like more inside information? You betcha. But in terms of the overall amount of information available to the analytical community today, they cannot complain. It is certainly a lot of information that is available there. And if $40 billion would buy you that estimate in 2002, shame on us. If you cannot do better than that for $40 billion, somebody ought to go to jail. And those who would like to blame our problems and troubles on the policymakers, at least from my experience, that will not cut it either. We truly, sincerely, deeply believed the flawed judgments that we presented to the president and to others in the cabinet.

Now, you are probably asking yourself at this point, Carl, if it is not the people, if it is not the money, if it is not the collection, what in the world is it? Well, that is a fair question, and unfortunately, I can only give you some preliminary, not-so-good answers. As I said before, I do not have any magic solutions, and there are a lot of people smarter than I am who have been befuddled and frustrated by these problems. Now, one, I would agree that the DNI [Director of National Intelligence] system that the president and the Congress have come up with is a good first step. If anything, I would argue for more budget and operational authority for the DNI. But I would be quick to say that I do not think that you can solve the problems we face by organizational changes alone. I think that that has been one of the mistakes that we have made in the past. What I would focus most of my attention on is analysis. I think that we can make dramatic, significant improvement relatively quickly on the quality of our intelligence analysis. Now, that is, albeit, based on the fact that we are starting from such an abysmally low level. And if you are starting from crap, making it a little bit better is a lot easier than some other things that we might have to do, particularly when we are spending all this money on collection and all these other things. You could double the collection budget and I would argue that you are going to get a minimal difference in the quality of the product that goes to the president. You do not have to double anything to improve the intelligence analysis.

Now, part of this is that we have about 90 percent of our workforce, our analytical workforce, doing current intelligence. They are reporters; they are reporting the news. Now, this is an important function of the intelligence community—do not get me wrong. I believe that that is clearly something that we do and, in fact, we do well. No one could say that the current intelligence provided over the last several years has not been excellent. At $40 billion, it better be. But when you have 90 percent of your people doing that, it is overkill. You are actually wasting valuable resources on things that could be done in different ways. The fact is that historically, something less than a third of our analytical force could produce as much current intelligence as anybody could read in a lifetime, and that instead of having 20 or 25 percent of our people doing that, we now have 90 percent doing that. And in that mode of current intelligence, my rough estimate is we probably use less than 5 percent of the billions and billions of pieces of data that we collect every day. There is just so much that we can do with that 5 percent.

Now, in the past, something like 80 percent of our analysts were doing something else, and that was research. It starts from a different premise than current reporting. Current reporting reports on what happened last night or last week. Analysis starts from a different perspective. What is the problem? What is the question that a policymaker has? Once that question has been identified, then an analyst turns to the data that has been collected secretly, the open source data, and tries to formulate an answer, provide new knowledge, trends, basic facts of the case. The fact is that nobody is doing that anymore. And if no one is doing that, not only are you not able to respond to the policymakers' major questions and dilemmas, but current intelligence cannot withstand the lack of new knowledge being pumped into the system.

Finally, because I am reaching the end of my fifteen minutes, what you really need here is a culture change—nothing short of a culture change in the way we do analysis. If we practiced medicine the way we practice intelligence, half of the people in this audience would be dead today. The fact is that what analysts do today is that they visually observe the problem. They take the temperature and the blood pressure and, from their own experience, try to tell you what is wrong with what is going on in Egypt or Israel or China or in terrorism. There are no MRIs [magnetic resonance imaging] being done. There are no blood tests being done. There are no colonoscopies being done. And the fact is that there is no *Harvard Medical Journal* or other research to support it, and there are no drug companies producing medicine—all we have got is what we can see most visibly from our current collection flow of information. As long as that remains the case, it is not going to get better.

We have to go back to fundamentals and go back to creating new knowledge. All of this money that we are spending to collect it—we actually have to use it. Do we have to use 100 percent? Go from 5 percent to 100 percent? I would be happy if I could tell you that we have used 15 or even 20 percent of the information being collected. That sort of tripling or quadrupling of the use of information we have to formulate our guesses would, overnight, improve the quality of our intelligence. Beyond that, it is something that I am glad that I am now worried about colonoscopies and MRIs and blood tests, because this problem, obviously, is something I was not able to solve on my watch. But I hope the future generations will finally come to grips and get a handle on it. Thank you.

NOLAN: Thank you Carl. I think we have a diverse panel, so perhaps we could get a somewhat more pragmatic and jaded view from Dennis. It is not a very optimistic, rosy picture you paint Carl, but thank you very much. Dennis.

DENNIS M. GORMLEY: Yes, it is important to note that none of us shared our viewpoints before we assembled here today. But certainly, based on Carl's remarks, I think nothing that I say will seem terribly more critical than what Carl's observation suggested, but they are certainly consistent. I want to talk about the inevitability of surprise.

If the past is any prologue to the future, it is difficult to conclude that either policymakers or intelligence officials can avoid the inevitability of surprise. And I say this in spite of all the intelligence reforms now taking place to deal fundamentally with the very same pathologies identified after every major intelligence failure, from Pearl Harbor through September 11th. The commissions form, investigations occur,

Dennis M. Gormley

hearings galvanize the public, organizational changes follow, and so do further surprises. But what makes the prospect of surprise as a constant of international affairs wholly unacceptable is that the next terrorist attack on U.S. soil could be a truly catastrophic one, involving a weapon of mass destruction with untold and long-lasting physical, economic, and psychological damage and societal trauma. In just about every regard, the consequences of such an attack would change fundamental assumptions about American and global security. Today's very legitimate concerns about abridgments in civil liberties would become decidedly secondary considerations in the aftermath of a surprise WMD [weapons of mass destruction] incident on U.S. soil. Now, this is not to exaggerate the threat of such an attack; it is simply to emphasize the huge stakes involved.

History also tells us that intelligence failure is just as much a failure of policymaking as intelligence: failure of policymakers to grasp the importance of the intelligence presented to them, and their failure to take actions that might clarify threat ambiguity. Certainly, Pearl Harbor stands as a classic example, but the illustration that reminds me most of the setting prior to September 11th is Germany's successful attack on France in May of 1940. Although France and Britain were both better equipped than the Germans—with more guns and men, better tanks, more fighters, more bombers—the German decision to attack through the Ardennes Forest successfully surprised them. In a superb new piece of historical analysis, Harvard historian Ernest May argues that Hitler and his generals prevailed against a stronger set of adversaries because they perceived and effectively exploited weaknesses in French and British governmental processes and behavior. Around these weaknesses they designed their plan of attack. In spite of ample intelligence on German preparations, which indeed included British and French spies in Berlin, French and British decision makers took no time to understand how and why German operational thinking might depart from their preconceived notions. They simply neglected to prepare for the possibility of surprise, and when it happened, they could not react quickly enough to forestall its effects.

The failure to perceive and process information correctly is a pathology equally germane to policymakers and intelligence officials. In the case of intelligence analysts, it relates to certain cognitive biases, both institutional and individual. It must be addressed to improve the analytic process. As for policymakers, even if the best intelligence is presented to decision makers disinclined to take political risks, to clarify ambiguity, such policymakers will find sympathetic domestic and foreign advisors and allies who will help them explain away the need for action. So what can be done? Any quest to fix intelligence merely through organization will be futile, insofar as it avoids the more prosaic but much more critical area of intelligence effectiveness. This depends far less on structural reform than on the quality of collected intelligence, on the nature of the analytic process, and ultimately on the relationship between intelligence and policymaking officials.

Let me say just a few things about each of these aspects. In regard to intelligence quality, simply put, low-quality intelligence is more likely to produce analytic error and is more susceptible than high-quality intelligence to political manipulation. Limitations in the availability of high-quality human intelligence and overhead recognizance imagery made assessments of Iraq's WMD holdings more susceptible to various individual and institutional pathologies. After September 11th, most attention has focused on better and more human intelligence. More agents with the appropriate skills and training may produce higher-quality dots, but the challenge of penetrating the inner sanctum of terrorist organizations should not be underestimated, nor should the peculiar demands of maintaining quality control over source information. More and better case officers will only furnish an incremental improvement in the quality of collected information. The issue of quality is more problematic with regard to technical intelligence sensors. Intelligence failure is virtually assured when a predisposed analytic mindset is combined with predictable overhead intelligence collection systems. Yes, we still need to penetrate denied areas, but we need more unpredictability and far more persistence built into our technical intelligence sensors. The dismal technical and financial state of the future imagery architecture does not augur well for the future. We need to ask more from our research and development investments to enable persistent coverage and to equip even our human spies, literally, with what one recent observer referred to as the capacity to penetrate not just denied areas, but denied minds.

With respect to improving analysis, virtually, every post–Cold War intelligence commission that has met has illuminated the intelligence community's deficits in analytic performance, but little progress has occurred. The chief analytic shortcoming that invites error and susceptibility to political manipulation is the decidedly unscientific nature of the current analytic process. In commenting on my colleague David Kay's disclosures in February of 2004 about the failure to find WMD in Iraq, David Brooks of the *New York Times* stated that the problem with the CIA was that it depended too heavily on scientific methodologies that all but eliminated the individual's intuitive and imaginative skills in analyzing information. Brooks formed this judgment by perusing the CIA's website, which does, indeed, convey the notion of a rigorous methodological approach to intelligence. But the actual record, documented powerfully in a new book, which I highly recommend, by Dr. Rob Johnston, called the *Analytic Culture in the United States Intelligence Community: An Ethnographic Study*, shows woefully little rigorous analytic tradecraft, but rather, idiosyncratic methods and techniques having more to do with writing and communication tips than with any systematic use of methodological tools that might help eliminate individual and institutional biases. Thus, animating the intelligence analytic process with more science and less art stands as a critical test of change within the intelligence community. Otherwise, intelligence will be nothing more than a classified CNN, with little or no value added to the policymaking process.

Now, with respect to harmonizing intelligence and policymaking, with so many failures to contend with, the intelligence community may be tempted to reestablish its independence and integrity by distancing itself from policymakers. This would be counterproductive and, indeed, even dangerous. The character of today's unique threats reinforces a closer harmonization of intelligence and policymaking. Policymakers will always seek actionable intelligence, but unambiguous intelligence is the exception, rather than the rule. Belief that getting too close to policymakers emanates from a perception of a neat, but entirely erroneous division of responsibilities: that intelligence officials resolve ambiguity about adversary behavior, and policymakers implement responses only when intelligence is actionable. The fact is that warning is a two-sided game. Our adversaries' behavior hinges frequently on the actions or inaction of U.S. decision makers. Intelligence officials must be intimately aware of what our own government is doing and must be equally involved with policymakers in crafting probing actions that clarify threat ambiguity. The attack on the USS *Cole* by al Qaeda operatives in the Yemeni port of Aden in October of 2000 illustrates to me both the absence of such an intelligence-policymaking harmonization and how closer coordination might have prevented the attack. Of course, one needs to be aware of retrospective coherence. It always looks better in the aftermath to put the pieces together. Intelligence was ample, but ambiguous at the time, with lots of strategic warning, but no precise information about place or time. But we surely ought to have known about the dangers of taking a vessel into Aden. Three years earlier, after the Khobar Towers attack in June of 1996, an NSC [National Security Council] official was chartered with going to the region, doing a detailed evaluation of vulnerabilities, and preparing a detailed memorandum. He specifically called particular attention to the vulnerabilities associated with ship visits to Aden. Moreover, the ambassador, Barbara Bodine, had previously advised the Central Command to cancel ship visits due to lack of progress by Yemeni security in dealing with al Qaeda terrorists. Given the buildup of tactical warning about terrorist attack somewhere in the region, one would have thought that a more careful vetting process would have preceded the October 2000 ship visit. Yet policy coordination only occurred between [the Department of] State and CENTCOM, a routine procedure. Both, though, had keen interests at the time in making the visit: State, to bolster its diplomatic ties with Yemen's new pro-Western government, which had recently ousted Marxists from power, and CENTCOM, which coveted assured access to facilities throughout the region. Had such a decision been elevated to the NSC level, where all the bureaucratic stakeholders—policy, operational, and intelligence officials alike—would have been involved, there might have been more thorough consideration of the broader strategic and tactical context. I doubt that a ship visit request would have been blocked, but I would like think that a more thorough examination of the threat context might have led to at least one of several possible probing actions, such as CENTCOM making it known that the ship would enter the port under heightened security or, indeed, even arrest the suspected terrorists with ties to al Qaeda prior to the visit. In any event, such probing actions might have revealed patterns of terrorist behavior more clearly and thus made the attack preventable.

Some final thoughts: none of the changes outlined here will be easy. Moving from a conservative, incremental approach to intelligence collection R&D [research and development] to one more willing to make huge leaps in capability will be a daunting challenge. Entrenched government bureaucracies supported by long-time congressional advocates with huge stakes in the present model are an obvious impediment to change. While there are signs of a willingness to introduce more formalism into the analytic process, the revolution in analytic affairs requires change from below as well as above. The well-known outliers in the system need to play a more central role in fostering change, with much greater attention given to examining the benefits against the risks of network derangements for broad intelligence community collaboration, and much more training, education, and outreach with academia and nongovernmental organizations. But even if the quality of intelligence and analysis improves, a more thorough integration of intelligence in policymaking will not happen until additional bureaucratic changes are made. One modest idea is more liberal rotation of midlevel intelligence officers into policy organizations. In today's information-abundant context, a new contract must be forged between elements of the government with decidedly different cultures: an intelligence community preferring to reflect and assess, and policymakers more prone to act or ignore, but in the end, shape outcomes. The principle intelligence challenge is to furnish policymakers with stratagems for stimulating responses from adversaries that will help clarify their emerging conduct. Still, as history sadly testifies, none of this is likely to make being surprised vastly less probable. But a combination of reducing our vulnerabilities and greater attention to systematically clarifying uncertainties in adversary behavior is about the best we can hope for. That, indeed, was the message of Roberta Wohlstetter's classic treatment of Pearl Harbor written forty-three years ago, and it is equally compelling today. Thank you.

NOLAN: Thank you very much, Dennis. David.

DAVID A. KAY, PH.D.: Thank you very much, Janne. When Janne called to ask if I would appear on this panel, as I usually do when Janne calls, I said yes. And then I asked, "What is it about?" And she said, "Oh, we are going to discuss intelligence failures, and you have been involved in so many failures, no one could do it better." You know, even as a dumb Texan, I thought, this is probably not the way I want to headline my resume. And then she said, "And you explained it so well to the congressional committees that were investigating it." I thought, that is the second thing I do not want on my resume at the top. I may be the only one in this town who felt sorry for Mike Brown yesterday. But that is life.

David A. Kay

The great advantage of coming last is, the wisdom has already been poured out, and the best I can hope to do is try to shake it up, organize it in a slightly different way, which maybe will get you to think about the pearls of wisdom a second time. What I have tried to do is try to think back—why intelligence has such a difficult time in dealing with strategic surprises—and then to think of some general systemic challenges that I think cut across the community and, in fact, for those of you who are still active in it, are going to be the bread and butter of what you are going to have to face.

First of all, I think intelligence historically has had an extremely hard time with anticipating or recognizing breaks with previous, understood patterns of behavior and the risk calculus. Just think back to the Cold War—and the list is very long that you can pull out—but think of the Cuban Missile Crisis, the Soviet invasion of Czechoslovakia, the Soviet invasion of Afghanistan, and probably most startlingly of all since so many intelligence assets were deployed against it, the Soviet biological weapons program, which for those of you who have not followed that, we now know that the Soviets actually deployed smallpox on the nosecones of intercontinental ballistic missiles. We missed everything about the Soviet program. And we essentially did because in each of these cases, it was outside our understanding of the paradigm of behavior and risk calculation of the Soviets. That is one of the most dangerous things you can have—when you think you fully understand another state, another interest group, some risk pattern and how they behave, and you exclude from your analytical paradigm looking at the outliers; it might be completely different from the way they behaved.

The second class are those actors or situations with whom we have little experience, understanding, and little collection. Here again, there are both historic ones going back a number of years as well as current ones. I would put the Iranian revolution as an example there. We had very little coverage, very little analysis of the rag-tag band of mullahs, theoreticians, and cassette purveyors who were challenging the shah. We just did not collect against it, did not understand it, and it was not high in something we had experience with. I would say North Korea, on any given day, I would also put in that box. Although we have had over fifty years of dealing with them, we essentially have little experience, little understanding of what really goes on in Pyongyang and almost no—"almost" is probably an exaggeration, let me say no—collection that goes against it. Iraq: Iraq pre–Persian Gulf

War, Iraq pre-OIF [Operation IRAQI FREEDOM], and by and large, Iraq on any given day, too. We just have had less experience understanding their collection against them. The Iraq insurgency is another example of that. When I entered this game, Vietnam was the trauma we were all going through, and we seem to have washed out of our collective system, both military and intelligence, what we really learned, a very hard way, about insurgencies and how they operate, how to understand them, and, God help us, how to measure your success against them; all of this seems to have gone.

The third category is actors that we think we understand—and we understand too well. The first example, and one that is current and I quite frankly think will be on the forefront of national security policymaking for the next twenty years, is the Indian nuclear test. You go back through the analytical product preceding the Indian nuclear test, and you had detailed explanations as to why the Indians would not go to a new open test of their nuclear warhead. Our understanding of how they viewed their deterrent and the competition with Pakistan and the rest of the world, we thought was so good, that empirical collection evidence was pushed aside because it was ambiguous and really did not mean it. All collection is always ambiguous, but the mindset just excluded it. The second example that worries me far more today is Mexico. We are becoming a nation with a very substantial Hispanic population. Mexico has been an important neighbor in many ways. We think we understand Mexico. I would argue we do not understand Mexico, and we particularly do not understand what is driving the society, the state, and the economy—and that is one of the national security surprises likely to bite us, and it will be because we know Mexico too well. They are among us.

The fourth category is those actors in situations where policymakers have ruled out intelligence collection and analysis. Saudi Arabia is certainly among those. You could not even list Saudi Arabia as a denied hard target in open intelligence collection, writings about open intelligence. I would also put Israel on that same list. Policymakers essentially exclude the full range of collection and analysis that you would bring to most normal targets and countries with regard to those two. There are others that emerge at various times.

Finally, the fifth challenge: I would certainly put an atmosphere of zero accountability. It is not because I like to see people hung from yardarms—although I must say it does have a certain redeeming quality at times; it is probably better than rewarding them for failure—but there is something Admiral Crowe will be familiar with and certainly every young midshipman, as I recall, learns, and that is the responsibility of command. I do not care whether your destroyer hits a sandbar, a Mexican fishing vessel, the dock as you are trying to maneuver in, or an undersea mountain as you are zooming to R&R in Australia. The captain is responsible for everything that goes on in his ship and is held responsible, even though, as there are in all failures, multiple explanations and multiple causes. The reason for that is because it communicates throughout the service the seriousness of your actions and responsibility. If you loosen up and deny that, the whole system goes to hell very quickly. I would argue that in the intelligence system, the lack of accountability for failures has not only left people in place who committed failures, it has communicated a lack of seriousness about the whole purpose of the enterprise. And that is, in many ways, the one that worries me most about strategic surprise; you can wash it off, no one is accountable, it will go ahead.

Now let me hit five for six systematic challenges I think you are going to face that are really different. One is clearly the rapidity of change. I came into this game as a Soviet specialist. We probably developed a better understanding in the U.S. intelligence community of events in the Soviet Union than most Russians had of their own system. Our stovepipes were slightly broader than the Russian's stovepipes. We focused a lot of collection effort on that, and it was a huge, dominant driver of U.S. intelligence for forty years. But it principally concerned one element of Soviet society in military power, the one that made the biggest difference to us, and that is the strategic nuclear option. We came away from Pearl Harbor understanding that never again should we allow an opponent to have sufficient military power that in its calculus it would make sense—wrongly in the case of the Japanese, I think we also understand now, but in their own logic—it would make sense for them to attack us first. So we had to focus our efforts to understand that under no circumstance would any Soviet leader ever believe, looking at the United States, that they had more military power or enough military power to justify a strategic strike against us. And we spent a tremendous treasure to be sure that they understood that they did not, and that we understood what they were doing.

The world we are in today, the change is much more rapid, and it quite frankly is broader as well. So the task before the intelligence community is not a single target, even a target as big as the Soviet Union, and it shifts. How many analysts today do you think fully understand the information revolution and the tools that are given to them to understand it? It is amazing as you walk through the halls in—and I speak to the one I know best—the CIA, the tools that the analysts have available to analyze the flood—and Carl described it; it is a wealth—of collection data that in one's earlier life, one could not even imagine having on call. Unfortunately, the analytical tools to deal with it are not much different than, in fact, were available when Carl and I were much younger, and yet what they are being asked to understand about other societies is just much broader. There is also the issue of the target set, which has grown. It is no longer this piece of Westphalia 1648, billiard-ball model of states. It is groups, acting sometimes with state endorsement or state aide; it is other times groups acting completely independent of states, in an atmosphere in which about two-thirds of the states in the world essentially should be in Chapter 11 bankruptcy. They are failing states, unable to exercise military, economic, and legal sovereignty over their own, and so the rise of organized crime, illegal transport in human, WMD and proliferation technology. All of this is emerging, and yet we expect the intelligence community to keep on track.

The third one is one of failing standards of excellence, and let me be clear here. I think the failing standards of excellence applies greatly to the analytical management and tools available, but I also think we would be less than honest if we did not say there is a falling standard of excellence with regard to those who go into the enterprise themselves. And this is because of the nature of competition in American society for that type of expertise. When I came out of Columbia as a graduate student with Soviet expertise, there was a limited range of employers around. Universities, if you wanted to teach. By and large, business was not a competitor for that sort of expertise. And there were the intelligence community and a few research and think tanks around. The intelligence community indeed got the best of a generation, of several generations of Russian expertise. Today if you go out and say I want to hire the best expert on biotechnology, you are competing not with just the universities—and the universities are as fierce competitors in this as they, in fact, are going after the grant money as well—but you are competing with American industry, foreign industry, a lot of other places that want that expertise. Every Wall Street broker firm wants the best biotech analyst, and they are out there in the same market for it. There has also been a loss at the experience level. The average tenure in the CIA, DIA, and analytical positions today, is between three and five years, depending on whose figures you believe, at the unclassified level. This is a tremendous drawing down of the wealth of experience. Now, I quite agree with Admiral Crowe on the importance of new blood. It is certainly true that in understanding the change the Soviet Union was going through at the end of its existence, we were impeded by a group of analysts who, in fact, had invested their lives, their careers, and focused on the old Soviet Union and had a hard time getting their mind around a very different process that was going on. But quite frankly, if I had to worry about that versus the current trend, in which we have experts on very, very important regions of the world who have relatively little experience as analysts and almost no experience with the actual countries themselves . . . you will scratch long and hard in the U.S. military, the CIA, and the DIA, to try to find someone who has actually ever lived in Iran, has served in Iran, knows anything about Iran on a first-hand basis, and the same thing is true of a very large number of variants. And one reason this is important and it affects the relationship of policymakers is, you send an analyst in to brief the vice president, for example, on events in Iran and Libya, on the world's energy market, and they've got to compete with a guy who has been there, done that, talked that walk, walked that talk, knows those intimately; and you've got someone who has been on the job for three to four years, out of an American university, who has never served there, and they are telling him how events are going there. That really does affect them.

And finally, probably the largest challenge in this area, and let me end very quickly: loss of information dominance. I come from the period when, in fact, you really knew secrets and you could whisper things, even about current intelligence, that people could not get off the air. That is no longer true. I quite agree with Dennis. Really current intelligence, I think, has become a vast sucking chest wound for the intelligence community, and a nonproductive one at that. And finally, let me conclude by echoing the comments of several others. We've got to learn to use competition rather than attempting to exclude it, and the intelligence community, quite frankly, is an exclusionary service. If you are not in the brotherhood, you are outside the brotherhood. The battles have been made toward open-source information. Quite frankly, open-source information is not the solution. We need open analysis and competition about ideas. And if you look, quite frankly, at what is classified, there is no reason that matters to the policymakers for virtually 80 percent of it to be classified. Large areas of that could be openly submitted to competition for analysis, and the quality of the analysis, as well as the experience level of the analysts, would improve very quickly.

NOLAN: Thank you very, very much. It is time for responses and comments and questions. If you could stand, please, and identify yourself, someone will bring you a microphone. Oh, that is better. It is not possible that you were rendered speechless by this panel.

AUDIENCE - SIMIN CURTIS: I am here with the Ridgway Center. I am also in the private sector, Greycourt & Company. My question is to either Carl Ford or David Kay. Earlier this year, George Tenet came to Pittsburgh and spoke at a cancer benefit. He was a private citizen, of course, and someone was asking him about his slam-dunk comment, and he could not really talk about that. But what he did say—sort of what I remember—is that the CIA can never talk about their successes. I sort of wanted you to comment on that, and also ask whether you believe that we are, in fact, doing a better job since 9/11 at detecting terror cells and destroying them. And are we safer since there has not been an attack on our soil since then, or are Madrid and London just sort of a precursors to what we can expect in the future?

FORD: Well, it has been my experience that there is a difference between the capability of the intelligence community and what it actually produces. There are a lot of smart, capable people who spent a good portion of their lives studying particular countries, regions, or issues, and I have always found that they had information and knowledge that was useful to me. But the product that we produce in the intelligence community is, and I cannot think of a better word, crap. And to those who believe that because you do not have a clearance or that you do not have a need-to-know, that there is a lot of good stuff out there that is going to the president and the secretary of defense, the secretary of state, and I could tell you what we really know—well, I have got bridges in Arizona to sell you. As far as I am concerned, the NIE key judgments that are now unclassified give you a window into the best production of the intelligence community.

KAY: Well, let me just add, it is really hard to have a discussion about we are right, but I cannot tell you when, and, yeah, we were wrong, and we are at war because of it. One thing I know; the other is hidden in this murky land. I do not want in any way to denigrate the patriotism and dedication of the people who are involved in the intelligence enterprise. I've got the greatest of admiration for what they are trying to do and their successes. I think, by and large, if you look at the number of intelligence failures that really are strung like a not-very-pretty pearl necklace over the last twenty years—I do not know if I would use Carl's scientific term of "crap," but as a Texan, we have better, more descriptive terms for that. I hasten to add I am not an Aggie. My Aggie friends have even better terms for it. I do have Aggie friends, for some of those who doubt it. I think, not to recognize that it is a broken system is what, in fact, is going to leave the system broken. And the cop-out that "well, we were right, I just can't tell you when," is genuinely a cop-out that is not worthy of the dedication of the men and women who serve, nor of the policymakers who, in fact, have a right to expect a much better product than they are given. So that argument does not wash well with me.

FORD: If I could just add one brief comment, just sort of as an example, and it may not be representative of anything other than my own experience. When I was NIO [National Intelligence Officer], and I was there for about three and a half years, I wasn't reading all of the raw traffic. I had an assistant and a secretary who would filter out a lot of stuff, but I read a lot of things that were coming in. But I did read every single publication done by anyone in the community having to do with East Asia, and I had a simple proposition in my mind as I would read that product. If I could say to myself, "Wow, I did not know that; that is interesting," not only did I write the article down, I tried to find the author of that piece. And I would either see them personally or call them on the telephone and say, "Hey, good work." The problem was that in three and a half years, and probably a rough estimate of maybe 12,000 or 14,000 different publications, I had said "I did not know that" less than ten times. And among those ten, less than ten, publications, a number of them were economic in orientation. I can't even balance a checkbook. So someone who knew something about economics probably said, "Well, I already knew this, too." But that was the sort of dimension of it. When I then went and changed jobs and went to the Pentagon, I kept that up over another four years. The number of documents I read expanded to different geographic regions, and the amount of raw intelligence was drastically reduced; but after seven and a half years, I was still on five fingers and ten toes on the times that I could say honestly and sincerely, "I did not know that," when I read a publication. Now to me, that is a broken system. If our experts cannot write things that I did not know before I read the report, something is terribly wrong.

GORMLEY: Let me add to the issue, focusing on the question that relates to successes, and I certainly cannot speak to when the next surprise will occur. I simply talked about the huge consequences of WMD. But in terms of successes, those successes are not advertised, and there is some open record with respect to, for example, the successes in wrapping up terrorist groups, between [Operations] DESERT SHIELD and DESERT STORM, when Iraq challenged us and said that we were going to send terrorist groups. There was an enormous acceleration of collaboration amongst elements of the intelligence community, which all came apart in the aftermath of DESERT STORM. And I think there is an object lesson in that, and it speaks to the importance of strategic context. It informs your willingness to take decisions to clarify ambiguity. And the danger is that, as time passes and the strategic context shifts, you create a lulling effect as a consequence, and you may be less prone to take those actions that clarify ambiguity. So what I fear is, to the extent that time passes with success in precluding attacks recurring on U.S. soil, that it may well lull us into an unwillingness to take certain actions that we need to take to clarify ambiguity. So that is an important, critical factor that we need to pay attention to, and we need to repair the institutions to deal with clarifying ambiguity on a permanent basis, independent of the strategic context.

AUDIENCE - DAVID BUFFALOE: I am Captain David Buffaloe, U.S. Army Joint Staff intern. I was wondering if anyone on the panel would care to speculate on potential future threats. The first one is the failure of capitalism to achieve widespread prosperity in the former Soviet Union. What could that spell for the United States, if a failed Russian state were to occur with its vast WMD resources? The second would be, if widespread dissent and anger amongst the Arab populace could potentially cause a fall of the House of Saud, what could that potential mean for the United States with its vast natural resources?

NOLAN: Two excellent questions. Who would like to take one or both? Come on guys, this is a panel of courage here.

KAY/GORMLEY: I think a former chairman should address that.

NOLAN: I could certainly speak to the second one, which is only to say that the second issue—the discussion of the internal stability in Saudi Arabia—has been analyzed much too little and is not debated openly. The reluctance to take this on, even in the academic environment, is reflective of some of the lessons I think we learned with the fall of the shah of Iran. The outcome of that, given the dependency—reverse dependency, in this case—of the United States on the strategic relationship and partnership, actually precludes an open and informed discussion of what we would do in the event that instability arises, and this is very much the case. When it was quite clear to many, not even experts, that the rule of the shah was problematic and certainly not eternal, many people who did raise issues about that regime found themselves silenced in a variety of ways. The collective tended to say, because we have such important strategic interest in the Persian Gulf, therefore, the shah will live forever somehow. But punishing the people presenting information, becoming inadvertent dissenters, is a very fascinating topic, and it pertains, I think, very, very much to the nondiscussion about Saudi Arabia. There is no good reason for it other than the observation of codes of conduct that themselves need to be our fight and talked about more openly, because they contribute directly to the failure of imagination or, if not failure of imagination, the failure to communicate that imagination in any way that does not result in career suicide—which I may have just committed. But I don't care.

KAY: Can I just add, I think these are two examples of where you ought to understand what you can ask of the intelligence community. You cannot ask and expect an answer of the intelligence community, is the House of Saud going to fall in 2012 in June? What you can expect, and should hold the intelligence community to telling the policymakers, is, there are pressures, there are processes, there are things happening in Saudi Arabia—to use your two examples—and Russia that, in fact, hold the prospect of leading to . . . and you policymakers had better think about how you deal with it. Now, there is a tendency when the prospect of a problem is so awful. For any of you of my age who ever used to play war games, every time you exercised the nuclear option is when the game ended. I mean, no one wanted to think through the process of after you called for the nuclear option, so you ended it—consequently, very seldom did you think that process through. The same thing is true about something truly horrendous: the fall of the House of Saud and the implications that would have for U.S. national security, economic security; Russia falling into chaos, a failed nuclear state as capitalism fails and whatever breaks out afterwards. But you can expect the intelligence community to be able to tell policymakers about developments that, in fact, hold the possibility of that, having and emphasizing it. One problem is—and it is the nature of the collection process—overhead collection is far better at counting things than it is at telling you about social processes that are going on. I remember a German friend of mine—as I was bemoaning what had happened to us in Iraq and failing to recognize how corrupt that state had become after 1995 and the implications that had for WMD, any prospect of having WMD capability—saying to me, "Don't feel so bad; we didn't even understand that the DDR, the East Germans, could not collect their own garbage until after the fall." Collection capability was not focused on societal processes and warning policymakers of the broader implications, which indeed are national security implications, the economic security implications. That is the responsibility of the managers of the process, and it is one that I am a very harsh critic of. What appears in the presidential daily brief is the worst of current intelligence mania. Instead of reporting that the ruler of X state is engaged in some shadowy activity with gem stones or something worse than that or sometimes not even worse than that, they should be raising to the president's level that 35 percent HIV-positive in the Russian strategic rocket force, plus this and this means that whole prospect, that whole enterprise, may fall apart. Focusing analysis and policymaking thought on that should be the mission of managers of the intelligence community, and it is not a mission they rise to very often.

CROWE: If you are concerned about whether the policymakers are aware of what you talked about or not, you shouldn't be, because on the particular subjects you mentioned, the U.S. government has pushed that information up to the top. I can speak from some experience on that, for example, Saudi Arabia. But concluding that Saudi Arabia is going to fall and is going to present a problem for the United States does not take into account the entire spectrum of problems a change in policy would involve in the United States, not only vis-à-vis a foreign country.

And some of these problems are such that, even if you concluded it, and even if you knew what you do not know, I am not so sure that policy would change very much. You've got some current examples, one being Pakistan. We have forged a relationship with Pakistan for short-term reasons; that is very important and very helpful, and probably for long-term reasons that is a major problem. But would you change, give up the short-term interest in order to worry about the major problem? You might, an analyst might. But the policymaker who deals with the United States government, who wants to get reelected, has got a lot of pressures on oil, etc., etc., energy—no, he is not going to give up the short term. And the way you are going to solve those problems is, when it happens, you are going to deal with it. Not the neatest, tidiest way to do business, but in the world of politics, that is realistic.

Mr. Kay said he thought that policymakers had a right to demand greater product. I am not so sure that is true. If they are aware of the vulnerabilities, the fragility of intelligence and its limitations, that in some cases getting what you might call shoddy or mediocre intelligence is the best we can do—a policymaker should understand that, and he has got to make his policies to hedge on what he does not know. The idea that if he makes a mistake, it's always intelligence's fault is not true. In battle, very seldom does a military commander have complete intelligence, but he still has to fight, and he still has to win or lose, and he doesn't have time to say, "Well, let's blame the intelligence people for this." He has got to deal with the fact he does not know everything. And the policymakers in the U.S. government do not know everything, and they never will. I guess my instinct would be to blame the policymaker more than the intelligence, but that is a bias that you can afford when you get to be my age.

FORD: One simple experiment that you can try, particularly those of you in the military who have tasking authority, go back tomorrow and ask your intelligence experts. Because I think we all agree that these two questions are pretty important and that somebody ought to have been looking at them. They may not have the best answers, but they ought to have been looking at them. So ask them to give you a bibliography of the products over the past five years that deal with these two questions, in any form or fashion, even if it is only an incremental part, and to give you, in their judgment, the five best products that they use to make judgments about those questions. I guarantee you, the hard part will be trying to come up with five. The bibliography will probably be a simpler task—they ought to be able to do that within a few hours—but give them a day and see what comes back. And then read what you get and make your own judgment. Don't believe me; don't believe other people. Take your own survey of what you get back when you ask a question as important as what is the future of Saudi Arabia–U.S. relations and what could go wrong there. Ask the question and see what you get back.

CROWE: Incidentally, we were looking at the questions you asked when I was chairman. Some of the major military victories of history have been forced when the commanders said, "I disagree completely with the intelligence, and I'm unwilling to run the risk." Politicians are not liable to say that.

FORD: Those are the smart people.

KAY: Again, let me just say, I think Admiral Crowe made an important point that I do not think is considered often enough. I think it is a combination of responsibility of the policymakers and of the intelligence community, and it is an example of Gresham's Law ["bad money drives good money out of circulation"] operating. You know, Lyndon Johnson used to say he would like to find a one-armed economist, because every time he asked an economist, the answer would be, on the one hand, on the other hand, on the third hand, on the fourth hand. Policymakers do not like ambiguity in response to questions. Now, moral courage on intelligence managers would, in fact, lead them to emphasize the limits of their knowledge and the knowability when they are engaged in discussions with policymakers, even if policymakers would not like to hear it. I think if you look over the course of the last two decades, you would find that people who manage intelligence services have been willing to trade intellectual honesty as to the limitations of the analysis for access to the policymakers by giving them a certainty that the data, in fact, do not have. Now, to argue who is at fault—well, ultimately, in fact, the policymakers are at fault. Anyone who tells anyone in the White House office about anything more mundane than the time of day, and maybe even on that, and gets an answer back, "it's a slam-dunk," deserves to be grilled, slashed, burned by the process itself—which says nothing is that simple and that compelling; let's understand the limits of the data you have. We seem to have lost that intellectual rigor, and it has been lost from both sides there. I think we are suffering from that.

NOLAN: I think, certainly with the various commissions, recommendations are unanimous that there should be more team B exercises and more questioning of mindsets. Those two topics that you raised—the failure of capitalism in that region of the world and Saudi Arabia—should be at the very top of the list. This is part of the implementation of commission recommendations, where there is often a big disconnect between the announcement of the conclusions and the actual implementation strategy. There are questions. Let's get you a microphone.

CROWE: Why aren't you up here, General?

AUDIENCE - LIEUTENANT GENERAL JOHN F. KIMMONS: I am J. F. Kimmons. I am the Army G2, and I appreciate the thoughtful comments that have been made this morning. I think they are very insightful. I am in the position of having to try to fix this as we go, because we have a lot going on right now with an ongoing war on terrorism and a lot of other regional crises present on the agenda. I have worked with David Kay on some of this over the last four years. These are hard problems. Whoever made the comment that if it was easy, someone would have already done it—that is very apt. We do have a lot of very bright and dedicated people, and I think the challenge we face is how to turn this to our advantage. We have some asymmetric advantages here in America. We are candid, more than most of our friends and allies, in admitting where we have come up short and are certainly devoting a great deal of money and attention on how to fix this as we go. The commissions that have reported out, the fixes that have been put in place, the establishment of an NDI—a small step, but at least a step, probably in the right direction—come to mind. Unlike Carl Ford, I read things all the time that I did not know before, but that is probably a reflection on me, not on the quality of the work. My experience over the last thirty-one years is that we are paid to take into account all of the information we can put our arms around and deliver intelligence assessments when they are required, not when we are fully satisfied we have all the facts and figures. The challenge is how to do that with full integrity, do that with absolute rigor, and still meet your deadlines. We are called upon to take all that ambiguity and render judgments, and then attempt to confirm or deny with all-source intelligence and other sources that our judgments are correct. And if they are not, we have to have the moral courage to go back and tell the boss we got it wrong, it has changed. I think that has always been the dynamic; the challenge is how to do it better, how to gain access to more information faster for a more complete, less biased view. But you still have to, at the end of the day, meet your deliverables. You have to render your judgments. And people make life-and-death decisions on the strength of your judgments at every level, from battalion level all the way up to the strategic level. If we do not do that with full candor and with full rigor, shame on us. We are accountable, and we need to be accountable for that. But at the same time, I think that the practical challenge is how to do this better.

Now in 2005, in the fourth year of war, we have a lot of people engaged all over the world, and I would appreciate your comments, any or all of you. As a community, and I am a part of it, one of the things we are focusing on, and that George Tenet attempted to put in place before he left, was addressing the issue of information sharing: how to do that and how to create a flat network without compartments and stovepipes so that we can collaborate at all levels with all of the information or virtually all of the information available, unclassified to highly classified, in near real time, to take advantage of windows of opportunity, to recognize significance, to understand associations, and to try to understand the full context for the little ambiguous bits and pieces that we see every day. Again, we have got to make the judgments on call, because that is not negotiable. So, I think the steps that have been made—to better fuse intelligence, to empower our analysts at all levels with more and more information so they can see it, they can visualize it, and they can see how things interrelate, all these terabytes of information that go back years and years, information and papers that they will never have read, to understand that so they can collaborate meaningfully with each other faster, better, across the world, using globalization—I think strikes me is being a fundamental, critical step in getting this more right than wrong. And, of course, we get to test fire it and apply it in a war at a tactical level, but it has strategic implications. At the end of the day, you need better analysis, and the comments that were made in that regard, I believe, are absolutely spot on. But analysis is tough and it's an outdoor sport. And so enough, but I appreciate your thoughts. Thank you.

NOLAN: Thank you for your very thoughtful comment.

CROWE: General, the operative word you used that impressed me was "full integrity." It is just as wise to report we do not know, or we do not partially know, or we are not confident. You could meet a deadline, but you can say those things too, and it is imperative that you do if that is the case. The boss won't like it all the time, but who cares about that?

FORD: There also has to be some risk taking on the part of managers. I believe, and this is just simply my personal experience, that you could take two-thirds of our current analytical force and send them to the dark side of the moon, and it would take a good eighteen months for anybody other than their families to realize they were gone. The fact is that we are duplicating every day, over and over, stuff that a much smaller work force could do. So somebody just simply has to say, stop doing that, I want you to do something else. And if you take part of our people and say, do something else, they will do something else. They've got the collection, they've got the human brain power; somebody simply has to tell them to go do it.

For example, one of the things that shocks people is, they ask me, "What about Korean weapons of mass destruction?" and I say, "Well, we probably knew a thousand times more about Iraq's weapons of mass destruction than we do North Korea." So take it from there; be comforted by that. But the fact is that we have a lot of very well-trained Korean specialists around DIA, NSA, in the Army, at INR, and at the CIA—wherever you go. Put seventy-five of those people together and say, "Think new thoughts; let's get to the bottom of this particular problem. We want you to think and work on that problem full time and tell us when you have something good. We are not going to ask you to do presidential daily briefs, we are not going to ask you to do PowerPoint presentations, we are going to ask you to use your minds to study that problem." If we can't afford to take fifty to seventy-five people and put them on North Korea, then what are we doing intelligence for? I guarantee you, for the next decade, the president, secretary of defense, secretary of state, everybody is going to want to know everything that we can find out about North Korea: how much food they have, what dialects they speak. The number of problems that we have with North Korea are so great that we cannot give them enough new knowledge about North Korea. We got the people, we got the money, we got the time, and you are still going to get your PDB [President's Daily Brief]. Go do it. But somebody has just simply got to take those people and put them on the priority.

I'd put some on Iran, too. I am not the smartest person or the sharpest tack in the drawer, but the fact is that we are going to be focused on Iran. How about China? Those are not hard questions for managers to answer. The question is, take the people and resources and go do it, but talk about quality, not quantity, talk about getting the job done better. And remember, as everybody said here, I always referred to intelligence as WAGS. I don't do that as a pejorative; I think it is an accurate statement of what we do as analysts: WAGS, wild ass guesses, okay. But I would rather have one of my old INR analysts who had been following the problem for twenty years guess for me, than one of those three-year wonders at CIA. Expertise matters, experience matters, and in intelligence it matters even more because you are guessing. You are making educated guesses, hopefully, you are doing it based on research and evidence, but in the end you are telling the policymaker your best guess. That is something that you cannot get away from, and if the policymakers forget it, shame on them. If intelligence officers forget it and talk about slam-dunks, shame on them.

CROWE: When you organize this trip to the dark side of the moon, I got a long list that I would like to add to that.

NOLAN: See if we can give quick responses so we can have a few more questions.

GORMLEY: I have a recommendation that is very specific. If all these commissions talk about changing mindsets and you change mindsets through the collaborative process, taking the three-year wonders in the CIA and affording them the opportunity to collaborate with a few experts who remain in various parts of the intelligence community, even some outliers, why doesn't that occur more systematically? David talked about the tools that are used in the intelligence community, how shocked we are at how abysmally—you walk into a modern corporation, you see all of these IT tools, they are not used because of another thing that Carl said, risk. The risk you need to take is to look at the risk-benefit calculus over implementing more formalism in the analytic process through the use of information technology tools. They are not a salvation, but they certainly allow for much improved collaboration across the full breadth of the intelligence community. That risk-benefit tradeoff now errs decidedly on the side of "we do not want to take any risks." Software tools are readily available; DARPA spends millions and millions of dollars on developing these tools—none of which find their way into the intelligence community because of concerns about collaboration and the associated risks of that collaboration. So something needs to be made to break that phalanx of erring on the side of no risk and not considering the enormous benefits associated with that collaborative process.

KAY: General Kimmons, I think we all feel and understand the intense pressures you work under, as you've got men and women who are putting their lives daily at risk and, in fact, are losing them. I don't think anything we are going to say is going to be very helpful to you in that regard. I mean, it is just a pain, as I know you know, you have to bear and do the best you can. I do think there are some solutions and some steps—probably not solutions, but steps—that need to be taken that will at least make your successors' task a little bit easier, and that is, I think we ought to recognize we have a broken bottle. We've divided the intelligence world into collection systems, into human intelligence collectors, which exist quite different from the technical world of intelligence collection, and then we've got the analysts. That is the model that grew up in the early years of the Cold War and has been perpetuated for a lot of reasons that we don't have time to go into here. That's absolutely the wrong model, and let me give you a real-life military example of where you broke that model: when Bill Owens said, "Look, we don't have to drop 500-pound iron bombs on every bloody power station wherever you are." There must be a way to think through the systemic problems of how they exist and understand the choke points. That was the rise of a Joint Warfare Analysis Center, JWAC. You know, we've lost in the intelligence community—I know DIA and the military has it; CIA actually doesn't have it—the expertise of thinking about targeteers and targeting. We, in fact, need people who say, whose job is, "the problem is, how about the stability of Saudi." If want to understand and get a better answer for the boss than I have today, what do I need to bring to bear? And you don't get it by going out to NRO, or going to CIA, the DO [Directorate of Operations], or going to the intelligence analyst at either DIA or the CIA and asking those as stovepipes. You bring them together and say, "I don't want to develop any more collection systems that, in fact, don't have input from my analysts and my targeteers that will give me answers that are relevant and understandable to them." Dennis mentioned—and we cannot say very much more about it than it is an utter disaster—the future imagery architecture is a classic example of giving technical weenies their head and telling them to go out and think bold thoughts about collection systems, when they are uninformed by the questions analysts have to answer for the boss. The targeteers know where the answers may be, if you can only get me into that place, whether it be a denied mine or a denied area. I really think that it is the responsibility of people like you to go back and rethink that model and break it and put it together in a way that makes sense and gives your successors, probably not you, the quality answers that your boss wants. Until we do that, we are going to spend a lot of money, waste a lot of effort, and the product is still going to be—to use the scientific term of Carl—crap.

NOLAN: Maybe a lot of us are going to be on the dark side of the moon. Not for reasons of having very challenging and certainly very difficult problems being put forward, which are welcome, but there was a question over here earlier. I think I would like to take two or maybe three more questions and let each of the panelists respond with a summation. Over here. This gentleman needs the microphone.

AUDIENCE - WILLIAM RUDOLF: Thank you. I am Bill Rudolf of the National Committee on American Foreign Policy. I wanted to ask you, in terms of avoiding surprises, to what degree are we spending money and should we spend money and effort in infiltrating those whom we identify as potential enemies and potential military or nonmilitary enemies of the United States, and how long, in your view, will it take to infiltrate foreign potential enemies?

NOLAN: Thank you. Let's take two more questions. There is someone over here, back on that back row there.

AUDIENCE - HERMAN COHEN: Hi, I am Herman Cohen. I was the deputy assistant secretary for INR for four years, and I consider that one of the richest experiences I ever had. That was twenty years ago, and I am quite sorry to see that the research element has really gone down hill. I had a question for Mr. Gormley. On your USS *Cole* example, okay, it was policy that it was a good thing to send the *Cole*, but wasn't there a G2 in CENTCOM who was aware of the dangers? And couldn't he tell the commander, look, it is policy, you want to send it, that's fine, but if you see a small boat coming, shoot first and ask questions later. Isn't that type of analysis getting out there?

NOLAN: There is a question in the back row and one right here, and that is all we can take. Each of the members of the panel will respond.

AUDIENCE - LUKE GERDES: My name is Luke Gerdes, and I am with the Ridgway Center. My question is also for Professor Gormley. It deals with his pessimistic view on structural reform. As you guys have all emphasized, innovation is very necessary for the intelligence community to improve. My concern is, can a highly bureaucratic organization, such as the intelligence community, going to be able to do so. In fact, that has been the conclusion drawn by every theorist that has tackled organizations as a subject since Max Weber first published his work on bureaucracy in the 1920s. I don't mean to overstate the case, but given this recognized need for innovation and bureaucracy's well documented inability to do so, can effective reform take place without at least some structural reform that moves away from bureaucracy and centralization?

NOLAN: The final question in the back, right there.

AUDIENCE - ANNA WEISFEILER: Hi, my name is Anna Weisfeiler; I am a grad student. I was wondering what your opinion is of DNI and whether you think that will be an effective method of shifting analysis more toward transient insights, as you said we should be doing.

NOLAN: We have questions about infiltrating enemies, about the *Cole* specifically directed to Dennis Gormley, about network organizations and reforms, and about the DNI. You can talk about whatever you like. Admiral Crowe.

CROWE: I would like to mention the *Cole*. Yes, that information gets out and that is proper, but when a ship is sent in there, the commanding officer still has the responsibility for the safety of the ship. His superior has the responsibility to make sure he is aware of the ambiance and the general mood, tone, etc. He was. But he sends his ship in with confidence that the ship is worrying about its own security, and if something like that happens, there is accountability in the Navy, and it is still the commanding officer's responsibility. Incidentally, we had plenty of evidence in the past that something like that might happen. Rather than answer some other question, I just want to make one final observation. I couldn't help thinking—and I don't know if you'll find this comforting or not—but I had a lot of very long conversations with my opposite number, Marshal [Sergei] Akhromeyev, who was the chief of the Soviet general staff at the time. In fact, he and I, and I hesitate to say this, we almost became friends. I know it was unfashionable, but he had the same concerns about his intelligence that we have heard voiced here today, and he was very depressed about the quality of Soviet intelligence and their inability, etc., etc. In fact, he used the analogy that we, in the Cold War, were passing trains in the night, that we never understood each other. But he was very quick to criticize his own system, and, as I say, you may find that comforting.

NOLAN: Final words, Carl.

FORD: Just a final comment on organization and bureaucracy. As I suggested, I think that the current system is broken. And I also said I think that the DNI is at least a step in the right direction, but I think that the DNI should use this as an opportunity to create what David referred to as a new model for intelligence. We simply can't continue to do it the way we have done it. We can't make incremental changes. We have to come up with a whole new paradigm for the way we think about, at least, intelligence analysis, and how we weave together a collection and analysis. And that is something that is going to require a centralized authority. My guess is that it is going to mean greater decentralization within the intelligence community. Innovation and innovative thinking rarely happens in a large bureaucracy. You also need the competition and infighting that goes on when several different organizations are rushing to try to solve the same problem. I am also struck by the way that our colleagues in the scientific community do it. That is, they find someone who has a lot of experience and they have a question that they are trying to answer, whether it is a cure for some sort of cancer or whatever it might be, and that person is given responsibility to put a team of people together to try to focus on answering that question. That is what the organization and the team are based on—the problem and the question. Right now, our bureaucracy is formed, and then we try to bring the questions into that existing bureaucracy. I think we have to change that paradigm around and focus on organizing around problems that need to be solved, rather than using our existing organizations.

NOLAN: Dennis and David you have two minutes each.

GORMLEY: Two minutes, okay. Nobody answered infiltrating the adversary. I will take a stab at it. I had the former head of KGB [Soviet Committee for State Security] operations, the head of what they referred to as Washington Station, in my class at the University of Pittsburgh two weeks ago, and the question of penetrating al Qaeda operations came up. The best that he could give was, go to the mosques and collect information. I am sure we do that. But infiltrating inside these organizations is a daunting problem. How long will it take with new training in language skills and cultural sensitivity, etc.? It will take a long time, and it is a serendipitous process. On G2, I think Admiral Crowe answered the question appropriately. Let me simply say that the messenger—the individual from the National Security Council who was charged by the then-head of the National Security Council to go out and look at vulnerabilities, military vulnerabilities in various regions of the world—the messenger was shot. His top secret memorandum was leaked to *The Washington Post*, and the military essentially said, stay out of our business. It is, indeed, ultimately the military's responsibility, and the actions they take with respect to rules of engagement become critical in that regard. On Luke Gerdes' question on networked organizations: I didn't mean to suggest that radical changes need to take place. Carl Ford just mentioned some that I would endorse, and that is going to a more networked organization, and maybe the first step toward that is the suggestion I made with respect to putting midlevel intelligence officers out into the network and allowing for that collaboration. A networked organization won't work without true, significant, revolutionary improvements in collaboration, akin to what goes on in modern industry today. So that is an essential element of it. I'll end it there.

NOLAN: David, you have the last word.

KAY: Okay, just a couple of comments. Let me take first the infiltration one, as well. I don't want to be too pessimistic, but let me give you a fact that is now declassified. Not at any time during the Cold War did the U.S. government have a single penetration operating at the Politburo level of the Soviet Union. Sure, we had people at other levels who we managed or usually walked in. They were generally not recruited, and that was a relatively easy target. You can double the money spent on human intelligence today, and unless you break the model, you are not going to get any better. How do you expect people who operate out of embassies—and principally that's where they operate out of these days—to penetrate people like al Qaeda? Al Qaeda is a particularly a hard target. Sure you can get the paper hangers, the document forgers, the gun runners, but to expect that you could penetrate the senior planning level of al Qaeda on our present model, I think, is just a hopeless task. On the DNI, there is a general rule we all know from our own life. It is awfully hard to be better than your customer, unless the customer is demanding better intelligence. Let me single out J. F. Kimmons. General Kimmons understands when the commander is not happy with the quality of intelligence he is giving, as he was not at certain times in Iraq. Tremendous changes can be made in the organizational structure, the way you organize it and collect intelligence, but you had a very unhappy customer at that point. Unless, at the very top level of policymakers, there is a tremendous revulsion against the intelligence product and a demand for better, I don't think any reorganization of the deck chairs is going to produce very much. And quite frankly, my pessimistic view is that, unfortunately, the intelligence policymakers have concluded it is crap, it is unlikely to get better than that, and in some ways it serves our interests, it opens up our operational freedom, if everyone recognizes it as that. They are not willing to endorse, encourage, and break the china necessary to do the fundamental reorganization. Until you break that china and do that because you are an unhappy customer, I do not think you are going to be successful.

NOLAN: Thank you very much. Please join me in thanking the Army and this panel for their candid remarks.

PANEL IV

UNDERSTANDING THE NEXUS OF PROLIFERATION AND TERRORISM

Co-sponsor: Woodrow Wilson International Center for Scholars

Moderator: Robert S. Litwak, Ph.D., Director of the Division of International Security Studies, Woodrow Wilson International Center for Scholars

Shahram Chubin, Ph.D., Head of Academic Affairs, Director of Research, Geneva Centre for Security Policy

Bruce Hoffman, D.Phil., Corporate Chair in Counterterrorism and Counterinsurgency, The RAND Corporation

Mitchell B. Reiss, D.Phil., Vice Provost, College of William and Mary

Panel Charter

JIM LEHRER, Moderator: ...So it's correct to say, that if somebody is listening to this, that both of you agree, if you're reelected, Mr. President, and if you are elected [Senator Kerry], the single most serious threat you believe, both of you believe, is nuclear proliferation?

GEORGE W. BUSH: In the hands of a terrorist enemy.

JOHN KERRY: Weapons of mass destruction, nuclear proliferation....

—Presidential Debate No. 1, September 30, 2004

As time allows us to gain perspective on the events of September 11, 2001, many scholars have come to the conclusion that those attacks did not, in fact, change the structure of international relations. Instead, they highlighted the glaring vulnerability of free nations and ushered in a new era of danger for Western-style liberal democracies.

There seems to be agreement on the composition of this danger. At the first presidential debate in 2004, both President George W. Bush and Senator John Kerry recognized the "nexus" of nuclear proliferation and terrorism as the most

Left to right: *Robert S. Litwak, Shahram Chubin, Bruce Hoffman,
and Mitchell B. Reiss*

serious threat facing our country. But what is this nexus, and how can we study it effectively?

This panel attempted to provide greater analytical and policy clarity to this nexus between proliferation and terrorism. Perspectives came from several critical areas. The depth of academic talent and practical expertise on this panel—composed of world-renowned terrorism experts and those who planned the American policy response to these threats—helped guide the discussion.

Discussion Points

1. How might a terrorist group gain access to nuclear and other unconventional capabilities?

2. What strategies can be adopted on the state level to deter the direct transfer or prevent the leakage of such capabilities to nonstate actors, such as al Qaeda?

3. In fashioning these strategies, what are the roles of deterrence, military preemption (or prevention), and capacity building?

Shahram Chubin, Ph.D.

• Rogue states have historically been "underestimated or understudied," but they are not new. During the 1990s, the central question was, can rogue states be deterred, and if so, by what means? Some drew the conclusion that rogue states are irresponsible. Consequently, they attempted to link terrorist attacks to these states. It was readily apparent in the 1990s that terrorists were prepared to inflict mass casualties. Following from that assessment was the conviction that terrorists would seek to acquire the means to carry out these attacks from rogue states.

Inexorably, the notion of regime change took hold. Aum Shinrikyo clearly did not fit this profile. It carried out its 1995 attacks on the Japanese subway system as a transnational actor, independent of any state support (a fact that was largely ignored at the time). Similarly, the 2001 anthrax mail attacks in the United States show no evidence of state sponsorship. We all missed the most significant development in the post–Cold War era, the emergence of transnational autonomous organizations like al Qaeda. Nevertheless, there was a continuing focus on states—a state-centric analysis of the terrorist-WMD threat.

• What do we know about the terrorism-WMD nexus? For one thing, we know that some terrorist groups seek WMD. However, not all terrorist groups with terrorist aims seek WMD. For another, we know that some terrorist groups do not depend on states for their existence. They have their own organizing and financing networks. In addition, we know that some governments have cooperated with terrorist organizations. However, we know of no case where a government has transferred a weapon of mass destruction to a terrorist organization.

• With respect to Iran, we know that Tehran has used terrorism strategically against U.S. Soldiers and diplomats, has encouraged cooperation among Shi'a in the Middle East, has transferred missiles to Hezbollah, has supported terrorism for bargaining purposes, and has hosted at least some terrorist elements. Iran has reportedly offered to share missile technology with its neighbors. The current Iranian president made the (mis) statement that Iran would be willing to share nuclear technology with its Muslim neighbors. Iran is suspected of developing biological weapons (BW) and chemical weapons (CW) for offensive capability. Yet, the direct transfer of WMD by Iran to terrorist groups is highly unlikely. The regime has not stayed in power for a quarter of a century by behaving this recklessly. More problematic, however, is the use of a controlled group to execute an order under specific circumstances. What would these circumstances be? The outsourcing of WMD to a terrorist group would be most likely when the regime itself feels under direct attack. The most troubling scenarios are the "insider" problem (where a rogue faction or institution transfers WMD) and the "leakage" problem (where technology or material is stolen or sold).

• The biggest U.S. mistake with respect to dealing with Iran is loose talk and wishful thinking about regime collapse. U.S. policy, ostensibly, is aimed at persuading Iran to change its policies. But, in practice, which policies would Tehran have to change that the United States would settle for? The United States needs to be reasonable and specific in its expectations toward Iran, lest it back the regime into a corner, raising the risk that Tehran might commit the very act the United States wishes to avoid.

• International legal arguments aside, in theory, a policy of preemption is enticing. The notion of a preemptive attack on North Korean nuclear installations is appealing, but what of the feasibility and probable adverse consequences or the problem of faulty or inadequate intelligence? In practice, then, it is difficult to find cases where preemption would work. If a policy of preemption is thus inadvisable, then what of deterrence? The case of Iraq weakened the credibility of deterrence. The case of the homegrown terrorist reveals that military means have no deterrent value. We are therefore drawn to the policies of denial and prevention. Getting governments to set and adhere to international standards is of critical importance. To be sure, cooperative threat reduction (CTR) is not easy, given the premium all governments place on secrecy, not to mention national pride and the problem of corruption. Nevertheless, perhaps UN Security Council resolution 1540 could be used as authority to develop a mechanism for setting international standards for best practices to secure companies against the knowing transfer or leakage of dangerous technologies.

Bruce Hoffman, D.Phil.
_____

• The "missing third dimension" is a terrorist group's own WMD research and development activities. When terrorists look toward these weapons, the expectation now is that they will deliver an enormous psychological blow to their adversary. There is no doubt about al Qaeda's lethal intentions. There is also clear evidence that al Qaeda made numerous attempts to acquire WMD capability from rogue scientists and insecure installations, and put in place parallel chem-bio research programs. Their interests were matched with at least nascent capabilities.

• As easy as it is to fabricate ricin and some other pathogens, it is very difficult to disseminate the substance. But if you look carefully at the British case, the group seeking to employ ricin was rather more sophisticated than had initially been assumed. This suggests that even those groups that are on the low end of the terrorism food chain, though under no illusions they could kill thousands, understand the profound psychological damage they could inflict. Mere contamination is enough of an accomplishment for them. So, even though mass attack cannot be totally discounted, the immediate future threat of contamination looms large. Terrorists have learned profound lessons from the 2001 (as yet unsolved) anthrax attacks: that such attacks produce unsettling effects (fears and anxieties) throughout society, that miniscule traces of a pathogen can shut down major federal buildings for four months or even years, that decontamination costs ($41.7 million, in the anthrax case) can be enormous.

• To counter such threats, the military has a role to play. U.S. Special Forces can be enormously helpful in conducting strategic reconnaissance. But with respect to the threat of contamination, questions of response and remediation loom largest, although prevention is still important.

Mitchell B. Reiss, D.Phil.
_____

• The first challenge in addressing the terrorism-WMD threat is coming to terms with the multitude of forms this threat may take. This entails determining whether there is any hierarchy of threat among chemical, biological, nuclear, and radiological. Each of these threats calls for a different type of response.

- With respect to the nuclear threat, there is ample evidence of terrorist interest in acquiring such weapons. Al Qaeda continues to pursue its strategic goal. Analytically, then, there are four pathways for terrorists to acquire such weapons: (1) develop the weapons themselves, (2) steal the weapons, (3) buy the weapons, (4) obtain them from states through "inadvertent" transfer (e.g., state collapse, where either chaos or the emergence of a new regime with an ideological affinity to the terrorists could render the weapons accessible). The last pathway is the most worrisome.

- The good news is that there are already mechanisms in place to reduce the likelihood that nuclear weapons will fall into the hands of terrorist groups. There are a number of cooperative threat reduction programs. There are bilateral and multilateral export controls in place. Besides these measures, there are other policy options at our disposal, ranging from active denial (e.g., interdiction and military preemption), to passive denial, to engagement of a potential supplier (e.g., Iran).

- In the case of North Korea, the United States has opted for engagement through the Six-Party-Talks approach. The key to further progress in this effort in the coming round of negotiations in Beijing is the sequencing of who does what when. With respect to Iran, military preemption seems impractical and potentially counterproductive. The conventional wisdom is that the United States does not want to engage Iran. But what is seldom noted is that there is no evidence Iran wants such a dialogue, certainly not at this time. Nevertheless, the United States has not explored directly how much flexibility Tehran might have in its position on nuclear programs. Were we to do so, and were the effort to fail, then at least we would be in a position to win diplomatic support for tougher action.

Question-and-Answer Period

- How can we capture the general sentiment that the terrorism-WMD threat is real and translate this into concrete policy? Chubin advocated that our statements and actions must be grounded in UN standards, not just U.S. standards, because other governments find it easier to adhere to UN standards rather than American ones.

- Have our efforts to defeat terrorism thus far been successful? According to Hoffman, there have been very clear successes, such as killing and capturing al Qaeda members in Afghanistan or apprehending them and other terrorists elsewhere. Reiss added that there has been no attack on the U.S. homeland since 9/11. Nor has any government allied with the United States against terrorism been overthrown. But these achievements should not lull us into complacency. The terrorist threat is formidable. The campaign against terrorism is far from over.

- As terrorists have shown that it does not require physical destruction to accomplish their goals—that mere disruption of our economic and social systems is effective—should we not be doing more to secure ourselves against cyber-attack? Hoffman replied that, given our great dependency on cyber systems, it is wise to spare no expense or effort to guard against cyber-terrorism. But we should also employ the Internet more effectively against terrorists—"contest the ground in virtual space"—so as to make progress in the battle of ideas, which is an integral part of combating terrorism.

Analysis

Panel IV provided wise counsel to decision makers charged with developing strategies intended to defeat terrorist acquisition and employment of WMD. Four key points are particularly instructive. First, there are two certainties with respect to terrorists and WMD—those interested in mass casualty attack are seeking WMD capabilities and will employ WMD should they either develop or acquire them. Second, state sponsorship is not the sine qua non for terrorists of strategic significance. Thus, deliberate transfer of WMD capabilities between rogue states and terrorist actors is among the lowest probability (and, arguably, most manageable) circumstances with regard to the issue. Third, rudimentary, nascent, "homegrown" terrorist capabilities promise significant strategic effects if skillfully cultivated and employed. Finally, a loss of responsible control born of state weakness, failure, or corruption presents a particularly complex challenge, trumping many threat reduction efforts and assumptions on state rationality.

With regard to the first issue, all panelists agreed that select terrorist groups are acutely interested in acquiring WMD capabilities. To those pursuing WMD, possession implies increased prestige and employment promises immediate, far-reaching effects and strategically significant outcomes. Shahram Chubin pointed out that acquisition of WMD capabilities is not a desire common to all terrorist groups. He argued that many are happy to limit themselves to conventional forms of resistance, and thus, the problem is bounded.

The second issue concerning state sponsorship is more controversial and strikes at the heart of the Bush doctrine of preemption. Shahram Chubin and Bruce Hoffman understandably were more forceful in making this argument. Both observed, in their own way, that terrorist groups were increasingly independent and self-sufficient. Thus, many are capable of pursuing discrete strategic objectives without the benefit of state sponsorship. Chubin, citing Iran in particular, indicated that rogue states are likely more rational than conventional wisdom would indicate. The implication of this is clear. Many suspected proliferators are deterred from collusion with terrorists as a matter of policy, as they clearly understand the grave challenge it may entail with regard to regime survival.

On the third issue, Hoffman was particularly thoughtful. He argued that al Qaeda and associated terrorist groups have a long, documented history of trying to both acquire and develop WMD. He contended that terrorist development programs are potentially more consequential than often thought. In his view, "contamination" with chemical, biological, or radiological agents alone may be enough to effect strategically significant levels of unease and disruption on target societies. He pointed to both the anthrax incidents in the immediate post-9/11 period and British discoveries of ricin production in the heart of London as harbingers of a current and future threat from the innovative, diffuse, and sophisticated development and employment of WMD-like capabilities by substate actors.

Finally, with regard to the fourth issue and a loss of responsible control, both Chubin and Mitch Reiss were instructive. Chubin's ideas with regard to rationality only hold to the extent that state WMD capabilities remain under effective and responsible control. Reiss argued that the prospect for some "inadvertent" transfer because of a loss of responsible control is, in fact, the most worrisome prospect with regard to WMD. In his view, state failure looms as one key consideration for future proliferation.

This final point bears some deeper examination. The increasing proliferation of nuclear weapons beyond the bounded community of recognized nuclear powers and their regimented procedures for positive control is particularly troublesome. Pakistan, India, North Korea, and South Africa have acknowledged current or past possession of nuclear capabilities. It seems apparent that Iran is, at a minimum, experimenting with the development of standing nuclear capabilities as well. Finally, Israel has been a widely acknowledged nuclear power for decades, in spite of its own policy of deliberate ambiguity. And this represents only what we know.

None of the new nuclear states, it would seem, are socialized in those norms of nuclear surety that have evolved throughout the Cold War. Substantial internal and external security challenges in any could threaten responsible control of nuclear materials. Some have known formal and informal associations with international terrorism. Finally, the foundations of responsible and effective governance in a number of the states are fragile and may be vulnerable to sudden, serious dislocation. These considerations, when combined with the dubious control of the Russian nuclear arsenal, should cause significant concern within American national security elite. The potential weakness, failure, or substantial corruption of a nuclear state, in particular, puts the most dangerous strategic capabilities only a few degrees of separation from the world's most irresponsible actors.

In its September 2002 National Security Strategy, the Bush administration cautioned that the greatest danger to the United States lay at the "crossroads of radicalism and technology," where "shadowy networks of individuals" and modern technologies came together. In the twenty-first century, combating this threat will require a variety of state and nonstate tools and policies designed for both nonproliferation and counterproliferation. Finding the right balance between the two is paramount if we are to succeed.

Transcript

ANNOUNCER: Ladies and gentleman, please welcome the moderator of our fourth and final panel, the director of the Division of International Security Studies, Woodrow Wilson International Center for Scholars, Dr. Robert S. Litwak.

ROBERT S. LITWAK, PH.D.: The Woodrow Wilson Center is honored to have been asked to participate in this year's Eisenhower National Security Conference as the sponsor of this panel. Our president, former Congressman Lee Hamilton, commends General Schoomaker for his leadership in organizing this forum, which contributes to the nation's dialogue in international security. For those not familiar with the Woodrow Wilson Center, which was established by an act of Congress as the official memorial to our twenty-eighth president, it is an agency of the Smithsonian, located right here in the Ronald Reagan Building. The center sponsors a residential fellowship program and approximately 700 meetings per year with a primarily international focus. You can find out more about the center on our website, www.wilsoncenter.org, and you would be welcome to participate in our public meetings.

This month marks the fourth anniversary of 9/11. A former U.S. official declared that the date of this mass-casualty attack on the American homeland would, henceforth, be a demarcation point as stark as BC and AD in U.S. foreign policy. In terms of its searing impact on the nation's psyche, 9/11 is rightfully grouped with Pearl Harbor and the Kennedy assassination. But despite the widespread view that everything has changed, Osama bin Laden's attacks on the icons of American economic and military power, Wall Street and the Pentagon, did not alter the structure of international relations. Rather, 9/11 marked for the United States the advent of a new era of vulnerability, more dangerously unpredictable than that of the Cold War. The hallmark of this new era is what the Bush administration has called "the nexus of terrorism and WMD." That is the link between the terrorists groups' political intentions and their potential access to capabilities for inflicting horrific mass casualty attacks with weapons of mass destruction. 9/11 highlighted the danger posed by the availability of the means of mass violence to an undeterrable nonstate actor such as al Qaeda. Equally significant for U.S. national security policy, the 9/11 terrorist attacks also starkly recast the debate about state actors, most notably the countries designated by the Bush administration as "rogue states." In branding Iraq, Iran, and North Korea, the core group of rogue states, as the "axis of evil," President George W. Bush explicitly pointed to the threat that a state sponsor might transfer a weapon of mass destruction to a terrorist group, thus "giving them the means to match their hatred." In this new era of vulnerability, the administration's 2002 National Security Strategy document elevated military preemption "as a matter of common sense." Iraq's reported links to al Qaeda were a major element of the Bush administration's case for preventive war in Iraq. In the 2004 presidential campaign, both presidential candidates agreed that the greatest security threat to this country was a nuclear weapon in the hands of a terrorist group. This panel will therefore focus on this issue of the nexus, the link between proliferation and terrorism, and between state and nonstate actors. How might a terrorist group gain access to a weapon of mass destruction, particularly nuclear weapons? What strategies can be adopted on the state level to deter the direct transfer or prevent the leakage of such capabilities to nonstate actors, such as al Qaeda? In fashioning these strategies, what are the rules of deterrence, military preemption or prevention, and capacity building?

To address these questions, we will hear from three distinguished specialists. Shahram Chubin is head of Academic Affairs and director of research at the Geneva Centre for Security Policy. He has taught at the Graduate Institute for International Studies in Geneva, and has been director of regional security

Robert S. Litwak

studies at the International Institute for Strategic Studies in London. He is also a fellow at the Woodrow Wilson Center. Dr. Chubin is an expert on international security in the Middle East, whose work has focused, in particular, on Iran. For the IISS, he authored *Whither Iran? Reform, Domestic Policy, and National Security* and is currently completing a major study on Iran's nuclear program. Bruce Hoffman is director of the RAND Corporation's Washington, D.C., office. He is also an adjunct professor at Georgetown University School of Foreign Service and is a senior fellow of the Combating Terrorism Center at West Point. I'd also mention that Bruce Hoffman and I co-organize a monthly series of meetings under the rubric of the Eisenhower National Security Series on Terrorism and Homeland Security. Dr. Hoffman is the author of one of the classic works in the terrorism field, *Inside Terrorism*, an updated, post-9/11 version of which will be published next year. During spring of 2004, he was the senior advisor on counterterrorism to the Office of National Security Affairs in the coalition provisional authority in Baghdad and has testified before Congress on the subject of terrorism broadly. In 1994, he received the U.S. intelligence community's highest award for a nongovernment employee. Mitchell B. Reiss, our third speaker, is vice provost for international affairs at the College of William and Mary in Williamsburg, Virginia. He was director of the policy planning staff at the Department of State from 2003 to 2005, as well as President Bush's special envoy for the Northern Ireland Peace Process, an assignment he continues to serve. Prior to moving to William and Mary, Dr. Reiss helped manage the start-up and operations of the Korean Peninsula Energy Development Organization, or KEDO, which is a multinational organization. He is a lawyer by training and has also been a guest scholar at the Woodrow Wilson Center, where he started the nonproliferation program that we continue to this day. He is the author of an excellent book, *Bridled Ambition: Why Countries Constrain Their Nuclear Capabilities*. The panelists will speak in the order of my introduction, each for about fifteen minutes, then we will open it up for questions and comments from the floor.

SHAHRAM CHUBIN, PH.D.: Thank you very much. Fifteen minutes is not a long time. I will try to make it a rapid fifteen minutes. It is very common to hear senior intelligence officials on both sides of the Atlantic say it is only a question of time before some terrorist group uses weapon of mass destruction. What I want to do is talk about three to four different parts of this issue. One is the background, as briefly as possible. Secondly, what do we know about this nexus, if anything? Thirdly, talk a little about Iran; and fourthly, to make an attempt to answer some of the questions that were posed to us in terms of policy.

You remember at the end of the Cold War, somebody coined the phrase that "we've slain the dragon, and now the forest is full of serpents." Those serpents were rogue states. Rogue states were those states that sponsored terrorism and sought weapons of mass destruction. There was a debate, though you may not recall it, in the United States about whether these states were deterrable or not, and if so, how were they to be deterred: by decapitation, by targeting the regime leadership, or what. As an aside, I should say that in the '90s, as a result of Iraq's behavior even under sanctions, and then afterwards, Korea's behavior in 1994, the belief, I think, became widespread at the end of the '90s that these rogue states were not reformable. Certainly they were not trustable, because if you had agreements with them, as in the 1994 agreed framework, they wouldn't hold to them. And so this led inexorably to something that was coined pretty much by the current administration, the notion of regime change. The idea was, of course, that these rogue states are irresponsible, irresponsible in the sense that they have links to terrorists, and consequently there was an attempt every time there was a terrorist act to find the link to the rogue state.

Do you recall in 1993 the World Trade Center bombing? I recall two things about that in the community that I have traveled with. One was the attempt by some people to link it to Iraq. And the other was the question raised by it, which was, okay, it wasn't successful this time, but what if they had had weapons of mass destruction? And this reflected the focus on an emerging mass-casualty terrorism that Bruce might mention later on. But in any case, it was clear that terrorists were prepared in the '90s and certainly later to inflict maximum damage, and if possible in some cases, they had no inhibitions if they could get their hands on weapons of mass destruction. And the question was, where would they get them? Well, logically they would get them from these irresponsible states.

Now, in 1995, Aum Shinrikyo, as you recall, detonated or tried to use biological, chemical weapons in the Tokyo subway. There is a great deal of focus on that episode, in terms of the fact that they had tried to use a so-called weapon of mass destruction. What was missed about that event—apart from the fact that they couldn't deliver it properly, despite lots of money and scientists and so on—what was missed about that event was that this was a transnational, autonomous terrorist group. It is only in retrospect that we noticed that they were acting on their own behalf, and they had sought weapons of mass destruction and had gotten them, but had not been able to deliver them properly. There was a continuing focus up until the year 2000 on states, state-centric analysis, and I think we missed, all of us, the emergence of independent, transnational terrorists. I mentioned the World Trade bombing because, of course, between 1993 and 1998 there was no hint that this might have been from some transnational grouping. In fact, it turned out from about 1998, when al Qaeda started claiming it, that we had underestimated and understudied this new phenomenon, and we had a very strong incentive to make it state-centric.

Shahram Chubin

Now 9/11, of course, confirmed that these transnational terrorist organizations sought to create maximum casualties, and we know later on that they also sought weapons of mass destruction. Now what do we know about this nexus? Well we know that mass-casualty terrorism exists; we know that some of these terrorist groups seek weapons of mass destruction. It is extremely important not to conflate this problem. Not all terrorist groups—I think that Mitchell knows this best—in Northern Ireland or in some cases in the Middle East seek weapons of mass destruction. These are terrorist groups; they have terrorist aids, but they are not seeking weapons of mass destruction. They are political, if you like, politically inclined terrorists. Some of these autonomous transnational terrorist groups do not depend on states for their existence and have their own organizing and financing, as we know, and their own agendas—mainly al Qaeda, but I've mentioned Aum Shinrikyo, and there may be others in the future. We also know that some governments in the past have used international terrorism for their own purposes, and we also know those governments have also sought or are seeking weapons of mass destruction. Libya in the past, Pakistan, Kashmir, Iran, Hezbollah, and that doesn't exhaust the list. And we know that sometimes these terrorist links with governments were very close indeed, and sometimes even indistinguishable. And we know that at least one government, a friendly government, Pakistan, has had official elements cooperate in spreading sensitive materials, designs and plans. So it is very hard to know whether to categorize Pakistan as a leak or a transfer, and certainly it is a case of an insider dealing with this. We know that the other case of an insider—I think we know, though it is not proven in the courts—the other case of insider WMD [weapons of mass destruction] dealing was in this town, with the spreading of pure anthrax. And here the aim seems to have been more as a warning than to spread mass-casualty terrorism, but again it was an insider issue, from within a laboratory, probably. Finally, at least finally for me, what we know about this nexus is, we know of no case where a government has transferred deliberately weapons of mass destruction to a terrorist group.

Let me move to Iran very briefly. We know that Iran has used terrorism strategically in the Iran-Iraq war against American Soldiers in Beirut and elsewhere—and not just Soldiers, also U.S. diplomats in the embassy. We know that Iran has encouraged fear in cooperation with the Sunnis in the Middle East, not just Hezbollah, Islamic jihad, Hamas. We know that Iran has transferred long-range—in the context, long range—surface-to-surface missiles to Hezbollah. We don't know who controls them, but we know Hezbollah has them. They may be under the control of Iranians; they may be under the control of Hezbollah. And we know that Iran continues to support terrorism for leverage and bargaining purposes in the Middle East and is at least the host to some al Qaeda elements. We also know that Iran has offered to share missile technology with its neighbors, though there have been no steps in that regard, as far as I know. And most recently and surprisingly—and is obviously a misstatement, but it is still a statement—the new president of Iran has offered to share nuclear technology with his Muslim neighbors. We know that Iran is suspected by this government of developing BW [biological weapons] and CW [chemical weapons] for offensive capabilities, and we know also that it is developing the basis for a nuclear option, if not nuclear weapons themselves.

Now, it may be that you can sort of describe the duck and at the end of it say, "But it's not really a duck," and that is what I am about to say. I think that direct transfer of technology or weapons in the category of weapons of mass destruction to a terrorist group is highly unlikely, despite all the things that I have just said. Now, it seems to me, more problematic is the use of a controlled group to execute an order under certain circumstances. I would think that under the circumstances, if I would envision that that might happen, it would be sort of an outsourcing of an attack on the United States target or United States homeland, under the conditions in which the regime felt itself under direct threat. I think under those circumstances, if they couldn't deliver it themselves, they'd get somebody who could. That seems to me the most likely and plausible.

Otherwise, far more serious, and this, I think, is a general proposition that I have put on the table, is the leakage of materials, the insider problem. The insider problem in Pakistan is not unique. Who controls the nuclear program in Iran? The revolutionary guards. Are there ultranationalists or ideologues in there? Are they vetted? What is the standard of safety and security of those facilities? Or once those facilities indeed become sensitive with fissile material, what would the standards be? There may be mercenary motivations. U.S. policy toward Iran—sitting next to Rob, I don't really need to have a number light to go into all the mistakes that have been made on both sides, but I am talking about U.S. policy here. Perhaps the biggest mistake is that. The fact is there is no side of the regime spontaneously collapsing, and talk of regime change makes it difficult to have a basis for negotiations. U.S. entanglement in Iraq, of course, has changed the leverage. The leverage that was on the U.S. side in 2003 is now on the other side. And the unwillingness to engage, of course, runs on both sides. Neither the U.S. nor Iran has been enthusiastic. The U.S. policy in effect today, I think, is one of policy change. In other words, Iran should renounce weapons, certain activities; in exchange the United States will renounce attacking it. But in practice, it is very unclear which policies have to change for the United States to be happy, and if it is all of Iran's policies, then it is indistinguishable from regime change from the point of view of the Tehran government. So it seems to me, one has to be very clear as to what it is we want that regime to do and what we would settle for.

I haven't gone into this business about having promoted rogue states into the category of an axis of evil. Then it becomes very difficult to negotiate with evil. The vice president of this country has said many times, "One doesn't negotiate with evil, one destroys evil." This is not the basis for diplomacy. And if you don't have diplomacy in cases like Iran and North Korea, you have to resort to either the possibility that they will collapse, or that if they don't, that you will be stuck with living with the problem. One comment—I will come to the policy part, I don't want to take too long, though certain questions raised by the chairman and in notes to us—the limits of deterrence. Deterrence is fine, and preemption in the case of direct transfer: if you have evidence of direct transfer by the government to an entity, the idea that if you do that, you will be hit. The problem with that is that even in the clear cases, there are difficulties. We saw in Iraq the problem of intelligence. Take the case of Pakistan. Has the American reaction to what happened in Pakistan increased the credibility of deterrence to future parties to do that? As I said, was it a transfer or was it leakage, or was it a bit of each? The third case is North Korea. I would have thought that even if you knew that North Korea was going to have or had terrorist groups under its control and had passed material on, the notion that if you attack North Korea—you have to ask yourself what the consequences of an attack would be in the North Korean context, whether it is practical and feasible, and whether it would achieve the results you wanted. So what I am suggesting is that it is very, very hard in most cases—the practical difficulties, the intelligence difficulties, and the outcome possibilities—to think of cases where preemption or deterrence, in terms of actual use, implementing the deterrent, can be very practical. And somehow the deterrence has been weakened by the U.S. reactions so far, both in the case of Iraq and the case of nonreaction of Pakistan.

The question of attribution I mentioned before, the World Trade Center, for five years or longer, people were trying to insist that Iraq was responsible. There is another problem, which is homegrown terrorists. I don't know how you can leverage military power to deal with the sorts of things that some terrorists in London were doing in trying to create ricin. So there are inherent limits to what you can do with military power except as a deterrent against states that willfully and clearly are going to transfer. You can hold states responsible and accountable for what happens on their soil, but that is different from actually being able to use military power. It seems to me much more important is the denial and prevention. The denial and prevention then leads you to the sort of things of you already have been doing, thanks to Senators Lugar and Nunn , and no thanks to various administrations that have cut back on that effort, and no thanks to the tardy and unfriendly and unhelpful cooperation of certain governments. You may have read an article in Monday's *Wall Street Journal* and another one today that show that the Czechs are being much more helpful. But CTR [cooperative threat reduction] and getting governments to have international standards in terms of their facilities, their labs, their scientists, and their technicians is terribly, terribly important, it seems to me. That is the critical area that I would put my money on. So my point is basically that while this is a security issue, it is not primarily a military issue. One of the key things, of course, with the CTR is that you have pride, on the one hand, you have secrecy and the tradition of nontransparency. You also have corruption that is very clear. There has been corruption on the Russian side. We have somebody in Switzerland who is being torn between extradition attempts by the Russians and by the Americans, who is the head of the Russian nuclear program, who seems to have filtered off some money for CTR. But many types of CTR equivalents for the buyer area are terribly important, it seems to me.

And finally I would say one thing: there is a company in Switzerland, called, I think, SGS [Société Générale de Surveillance]—I don't know, I'm not trying to get you to buy shares in it or anything—but there is a company called SGS and basically what they do, they go around putting a stamp of good housekeeping on companies. They put a stamp on it that says ISO, International Standards 2005–2006. They make a lot of money out of this. But basically they audit, as it were, what companies are doing in terms of their standards. It seems to me that you need something like an ISO that is internationally agreed standards. You have the United Nations Security Council resolution 1540, which requires states to report every year to the Security Council what they have done in terms of making sure that their facilities are secure, and that there is legislation against terrorist access to weapons of mass destruction. But that is just the legal part of it. What you need is a much a stronger best practices internationally. The United States has, after all, many facilities that it maintains secure presumably, or more or less secure, and presumably has an idea of certain standards. That, I think, is the way to go, because it seems to me it is the interface between the labs and the materials and the state and any group that might want to get them. It is that interface that is the most critical.

LITWAK: Thank you, Shahram. Bruce Hoffman.

BRUCE HOFFMAN, D.PHIL.: Thanks very much, Rob. When Rob circulated the notes for this panel, he asked us to answer the bottom-line, fundamental question of this session, which is, what is the most likely route of WMD acquisition by

Bruce Hoffman

a terrorist group? Is it leakage from state arsenals, or is it the deliberate transfer? And in thinking about this—point of fact, I am not going to address any of those elements. Now that is not to say that one could ever prudently discount the possibility of terrorist groups obtaining, either from leakage or deliberate transfer, a weapon of mass destruction. But I think by focusing on those two elements, we are missing a very important third element or third dimension, and that is the terrorists' own research and development efforts. That is actually what I would like to address. And also, I don't want to speak about it within the context of WMD, but rather to hone it a bit more sharply and talk, rather, about CBRN, about chemical, biological, radiological, and nuclear weapons.

In view of, I think, the very specific and individual fabrication and dissemination requirements that each involves—and, indeed, they have very different destructive and lethal potentials—there is another element that is also important: when terrorists look toward these weapons, it may not be exclusively or even deliberately because of their lethal or destructive capabilities. It may be because of the profound psychological impact, the profound psychological repercussions, the corrosive effects that use of these weapons could have not only on societies' own well-being and state of security, but. indeed. even on national economies. That said, though, I do not think there can any longer be any doubts about al Qaeda's own lethal intentions and, indeed, its CBRN ambitions.

As long ago as 1982, bin Laden made known his intention or desire to acquire a nuclear weapon, and serious efforts commenced the following year to do so. And we know, as well, that in 1994, an emissary of bin Laden, Mamdouh Mahmud Salim, was arrested in Germany while attempting to procure enriched uranium. In 1998, of course, bin Laden proclaimed that al Qaeda itself is divinely entitled to use nuclear weapons and, in addition, declared that it is every Muslim's duty to acquire a weapon of mass destruction for use against the United States. Now significantly, I think, especially during this time period, almost like the Aum Shinrikyo group, the Japanese apocalyptic movement that Shahram described, al Qaeda similarly was frustrated in its attempts to procure these weapons either from renegade scientists or from the stockpiles of established nation states. And al Qaeda, much like Aum Shinrikyo, embarked on its own very ambitious and very credible research and development program. We know, in fact, from Graham Allison's magisterial book on this subject, that literally on the eve of 9/11, bin Laden and al Qaeda had entertained two visiting Pakistani nuclear scientists. Even as one of the most consequential terrorist acts in history was unfolding, bin Laden was still pursuing the option of developing or acquiring a nuclear weapon—in this case developing one—as well as a range of chemical and biological and radiological weapons.

Indeed, information that has subsequently been uncovered by our military forces in Afghanistan reveals precisely al Qaeda's homicidal intentions in these respects. We know that in April of 1999, bin Laden's deputy, Ayman al-Zawahiri, sent a directive to al Qaeda's deputy chief of military operations, Abu Atef, who was killed in a U.S. air strike in November 2001 in Afghanistan, directing Atef to focus on redoubling al Qaeda's efforts to develop a biological weapon, with the phrase, something to the effect that, "This, as we know from my observations, is what most terrifies our adversaries. Why aren't we doing more in this respect?" And indeed, al Qaeda did put into motion a very ambitious research and development program. Hambali, for example, the Jemaah Islamiyah operations chief and disciple of Khalid Shaikh Mohammed, has revealed how he was tasked in establishing a bioweapons or bioterror facility at the Kandahar camp run by al Qaeda. We also know that a parallel track was being pursued at the same time at al Qaeda's camp in Daruta, where not only were biological weapons and anthrax and a ricin capability being pursued, but also chemical weapons were being developed or being used in experiments against living subjects.

So here it is here clear that al Qaeda's interests were matched by at least nascent capabilities and at least the intention to develop those capabilities. I think the paradox, though, that we face today is that although terrorists undeniably remain intent on killing in mass, they also, very significantly, I believe, recognize the potential psychologically corrosive impact of even a mostly nonlethal attack involving some unconventional chemical or biological or radiological weapon. And here, as Shahram described, I think a key indicator in this process was the raid staged by British police on a safe house in London in January of 2003. Now in point of fact, ricin was not discovered there. In fact, the sensors that the authorities in Britain used, for obvious reasons, were calibrated to have a very high false-positive reading, to ensure that if there was any possibility that one of these weapons was present, it would be detected. But in point of fact, Porton Down and other British facilities weren't able to authoritatively determine that there was ricin. What instead was discovered were photocopies of plans to fabricate ricin, which—even though it's the third most toxic substance known to mankind, behind plutonium and botulitum—is nonetheless extraordinarily easy to fabricate, basically derived from ordinary castor beans. But as easy as it may be to fabricate ricin, it is as difficult to disseminate in any mass killing form. And this is why many commentators looked at this group—in many cases, adolescents or postadolescents, Algerians in their late teens or early 20s who were apprehended—and dismissed them as a bunch of idiots, basically.

Well, attempting to fabricate ricin: it may be easy to fabricate, but it is impossible to kill lots of people. But if you look very carefully at the court transcripts or at least one member of that gang—the leader, who, in fact, stabbed to death one of the British officers who had arrived to search the house—one finds that this was a rather more sophisticated group than we had hitherto imagined or understood. Even though they were comparatively low on the terrorist food chain in terms of sophistication or capability—this was the same type of people who a decade ago would have been sitting in the basement of the safe house, fabricating or building pipe bombs—it is alarming because now even terrorists on the low end of the food chain are thinking undeniably in unconventional weapons terms. But they had no illusions that they could kill lots of people with the ricin. They knew full well the limitations of this particular weapon, but equally so, they understood the profound psychological impact that the use of a biological weapon could have on British society; the fear and anxiety that it would generate; the undermining of trust and confidence in the authorities; and, not least, the harm that it would effect or do to the British economy. Their plan was not to kill in mass, as many of the newspapers described it, but rather it was to contaminate orange juice containers in supermarkets, to contaminate hand lotion and body lotion moisturizer in pharmacies—and only to do that in a handful of cases, because even these relatively unsophisticated terrorists understood the asymmetrical psychological impact that it could have on society.

However, the threat of a mass CBRN attack cannot be discounted. In fact, we know that a little more than two years ago, in May 2003, bin Laden obtained a fatwa, a religious ruling, from an influential Saudi cleric that would allow al Qaeda to use a nuclear weapon against the United States. And even more recently, we know that in April 2004, arguably the archterrorist of our time, Abu Musab al-Zarqawi, who is particularly active in Iraq, had amassed some twenty tons of chemicals and explosives, which he intended to use to stage simultaneous attacks in Amman, Jordan, against the prime minister's office, the offices of the general intelligence department, and the American embassy. According to Jordanian authorities, an estimated eighty thousand civilians could have been killed or seriously injured in that attack. So we cannot, by any stretch of the imagination, assume that terrorists have left the business of attempting to and seeking to kill in mass.

But I think that, for the immediate future, the threat of contamination looms largest. Let me say why. And Shahram mentioned this: one of the profound lessons from the as-yet-unresolved anthrax incidents that occurred in New York and Washington, D.C., and Boca Raton, Florida, in September and October of 2001, is not only the fact that the cases themselves remain unsolved, but the profoundly unsettling impact that these incidents had on the population, in particular of Washington, D.C., and New York City. And in this respect, I think, for any terrorists who were observing the anthrax exposure cases as they unfolded, they understood very clearly that you do not necessarily have to kill three thousand persons again to sow widespread fear and concern, not just in the two cities or the three cities that were affected, but literally throughout the country and arguably throughout the world. Because what we saw is that even the deaths, the tragic deaths, of only five persons was sufficient to generate precisely those same profound fears and anxieties.

Also, looking back on the anthrax exposures, they created enormous diffi-culties that I do not think anyone had fully anticipated. No one, I think, in their right minds imagined that a miniscule amount of even pure anthrax, such as was discovered in the office of Senator Daschle in the Hart Senate Office Building, would result in the closure of that facility for four months and the enormous and formidable problems of decontamination that attended it. No one would imagine that the anthrax, the traces of anthrax, discovered both in the Brentwood postal sorting station downtown here and in the sorting station in Harrison Township, New Jersey, would result in those two facilities remaining closed for nearly two and three years, respectively, before they were declared clean and inhabitable. And I do not think that anyone at all reckoned on the extraordinarily high costs that were entailed in this decontamination process. At the end of the day, it cost $41.7 million to decontaminate the Hart Senate Office Building, which is nearly twice the initial estimate. The American Media Building in Boca Raton has been estimated at nearly $100 million to decontaminate and remains completely sealed to this day. So here we can see an important terrorist incentive: to use the biological or radiological weapon not so much or not primarily to kill or destroy, but rather to contaminate, to render inoperable for a prolonged period of time, a prime piece of commercial real estate, an iconic landmark, or a vital government facility, and thereby to prolong the terrorist incident, to keep it in the news, not just for days, but for weeks, months, and even years at a time, and therefore continually heighten fear and uncertainty and—as terrorists have always sought to do—undermine confidence in government and political leadership.

So in conclusion, what does this all mean and what can we do about it? I think with respect to both mega capabilities that terrorists might seek to develop and, indeed, even the more modest research and development efforts, the U.S. military already has a sterling capability of its own in the U.S. Army Special Forces. Although a lot of attention in recent years has been devoted to the activities of Special Forces in the war on terrorism—particularly its direct action mission in hunting down high value targets, whether in Iraq or Afghanistan or elsewhere—what we often forget is that strategic reconnaissance is a core Special Forces mission. This is precisely the capability that would prove enormously useful to obtain evidence, surreptitiously or clandestinely, of terrorist development. That provides or affords the national command authority with an option where air power either cannot go or is inap-propriate, to use a ground-based attack capability to neutralize these threats. With respect to the threat of contamination, here, just days after hurricane Rita and less than a month after hurricane Katrina, the question of response and recovery looms largest. While prevention and preparatory efforts, as we have learned with natural disasters, even with terrorist-induced ones, are of critical importance, we cannot afford to neglect recovery and remediation, especially in the event of a bioterrorist or chemical or radiological attack. And to date, many of our efforts in these realms, particularly in the CBRN area, have been inadequate in terms of the recovery and remediation—not least, the profound economic effects and fallout that would be caused. Hitherto, terrorist interests and capabilities have yet to fully converge in this vital area of using unconventional weapons effectively against population masses. But as many observers say, if only at the level to achieve a profound psychological impact, it is, indeed, only a matter of time. Thank you.

LITWAK: Thank you very much, Bruce.

MITCHELL B. REISS, D.PHIL.: Thank you, Rob. I'd also like to thank General Dayton—I have to note that he is a William and Mary alum—and the U.S. Army for this conference today. The first challenge in understanding the nexus of proliferation and terrorism is coming to grips with the irritatingly imprecise terminology of WMD, which literally covers a multitude of sins. Chemical weapons, biological weapons, radiological weapons, and, of course, of nuclear weapons—which threat is covered when you see the term "WMD"? Are they all equally plausible? Is there any hierarchy of threats that we need to understand and address?

Without greater clarity, it is difficult to understand intelligence community assessments, their efforts, and their successes because each of these weapons poses very different threats, presents very different consequences, and suggests different policy remedies. A lack of clarity with WMD was present at the creation. I have been able to find the earliest reference to the nexus of terrorism and WMD back in 1993, when the CIA director, Jim Woolsey, first warned of the terrorist attack using WMD, but did not specify which type of WMD. Earlier this year, Porter Goss did the same thing, stating that "it may only be a matter of time before al Qaeda or another group attempts to use chemical, biological, radiological, and nuclear weapons."

Now, this afternoon, I want to focus only on nuclear weapons and the potential nexus with terrorism. For starters, there is ample evidence that terrorists are interested in acquiring nuclear weapons. George Tenet, when he was CIA director, stated publicly in March 2004 that "al Qaeda continues to pursue its strategic goal of obtaining a nuclear capability." Earlier this year in congressional testimony, the FBI director, Robert Mueller, and DIA director, Admiral Jacoby, reiterated the sentiments expressed by George Tenet. Now, analytically there are four pathways for terrorists to acquire nuclear weapons. First, terrorists could develop these weapons themselves, at least in theory. This is judged the least likely scenario because of the cost involved, the scope of the effort required, the scientific and technical competence that would be needed, and the sheer amount of time that they would have to keep it secret so that it could not be discovered and eliminated. Tom Finger, when he was head of INR [Bureau of Intelligence and Research] at the State Department, said in February of this year, "We have seen no persuasive evidence, no persuasive evidence that al Qaeda has obtained fissile material or ever has had a serious and sustained program to do so." The second and third acquisition paths are for terrorists to steal or buy fissile material or nuclear weapons from nuclear weapon states. And the fourth acquisition path is by states transferring this fissile material or nuclear weapons to terrorists.

Under this general category, there are a variety of scenarios under which this might occur. First is what might be termed "inadvertent transfer." A nuclear weapon state could collapse. North Korea is most frequently mentioned here and, I should add, is the one most frequently hoped for here, but Pakistan is also sometimes included in these discussions. In a situation where state control evaporates, the fear is that the fissile material or the nuclear weapons themselves would scatter before the United States or the international community had a chance to secure them. A second scenario would involve a state selling fissile material or nuclear weapons to terrorists. To the best of our knowledge, no state has ever done this, but we do know that North Korea has sold ballistic missiles around the world, and Shahram

Mitchell B. Reiss

has also mentioned Iran's commercial ambitions with ballistic missiles and other technology. The DIA director, Admiral Jacoby, has admitted publicly that we do not know under what conditions North Korea would sell nuclear weapons or technology, and Tom Finger has added, "There is no convincing evidence that the North Koreans have ever sold, given, or even offered to transfer such material to any state or nonstate actor, but we can not assume that it would never do so." The third scenario is a state transferring fissile material or nuclear weapons because of ideological affinity, and this might be the most difficult of all the acquisition paths to counter. There is less concern with North Korea on this score than Iran, largely because Juche does not travel very well outside of Northeast Asia. But let me read an excerpt from the address of the new Iranian president to the United Nations General Assembly last week—and I should say, Shahram is helping me with the pronunciation of his name, but until I have more coaching, I am just going to keep on calling him the new Iranian president. He stated, "The Islamic Republic of Iran is prepared to engage in serious partnership with private and public sectors of other countries in the implementation of the uranium enrichment program in Iran." Now, this statement raises more questions than it answers, questions that the new president refused to answer with the media afterwards.

So what can we do to address these challenges? What strategies can we develop to reduce and eliminate the chances that terrorists will acquire nuclear weapons? The good news is that we already have a number of programs in place to deal with these four acquisition paths, and I am sure they are familiar to people in the audience—programs like CTR, the Nunn-Lugar programs, bilateral and multilateral export controls, and the like—but from a policy perspective, they fall into four conceptual categories. It's just a useful sort of framework for thinking about the issue. The first is denial, and this comes in two flavors: passive denial and active denial. Passive denial includes export controls. Active denial includes interdiction efforts, like the Proliferation Security Initiative, PSI, and it also includes military preemption. The second conceptual category is deterrence, the third is containment, and the fourth is engagement or what is sometimes called diplomacy. How do these work, how does this menu of policy options or approaches work with the two cases that are most prominent today, North Korea and Iran?

With North Korea right now, we are trying to engage with our partners in the Six-Party talks in Beijing, and we have had some good news recently out of Beijing. Now, immediately after the North Koreans left, they issued some statements trying to walk a few issues back or perhaps, in their mind, to clarify some of the terms of the joint statement. Based on my experience in dealing with the North Koreans, I think that these statements are best understood as they are trying to position themselves for the next round of talks, they are trying to reframe the issues to give themselves as much negotiating leverage as possible. It should be anticipated that they are going to do that, and I wouldn't read a whole lot more into it, at least not at this point. The key for this coming round, which is scheduled to take place sometime in November again back in Beijing, the key for this coming round and all subsequent rounds is going to be the sequencing of who does what when, and those issues really have not been addressed yet. I am sure the governments have not spent as much time as they will be spending in the next few weeks in order to figure out what they are going to be doing in terms of sequencing. We will have to wait and see how it goes.

With Iran, the real concern is with the regime's preexisting relationship with terrorism, as Shahram mentioned. According to the State Department, Iran is the largest state sponsor of terrorism in the world today. So let us look at the policy options that are available for dealing with the Iranians. The concern that I have is that two out of the four policy categories I mentioned, deterrence and containment, aren't going to be sufficient to prevent the transfer, the migration of nuclear weapons or fissile material from the regime in Tehran to their partners in terror, especially Hezbollah. The third category is denial, and there has been an awful lot of loose talk devoted to active denial, in other words, military preemption. I say loose talk because I think it is premature at this time to really be raising those options in a public forum, certainly by U.S. officials, and it may even be counterproductive in terms of what it is we want to achieve with the Iranians down the road. And that leaves one last option, and that is engagement.

Now it is clear that we need to have a dialogue with Iran, at least it is clear to some people. The conventional wisdom is that the U.S. government does not want to, and if that is true, I think it is only part of the picture. I think that it omits the other side of the equation. There is absolutely no evidence that Iran wants to have a dialogue with the United States, certainly not at this time. Now, it is not to prejudge whether engagement will take place in the future—as I said, I think it is in both countries' interests to explore the options—but let me be clear: engagement is not a panacea. But I think that we do ourselves some credit in a variety of ways if we are willing to sit down with the Iranians. First of all, we are not sure until we explore with them directly how much flexibility they have on this issue and other issues of concern to us, not least their meddling next door in Iraq. And if it fails, if the discussions do not lead to any attractive results for us, then the United States would be better positioned to win diplomatic support from the countries in Iran's neighborhood, as well as in Europe, on the Board of Governors [of the International Atomic Energy Agency] in Vienna, and hopefully at the UN Security Council that would allow us to pursue other options. Why don't I stop there.

LITWAK: Thank you very much, Mitchell. We have a little over half an hour for discussion and questions from the floor. I would like to take the prerogative of the chair to spend maybe the first ten minutes just asking a few questions to direct the conversation and, in a telegraphic delivery style that was necessitated by the format here, to allow our speakers to extrapolate from their verbal remarks. Listening to the presentations—and we had some extremely useful lay downs on the issues by our speakers—on this nexus issue, three pathways were identified, each with some offshoots: direct transfer as a conscious state policy, leakage, and the third that Bruce focused on was indigenous development. Let's just focus for a minute on each of those different pathways.

From Mitchell and for Shahram, let us start with the root that has gotten probably the most attention in Washington in recent years, which is the direct transfer that the president has referred to; that is really the crux of what the nexus issue is about. Listening to both of you, one gets the sense that one can really get a lot of leverage through deterrence, and yet, in our dealings with these two hard case countries—Mitchell has dealt extensively with North Korea, and Shahram obviously works on Iran—we have conflated the issue of behavior change and regime changes. There is clearly in Washington a division within the administration on what are our objective is. Therefore, we have made the character of the regime a central issue. When people talk about, say, counterproliferation strikes on facilities for the target state, it is indistinguishable from the regime change option, okay. The much-maligned October 2002 National Intelligence Estimate [NIE] on Iraq in the analytical section argued that the one scenario under which Saddam Hussein might transfer to al Qaeda would be the march-on-Baghdad-regime-change scenario. So, just focusing on this first pathway of direct transfer, could I get a reaction from the two of you in the context of North Korea and Iran, whether the conclusion that was in the October 2002 NIE on Iraq would hold in the cases of Iran and North Korea, that short of overt regime change, there is not a strong incentive for either of those countries to transfer. I don't mean to put words in your mouth. It is not a leading question; there is emphatically a question mark there.

CHUBIN: Well, as far as Iran is concerned, they have kept Hezbollah on a very tight leash. I think that if you talk to the Israelis, they will tell you that since their withdrawal, Hezbollah has been relatively restrained, I mean compared to activities beforehand, and part of the reason is because it is also a political party and it fears retaliation. If Hezbollah were to start freelancing attacks on Israel, Israel would take down some of the power stations in Lebanon and then other targets, and Hezbollah would be directly responsible. So there are restraints built into Hezbollah's activities that come from its location. I mentioned the missiles provided to Hezbollah before the Israeli withdrawal—that was intended as a sort of compensating deterrent, if you like, strategic deterrent against Israel, if Israel were to attack Iranian facilities. It was not intended to be the precursor to a war between Iran and Israel. So, I cannot imagine the direct transfer of material. I also mentioned that it is not clear who controls these missiles, whether it is Hezbollah or the revolutionary guards attached to them. I cannot imagine that the Islamic Republic of Iran would so little value its control over Tehran as to hand over its future destiny to a group of other people to do what they wanted with it, whether it is Hezbollah or somebody else. This is not the action of a regime that has managed to stay in power for twenty-seven years.

REISS: Let me do something I used to do a lot when I was working full-time at the State Department, which is answer a question by asking questions. One of the first things that I asked the intelligence community to do when I started at the State Department, with respect to exactly to this issue, was to try and answer three questions for me with respect to North Korea. Has North Korea ever transferred any form of WMD? The second question was if not, why not? And the third question was, if not, under what circumstances would they revisit that decision and come out the other way? And so, I think, analytically, you come to a conclusion pretty quickly that WMD are viewed by many regimes as falling into a different category—at least, you would argue, the nuclear side, to be more precise about it. Now, it does not mean that you can guarantee anything, but again, I thought that that was interesting, to look at the record to see what motivations they have had to behave the way they have done, and under what circumstances that might change. To flip it around, there is a real difficulty in whether or not we would ever know if they transferred these items. PSI [Proliferation Security Initiative] is useful for a number of reasons, but with North Korea, you need to start with the reality that South Korea and China are not members of PSI, and PSI is mostly effective on the high seas, and you've got land borders on North Korea. Twice a week, there are plane flights in and out. So there are other ways of getting things out, and we are really talking about something the size of a grapefruit. So the other reason not to get too overconfident about whether they would transfer or not is that we might not know until it is far too late.

LITWAK: Thanks, Mitchell. Let me conflate the second two pathways into my final kind of initial round of questions, and then we will open up the floor.

We talked about there was a sense that the direct transfer scenario is deterrable, and the condition under which they would likely do a transfer is arguably tied in with a credible threat to regime survival, at which point, all bets are off for both us and for them. The leakage and indigenous capability of pathways—let me just tee up a question on that, and we will invite Bruce to come in on this. On leakage and indigenous capabilities, how far will effective state strategies get you there? I mean, we talked about nonstate actors as if they are existing in some Cartesian space that is not on this planet. We may not have leverage on nonstate actors, but we do have leverage on states, and we still live in the Westphalian system. If you have effective strategies that help develop state capacity—capacity either for Somalia, which cannot control its territory, or for Russia, which cannot control its technology—how far does that get you? And if you can create political will in a country like Pakistan, how far can that get you in dealing with the leakage or the indigenous capability issue? It won't get you all the way there, and it may not deal with, say, the ricin production in London, but what is your sense about how far that gets you?

HOFFMAN: Well, in the case of weapons like anthrax or ricin, it can get you some distance, perhaps—not completely because there is still a question of having a safe haven to organize these laboratories. After the invasion of Afghanistan, when al Qaeda's capabilities were compromised at Kandahar, they packed up and left and went to the Pankisi Gorge in Georgia, so there is clearly a role. In fact, one of the principals fled back to Paris, France, where he was subsequently arrested. So there is a role for states to play in that respect: monitoring, good intelligence, and good countermeasures. In essence, I think that the problem is that, of course, this is a capability that could be completely indigenous. Just as this group of morons in essence was downloading a formula for ricin from the Internet—and not even from al Qaeda sites, but from American white supremacist sites, in fact—and had the potential to fabricate these materials that could not cause tremendous physical harm, but would be enormously significant psychologically, you could have a farmhouse in Vermont or a ranch out in Montana where there was no risk of transferring materials from country to country, but rather clandestinely they were being developed.

LITWAK: You do not need a huge Kandahar facility to do this then?

HOFFMAN: No. Again, it depends on what the goal is—to kill lots of people, of course [you need a huge facility]. But probably for a psychological and destabilizing impact on the economy, no, very small.

LITWAK: And you distinguished between the chem/bio side and what Mitchell was talking about on the nuclear side. Where you do need more of an infrastructure if you want to go for the bomb, not as sort of a dispersal of radioactive material?

HOFFMAN: Precisely. When we are talking about nuclear, then it is appropriate to refer to it as a weapon of mass destruction, because of the four, that is truly the only one.

LITWAK: Shahram or Mitchell, do you want come in on this?

CHUBIN: I have not yet emphasized two things. One is this excellent book by Allison. There is a statement—I think it is on page 156—in which he conflates all terrorist groups. It is at the end of the first section. He ends up saying that there are many terrorist groups out there, from Hezbollah through al Qaeda, that want to get nuclear weapons. Well, my first question is, are there really? I don't think that is the case at all; many terrorist groups out there are not interested in any of these things. But the other point I would emphasize is the United Nations Security Council Resolution 1540. Though nobody can agree in the UN because it is a highly political issue about who the terrorists are and even the definition of conventional terrorism, there is absolutely no dissent to the proposition among states that the dissemination of weapons of mass destruction to nonstate actors is a threat to all states. I think it is an important point to build on. There is no state out there that says, no, this is a bad idea.

LITWAK: Did the Iranians, particularly, comment on 1540?

CHUBIN: They supported it. And if you go to the UN website, you will find that they have annual reports from Syria, Iran, and others.

LITWAK: Mitchell, do you want to comment on that?

REISS: Yes, I think Shahram is exactly right. But the frustration for the U.S. government is translating that general sentiment into concrete policy support, and so a lot of countries are really not going to put their money where their mouth is, in terms of being against terrorism, against WMD proliferation. All of these things are wonderful, but when it comes to a vote in the Board of Governors in Vienna, when it comes before different bodies, they are not sticking their heads up above the parapet. A lot of it is free riding; a lot of it is the fact that we are not as popular as we once were in the world. There are a variety of reasons for it. But the real challenge, if you are sitting in Washington, is to try to figure out a way to capture and mobilize the general sentiment that Shahram has identified and channel it into policy support. And that has proven to be very, very difficult.

CHUBIN: Can I just say one thing on that. The reason it is difficult is, it is seen as an American policy, rather than international norm. The United States has made everything so personal and bilateral that, of course, people aren't going to jump on the bandwagon of the United States if it is a U.S. thing. The fact is, the United States is the most competent country, and it has more experience with dealing with plant security and other issues. But that is why it has to be grounded in international standards. That is why I mentioned the UN—not because I am starry eyed about it, but simply that other governments find it easier to adhere to the UN's standard rather than U.S. If it is a question of either you are for us or against us, then the answer is, you know . . . and I was not talking about terrorism. On terrorism, there are disputes, and I am sorry to hear it after 9/11. It is a shame that people still think there are any causes worth killing innocent civilians over. Unfortunately, that is still the case. People talk of resistance, occupation, and all of this stuff, but on the question of transfers of weapons of mass destruction to nonstate actors, all states agree. The question is how to operationalize that, and I suggested that maybe you could go beyond the annual reports to the UN on certain international standards about facilities.

LITWAK: Okay, thank you. We have about twenty minutes left. Let's open it up now for questions and comments from the floor. There are microphones in the room. If speakers could please identify themselves. Who would like to be the first?

AUDIENCE - GEORGE MAURER: George Maurer, Key West. A couple of months ago, I tried to get confirmation of the terrorism statistics, both in the country and the world. I tried to get the office of the National Counterterrorism Center. Nobody in Washington, D.C., except a secretary in the State Department who formerly worked in that office, knew where it was. George Bush did because he went there a couple of months ago, and it is in McLean, Virginia. But his White House, his press secretary, they did not know where John Negroponte is.

LITWAK: Do you have a question, sir?

MAURER: Yes, and the question is this: the National Counterterrorism Center, on its website—not *its* website, the website of MIPT [National Memorial Institute for the Prevention of Terrorism], which is www.tkb.org—says that the total number of terrorism incidents from January 1, 2005, to July 6, 2005, were 2,418 fatalities, 4,575 injuries worldwide. For 2004 it was 4,986.

LITWAK: I think we had better move right to your question.

MAURER: And the question is this: if the fatalities and injuries are around 10,000 per year fatalities, injuries 5,000 worldwide as compared to a couple of thousand worldwide in 2001—question number one, are we winning or losing the war on terrorism if it is twice as much now worldwide? Question number two, is it worth this effort?

LITWAK: Okay. Bruce, why don't you answer.

HOFFMAN: Well, the TKB website address stands for "the knowledge base," and what MIPT is trying to do is to pull together diverse sources of information on terrorism. The short answer is, it depends how and what you are counting. This was one of the controversies this year. On why global patterns of terrorism, for the first time, I believe, in twenty-plus years, were not released is because, not inappropriately, a different metric was introduced. It was counted differently, many more domestic. This and, I think, the conversions of domestic and international terrorism have grown so profoundly, for the first time incidents that hitherto were dismissed as just examples of localized or parochial conflicts were now included. So the numbers changed for that simple reason. I think that the broad picture is that, indisputably, terrorism remains a profound problem of international security. But by the same token, we have known this for many years. And far more Americans, for example, are killed on the roads in auto crashes than from terrorism worldwide. But we know, too, that terrorism, though, is a different kind of problem that threatens not just the authority of nation-states and of governments, but, as I said earlier, that undermines popular confidence. After all, I think the fundamental expectation of citizens anywhere is that their government will protect them, so even if terrorism may not kill as many people as disease or as auto accidents might, it still has a very profound effect, not just on the political system, but on the fabric of trust within society. Are we winning or losing? I think it is a long struggle. That is the very short answer. I think in many respects, we are winning. As the president has said, we have killed or captured 75 percent of al Qaeda's leaders. Our allies and friends throughout the world have apprehended themselves upwards of 4,000 al Qaeda operatives. We have, of course, destroyed al Qaeda's infrastructure in Afghanistan, and those, I think, are very clear successes. But I think, by the same token, what we understand now, four years into the struggle, is that we are up against a very determined and a very formidable adversary. And despite those successes, this adversary is still able to recruit and to attract new sources of support, whether it is personnel or finances, to sustain the struggle.

REISS: Can I just add, there are two other metrics for judging the success. There has not been another attack on the United States since 9/11; that is not trivial. And there has not been the overthrow by jihadis of the regimes that Osama bin Laden so vehemently opposes—again, a nontrivial accomplishment.

LITWAK: Yes, microphone over here.

AUDIENCE - PATTI BENNER: I'd like to invoke the audience prerogative to alter the topic a little bit. I know that you are talking about proliferation and terrorism in the nexus, but the dominant discussion has really been CBRN. When we talk about "it's not just destruction and death, it is also disruption," I am immediately taken to the cyber and information world, upon which we have become, obviously, very, very dependent. And there is a certain amount of vulnerability there, simply based on dependence. So, in altering the topic, I am wondering if it is time—given that we recognize it's not just destruction, it is disruption, it is undermining confidence—that we begin to expand how we think about all of this to include the cyber and information side. I would like to hear Bruce Hoffman's thoughts on that first, if you would.

LITWAK: You've taken charge of the panel. That's okay, but I'd like to hear … Mitchell did you get into this issue much when you were at policy planning?

REISS: No.

HOFFMAN: Well, my gut response—and I don't mean this to sound dismissive, because you do have a point—but my gut response is that when we tend to think of terrorism and cyber threats, we think mostly of terrorists using offensive tactics to disrupt networks. I don't mean to be dismissive, I think that is enormously important, but by the same token, I think one of the areas where we are losing the war on terrorism is in not engaging in the war of words and the propaganda. The terrorists have taken the Internet, which ten years we thought would be this enormous engine of education, enlightenment, and turned it into basically one of the most effective purveyors of the most base and coarsest conspiracy theories and lies. They have taken a vacuum and they filled it. I think our efforts in public diplomacy and in information operations have to, indisputably, include contesting this ground in virtual space, for example, as well as over the established media, whether it is the print media or television and radio. Interestingly, to date, there has only been one instance, at least that I know of, where terrorists have engaged in that kind of offensive information operation, and that was when the Liberation Tigers of Tamil Eelam in November of 1987 shut down the Sri Lankan embassy servers in Washington, Ottawa, and Seoul. And that was before 9/11. There was one instance only when terrorists hijacked a plane and purported to crash it into a city below—and that was, of course, in 1994 in Paris—and we dismissed and forgot about that example, which was so enormously relevant to 9/11. So I don't think we can ignore this threat at all. But it does then become a question of prioritization and that we obviously can't defend every target all the time. And that, I think, is the main challenge that we face—to have this very nimble and very flexible response capability that is capable almost of covering the waterfront, but at the same time can shift when we see new inroads being made in innovative areas. So, the bottom line is, I don't think we completely ignore that threat, but it hasn't, to date, been a front-burner one, and terrorists seem much more interested in getting onto the Net than taking it down.

LITWAK: Thank you. Other questions or comments from this side? Oh, yes.

AUDIENCE - ANN KHALIL SARKIS, RN: Dare I admit I work at the FBI? I am an analyst there and a very low-ranking person, so I really have nothing to lose by asking this question. Looking at some of the biological threats around the world, we are looking at the weapons of mass destruction. I want to weigh that against some of the issues of softer targets, such as Boston, for example. The health of a nation and force protection become national security issues for every country, and we know, simply, that influenza kills twenty thousand people in the United States every year: three hundred thousand people get influenza, twenty thousand die. That is just a normal course of disease. Looming on the horizon is the avian influenza pandemic that the entire world is concerned about, and rightly so. It will kill millions if it occurs. What is the probability, in your mind, of an exploitation of this softer target by the terrorists, keeping in mind that they do have some pretty bright minds at their top echelon of planning? It becomes a global security issue, and I think that is how the United Nations is looking at that. Do you have any comments on that kind of scenario occurring? I know that we, again, look at the weapons of mass destruction at a very high level, but the softer targets—it is quick, it is easy, it is inexpensive, and it is very real. Any comments?

LITWAK: Thank you very much for that question because, as Bruce mentioned in his presentation, Osama bin Laden's early interest was biological because of its terror impact. And Mitchell, in focusing on the nuclear, said that you need a real infrastructure if you want to get serious on the nuclear side, in terms of weaponization. Do advances in biotechnology permit more diffusion to these sorts of indigenous production facilities, where you don't need a lot of infrastructure and, therefore, are harder to get leverage from these state strategies of controlling them? I am not talking of going to one of the Russian former biolabs and getting a deadly toxin, but the kind of manipulation that university bio departments are able to do now, where you don't need to have a Los Alamos type infrastructure or to fabricate it.

HOFFMAN: I don't know.

LITWAK: I mean, could a person have done, let's say, the anthrax attack in Washington without access to a lab or some type of facility that a state could get leverage on and control?

HOFFMAN: I think the anthrax, and the fact that it was such a high weaponized grade, suggests that they needed a fairly sophisticated laboratory and the ability to do so. But by the same token, before the exposures, we had imagined that that was a capability that resided only in established nation-states or in formal research facilities, not that an individual could do so flying under the radar, where it would be impossible for us to detect. I think the question whether avian flu or other types of diseases might be harnessed by terrorism is, of course, entirely possible. I don't think there is any terrorist analyst who would say it couldn't be, but the question is one of control. And that may have influenced, actually, terrorist interest in this area. Even in al Qaeda's case, when they have attempted to develop these weapons, the difficulty is to control them and to apply them against their enemies very specifically, and some of these weapons then become outside the realm of being able to limit their effects.

REISS: Let me just say that it is my understanding that there are really two hurdles that need to be overcome. One is, as Bruce mentioned, a weaponization issue. It is not enough to just cook it up in your kitchen; you actually have to figure out a way to put it in a weapon and then deliver it. I am told that that is actually a little bit harder than it may seem. The second is that you have to develop a bioweapon in a way that it is fatal, but slowly fatal. The problem with the Ebola virus, as I understood it, is that it worked too fast and it killed people too quickly, before they could infect others. And so what you really need to do is that you need to have something that incubates in a person so that they can be the carrier and infect other people before they die. And again, I am told by people much more knowledgeable than myself, that this is another hurdle. It is not so easy to calibrate something like that.

LITWAK: Thank you very much, Mitchell and the panel. One of the objectives of this meeting is to look at some of the major trends in the international security field. This forum provides an opportunity to look at phrases like "the nexus of proliferation and terrorism" and to bore in and say, what do we mean by the nexus, what are the conditions under which a state might transfer, how might a nonstate actor acquire it? Where one comes out on these questions, that becomes a critical threshold assumption that drives policies. If you posit that a particular state is going to transfer this capability to a nonstate actor that could have an incentive to do it, that is a huge going-in assumption. So the occasion of this conference, to bring together experts and the participants to focus on these core issues that underpin our policies, is an important function. We are, again, very grateful to the Army and General Schoomaker and his colleagues for making this possible. Woodrow Wilson Center was institutionally very pleased to participate. I would like to thank our panel, and I would like to thank all of you for your attention. Please join me.

MAJOR GENERAL KEITH W. DAYTON: Robert, you caught me by surprise. I wasn't ready. Thank you. This is an issue that we will be dealing with for many years. General Abizaid is fond of talking about the long war. This is an integral part of the long war, and it will be a shaper of our national security. I feel a little bit better that maybe I don't need to worry quite so much about state transfer. But I feel a lot worse realizing that you really could cook something up in your basement, and if you killed five or ten people, that you'd get a lot of press over it—you've accomplished the same purpose—and that is very very worrisome. So again, thank you, panel. I am sure we will talk to you again.

We are going to take a break here for about thirty minutes. The place to take the break is not where we usually take the break, but it is in the atrium area. I don't know why we are doing that, but we are. I think it has something to do with security in the amphitheater and all that. And then at 3:00, we will start again in the amphitheater with Congressman Ike Skelton, who is always an interesting man to listen to. He has agreed to take questions and answers at the end of his pitch, and then that will conclude our conference. I'll make a few closing remarks after that. So right now we will just take a break. And again, thank you very much, panel, for everything.

CLOSING ADDRESS

BUILDING AN EFFECTIVE NATIONAL SECURITY CADRE FOR THE FUTURE

U.S. Representative Ike Skelton (D-MO), Ranking Member, House Armed
    Services Committee
Introduction by: General Peter J. Schoomaker, Chief of Staff, United
    States Army

Summary

U.S. Representative Ike Skelton

- Today the U.S. military is fighting in Iraq and Afghanistan, participating in rescue and cleanup operations on the Gulf Coast, and rooting out terrorists around the world. Military forces are serving everywhere in difficult circumstances.

- In assessing future threats and determining how best to apply military power, we must be forward looking and flexible in our thinking. Iraq is indeed important. If we fail in Iraq, that country is likely to become a nest for terrorists. But we must look ahead to other possible confrontations as well. The threats we know are formidable. They range from Islamic extremism to the proliferation of weapons of mass destruction, and to the possibility that terrorists might acquire such weapons. At the same time, we must be prepared for traditional state conflict even as we strive to avoid it. To wit, the Taiwan Strait is the most dangerous part of the world. China is developing strategic relationships, particularly in areas important to U.S. interests, such as Africa, Central Asia, and South America. Chinese missile technology is steadily improving, and the Chinese military is able to field an increasingly sophisticated navy and air force.

- The tragedy of Hurricane Katrina has drawn to the Gulf Coast a wide range of private and public actors. Here, too, the U.S. military has been called upon to compensate for the lack of strategic foresight. On July 3, 1863, as broken units and bleeding men retreated at Gettysburg, General Robert E. Lee apologized for having overridden the wise counsel offered him to cut off Union supply lines. As did Lee, our military leaders sit today astride a transitional age. New technology provides advantages to us but also to our adversaries. New technology has added a huge layer of complexity to the battlefield. Great efforts are underway to pursue even more new information-age technology. Global air dominance, enhanced capability to patrol seas and littorals, and more sophisticated Army combat systems are important. But single-minded pursuit of new technology runs the risk of neglecting the human side of the equation. We need a similar commitment to improve our servicemen's ability to understand the art of warfare. "The tools matter less than the talent, the training, and the dedication of the Army....We can't have a masterpiece without a master."

- The machine-age personnel system must be disassembled and put together in ways that capture agile and innovative people. Warfare is more complex not just at the senior officer level but at lower levels as well. Flexible pay systems are needed to compensate Soldiers to buy time to master their profession at each level. We must also make the proper investment in the size of our forces. It is not enough simply to spread deployments. We need a "deep bench" to develop the capabilities needed to face the multitude of current and future security challenges.

- The demands placed on our Soldiers raise the real danger of breaking the Army. Recruiting efforts are not attaining their goals. The retention rate is less troubling, but for how long? Our country is not making a clear and compelling case why our young people should serve. All leaders in all professions at every level must call upon our nation's youth to enter national service, and to explain why. The cost of preparing for the future pales in comparison to the consequences of failing to do so.

Question-and-Answer Period

- Is sacrifice in the service of the country spread evenly? Regrettably, sacrifice is uneven. There is a core of decency and goodwill. We must work through the negativism to tap this wellspring of American nobility—this sense of common purpose and shared sacrifice.

- What could be done in terms of education and training to improve the capacity of our military personnel? We could be more attuned to different cultures and languages. That is essential. Efforts are being made in this regard. They should be augmented. Several groups have studied in depth the subject of professional military education (PME). Their reports and recommendations are finally being dusted off. Let us recall, however, that Goldwater-Nichols was bitterly resisted by the services. Let us hope that this time the services will, on their own, implement the changes needed.

- How can we make better use of the concept of the citizen-soldier? The major challenge today is interesting people in and getting people to join the armed forces; only then will we work out their specific uses. And while serious efforts are being made to generate that interest, we must extend to those who have served, and are serving, in our armed forces our deepest appreciation for their contribution and their personal sacrifice.

Analysis

Congressman Ike Skelton left no doubt that he has been at the center of congressionally induced military reforms for many years. His emphasis on the importance of the "masters of tools," meaning military personnel, certainly appealed to many in the audience. Likewise appealing was his emphasis on the need to revise Department of Defense (DoD) personnel systems and enhance the quality and relevance of military education as the means to increase military leaders' intellectual skills. As is often the case, the devilish details of his proposed PME model began to draw the opposition.

Congressman Skelton is certainly correct that Goldwater-Nichols was resisted by the services and, in retrospect, that resistance was largely unwarranted and slowed the progress toward a desirable goal. He implied that resistance to the proposed PME model is equally unwarranted and that motivations are similarly shortsighted. His extension of similarities between the Goldwater-Nichols legislative "fight" to that about PME is somewhat convincing when that portion of PME being considered is about making curriculum more "joint," because issues and reasons for resistance are similar. When he extended that logic to resistance to curriculum revisions designed to make military personnel "more attuned to different cultures and languages," he oversimplified and did injustice to a complex issue.

Most DoD educators would agree that effective leaders must be sensitive to cultural differences, whether those differences are based on ethnicity, organizations, or any other source. Agreement also exists that there is an advantage to extending that sensitivity to your own forces, those you are trying to help, and to those who are the enemy. The motivation for sensitivity to each of these groups is different, and the required degree of understanding may be different. How to best create knowledge about other cultures, of which language is only one artifact, and how to create "attunement"—whether that means real understanding, empathy, or sympathy—are all questions with long histories of debate among educators. For certain, being aware that cultures are different (Anthropology 101) is different from learning a language (Spanish 101 through immersion), is different from immersion into another aspect of a culture (advanced religion course), is different from understanding a culture (living in it for a long time), is different from respecting a culture, meaning a complex collection of cultural artifacts (no known method), etc.

Congressman Skelton is correct, and most DoD educators agree, that PME needs to change, as has been the case many times in our history. He is correct that the services must enter the debate with an open mind and set aside self-interest for the good of common goals. He will get some disagreement about the identity of those common goals and much more about how best to reach those goals. Those proposing a new model must be equally open-minded and acknowledge that debate is desirable and that their opponents may have a few good points about issues that have for many years vexed our nation's leading educators.

Transcript

ANNOUNCER: Ladies and gentleman, please welcome back your master of ceremonies for the Eisenhower National Security Conference, Major General Keith Dayton.

MAJOR GENERAL KEITH DAYTON: Well, thank you. We have given you the previews of upcoming attractions, so now what I would like to focus on is our culminating event of this 2005 conference, which will be an address by Congressman Ike Skelton, Democrat of Missouri, the ranking member of the House Armed Services Committee. He is going to address you with his thoughts on how we can build an effective security cadre for the future. There are a couple of quotes by Abraham Lincoln, that great Midwestern philosopher, that may relate a little bit to this conference and to this theme. The first one—and it does not read that well in the twenty-first century—but he said, "If you could first know where we are and whither we are tending, we can better judge what to do and how to do it." That is pretty good. And then he said, though in a more lighthearted vein, "You know, the best thing about the future is that it comes only one day at a time." Well, I think that is something we are going to address here this afternoon because our speaker is going to ask that question, but he is also going to ask the question of how do we plan well beyond tomorrow. Now, I am not here to introduce him. We are privileged to have the chief of staff of the U.S. Army, General Peter Schoomaker, who will introduce Congressman Skelton. General Schoomaker.

GENERAL PETER J. SCHOOMAKER: Thanks, Keith. Good afternoon, ladies and gentleman. It is a great pleasure to be back with you, and it is a great honor to be able to introduce our closing speaker this afternoon, Congressman Ike Skelton. I think, Keith, you had a good start on the introduction, because he is a very special person to all of us. He represents Missouri's Fourth Congressional District in the U.S. House of Representatives and has done so since 1977. He currently serves as the ranking Democrat on the House Armed Services Committee, and has done that since 1999, and is a member of the Tactical Air and Land Forces Subcommittee. Congressman Skelton was instrumental in the passage of the legislation called the Goldwater-Nichols Department of Defense Reorganization Act of 1986. He chaired a House panel on military education from 1987 to 1988, and has advocated to all of us better strategic thinking and improvements in the intermediate- and senior-level educational programs for our Armed Forces, for all four services. I know—since I consider him, quite frankly, to be a personal friend, and he has been for many years a mentor for many of us in his thinking—as we look ahead, both on the educational side and on the transformational side of our Armed Forces, that we look forward into the future. He has been a prosecuting attorney and he was a Missouri state senator, and I would like to say, just as a personal note, he also has raised his family to understand service to nation. He has two sons, one serving in the United States Navy and another serving in the United States Army, both officers, both fine young men, and it is a great privilege personally to know them. So without further ado, I would like you to give a very warm welcome to Congressman Ike Skelton as he comes to help us close out what has been a fine conference. He honors us with his presence, and Congressman, welcome, thank you very much for being here with us.

CONGRESSMAN IKE SKELTON: Thank you, General Schoomaker, thank you very much for your overly kind introduction. I appreciate it so much. And I thank all of you for inviting me to speak at this important conference. I am honored to have the opportunity to share my views, particularly some of the views on national security issues that demand our attention, and on what we must do to support and nurture the

Peter J. Schoomaker

exceptional military leaders we depend upon now and we will continue to call upon in the decades to come.

When I was first elected to Congress, I was invited to speak to a group of first graders in Independence, Missouri. Two of my staffers accompanied me, and due to the cold weather, they both wore trench coats. After trying to explain my work in Congress to the first grade class, I agreed to take some questions. One young student raised his hand, pointed to my staff, and asked, "Are they your bodyguards?" The next student asked, "Do you know Robert E. Lee?" As you will note, I will quote Robert E. Lee a bit later. A number of years ago, when I addressed military audiences concerning the need for reform of the Joint Chiefs of Staff and the need for more jointness, which of course culminated in the law known as the Goldwater-Nichols Act, many of my listeners reacted as if I had given them a dose of castor oil. After my comments today, some of you may think that my bottle of castor oil is not quite empty.

Today, our remarkable men and women in uniform are fighting the war in Iraq and the war against terror in Afghanistan. They are pursuing terrorists all over the globe, and they are cleaning up along the Gulf Coast. These campaigns and actions, like the scores of operations before them, demonstrate why our service people deserve the reputation as the world's finest military. They are serving every day around the world under the most difficult of circumstances. It is true that some of these challenges—particularly Iraq, but also the cleanup after the hurricane—have been made more difficult by the lack of strategic planning. Mistakes have been made. I have spoken about that elsewhere, and some of the time my warnings have fallen on deaf ears, but that does not mean I do not want our efforts to succeed. And while the wars we are fighting today demand our focus, we need to be careful that we don't become so myopic that we fail to see what else is out there. There are great challenges ahead. As we think about the future, we must, therefore, look beyond Iraq. This is not because Iraq does not have strategic importance; it does. If we fail in Iraq, we will be left with a snake pit of terrorism worse than Taliban-era Afghanistan. It is because there are other challenges on the horizon that have the potential to pose even greater threats if allowed to develop.

Ike Skelton

Our national power can be used to enormous good. We have a tremendous ability to prevent and defuse conflict, but we must be looking ahead to see any confrontations looming. I don't want to belabor this point, but just the threats we know make this a complex world. For example, the struggle against radical Islamists will be with us for decades. This radicalized group includes only a segment of those faithful to Islam, but the war in Iraq has made our efforts to work with the Arab and Muslim worlds more difficult. We face the proliferation of weapons of mass destruction to states like Iran and North Korea, which risks destabilizing regions and threatening our interests and our friends. Terrorists are seeking these weapons, too, and that may be the most dangerous threat of all. Weapons of mass destruction will arrive on our own doorstep, with devastating effect, if we cannot prevent it.

At the same time, we must be prepared for traditional state conflict, even while we work to avoid it. There are many examples, but the one that strikes me most is China. I traveled to China earlier this year, and I remain convinced that the Taiwan Strait is the most dangerous part of the world, but China poses greater strategic challenges for us. They study us rigorously, consistently, and in tremendous detail. Beyond that, they are developing a system of strategic relationships through aid and military-to-military ties, particularly in areas where we have pulled back, such as parts of Africa and in Central and South America. China, along with Russia, is extending influence among the small states of Central Asia. They are going to great lengths to steal American technology. Their shipbuilding has grown by leaps and bounds, and they are producing world-class fighter jets. Their missile technology is steadily improving, and, of course, they are a nuclear power. It is by no means ordained that we will fight China, but they are making every preparation for the day when they may have to fight us. They speak our language, and their officers have studied our doctrine and tactics.

That is just to name a few of the challenges before us. And with that said, I do not want to follow on with some statement like, "now that we know what we are facing," because we don't know. I am sure I have missed some obvious threats. If history is any guide, we should expect that something out there is waiting for us that no one has imagined yet. Let us return for a moment to the two biggest challenges facing us today: the ongoing insurgency in Iraq and the aftermath of the recent hurricanes, Katrina and Rita. The ferocity of both was unexpected, and the nature of the crises they represent has been determined by a full range of human interactions. This is not two great armies clashing on an open battlefield somewhere, each uniformly executing the will of a national power. We can probably handle that. This is about thousands, millions of people who come together, form associations, act, disband, and reform, seeking to fulfill the hierarchy of needs. They engage in commerce, political activity, organized violence, and unorganized violence—the whole range of human activity. In the case of Iraq, that is layered on top of an additional national or quasi-national military competition of sorts. In the case of Katrina, it is layered on top of a region somewhat underwater and left without even the most rudimentary infrastructure. These human interactions cause great uncertainty surrounding our military efforts. That is why success is not just a matter of doctrine or technology, but achieved also because our military understands people, cultures, and the root causes of problems or conflicts.

Although both the insurgency in Iraq and the consequences of a massive hurricane were forecasted with some accuracy by certain experts, neither were adequately anticipated or planned for at the national level. The result is that the burden of response and execution falls upon our men and women in uniform, and they are performing magnificently, in many cases making up for a lack of strategic foresight with an abundance of energy and old-fashioned common sense. But as we know, it has not gone flawlessly. This is not due to a lack of a good-faith effort on the part of our Soldiers, but it is, instead, because they have been at times ill-equipped, intellectually, for the challenges we have placed before them.

I recently had the occasion to walk the battlefields at Gettysburg. I have done that several times before, but this time I was accompanied by Major General Robert Scales, the former commandant of the Army War College. Bob Scales is a great American and a master historian, and this is what he told me: On the afternoon of July 3rd, 1863, as broken units and bleeding men streamed past General Robert E. Lee during their retreat back across the bloody field now known as Pickett's Charge, he greeted them solemnly. "I'm sorry," he said. "It is my fault." In contrast, two days earlier, on July 1st, federal troops were retreating back through Gettysburg toward Cemetery Ridge. A Confederate victory seemed certain. The next day, General Longstreet, commanding one of Lee's corps, argued that they should use the superior mobility of Lee's army to maneuver between the Union forces and their supply lines. Longstreet reasoned that an attack on the rail and telegraph lines to the north would cut off the Union forces' supply lines and communications links, and would force the Union to abandon its position and attack Lee across open ground. But Lee was not persuaded. Instead, he ordered Longstreet to make a frontal attack against the Union left and to take the heights at Little Roundtop. That decision cost Lee a third of his force. Unable to grasp the significance of what had just happened, Lee again ordered a frontal attack the next day, this time on the Union center. The results of Pickett's Charge are well known. So how is it possible that Lee, arguably the greatest general in the history of the United States, found himself on July 3rd looking into the eyes of his defeated soldiers, when victory had seemed so certain just two days before? Quite simply, Lee stood astride a transitional period, as warfare moved out of the agrarian age and into the machine age. New technologies such as the rifled musket, the train, and the telegraph were quickly changing the science of warfare, and Lee was unable to update his understanding of the art of warfare as rapidly.

Today, we stand astride a similar transitional period, as the machine age moves into the information age. New technologies are increasing our military capability almost daily, but new technologies are also empowering real and potential adversaries in unpredictable ways. When we consider these technologies are spread across the security landscape I outlined a moment ago, the result is an exponential increase in the complexity of the modern battlefield. To that we must add the dimension of human interactions I described when discussing Iraq and Katrina. People are coming together in new ways, as information technologies enable new forms of dynamic social, political, and economic interactions. For many, this is a welcomed change that holds great promise, but for some, this change represents something to fear.

Which brings me to my real point: the challenges before us place an enormous intellectual demand upon our military professionals. Their understanding of the art of war today is pretty good. Tomorrow it must be even better. The employment of a joint force, successful across the full range of military tasks and at every subordinate level, demonstrates today's height of expertise. Tomorrow, our forces must continue to perform with the same proficiency, but their task will be complicated by two factors: first, our transition to the information age, and second, our global relationships in regions of potential conflict. Now most of you understand this, either intuitively or as the result of your recent combat experience. Generally speaking, the language the services use to describe the requirement for high-quality people recognizes the need for this sort of change. I hear a lot about the importance of qualities such as vision, innovation, agility, adaptability, creativity, wisdom, as our Soldiers adapt to the pace and lethality of the twenty-first century battlefield. I see an enormous effort on the part of all the services to pursue new information age technologies as a means to further the science of warfare, and that is important. We need to ensure that our Air Force can establish and maintain global air dominance. Our Navy needs additional ships to control the seas and patrol the littorals. The Army is proceeding with the development of the Future Combat System. But in our urgency to adopt technological transformation, I fear we are neglecting the human side of the equation. We are devoting enormous amounts of money and talent to advance our weapons technologies, but I do not see a similar commitment to advance our service men and women's understanding of the art of warfare. While I do not pretend to understand the Future Combat System in all its complexity, I do know that it will be useless unless it is employed by those who understand how to use it effectively on the battlefield.

We spend a lot of time talking about new technologies, new platforms, and new gadgets. The reasons for that are pretty simple. First, of course, there is always a constituency somewhere whose interests are intertwined with the sale of a particular piece of equipment. The second reason is that it makes it easy to quantify the increase in capability we are buying: twice as fast, five times the range, ten times the payload. This is especially appealing to those who have only a rudimentary understanding of warfare, because how do you quantify the value of a Lee? Or of an Abizaid, for that matter? Imagine what might happen if a Rembrandt received a box of sixteen crayons, and an average Joe was given a full palette of oil paints, easel, and canvas. Which one is more likely to produce a work of art? The analogy may not exactly fit, but the point is clear—the tools matter less than the talent, training, and dedication that create the art. You cannot have a masterpiece without a master. I think we forget that sometimes in the realm of warfare.

If the complexity of the modern battlefield requires a deeper understanding of the operational art of war, we must push the joint professional military education system to meet that need. Today, the system is adequate, but it needs to get better. It must be rigorous and robust. It must give students the intellectual tools they need to fight the next war—not the war they are fighting today. The time spent at professional military schools needs to be longer, not shorter. I believe that the services will understand this message when I see student performance in their PME [professional military education] systems start to matter. Sure, selection matters. You need to go to this staff college or that war college to get promoted, but where does intellectual performance enter? I assure you that performance matters in nonmilitary professions. For instance, top law firms recruit only the top law school students, not mere law school graduates. Performance ought to make a difference in a military career as well. Because complex modern battlefields will likely be defined by many types of human interactions in the broad range of regions and circumstances as I described a moment ago, our forces must develop greater cross-cultural understanding at all levels. Accession policies should reflect that need. Perhaps we should require future officer candidates to study a relevant foreign language as a precommissioning requirement, for example. We must also expand opportunities for midcareer graduate level education. The graduates of these programs should then go right back into the operational force—not be shunted off to some utilization tour at the Academy, for instance. We must remove the stigma that exists today when officers take time out of their operational careers to pursue liberal arts graduate degrees.

These principles ought to extend into the noncommissioned officer corps as well, but I suspect you think I am describing the impossible. Presently, going to graduate school risks getting off the beaten path and being passed over for promotion. There is no time to cram more PME in today's career time line. Well, you are right. What really needs to happen is for the legacy machine-age personnel systems to be disassembled and put back together again in fundamentally different ways to meet the demands of the information age population they are trying to recruit, train, and educate. It is tough to see how the services are going to attract adaptive, innovative, agile people without adaptive, innovative, and agile personnel policies to suit them. Most important, this career time-line model, with all of the gates officers must hit in a certain sequence in a certain time to remain competitive for a promotion, must be seriously reviewed. It is a tyranny. Generally, promotion is associated with greater challenges and responsibilities, as well as a deserved pay raise, but since warfare is becoming more complex at lower levels, greater challenges and responsibilities are coming to officers as a natural course of their duties. As a result, it takes longer to develop the required expertise at each level, but we do not see recognition of that in today's compressed career time lines. A flexible pay system, not rigidly linked to rank, could probably compensate people throughout their service life and reduce the fiscal pressure Soldiers feel to get promoted. This would buy them the time that they need to truly master their profession at each level.

Napoleon said, "Ask me for anything you need, except time." How do we buy the time in the service lives of our officers so that they can develop the deep expertise that they will require? The only way to do it is to make the proper investment in the size of our forces. I have been calling for more active duty forces for years, and at no time has the need been greater. We need more forces just to meet the demands of today, to more evenly spread the load of these multiple deployments we are now experiencing. But just as important, we need these additional forces to buy time in the present to prepare for the future. Only with a deep bench can we meet the demands of today while providing our service members the opportunities they need to develop the expertise required at each level, to broaden their professional military education, to pursue civilian graduate educational opportunities, and to take the time needed to pause and reflect upon what they have learned and experienced. This is how knowledge turns into wisdom. But all of that is pie in the sky when we stop to consider the reality, which is that we are struggling to man the Army today. I have great faith in our Soldiers; they are wonderful. But I have been worried for quite some time that the demands we are placing on them are beginning to break the force. Public support for the Iraq war ebbs lower and lower. This is evident in the polls, of course, but more pointedly, it is evident in the recruiting stations across the nation. This is also reflected in the declining numbers of high school seniors who are willing to compete for appointments to the service academies. Iraq represents a looming crisis we did not expect when we began the war two and half years ago. The Army's recruiting numbers are below its goal this year, and next year looks tough as well. Retention is doing fairly well, but both recruiting and retention are truly indicators that fail to identify a problem until after it has arrived. Serious damage may have already been done. The signs of strain are unmistakable, if we want to think about leading indicators. The increasing rates at which Army marriages are failing bodes ill, as does the rise in junior officer attrition. The bottom line is that if some of these trends do not change, the Army may not recover fully for years.

This is a national security threat we can ill afford. I have spent a lot of time thinking about how to carry this message to the American people, since I do not believe the youth of America is unwilling or incapable of serving our country. I tend to think that our country is not making a clear and compelling argument about why they should. The former Speaker of the House, the late Tip O'Neill, used to tell a story about his first run for public office. He assumed that he did not need to campaign in his own neighborhood because he took their votes for granted. He ended up losing the election by 160 votes. Just before election day, an old friend told him, "Tom, I am going to vote for you tomorrow, even though you did not ask me to." The future Speaker was shocked and surprised by this. "Why, Mrs. O'Brien," he said, "I have lived across the street from you for eighteen years.... I did not think I had to ask for your vote." "Tom," she replied, "let me tell you something: people like to be asked."

This is a lesson for all of us to take to heart. People like to be asked, so today, I am asking America's young people to enter national service. I urge all of our country's leaders to make a similar call. Leaders at all levels, not just the recruiters in our neighborhoods, have a responsibility to ask our young people to serve our country. We cannot expect America's sons and daughters to volunteer for the military just because they live in the greatest country the world has ever seen, but when we ask young men and women to volunteer, we must be able to explain to these potential recruits, as well as their families, why service is so necessary. Essentially, the message must be this: the issue is no longer just about what is good for the war in Iraq. It is not just about losing a nation with the potential for representative self-government after so many years of tyranny. Nor is it about allowing a snake pit of terrorism to flourish in the heart of the Middle East.

Those reasons are powerful geopolitical considerations, but there are other compelling reasons for America as well. This is about what is good for the long-term health and security of our nation. If our military is going to make the transition from the machine age to the information age, we need that deep bench about which I spoke. That means significantly increasing the forces and populating them with high-quality people at a time when Americans' tendency to serve in the military is on the decline. We must turn that around. The best of America must continue to step up to serve, and we need them to come forward in even greater numbers. If they will not, our military will be unable to take the time to adequately prepare for the transformation to the information age, and the finest force in history will atrophy to the point where it will be unready to fight the next time it is called upon—whether that is responding to a terrorist attack, deterring a conflict on the Korean Peninsula or across the Taiwan Strait, or somewhere else we cannot yet foresee.

The cost of preparing for the challenges of tomorrow pales in comparison to the price we will pay should we be caught unawares. The future of our country depends upon the next great generation of citizens who will answer our call to service. Their contributions will shape the country that they hand down to their children and their grandchildren. I believe that young Americans understand this and they are willing to answer the call, but we must never take them for granted and fail to ask. Thank you and God bless.

DAYTON: Ladies and gentleman, Congressman Skelton has agreed to answer questions. I would simply reserve the right: I will call on people and he will answer the question. Do I have any questions out there? So let me start with you over here on the left.

AUDIENCE - JONATHAN CZARNECKI: Congressman Skelton, I am Jon Czarnecki. I teach with the Naval War College up in Monterey, doing a lot of stuff that you are already talking about. The first thing I would like to say to you is, thank you so much for your comments. We need that kind of support, certainly in the Congress, to keep on the joint path, and we wish it could be more as well. My question for you, though, sir, is when you finished up asking us to ask the American people, right here, it is kind of like almost preaching to the choir. Is anybody else asking the American people to provide the sacrifice of time, of sons and daughters, other than just simply to consume? Is there any movement in that direction so that we can challenge the people who we really need, sir?

SKELTON: I see a great void. There is a need and I see, frankly, very little in the terms of sacrifice. So many of the young men and young women who enter the military are military brats. It is in their blood. There are, of course, some who take advantage, whether of the Montgomery GI bill or for other, personal reasons. But people join for personal reasons. They are inspired by a member of the family, a friend, someone in uniform, or by a leader who had the good sense to speak to the young people and say, "We need you." We need more of that, much more of that. Members of the Congress have the opportunity to appoint young people to the various service academies. I know, as a result of the conversation I had with some college yesterday in some of the districts, the number of those young people who want to go to the academies is dwindling, but I think there is a great void of leadership, asking, and sacrifice. Very bluntly, sir, the only real sacrifice I see today is with the young people in uniform and their families. I was a youngster when the Second World War came along. Gas was rationed; it was difficult to get soap, so many things. Everybody had a victory garden, and my heroes were the young men who came back to Lexington, Missouri, in uniform. I do not see a comparable sacrifice today. That is why it is incumbent upon leaders—community, state, and national—to make the call to the young people for a noble profession or at least a part of their young lives. I wish I had a crystal ball to look into the future and say, that will be solved, but we need the leadership and the example and the sacrifice.

AUDIENCE - EXODIE ROE: Congressman, my name is Exodie Roe. I am a student at Dillard University in New Orleans and I want to know, do you feel that it will be in the national interest of our country for not just military troops, but for all Americans, to become more culturally compensated? Culturally compensated in the sense of learning other cultures and learning new languages besides our native.

SKELTON: The answer to your question of course is yes. It is going to be more and more important for those in uniform to understand cultures and languages; if you understand and learn the language, you learn an awful lot about a culture. But this is a very small world. My high school senior trip was from Lexington, Missouri, to Fort Leavenworth, Kansas. We left in the morning and came back by six o'clock in the evening. Today, high school senior trips are sometimes to England, to London, to Paris, to New York. The world has changed. It is important businesswise, it is important politically, and it is very important militarily to understand other cultures, and it is not just confined to military. I applaud those who study languages in high school and in college—and some difficult languages—because at the end of the day, ten, twenty years down the road, they are going to be needed. I especially applaud those in uniform who did the very, very same thing. The answer to your question is obvious. Thank you for asking.

DAYTON: Other questions? In the back, way up in the back.

AUDIENCE - DAVE LOUDEN: Yes, sir, my name is Dave Louden. This may be more of a question of consideration. Has the Congress considered partnering with industry, including the entertainment industry, to attend to the sense of self-sacrifice, to attend to the appeal to what is best in people, and perhaps, focusing that way, move away from some of the selfishness and the negativism that we see so much presented to our young people via the media, as a means of fostering a greater sense of patriotism? And I am not talking about selling a bill of goods. I am talking about rounding our young people in a good foundation of the freedoms that they enjoy. You know, wait for your answer.

SKELTON: When I was a boy, I saw the movie *Bambi*. Do you remember Thumper? Thumper said if you cannot say something nice, do not say nothing at all. In the political world in which we live, and really, if you study history closely, it has not changed that much on the negative end of it. The media has enlarged it a great deal, but the core of so much of what we attempt to do and what others attempt to do, there is a core of decency and good will and old-fashioned patriotism. We study our history in the early days of Jefferson and Jackson; those were unhappy days, and they were pretty mean cookies. We put them on a pedestal today, but they were tough guys, and I wonder what they would have been if they had a microphone and a television set in those days. But out of it all came noble causes. So let us not get tied down with the negativism around us. We have to work through that. There is enough of it floating around. Have faith in our country, have faith in the good that is in America. We are a very, very unique country, and we have to realize that despite all of the unpleasantness in the political rhetoric—you know, I have been in the middle of it now for a good number of years—there is a core of greatness and decency and nobility in what our country is all about. We should not forget that. When we are bombarded with the negativism, take it for what it is, but also remember underneath it all is a wonderful, strong country. The people in this audience are a reflection of that, and thank you for it.

DAYTON: Do we have another question? Yes, sir, back here in the back on the right.

AUDIENCE - LT. COL. JONATHAN DAGLE: Congressman, I am Lt. Col. Jon Dagle of the Air National Guard headquarters. I was very pleased to hear some of your calls for scrapping some of the antiquated personnel systems that we have in place today.

SKELTON: Did you see the civil generals flinch when I did that?

DAGLE: There was a summer study in the DoD called *The Military Officer of 2030*, which was conducted, I think, in the summer of 2003, and it called for many innovative procedures and changes to help encourage new and more innovative thinking in the personnel systems in and among the officers, the leaders who would be needed in 2030. I was curious if you are aware of that study and if you have any thoughts on that, or what your thoughts might be on how we can accomplish that.

SKELTON: I do not know the study, but let me give you a bit of history. The subject of professional military education had been studied by several groups, including one of General Russ Dougherty, one of the world's great guys. And those several studies on PME were put on the shelf, and they are still dusting off. And after we had the struggle, and I mean the struggle, of Goldwater-Nichols, which by the way was fought bitterly, and I underline the word bitterly, by the military—particularly those with four stars, service chiefs, chairmen—we got it done: had enough votes, both the House and the Senate, after four years of working on it, enough to override any detail that came along. Congress did that. The Pentagon did not do it. The White House did not do it. So the following year, as a result of some staffers who convinced me to become involved with the professional military education system, I did. And to a great degree, I was very pleased that the various services that were fighting us in the previous year and a half gave me three active duty O6's [colonels]—a fellow named Bob Natter, a fellow named Don Cliff, and a fellow named John McDonald—and a retired Air Force colonel named Mark Smith to work the issue of professional military education. The point is, we had to do it. We changed the system, the professional military education system, despite the fact that there have been studies by those in the Pentagon, by outstanding people. Your question is, can the services or will the services do this on their own? I hope so. If not, we may end up with a series of hearings, recommendations coming from the Congress. I hope it does not get that far because it is better if the services do it on their own and make the ends meet. But my two examples of jointness—Goldwater-Nichols and professional military education not happening within the services and having Congress do that—caused me to scratch my head as to whether the services will be able to glue together the personnel policies of which we speak. Am I too blunt, Colonel? I have been through two of these efforts myself, and I would tell you, I hope I am wrong.

DAYTON: Congressman, I would like to ask you a question.

SKELTON: No, you are not allowed to, General.

DAYTON: I am not as old as you think. One of the themes of this conference has been shaping national security, and it has become quite obvious to many of the participants that the military is only one piece of national security and in some ways, not even the largest piece. If we are going to get this right, we have to somehow figure out how to engage the entire United States government. You, as a father of Goldwater-Nichols, probably are uniquely positioned to answer a question that may seem rather trivial: is there a prospect for a similar Goldwater-Nichols for the United States government, or are we doomed to having these sort of warlords who preside over cabinets, and that is all we are going to have?

SKELTON: There have been recommendations, and I think one is forthcoming from the CSIS [Center for Strategic and International Studies] group that has been studying this. Knowing what we went through for the initial Goldwater-Nichols, it was painful—I am quite honest—and a four-year effort, and you are now speaking about something that includes other agencies as well. It would be a massive test to get that done. If it is done, in all probability, General, it would have to be done piecemeal or layer by layer. I do not think the political atmosphere would allow it to be done all in one fell swoop, as Goldwater-Nichols was. It is a massive animal you want to move, bigger than the military by far. Of course, the military will be part of it. We need a streamline. We need to make sure the left hand knows what the right hand is doing. It is cost effective, as well as effective for the citizens of our country. I do not hold out a great deal of optimism, except for the possibility of doing it on a layer-by-layer effort over a period of years. And you are going to have to do that, Congress is going to have to do it, of course, with cooperation from the various agencies. But it is going to take a consistent stream of thought because Congress usually thinks in terms of one-year or two-year cycles. This, of course, would be maybe even a decade of effort. I wish I had the easier, better answer for you, but I am not overly optimistic.

DAYTON: Thank you, sir. We have time for one or two more questions in the front.

AUDIENCE - MAJOR GENERAL MICHAEL W. SYMANSKI: Mike Symanski, assistant G3 for Mobilization and Reserved Affairs.

SKELTON: Nice to see you, General.

SYMANSKI: Thank you, sir. Can we make better use of the concept of the citizen soldier as we move forward from here? ROTC, for instance, has a component of education, or the way that we use our citizen soldiers has an operational reserve, compared to the strategic reserve concept. Are there any ways that we can do this better as we move out?

SKELTON: General, I do not know. I think your major challenge today is interesting people in and getting people to join the reserve component, much less worry about their use. I think they are being used today in ways that those who joined—at least over a period of time—in ways they never anticipated. Deployments, two deployments to the Middle East, we understand working on domestic problems such as Katrina and Rita—but you have a numbers problem with the active duty forces, and you have no place to turn except to the reserve, the guard and the reserve. Now, I have been saying since 1995, based upon General Ted Stroup's testimony, that we need at least 40,000 more active duty troops. If we had done that a number of years ago, we probably would not have the strain on the reserve units that we are having today. But they are being used today in ways that most of those young folks never dreamed about.

DAYTON: Do I have one final question?

SKELTON: Let me, General, thank you all for this opportunity to be with you. You seemed to have taken my castor oil quite well. I marvel at the young people in uniform and those civilians who support them. Cicero, the great Roman orator general, once said that gratitude is the greatest of all virtues, and I sometimes think that we do not say thank you enough for those who serve, for their families, for civilians who tear their hair to make ends meet on their behalf. So for whatever it is worth is, this country lawyer from Missouri wants to say a special thank you to you who serve so well and serve so ably. Today, you are the finest military in the world. Our job, jointly with you and with Congress, as well as those back home, is to keep you that way. That is the purpose of my comments today, and that should be our purpose in the days and years ahead. So, thank you for this opportunity, and I am proud of you. God bless.

DAYTON: Ladies and gentleman, if I can keep you for just another couple of minutes, we just need to close out the conference. I would be remiss if I did not recognize a few of the organizations that made this possible. They include, of course, as we said at the very beginning, the National Committee on American Foreign Policy, the Center for Humanitarian Cooperation, the Matthew B. Ridgway Center for International Security Studies at the University of Pittsburgh, and the Woodrow Wilson International Center for Scholars. But also I would like to thank all of you for being here, because even though there appear to be a lot of empty seats, your contributions are vital to making this work. You have seen what we are going to do next year. There is a series of these, about one a month, that leads up to the national level of conference in September, and I would encourage as many of you as can to come and participate. I would also be remiss if I did not note just a few other people and groups that were here. We had a Mr. Bill Angerman and MPRI, which did operations and logistics behind the scenes. Sharon Baker and a group called SYColeman did program integration and the strategic communications aspect. We had the Army television team. We had security teams here, whether you knew them or not, or whether you saw them or not, and an Army protocol team. We had Soldiers here—I hope you speak to them on the way out, if you have not already talked to them—from Charlie Company, 1st Battalion, 3rd Infantry Regiment, the Old Guard at Fort Myer. The Voice of God was Private First Class Mark Dewaegeneer, and we also had able support from the Ronald Reagan Building staff. But I want you also to know that we had a young captain who put all this together, probably not even thirty years old yet, Captain John Prior. He is probably not even in the room right now, but if you see John—John, are you here? Yeah, I thought so; he knew I was going to do this—but if you see him, thank him, because it is one heck of a lot of responsibility for a young fellow just at the rank of captain. We do not pay him nearly enough. I can say that because he is not in the room. But you know, it is the kind of quality of young officers that you have in the army today, and for all of you who are in uniform, you understand what I am saying. For those of you who are not, I think you also understand. So again, thank you very much. We will see you, I hope, at some of the monthly seminars, and if not, next year. Thank you very much.

BIOGRAPHIES

Ambassador Alyson J. K. Bailes

Before assuming her current position as director of the Stockholm Peace Research Institute, Alyson Bailes served as the British ambassador to Finland from 2000 to 2002. She previously held a number of foreign posts for the British government, including Budapest, Bonn, Hong Kong, and Oslo. In addition, Bailes worked in the Western European Department and the European Community Department, was the second secretary in the United Kingdom delegation to NATO, served on a special mission to the European Council, and was the deputy head of the Policy Planning Staff and head of the Security Policy Department at the Foreign and Commonwealth Office. In 1996 and 1997, Bailes was vice president for the European Security Programme at the Institute for EastWest Studies in New York. From 1997 to 2000, she was the political director of the Western European Union in Brussels.

Bernard E. Brown, Ph.D.

Bernard E. Brown is professor emeritus of political science at the graduate school of the City University of New York. He previously taught at Vanderbilt University and State University of New York–Buffalo, and has served as visiting professor at the universities of Rennes (France), McGill (Canada), Delhi (India), Dakar (Senegal), and Saigon (Vietnam). He earned his doctorate at Columbia University.

Brown is author, coauthor, or editor of more than a dozen books on comparative politics, French politics, and political theory. His books include *Comparative Politics* (10th ed., 2005); *L'Etat et la politique aux Etats-Unis* (preface by Maurice Duverger, 1996); *Socialism of a Different Kind: Reshaping the Left in France* (1981); and *Protest in Paris, Anatomy of a Revolt* (1974). He has also written many articles published in professional journals.

Among the articles Brown has written for the National Committee's journal, *American Foreign Policy Interests*, are "On the Breaking of Nations" (February 2005); "The United States and Europe: Partners, Rivals, Enemies?" (April 2004); "Europe Against America: A New Superpower Rivalry?" (August 2003); "Are Americans from Mars, Europeans from Venus?" (December 2002); "But What Is the National Interest?" (August 2002); "Europe's Rise—NATO's Demise?" (October 2001); "What Is the New Diplomacy?" (February 2001); "NATO Hits a Land Mine" (February 2000); and "Reinventing NATO" (February 1999).

Shahram Chubin, Ph.D.

Dr. Shahram Chubin, a Swiss national, was born in Iran and educated in Great Britain and the United States. Before joining the Geneva Centre for Security Policy, he taught at the Graduate Institute for International Studies in Geneva (1981–1996). He has been director of regional security studies at the International Institute for Strategic Studies (IISS) in London and a fellow of the Woodrow Wilson International Center for Scholars in Washington, D.C. Chubin has published widely in such journals as *Foreign Affairs*, *Foreign Policy*, *International Security*, *Daedalus*, and *Survival*. His recent publications include "Whither Iran? Reform, Domestic Policy and National Security" (London: IISS Adelphi Paper 342, 2002) and "Debating Iran's Nuclear Aspiration" (with Rob Litwak), (*The Washington Quarterly*, Autumn 2003).

General Richard Cody

General Richard A. Cody became the 31st vice chief of staff of the United States Army on June 24, 2004.

Cody was commissioned a second lieutenant upon graduation from the United States Military Academy. His military education includes completion of the Transportation Corps officer basic and advanced courses, the aviation maintenance officer course, numerous aircraft qualification courses, the Command and General Staff College, and the United States Army War College. General Cody is a master aviator with more than 5,000 hours of flight time.

Prior to his current assignment, he spent 32 years in a variety of command and staff assignments, most recently serving as deputy chief of staff, G-3, United States Army. Other key assignments include commanding general, 101st Airborne Division (Air Assault) and Fort Campbell; director, Operations, Readiness and Mobilization, Office of the Deputy Chief of Staff for Operations and Plans, headquarters, Department of the Army; deputy commanding general, Task Force Hawk, Tirana, Albania; assistant division commander for maneuver, 4th Infantry Division, Fort Hood, Texas; commander, 160th Special Operations Aviation Regiment, Fort Campbell, Kentucky; commander, 4th Brigade, 1st Cavalry Division; aide-de-camp to the commanding general, Combined Field Army, Korea; and director of the Flight Concepts Division.

General Cody has received numerous awards and decorations throughout his military career, including the Distinguished Service Medal, Defense Superior Service Medal, the Legion of Merit (with four Oak Leaf Clusters), the Distinguished Flying Cross, the Bronze Star Medal, the Meritorious Service Medal (with four Oak

Leaf Clusters), the Air Medal (with numeral device "3"), the Army Commendation Medal (with two Oak Leaf Clusters), the Army Achievement Medal, the Southwest Asia Service Medal (two battle stars), the Humanitarian Service Medal, the NATO Medal, and the Southwest Asia Kuwait Liberation Medal.

Eliot Cohen, Ph.D.

Eliot Cohen graduated from Harvard College in 1977 in government (political science) and received his Ph.D. there in the same subject in 1982. From 1982 to 1985 he was assistant professor of government at Harvard and assistant dean of Harvard College. In 1985 he became a member of the Strategy Department of the United States Naval War College. In February 1990 he joined the Policy Planning Staff of the Office of the Secretary of Defense, and in July of that year he was appointed professor of strategic studies at SAIS. In addition to directing the strategic studies program, he is the founding director of the Philip Merrill Center for Strategic Studies there. His activities include curriculum development and a university teacher training program. He was named to the Robert E. Osgood chair in 2004, and has twice won the school's Excellence in Teaching Award.

Cohen is the author of *Supreme Command: Soldiers, Statesmen, and Leadership in Wartime* (2002). His other books are *Commandos and Politicians* (1978) and *Citizens and Soldiers* (1985). He is coauthor of *Military Misfortunes: The Anatomy of Failure in War* (1990), *Revolution in Warfare? Air Power in the Persian Gulf* (1995), and *Knives, Tanks, and Missiles: Israel's Security Revolution* (1998), and co-editor of *Strategy in the Contemporary World* (2002) and War over Kosovo (2001). In 1991–1993 he directed and edited the official study of air power in the 1991 war with Iraq. For his leadership of The Gulf War Air Power Survey, which included 11 book-length reports, he received the Air Force's decoration for exceptional civilian service.

His articles have appeared in *International Security*, *Foreign Affairs*, *The National Interest*, *Studies in Intelligence*, *Commentary*, *Military History Quarterly*, *Foreign Policy*, and other journals. His shorter articles and reviews have appeared in *The New York Times*, *The Washington Post*, *The Wall Street Journal*, *The Times of London*, *The Chronicle of Higher Education*, *Slate*, *The New Republic*, *National Review*, and other publications. He is also the author of several widely used case studies for senior military and executive education.

In 1982 he was commissioned in the United States Army Reserve. His service included several years as military assistant to the director of net assessment, Office of the Secretary of Defense. He is a member of the Defense Policy Advisory Board.

Ambassador Herman J. Cohen

A retired career diplomat and specialist in African and European affairs, Ambassador Herman J. Cohen is president of Cohen and Woods International. Established in 1994, the firm provides strategic planning services to African and Middle Eastern governments and multinational corporations doing business in Africa and the Middle East. The firm is a member of the United States Corporate Council on Africa. Cohen's consulting activities include the development of energy-intensive industries in the Republic of the Congo, the mining of bitumen from oil sands in Nigeria, and the promotion of private investment in the Republic of Mauritania.

Cohen retired from the U.S. Department of State in 1993. His last position was assistant secretary of state for African affairs under President George H.W. Bush (1989–1993). During his 38-year career with the U.S. Foreign Service, he served in five African countries and twice in France. He was the ambassador to Senegal, with dual accreditation to the Gambia, from 1977 to 1980. During assignments in Washington, he also served as special assistant to President Ronald Reagan (1987–1989), principal deputy assistant secretary for intelligence and research, and principal deputy assistant secretary for personnel.

From 1994 to 1998, under contract to the World Bank, Cohen was a senior advisor to the Global Coalition for Africa, an intergovernmental policy forum that works to achieve consensus between donor and African governments on economic policy.

Cohen is a member of the boards of directors of the Council for a Community of Democracies and the Constituency for Africa. He has been a professorial lecturer in foreign policy studies at Johns Hopkins University's Paul H. Nitze School of Advanced International Studies since 1998. He is a member of the panel on Transatlantic Relations of the National Committee on American Foreign Policy. He is the author of a book on conflict resolution in Africa entitled *Intervening in Africa: Superpower Peacemaking in a Troubled Continent* (2000). This book won the award for distinguished writing on diplomatic practice for the year 2000 from the American Academy of Diplomacy.

Cohen received a bachelor's degree in political science from the City College of New York (1953) and a master's degree in international relations from the American University (1962).

Cohen's honors and awards include the French Legion of Honor, the Belgian Order of Leopold II, the U.S. Foreign Service rank of Career Ambassador, and the Townsend Harris Distinguished Alumni Award of the City College of New York. He is a member of the Council on Foreign Relations and the American Academy of Diplomacy.

Admiral William J. Crowe, Jr.

Admiral William J. Crowe, Jr., U.S. Navy, served as chairman of the Joint Chiefs of Staff under Presidents Ronald Reagan and George H. W. Bush, and as the ambassador to the United Kingdom under President William J. Clinton. He has more than 50 years of public service in military and civilian positions.

After graduating from the U.S. Naval Academy, Crowe served as assistant to the naval aide of President Dwight D. Eisenhower, executive officer of the submarine USS Wahoo, and an aide to the deputy chief of Naval Operations. In 1960, Crowe took command of the USS Trout, serving as commanding officer until 1962. He then earned a master's degree in education from Stanford University and a doctorate in politics from Princeton University. He returned to the Navy in 1966 to take command of Submarine Division 31.

During his ensuing naval career, Crowe was the senior naval advisor to the Vietnamese Navy Riverine Force, commanded U.S. forces in the Persian Gulf, served as deputy chief of naval operations for plans and policy, commanded Allied Forces in southern Europe, and was the commander in chief of the U.S. Pacific Command. In 1985, he was appointed chairman of the Joint Chiefs of Staff, a position he held for four years. In 1993 and 1994, Crowe chaired the president's Foreign Intelligence Advisory Board. In 1998, Admiral Crowe was appointed Chairman of the Accountability Review Board which investigated the al Qaeda terrorist attacks on U.S. embassies in East Africa.

Following a three-year assignment as ambassador to the Court of St. James (1994–1997), Crowe taught at the University of Oklahoma, George Washington University, and the Naval Academy. He is an advisory board member of Global Options, Inc., an international risk management and business solutions company headquartered in Washington, D.C.

Major General Keith W. Dayton

Major General Keith W. Dayton began his assignment as director of strategy, plans, and policy in July 2004.

Dayton was commissioned as an artillery officer through the Reserve Officer Training Corps in 1970. Prior to his current assignment, he spent 35 years in a variety of command and staff assignments, most recently serving as the director of the Iraqi Survey Group during Operation IRAQI FREEDOM. Other key assignments include deputy director for Politico-Military Affairs, Joint Staff; United States Defense Attaché, Moscow, Russia; senior Army fellow on the Council on Foreign Relations, New York; commander, Division Artillery, 3rd Infantry Division (Mechanized), Germany; and commander, 4th Battalion, 29th Field Artillery, 8th Infantry Division (Mechanized), Germany.

Dayton received a BS in history from the College of William and Mary, an MA in history from Cambridge University, and an MA international relations from the University of Southern California. He studied Russian at the Defense Language Institute and was a student of the Soviet Union Foreign Area Officer Overseas Training Program, the United States Army Command and General Staff College, and the Senior Service College Fellowship at Harvard University.

Major General Dayton has received numerous awards and decorations throughout his military career, including the Defense Distinguished Service Medal (with two Oak Leaf Clusters), the Defense Superior Service Medal, the Legion of Merit (with Oak Leaf Cluster), the Meritorious Service Medal, and the Army Commendation Medal.

Susan Eisenhower

Susan Eisenhower is president of the Eisenhower Group, Inc., which provides strategic counsel on political, business, and public affairs projects. She is a senior director of Stonebridge International, a Washington-based international consulting firm chaired by former national security advisor Samuel "Sandy" Berger. She is a distinguished fellow of The Eisenhower Institute, where she has served as both president and chairman.

After more than 20 years in the foreign affairs field, Eisenhower is best known for her work in Russia and the former Soviet Union. She has testified before the Senate Armed Services and Senate Budget Committees on policy toward that region. She is serving her fourth term on the National Academy of Sciences' Committee on International Security and Arms Control. In 2000, a year before September 11, she coedited a book, *Islam and Central Asia*, which carried the prescient subtitle, *An Enduring Legacy or an Evolving Threat?*

In 2000, the secretary of energy appointed Eisenhower to a blue ribbon task force, the Baker-Cutler Commission, to evaluate U.S.-funded nuclear nonprolifera-tion programs in Russia, and since that time she has served as an advisor on another Department of Energy study. In 2001, after serving two terms on the National Aeronautics and Space Administration Advisory Council, she was appointed to the International Space Station (ISS) Management and Cost Evaluation Task Force, which analyzed ISS management and cost overruns. Eisenhower is currently a member of the secretary of energy's Task Force on Nuclear Energy. She has served as an academic fellow of the International Peace and Security program of Carnegie Corporation of New York, and she is a director of the Carnegie Endowment for International Peace and the Nuclear Threat Initiative, co-chaired by Senators Sam Nunn and Ted Turner.

Within the last 10 years, Eisenhower has written three books; two of which, *Breaking Free* and *Mrs. Ike*, have appeared on regional best seller lists. She has also edited four collected volumes on regional security issues—most recently *Partners in Space* (2004). Her hundreds of op-eds and articles on foreign policy have been published in *The Washington Post*, the *Los Angeles Times*, *USA Today*, the *Naval Institute's Proceedings*, the *London Spectator*, and Gannett newspapers. She has provided analysis for CNN International, MSNBC, Nightline, World News Tonight with Peter Jennings, This Week with David Brinkley, CBS Sunday Morning, Good Morning America, the News Hour with Jim Lehrer, Fox News, and Hardball, as well as National Public Radio and other nationwide television and radio programs.

Carl W. Ford, Jr.

Carl Ford specializes in international policy and defense issues at Cassidy & Associates, a public policy consulting firm. Ford joined Cassidy & Associates in fall 2003, after three decades in the military, intelligence, and diplomatic services. He also serves as an adjunct professor at Georgetown University.

In May 2001, President George W. Bush appointed Ford assistant secretary of state for intelligence and research. He provided intelligence support and analysis to the secretary of state and other senior policymakers. He was also directly involved in policies related to the war on terrorism; the Iraq war and reconstruction; and issues related to the Chinese military, nuclear proliferation, the Middle East peace process, and the North Korean military threat.

Prior to his Department of State appointment, Ford established his own international consulting firm, which provided strategic and tactical advice to American companies doing business with foreign militaries.

Between 1965 and 1989, Ford served two tours of duty in Vietnam, was a U.S. Army military intelligence officer, a Defense Intelligence Agency China strategic intelligence officer, a military analyst specializing in China for the Central Intelligence Agency (CIA), a professional staff member for East Asia on the Committee on Foreign Relations, and the national intelligence officer for East Asia at the CIA. Beginning in 1989, he spent four years working at the deputy assistant secretary and acting assistant secretary levels in the Department of Defense.

Ford holds a bachelor's degree in Asian studies and a master's degree in East Asian Studies, both from Florida State University.

Ambassador Richard N. Gardner, Ph.D.

Richard N. Gardner, professor of law and international organization at Columbia Law School, is also senior counsel to Morgan Lewis, a global law firm. He is a former U.S. ambassador to Italy (1977–1981) and Spain (1993–1997). During his service in Spain, he received the Thomas Jefferson Award for his contributions to U.S. citizens abroad. From 1961 to 1965, he served as deputy assistant secretary of state for international organization affairs.

Gardner was a member of the President's Advisory Committee on Trade Policy and Negotiations and a U.S. delegate to the ministerial meeting of the World Trade Organization in 1999. In 2000, he was a public delegate to the United Nations General Assembly, and he has served as a special advisor to the United Nations on environmental matters. He is currently a member of the Department of State's Advisory Committee on International Economic Policy.

Gardner received his law degree from Yale Law School; a doctorate in economics from Oxford, where he studied as a Rhodes Scholar; and a bachelor's degree in economics from Harvard. His Oxford thesis, *Sterling-Dollar Diplomacy*, has been described as the "classic" study of Anglo-American economic collaboration in the creation of the Bretton Woods institutions and the General Agreement on Tariffs and Trade. He is the author of four other books and numerous articles on international affairs.

Gardner is a member of the American Academy of Arts and Sciences, the American Philosophical Society, and the Council on Foreign Relations. He is a member of the International Advisory Board of Grupo Santander of Spain and vice president of the American Ditchley Foundation.

Dennis M. Gormley

Dennis M. Gormley, a senior fellow at the Monterey Institute's Center for Nonproliferation Studies in Washington, D.C., is the author of "The Limits of Intelligence: Iraq's Lessons" (*Survival*, fall 2004) and *Dealing with the Threat of Cruise Missiles* (Oxford University Press, 2001). Gormley is also a senior lecturer on the faculty of the Graduate School of Public and International Affairs at the University of Pittsburgh. He has been a senior fellow at the International Institute for Strategic Studies in London and a visiting scholar at the Geneva Center for Security Policy in Switzerland.

Gormley served for 20 years with Pacific-Sierra Research (PSR) as senior vice president and director of its East Coast operations. He also served on PSR's board of directors. Before joining PSR in 1979, he was head of foreign intelligence at the U.S. Army's Harry Diamond Laboratories in Washington, D.C., for nearly seven years. Gormley has frequently chaired or served on Department of Defense advisory committees and often furnishes expert testimony to Congress.

Gormley received bachelor's and master's degrees in history from the University of Connecticut. After graduation, he attended Officer Candidate School and was commissioned a second lieutenant in the U.S. Army Ordnance Corps, serving on active duty from 1966 to 1969.

Judith A. Guenther

Judith A. Guenther has served on the Army Secretariat as the director of investment for the deputy assistant secretary of the U.S. Army (ASA) for budget since July 1999. She is the principal advisor to the deputy ASA for budgetary policies and issues involving Army investment resources (including procurement, research and development, military construction, and family housing).

Guenther began her federal career in 1981, working in the Army family housing program in Stuttgart, Germany. She came to the Washington, D.C., area in 1984 and has held a variety of program and budget analyst positions, both acquisition and nonacquisition related, in the Army Materiel Command, the Program Executive Office for Standard Army Management Information Systems, and the Office of the Director of Information Systems for Command, Control, Communications and Computers. She joined the Office of the Assistant Secretary of the Army (Financial Management) in 1993 as chief of the Military Personnel Division, where she was responsible for the military pay appropriation. Prior to her current assignment, she was chief of budget integration and evaluation, responsible for a variety of multiappropriation programs and processes. Before beginning her federal career, she worked in private industry as a program manager.

Guenther earned a bachelor's degree from Washburn University; a master's degree in public administration from George Mason University; and a master of science degree in national resource strategy from the Industrial College of the Armed Forces (ICAF). In addition to Senior Service College, she has completed the program management course at the Defense Systems Management College and the senior acquisition course at the Defense Acquisition University, ICAF. Guenther is a member of the Army Acquisition Corps, the American Society of Military Comptrollers, and the Association of the United States Army.

Bruce Hoffman, D.Phil.

Dr. Bruce Hoffman has been studying terrorism and insurgency for nearly 30 years. He is currently the director of The RAND Corporation's Washington, D.C., office and has served as acting director of RAND's Center for Middle East Public Policy and as RAND's vice president for external affairs. During spring 2004, Hoffman was a senior adviser on counterterrorism to the Office of National Security Affairs, Coalition Provisional Authority, in Baghdad. He has written books and articles on terrorism and testified before Congress on the subject. In recognition of his academic contributions to the study of political violence, the Queen Sofia Center for the Study of Violence in Valencia, Spain, awarded Hoffman the first Santiago Grisolía Prize and the accompanying Chair in Violence Studies, in June 1998. In 1994, he received the U.S. Intelligence Community Award Medallion, the highest award for a nongovernment employee.

Hoffman is a senior fellow at the Combating Terrorism Center, U.S. Military Academy, West Point, New York, and an adjunct professor in security studies at Georgetown University, Washington, D.C. He was the founding director of the Centre for the Study of Terrorism and Political Violence at the University of St. Andrews in Scotland. He has served as an advisory board member and consultant on terrorism, political violence, and security for many government and nonprofit organizations in the United States and the United Kingdom.

Hoffman received his D.Phil. in international relations from the University of Oxford in England.

David A. Kay, Ph.D.

President George W. Bush directed in June 2003 that the hunt for Iraqi weapons of mass destruction be transferred from the Department of Defense to the Central Intelligence Agency (CIA), and the director of the CIA appointed Dr. David Kay to lead that search and direct the activities of the 1,400-member Iraq Survey Group. In January 2004, having concluded that there had been no stockpiles of weapons of mass destruction in Iraq at the time of the war, Kay reported his findings and resigned his position. This report led to congressional hearings and the appointment of an independent commission to investigate the causes of U.S. intelligence failings prior to the war, including how this erroneous intelligence was communicated and used by policymakers.

Immediately after the Gulf War, Kay served as the International Atomic Energy Agency/UN Special Commission (IAEA/UNSCOM) chief nuclear weapons inspector, leading inspections into Iraq to determine its nuclear weapons production capability. He led teams that found and identified the scope and extent of Iraqi uranium enrichment activities, located the major Iraqi center for assembling nuclear weapons, and seized large amounts of documents on the Iraqi nuclear weapons program. He spent four days as a hostage in a Baghdad parking lot. He also led the analysis of the nature of the Iraqi nuclear program and its implications for nonproliferation and arms control activities.

Kay has served on a number of official U.S. government delegations and government and private advisory commissions, including the Defense Science Board, the Department of State's Advisory Commission on International Organizations, the Rockefeller Foundation's Advisory Group on Conflicts in International Relations, and the U.S. Delegation to the UN General Assembly. He has often testified before Congress, has published articles on weapons proliferation and terrorism, and is a frequent media commentator.

Kay holds a bachelor's degree from the University of Texas at Austin, and a master's degree in international affairs and a doctorate from Columbia University. He is a recipient of the IAEA's Distinguished Service Award and the U.S. Secretary of State's Commendation. Currently, he serves as an adjunct senior fellow at the Potomac Institute for Policy Studies and as a consultant concentrating on counterterrorism and weapons proliferation.

Kevin M. Kennedy

Kevin M. Kennedy is the director of the Coordination and Response Division, Office for the Coordination of Humanitarian Affairs (OCHA) of the United Nations in New York. Previous OCHA assignments include duty in Geneva with the Complex Emergency Support Unit and in New York as chief, Africa I (West Africa), and chief of the Office of the Undersecretary-General for Humanitarian Affairs. Kennedy also held UN field assignments in Somalia, Haiti, the Balkans, and East Timor, as well as numerous missions to Africa and Asia.

In 2003, Kennedy was the deputy humanitarian coordinator for Iraq and then the officer-in-charge of the UN Assistance Mission for Iraq. He most recently served as the acting resident/humanitarian coordinator for the Sudan.

Prior to joining the United Nations, Kennedy served in the U.S. Marine Corps as an infantry officer, retiring as a colonel in 1993. He served throughout the United States and abroad, including assignments in Vietnam, Lebanon, the Gulf War, Bangladesh, the Los Angeles riots, and Somalia.

Chaplain (COL-P) Douglas E. Lee

Chaplain Douglas E. Lee currently serves as the director of the Army Chief of Chaplains Reserve Components Integration in Arlington, Virginia. He assumed the responsibilities of the Army Assistant Chief of Chaplains for Readiness and Mobilization in October 2005.

Lee received his bachelor's degree in radio and TV production from the University of Minnesota, after graduating from the Covenant Theological Seminary in St. Louis with a master of divinity degree. After graduating from the seminary, he served as a Presbyterian pastor in three churches. He was commissioned to the Washington State Army National Guard in 1977. In 1982, he transferred to the U.S. Army Reserve. From 1977 to 1989, Lee served in various capacities as a Reserve Components chaplain.

In 1989, Lee joined the Army Active/Guard Reserve (AGR) program. In June 1998, he graduated from the Army War College at Carlisle, Pennsylvania, after which he received orders to the U.S. Army Reserve Command (USARC) as the command chaplain.

Lee's awards include the Legion of Merit, Meritorious Service Medal (oak leaf cluster), the National Defense Service Medal, the Army Commendation Medal, the Army Achievement Medal, the Armed Forces Reserve Medal (with 20-year device), the Army Reserve Components Medal, the Army Service Ribbon, and the Air Assault Badge.

Nancy E. Lindborg

Nancy E. Lindborg, Mercy Corps' president, joined the Washington, D.C.-based international relief and development organization in 1996. She leads Mercy Corps' strategic planning, policy and program development, and emergency response in areas such as Iraq, Afghanistan, the Balkans, North Korea, and Central Asia.

From 2000 to 2005, Lindborg served on the Sphere Management Committee, an international initiative to improve the effectiveness and accountability of nongovernmental organizations; she chaired the committee from 2000 to 2003. Lindborg was co-chair of the InterAction Disaster Response Committee from 1998 to 2002, and is currently a member of the CSIS-AUSA Blue Ribbon Commission on Post-Conflict Reconstruction.

Prior to joining Mercy Corps, Lindborg managed economic development programs in post-Soviet Central Asia and worked in the private sector as a public policy consultant in Chicago and San Francisco. She graduated with honors from Stanford University with a bachelor's in English literature. She also holds master's degrees in English literature from Stanford and in public administration/international development from the John F. Kennedy School of Government at Harvard University.

Robert S. Litwak, Ph.D.

Dr. Robert Litwak is director of the Division of International Security Studies at the Woodrow Wilson International Center for Scholars within the Smithsonian Institution in Washington, D.C. He is also an adjunct professor in the School of Foreign Service at Georgetown University.

Litwak is the author or editor of many books, including *Détente and the Nixon Doctrine*, *Security in the Persian Gulf*, *Nuclear Proliferation after the Cold War*, and *Rogue States and U.S. Foreign Policy*. In the mid-1990s, he served on the National Security Council staff at the White House as director for nonproliferation and export controls.

Litwak has held visiting fellowships at Harvard University, the International Institute for Strategic Studies, the Russian Academy of Sciences, and the United States Institute of Peace. He is a member of the Council on Foreign Relations. Litwak earned his doctorate in international relations from the London School of Economics.

Geoff Loane

Geoff Loane heads the regional delegation for the United States and Canada to the International Committee of the Red Cross (ICRC). He previously headed the ICRC delegations for Serbia and Montenegro in Belgrade, Serbia, Nairobi, and East Africa. Loane served as regional relief coordinator in Nairobi, where he initiated and led ICRC relief operations in Sudan (1989–1991) and Somalia (1991–1993). The Somalian relief effort involved more than 3,000 staff distributing 20,000 tons of food monthly to a million people.

From 2000 to 2002, Loane served as the head of ICRC relief activities worldwide. Based in Geneva, he managed and oversaw more than 70 delegations and a budget in excess of $150 million.

Loane has published a number of articles and books on humanitarian concerns. He was a senior scholar for the Conflict Prevention Network in Munich, where he prepared a series of research papers on humanitarian and political issues as part of the network's framework agreement with the European Commission and contributed to the establishment of policy in relation to new forms of conflict and humanitarian responses to them. While in the Sudan, Loane coordinated an extensive research project for the European Commission on the unintended consequences of humanitarian assistance.

Loane holds a bachelor's degree in social studies, a master of arts, and a certificate in social work from Trinity College in Dublin, Ireland.

Thomas Lynch

Thomas Lynch, minister-counselor in the U.S. Foreign Service, has been serving as the political advisor to the U.S. Army chief of staff, General Peter J. Schoomaker, since July 2004. He previously was the political advisor to the Combined Forces Command-Afghanistan; to Combined Joint Task Force 76 in Bagram; to the U.S. Joint Forces Command and the North Atlantic Treaty Organization (NATO) command in Norfolk, Virginia; and to the NATO Stabilization Force in Bosnia.

After studying European history at Vassar College and Sussex University, Lynch entered the Foreign Service in December 1975. Following a year in the Department of State's International Organizations Bureau, he learned Romanian and served two years in the U.S. Embassy in Bucharest. He covered meetings of the European Union (EU) heads of government and foreign ministers and U.S.-EU political relations for the U.S. Mission to the EU in Brussels from 1980 to 1983.

Lynch spent the rest of the 1980s and most of the 1990s working on East European and Russian affairs. He was the Department of State's Romanian desk officer (1984–1986), chief of the Political Section in Budapest (1987–1990), and chief of the External Political Affairs Section in the U.S. Embassy in Moscow (1991–1993). He served as the Department of State's director for Russian affairs (1994–1997) and U.S. consul general in St. Petersburg (1997–1999). Lynch also worked as a legislative assistant to the late Paul Simon, U.S. Senator from Illinois, and in the Department of State's Legislative Affairs Bureau.

Lynch was promoted to the Senior Foreign Service in 1995 and attained the rank of minister-counselor in 2001. His awards include the Department of State's Superior Honor Award (1989, 1997, 2001, and 2004), the U.S. Army's Outstanding Civilian Service Award, the NATO Medal for Service in the former Yugoslavia, and the William R. Rivkin Award from the American Foreign Service Association. He speaks French, Russian, Romanian, and some Hungarian.

Robert MacPherson

Robert MacPherson joined CARE in 1994 to organize and implement emergency response activities in humanitarian crisis situations. In addition, he coordinated all CARE land mine action programs worldwide. Since 1994, he has helped CARE respond to emergencies in Albania, Bosnia, the Democratic Republic of the Congo, Kosovo, Rwanda, Somalia, Sudan, East Timor, Afghanistan, and Iraq. As part of the United Nations' Operation RESTORE HOPE in Somalia beginning in late 1992, Macpherson served as deputy director for civil and military operations, prioritizing and coordinating multinational relief efforts. MacPherson is a retired U.S. Marine Corps colonel with 25 years of service, including Vietnam, Operation DESERT STORM, and Somalia. After completing active service with the Marines, he founded Enable, a humanitarian relief organization dedicated to assisting the survivors of land mines and war. Enable is a corecipient of the Nobel Peace Prize.

Janne E. Nolan, Ph.D.

Dr. Janne E. Nolan has been on the international security faculty at Georgetown University since 1994. She is the co-chairman of the project entitled, Discourse, Dissent and Strategic Surprise: Formulating American Security in an Age of Uncertainty, sponsored by Georgetown's Institute for the Study of Diplomacy and the John D. and Catherine T. MacArthur Foundation. In 2004, Nolan was appointed professor of international affairs and senior associate at The Matthew B. Ridgway Center for International Security Studies, Graduate School of Public and International Affairs at the University of Pittsburgh.

Nolan has held numerous senior positions in the private sector, including foreign policy director at the Century Foundation, senior fellow in foreign policy at The Brookings Institution, and senior international security consultant at Science Applications International Corporation. Her public service includes positions as a foreign affairs officer in the Department of State; senior representative to the Senate Armed Services Committee for Senator Gary Hart; and member of the National Defense Panel, the Accountability Review Board investigating terrorist attacks on U.S. embassies in East Africa, and the Secretary of Defense's Policy Board. In addition, Nolan has served on several congressionally appointed blue ribbon commissions and as a policy adviser to many presidential and Senate campaigns.

Nolan is the author of six books, including *Guardians of the Arsenal: The Politics of Nuclear Strategy*, *Trappings of Power: Ballistic Missiles in the Third World*, and *Elusive Consensus*. She currently is writing a book about discourse, dissent, and national security under contract to the Century Foundation of New York. Nolan edited *Ultimate Security: Combating Weapons of Mass Destruction*. Her numerous articles on international security and foreign policy have been published in *Foreign Affairs*, *Foreign Policy*, *The New York Times*, *The Washington Post*, *Science*, *Scientific American*, and *The New Republic*.

Nolan received her doctorate from the Fletcher School of Law and Diplomacy at Tufts University.

Ambassador Carlos Pascual

Carlos Pascual became the coordinator for the Office of Reconstruction and Stabilization in the U.S. Department of State (S/CRS) in August 2004. S/CRS leads and coordinates U.S. government planning to help stabilize and reconstruct societies in transition from conflict or civil strife so they can reach a sustainable path toward peace, democracy, and a market economy.

Previously, Pascual was the coordinator for U.S. assistance to Europe and Asia. He guided the development of regional and country assistance strategies to promote market-oriented and democratic states and to ensure that U.S. assistance reinforced American interests. He managed the allocation and implementation of $1.1 billion in annual assistance.

Pascual served as the U.S. ambassador to Ukraine from October 2000 to August 2003. He oversaw U.S. policy focused on promoting reforms critical to Ukraine's integration with the Euro-Atlantic community. Key priorities included strengthening grassroots democratic initiatives, promoting counterterrorism and nonproliferation, and building a strong private sector.

Pascual was a special assistant to the president and senior director for Russia, Ukraine, and Eurasia from July 1998 to January 2000. He advised the president on U.S. policy to advance security interests with Russia and reduce proliferation risks. He guided U.S. policy to encourage Ukraine's commitment to democratic and market reforms and to address stability, security, and democracy concerns in the Caucasus and Central Asia. From June 1995 to July 1998, Pascual was director for Russian, Ukrainian, and Eurasian affairs at the National Security Council (NSC), responsible for U.S. economic policy for Ukraine, Moldova, and Belarus.

Prior to his work at the NSC, Pascual worked for the U.S. Agency for International Development (USAID). He served in Sudan (1983–1986), South Africa (1986–1988), Mozambique (1989–1991), and in Washington's Africa Bureau (1991–1992). He became the director of the Office of Program Analysis and Coordination for the New Independent States Task Force in June 1992, and served as the deputy assistant administrator for Europe and the New Independent States at USAID from February 1994 to June 1995. There he oversaw budget and policy development for USAID's annual programs of $1.2 billion in the region.

Pascual is a 1980 graduate of Stanford University with a bachelor's degree in international relations. In 1982 he received a master's degree in public policy from the John F. Kennedy School of Government at Harvard University.

Mitchell B. Reiss, D.Phil.

Dr. Mitchell B. Reiss, vice provost for international affairs at The College of William and Mary in Williamsburg, Virginia, was the director of the Office of Policy Planning at the U.S. Department of State from 2003 to 2005. He provided independent strategic advice and recommendations on American foreign policy to the secretary. He was also the president's special envoy for the Northern Ireland Peace Process with the rank of ambassador, an assignment he continues to serve.

From 1999 to 2003, Reiss was dean of international affairs and director of the Wendy and Emery Reves Center for International Studies at William and Mary. He also held appointments at the Marshall-Wythe School of Law and in the Department of Government. Prior to William and Mary, Reiss helped manage the start-up and operations of the Korean Peninsula Energy Development Organization, a multinational organization.

As a guest scholar at the Woodrow Wilson International Center for Scholars in Washington, D.C., Reiss started its nonproliferation and counterproliferation programs. He has practiced corporate and banking law; was a special assistant to the national security advisor from 1988 to 1989; and served as a consultant to the Office of the Legal Advisor at the Department of State, the General Counsel's Office at the U.S. Arms Control and Disarmament Agency, and the Los Alamos and Livermore National Laboratories.

Reiss has a law degree from Columbia Law School and a D.Phil. from Oxford University. He has written two books on international security, contributed chapters to 11 others, and has published more than 60 articles and reviews.

General Peter J. Schoomaker

General Peter J. Schoomaker became the 35th Chief of Staff, United States Army, on August 1, 2003.

Prior to his current assignment, Schoomaker spent 31 years in a variety of command and staff assignments with both conventional and special operations forces. He participated in numerous deployment operations, including DESERT ONE in Iran, URGENT FURY in Grenada, JUST CAUSE in Panama, DESERT SHIELD/DESERT STORM in Southwest Asia, and UPHOLD DEMOCRACY in Haiti. He has supported various worldwide joint contingency operations, including those in the Balkans.

Early in his career, Schoomaker was a reconnaissance platoon leader and rifle company commander with the 2nd Battalion, 4th Infantry Division; a cavalry troop commander with the 2nd Armored Cavalry Regiment in Germany; and the S-3 operations officer of the 1st Battalion, 73rd Armor, 2nd Infantry Division, in Korea. From 1978 to 1981, he commanded a squadron in the 1st Special Forces Operational Detachment-D. Schoomaker then served as the squadron executive officer of the 2nd Squadron, 2nd Armored Cavalry Regiment, in Germany. In 1983, he returned to Fort Bragg, North Carolina, to serve as special operations officer, J-3, Joint Special Operations Command. From 1985 to 1988, Schoomaker commanded another squadron in the 1st Special Forces Operational Detachment-D. He returned as the commander, 1st Special Forces Operational Detachment-D, from 1989 to 1992. Subsequently, he served as the assistant division commander of the 1st Cavalry Division, Fort Hood, Texas, followed by a tour in the headquarters staff of the Department of the Army as the deputy director for operations, readiness, and mobilization.

Schoomaker served as the commanding general of the Joint Special Operations Command from 1994 to 1996. The following year, he commanded the United States Army Special Operations Command at Fort Bragg, North Carolina. His most recent assignment prior to assuming duties as the Army chief of staff was as commander of the United States Special Operations Command at MacDill Air Force Base, Florida, from 1997 through 2000.

Schoomaker's awards and decorations include the Defense Distinguished Service Medal, two Army Distinguished Service Medals, four Defense Superior Service Medals, three Legions of Merit, two Bronze Star Medals, two Defense Meritorious Service Medals, three Meritorious Service Medals, Joint Service Commendation Medal, Joint Service Achievement Medal, Combat Infantryman

Badge, Master Parachutist Badge and HALO Wings, the Special Forces Tab, and the Ranger Tab.

Schoomaker received a bachelor's degree from the University of Wyoming and a master's degree in management from Central Michigan University. His military education includes the Marine Corps Amphibious Warfare School, the U.S. Army Command and General Staff College, the National War College, and the John F. Kennedy School of Government Program for Senior Executives in National and International Security Management.

George D. Schwab, Ph.D.

George D. Schwab is president of the National Committee on American Foreign Policy. He also holds the title of professor emeritus of history and teaches at The City University of New York (The Graduate Center and The City College).

Schwab earned his doctorate from Columbia University in 1968 and began his teaching career at Columbia in the late 1950s. Since 1960, he has been teaching at The City University of New York. His courses include "History of the Cold War" and "From Appeasement to Detente and Beyond."

Schwab is the author, editor, and translator of numerous books and articles. His book, *The Challenge of the Exception: An Introduction to the Political Ideas of Carl Schmitt Between 1921 and 1936*, has been translated into Japanese and Italian. His translation (with Erna Hilfstein) and introduction to Carl Schmitt's *The Leviathan in the State Theory of Thomas Hobbes* appeared in 1996. A second printing of his translation of and introduction to Carl Schmitt's *The Concept of the Political* was published by The University of Chicago Press.

Edited books that deal with aspects of the Cold War to which Schwab has contributed chapters include *United States Foreign Policy at the Crossroads*; *Eurocommunism: The Ideological and Political-Theoretical Foundations*; *Ideology and Foreign Policy*; and *Detente in Historical Perspective*.

Schwab has lectured widely on his concept of "The Open-Society Bloc" at institutions such as the University of Freiburg and the Bundeswehrhochschule at Hamburg. He has also presented papers and participated at international gatherings in Tokyo; Paris (the Nobel Laureate conference at the Elysée Palace, 1988); Jerusalem; Washington, D.C.; and New York.

In 1974, Schwab cofounded the National Committee on American Foreign Policy with the late Hans J. Morgenthau. He has edited the committee's bimonthly, *American Foreign Policy Interests* (formerly, *American Foreign Policy Newsletter*), since its inception in 1976. Before assuming the presidency of the committee in 1993, he was its senior vice president and vice president.

Schwab formerly served on the board of directors of the Ralph Bunche Institute on the United Nations. In May 1998, he was made an Ellis Island

Medal of Honor recipient. In November 2002, he received the Order of the Three Stars medal, the highest award of the Latvian government.

U.S. Rep. Ike Skelton (D-MO)

Congressman Ike Skelton has represented Missouri's Fourth Congressional District in the U.S. House of Representatives since 1977. A House leader on defense issues, Skelton has served as the ranking Democrat on the Armed Services Committee since 1999. He is also a member of the Tactical Air and Land Forces Subcommittee.

Skelton was instrumental in the passage of the Goldwater-Nichols Department of Defense Reorganization Act of 1986. He chaired a House panel on military education from 1987 to 1988 and has advocated better strategic thinking and improvements in the intermediate and senior-level educational programs for the four services. A former chair of the Subcommittee on Military Forces and Personnel, Skelton has warned against further cuts in the defense budget and focused on efforts to improve military pay, health care, and quality of life.

As most of the Fourth Congressional District is composed of small towns and farming communities, Skelton also looks after the needs of rural America. He is a former chair of a House small business subcommittee and is past chair of the Congressional Rural Caucus.

Skelton has received a variety of awards and honors throughout his career. Among the many recognitions are the Outstanding Legislator Award from the Association of the United States Army, the Secretary's Award from the Department of Veterans Affairs, the James Forrestal Memorial Award from the National Defense Industrial Association, an honorary master's degree in strategic studies from the United States Army War College, and an honorary degree from the United States Marine Corps Command and Staff College.

A native of Lexington, Missouri, Skelton is a graduate of Wentworth Military Academy and the University of Missouri at Columbia, where he earned A.B. and L.L.B. degrees. He was named a member of Phi Beta Kappa and the Law Review. Prior to his election to Congress, Skelton served as Lafayette County prosecuting attorney and as a Missouri state senator.

Hernando de Soto

Hernando de Soto, president of the Institute for Liberty and Democracy (ILD), headquartered in Lima, Peru, has been honored by *Time* magazine, *Forbes* magazine, *The Economist*, and the German development magazine *Entwicklung und Zusammenarbeit*. *Fortune* placed de Soto's *The Mystery of Capital* on its list of the "75 Smartest Books We Know."

De Soto is a member of the United Nation's World Commission on the Global Dimension of Globalization, International Labor Organization, and the United Nations Development Program's Task Force to Examine Private Resources for Development. He also serves on the Expert Group on Development Issues, established by the Swedish government, and the Research Advisory Council of the Global Markets Institute at Goldman Sachs.

As their principal activity, de Soto and the ILD are designing and implementing capital formation programs to empower the poor in Asia, Latin America, the Middle East, Africa, and former Soviet nations.

De Soto was born in Arequipa, Peru, and did his postgraduate work at the Institut Universitaire de Hautes Etudes Internationales in Geneva, Switzerland. He has served as an economist for the General Agreement on Tariffs and Trade, president of the executive committee of the Copper Exporting Countries Organization, managing director of Universal Engineering Corporation, a principal of the Swiss Bank Corporation Consultant Group, and a governor of Peru's Central Reserve Bank.

In Peru, de Soto was President Alberto Fujimori's personal representative and principal advisor until de Soto resigned two months before the coup d'état. De Soto and ILD were largely responsible for modernizing and stabilizing Peru's economic system.

De Soto has written two books about economic and political development: *The Other Path*, published in the mid-1980s, and *The Mystery of Capital: Why Capitalism Triumphs in the West and Fails Everywhere Else*, published in late 2000. Both books have been best sellers and have been translated into some 20 languages.

Among the prizes de Soto has received are The Freedom Prize (Switzerland), and The Fisher Prize (United Kingdom). In 2002, he received the Goldwater Award (USA), the Adam Smith Award from the Association of Private Enterprise Education (USA), and the CARE Canada Award for Outstanding Development Thinking (Canada). In 2003, he was named the Downey Fellow at Yale University, and he was inducted into the Democracy Hall of Fame International at the National Graduate University. In 2004, de Soto was awarded the Templeton Freedom Prize (USA) and the Milton Friedman Prize for Advancing Liberty (USA), as well as the Royal Decoration of the Most Admirable Order of the Direkgunabhorn, 5th Class (Thailand). In 2005, he was awarded an Honorary Degree of Doctor of Letters from the University of Buckingham (United Kingdom); named the Most Outstanding of 2004 for Economic Development at Home and Abroad by the Peruvian National Assembly of Rectors; given the 2004 Peruvian Institute of Business Administration Award; presented the Americas Award (USA); received the Deutsche Stiftung Eigentum Prize; and was recognized for his outstanding accomplishments with the Academy of Achievement's Golden Plate Award (USA).

His Royal Highness El Hassan bin Talal

His Royal Highness Prince El Hassan bin Talal is the younger brother of His Majesty the late King Hussein of Jordan. Prince El Hassan had served as King Hussein's closest political advisor, confidant and deputy, and acted as regent in the king's absence. He has been decorated by more than 20 nations, and holds the order of Al Husseinbin Ali, Jordan's highest honor.

Prince El Hassan founded and is involved in a number of Jordanian and international institutes and committees. In Jordan, he chaired the committees overseeing the first four development plans. He founded the Royal Scientific Society in 1970, the annual Bilad Al-Sham Conference in 1978, and many other scientific conferences and institutions.

Prince El Hassan has chaired and been a member of a number of international committees and organizations, among them the Club of Rome, the Center for Peace Studies and Conflict Resolution at the University of Oklahoma International Programs Center, the International Board of the Council on Foreign Relations, and the Nuclear Threat Initiative.

Prince El Hassan is the author or co-author of seven books: *A Study on Jerusalem*; *Palestinian Self-Determination*; *Search for Peace*; *Christianity in the Arab World*; *Essere Musulmano*; *Continuity, Innovation and Change: Selected Essays*; and *In Memory of Faisal I: The Iraqi Question*.

After early schooling in Amman, Prince El Hassan graduated from Christ Church, Oxford University, where he earned bachelor's and master's degrees. He has also been recognized with honorary degrees from universities around the world, as well as numerous awards.

Howard Roy Williams

Before becoming president and chief executive officer of the Center for Humanitarian Cooperation, Roy Williams served as the director of the Office of Foreign Disaster Assistance, Bureau for Humanitarian Response (BHR/OFDA), of the U.S. Agency for International Development (USAID) from January 1998 until January 2001. USAID is the U.S. government agency that provides economic and humanitarian assistance worldwide. As head of OFDA, Williams oversaw disaster preparedness and relief and rehabilitation programs throughout the world.

Before going to OFDA, Williams was with the International Rescue Committee (IRC) for 12 years. He served as director of operations from 1985 to 1993, vice president for overseas programs from 1993 to 1996, and vice president for overseas policy and planning from 1996 to January 1998. During this time, Williams led efforts that resulted in the conceptualization, creation, and staffing of IRC's Emergency Preparedness Unit. He helped to establish and staff IRC offices in a variety of places, including Northern Iraq, Jordan, the Balkans, Kenya, Malawi, Rwanda, and Southern Sudan.

From 1979 to 1985, Williams served with the International Organization for Migration, formerly known as the International Committee for European Migration. He held the positions of chief of operations in Geneva, Switzerland; regional director in Bangkok, Thailand; and country representative in Kuala Lumpur, Malaysia.

From 1976 to 1979, he was assistant to the director with the American Council for Nationalities Services in New York.

Williams has a bachelor's degree from Columbia University. He also studied at the Columbia University School of Law.

GLOSSARY

ASEAN	Association of South East Asian Nations
Band Aid	Band Aid is a British and Irish charity "supergroup" founded in 1984 by Bob Geldof and Midge Ure in order to raise money for famine relief in Ethiopia
CBRN	Chemical, biological, radiological, and nuclear weapons
CENTCOM	U.S. Central Command
CEO	Chief Executive Officer
CFO	Chief Financial Officer
CFR	Council of Foreign Relations
CIA	Central Intelligence Agency
CSIS	Center for Strategic and International Studies
CTR	Cooperative threat reduction
DNI	Director of National Intelligence
ECOWAS	Economic Community of West African States
EU	European Union
EUCOM	U.S. European Command
FEMA	Federal Emergency Management Agency
G-3	Develops, articulates, and advances Army strategic vision, concepts, policies, and plans
G-4	U.S. Army logistics
GAO	Government Accountability Office
GATT	General Agreement on Tariffs and Trade
GMO foods	Genetically modified organism foods
HA	Humanitarian assistance
HACI	Hope for African Children Initiative

ICC	International Criminal Court
IDP	Internally displaced persons
IMF	International Monetary Fund
J-3	J-3 Operations Directorate is where U.S. Joint Staff's planning, policies, intelligence, manpower, communications, and logistics functions are translated into action
JAG	Judge advocate general
League of Arab States	The [Arab League] includes the Hashemite Kingdom of Jordan, United Arab Emirates, Kingdom of Bahrain, Republic of Tunisia, Democratic and Popular Republic of Algeria, Republic of Djibouti, Kingdom of Saudi Arabia, Republic of Sudan, Arab Republic of Syria, and the Republic of Somalia
MDG	Millennium Development Goals: The eight MDGs range from halving extreme poverty to halting the spread of HIV/AIDS and providing universal primary education, all by the target date of 2015. The MDGs form a blueprint agreed to by all the world's countries and all the world's leading development institutions.
MECA	Middle East Citizens Assembly
MERCOSUR	The MERCOSUR was created by Argentina, Brazil, Paraguay, and Uruguay in March 1991 with the signing of the Treaty of Asuncion. It originally was set up with the ambitious goal of creating a common market/customs union among the participating countries.
MNCs	Multinational corporations
NATO	North Atlantic Treaty Organization
NSC	National Security Council
NGO	Nongovernmental organization
NIE	National Intelligence Estimate
NTI	Nuclear Threat Initiative
OEF	Operation ENDURING FREEDOM—multinational operations in Afghanistan

OIF	Operation IRAQI FREEDOM—multinational operations in Iraq
OPEC	Organization of the Petroleum Exporting Countries
OSCE	Organization for Security and Co-operation in Europe
Phase IV	Post-conflict planning
PFM	Partnership for the Mediterranean
PFP	Partnership for Peace
PME	Professional military education
Porton Down	The United Kindom's Defence Science and Technology Laboratory, located in Porton Down, is a government facility for military bio-chemical research.
PSI	Proliferation Security Initiative
QDR	Quadrennial Defense Review
SACEUR	Supreme Allied Commander, Europe
SITREP	Situation report
Six-Party Talks	Meetings of the People's Republic of China, North Korea, South Korea, Russia, Japan, and the United States, held in order to find a resolution of the crisis over the North Korean nuclear weapons program.
SOUTHCOM	United States Southern Command
Treaty of Rome	The treaty establishing the European Economic Community (EEC)
UNDP	United Nations Development Program
UNHCR	United Nations High Commissioner for Refugees
WFDD	World's Faith and Development Dialogue
WMD	Weapons of mass destruction
WOCMES	World Congress of Middle East Studies
WTO	World Trade Organization

Co-Sponsors

Center for Humanitarian Cooperation

A not-for-profit organization founded by experienced professionals, the Center for Humanitarian Cooperation serves as a neutral party to foster functional cooperation among organizations concerned with humanitarian issues. It provides data for field operations by humanitarian agencies, facilitates sharing of resources by agencies with similar missions, and links governmental organizations with private and international relief agencies.

http://www.cooperationcenter.org

The Matthew B. Ridgway Center for International Security Studies

The Matthew B. Ridgway Center for International Security Studies is dedicated to educating the next generation of security analysts and to producing scholarship and impartial analysis that informs the policymakers who must confront diverse challenges to international and human security. The Ridgway research program analyzes the complex security dynamics of the 21st century global environment, concentrating on rapidly evolving and emerging security threats.

http://www.ridgway.pitt.edu

The National Committee on American Foreign Policy

The National Committee on American Foreign Policy is a nonprofit, independent foreign policy think tank that strives to identify and articulate American foreign policy interests from a nonpartisan perspective. Its foreign policy interests include preserving and strengthening national security; supporting countries committed to the values and practice of political, religious, and cultural pluralism; encouraging realistic arms control agreements; and promoting an open and global economy.

http://www.ncafp.org

THE WOODROW WILSON INTERNATIONAL CENTER FOR SCHOLARS

Established by an act of Congress in 1968, the Woodrow Wilson International Center for Scholars is our nation's official living memorial to President Woodrow Wilson, a distinguished scholar and a national leader. The Wilson Center is a nonpartisan institution, supported by public and private funds, engaged in the study of national and world affairs.

http://www.wilsoncenter.org

CONTRIBUTORS

STRATEGIC STUDIES INSTITUTE

The Strategic Studies Institute (SSI) at Carlisle Barracks is the U.S. Army's premier institute for global and national strategic security research and analysis. It is the Army's think tank for the analysis of national security policy and military strategy.

Its primary function is to provide direct analysis for Army and Department of Defense leadership, and to serve as a bridge to the wider strategic community. SSI is also the focal point for research at the Army War College, providing research and expertise for curriculum development and assisting other members of the faculty in research projects.

SSI is a unique organization that links the Army to the American and international strategic communities. It is the only research organization in the United States that focuses on the strategic role of land power.

SSI collects the wisdom of the wider strategic community for Army senior leaders and explains the role of the Army and landpower to both the strategic community and national decision makers. It does this through rigorous, independent analysis by a professional staff second to none assembled at any institution. Analysis of these conference presentations is but one example of the depth and breadth of study done at SSI.

AMERICAN UNIVERSITY'S WASHINGTON SEMESTER PROGRAM

The aim of the program is to provide students with firsthand exposure to the policy process and to help them plan and acquire skills for professional careers in public service. The program has three components: an eight-credit seminar, which incorporates meetings with public officials and other practitioners; an internship; and a research project. On average, nearly 500 third- and fourth-year undergraduates from universities around the United States and from abroad participate in this program. They live, dine, and study together on the AU Tenley Circle campus. The thirty students who contributed to the Eisenhower National Security Conference are members of the U.S. Foreign Policy unit of the Fall 2005 Washington Semester Program.

PARTICIPANTS

Songhyun Baik
Korea University

Elizabeth Bradley
University of Texas - Austin

Brian Campbell
Gettysburg College

Viviana Carlessi
Universita Degli Studi di Bergamo

Colin Conerton
Tufts University

Everett DePangher
Santa Clara University

Kathleen Emberger
Ursinus College

Saori Goto
Keio University/JSAF

Kent Harkness
Santa Clara University

Katja Kola
Universitat Regensburg

Victor Lin
Clark University

Joseph Macdonald
Audencia

Shawn Mayo-Pike
Saint Lawrence University

Alex Mazelow
McGill University

Mona Moayad
University of Texas-Austin

Ionut Popescu
Occidental College

Christiane Puia
University of Munich

Stephen Roques
Loyola University

Paul Schneider
Rhodes College

Ashley Seawright
Tufts University

Allison Simonton
St. Olaf College

Susanna Svensson
Karlstad University

Alexander Truelsen
Trinity College

James Turitto
University of Vermont

Meaghan Ursell
Dalhousie University

Philip Van Orden
Susquehanna University

Brandon Wheeler
Clarkson University

Gregor Young
Duquesne University

www.ingramcontent.com/pod-product-compliance
Lightning Source LLC
Chambersburg PA
CBHW051954280526
45793CB00005B/714